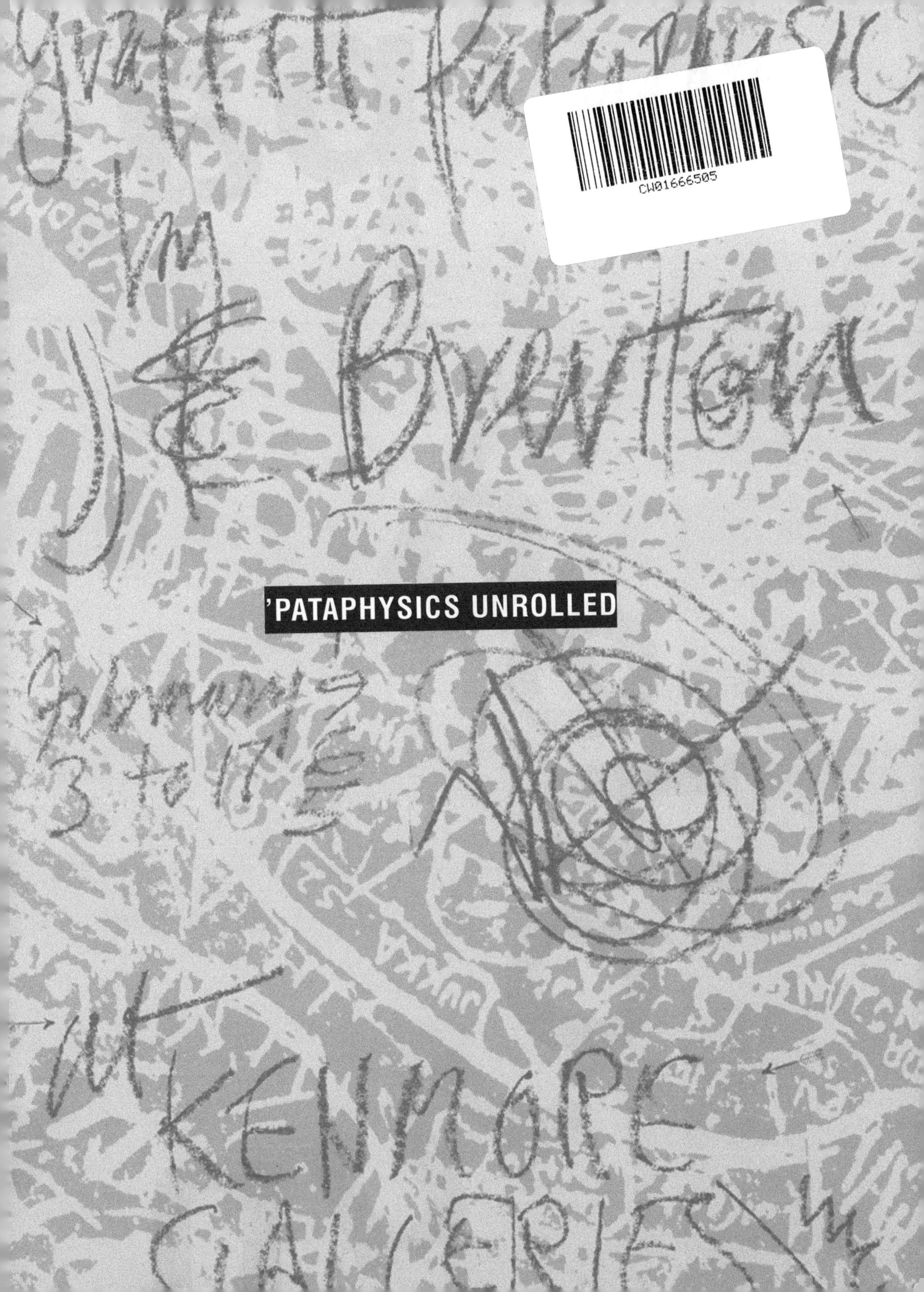

’PATAPHYSICS UNROLLED

unrolled ’pat

'PATAPHYSICS UNROLLED

EDITED BY KATIE L. PRICE

AND MICHAEL R. TAYLOR

The Pennsylvania State University Press,

University Park, Pennsylvania

Library of Congress Cataloging-in-Publication Data

Names: Price, Katie L., 1985– editor. | Taylor, Michael R., 1966– editor.
Title: 'Pataphysics unrolled / edited by Katie L. Price and Michael R. Taylor.
Other titles: Refiguring modernism.
Description: University Park, Pennsylvania : The Pennsylvania State University Press, [2022] | Series: Refiguring modernism | Includes bibliographical references and index.
Summary: "A collection of critical and creative essays exploring pataphysics, a late nineteenth-century French absurdist precursor to Dadaism, surrealism, and the Theater of the Absurd. Reveals how pataphysics has been a platform and medium for persistent intellectual, poetic, conceptual, and artistic experimentation for over a century"—Provided by publisher.
Identifiers: LCCN 2021046695 | ISBN 9780271089591 (paperback)
Subjects: LCSH: Pataphysics—History.
Classification: LCC CB430 .P38 2022 | DDC 153.3—dc23
LC record available at https://lccn.loc.gov/2021046695

Printed in the United States of America
Published by The Pennsylvania State University Press,
University Park, PA 16802–1003

The Pennsylvania State University Press is a member of the Association of University Presses.

It is the policy of The Pennsylvania State University Press to use acid-free paper. Publications on uncoated stock satisfy the minimum requirements of American National Standard for Information Sciences—Permanence of Paper for Printed Library Material, ANSI Z39.48–1992.

Additional credits: Page i, James E. Brewton, *Graffiti Pataphysic*, 1965 (plate 8); pages vi–viii, James E. Brewton, *Alfred Jarry in Paris*, ca. 1966 (plate 14); pages 17, 95, 171, and 223, James E. Brewton, *The Pataphysics Times*, 1964 (fig. 6.2). Images courtesy of the James E. Brewton Foundation.

And behold, the wallpaper of Faustroll's body was unrolled by the saliva and teeth of the water.

Like a musical score, all art and all science were written in the curves of the limbs of the ultrasexagenarian ephebe, and their progression to an infinite degree was prophesied therein.

—Alfred Jarry, *Exploits and Opinions of Dr. Faustroll, Pataphysician*

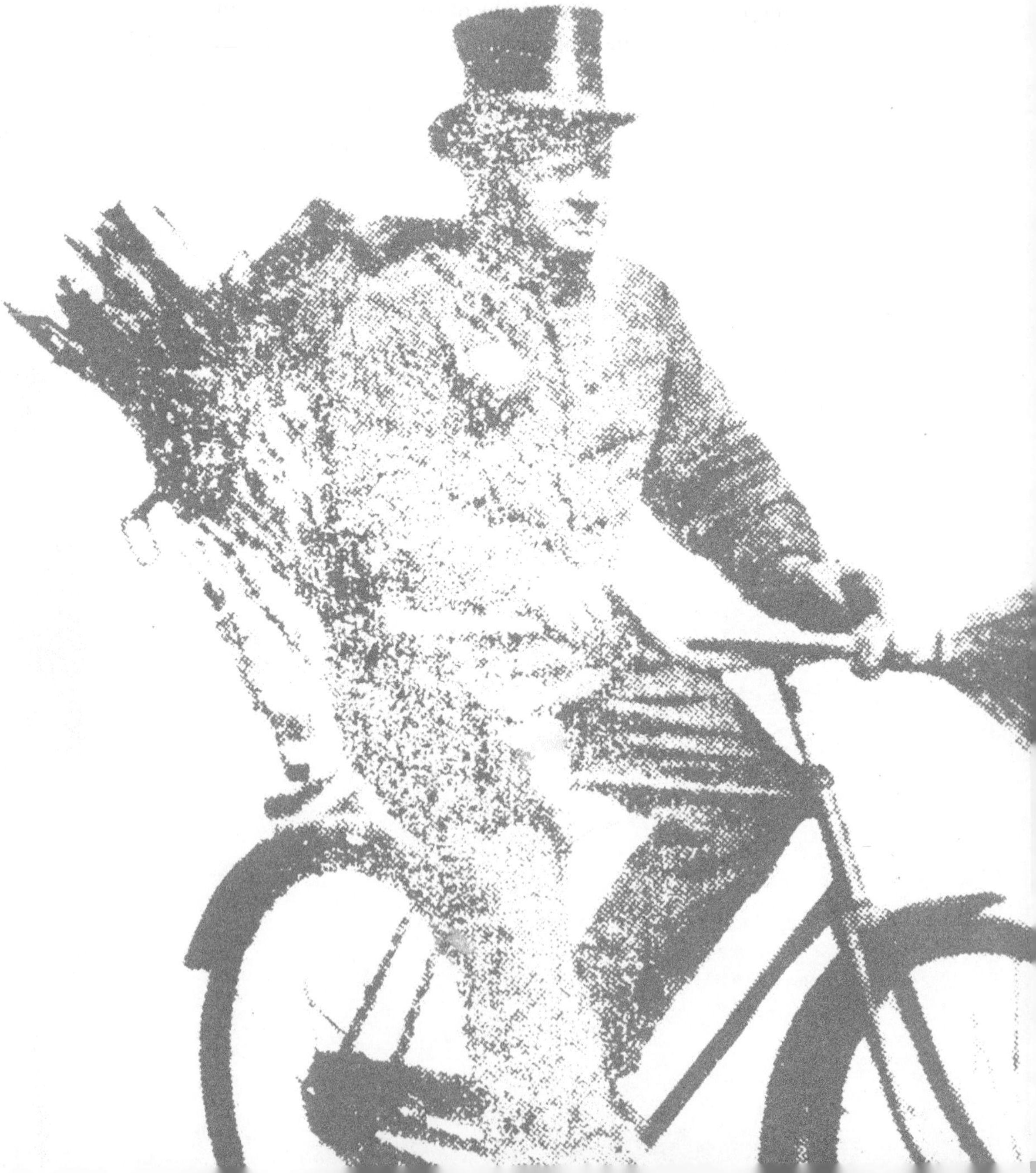

Contents

Part 3: "Written in the Curves of the Limbs": Pataphysical Criticism

Part 4: "Progression to an Infinite Degree Was Prophesied Therein": Pataphysics' Possible Futures

Illustrations

Color Plates (after page 116)

Figures

Acknowledgments

In many ways, this book is indebted to the city of Philadelphia. Early ideas for the volume emerged out of *Philadelphia à la Pataphysique*, a series of events that took place in Philadelphia in March 2014. The programming was capacious, including a conference, three exhibitions, two film screenings, a poetry reading and a musical performance. It was during this time that many contributors to this volume met to explore the vibrant life of pataphysical experimentation in the twenty-first century and discussed—surely over one too many drinks and, yes, some absinthe—the need for a book that captured the vitality of the moment and documented the rich history of pataphysical experimentation from Jarry into the present day. The participants of *Philadelphia à la Pataphysique* are throughout these pages, even when their names do not appear: Charles Bernstein, Christian Bök, DJ Spooky, Craig Dworkin, Jill Fell, John Heon, Andrew Hugill, Aaron Levy, Steve McCaffery, David McKnight, Line McMurray, Robert Cargni Mitchell, Christine Poggi, Gerald Prince, Jean-Michel Rabaté, Sid Sachs, Emily Brewton Schilling, Mari Shaw, Linda Klieger Stillman, Michelle Taransky, Christopher Vandegrift. The vibrant arts scene and spirit of collaboration in Philadelphia made this possible: in particular, International House (now in ethernity); Kelly Writers House; the Kislak Center for Special Collections, Rare Books, and Manuscripts; and Slought. In addition to the book before you, the success of *Philadelphia à la Pataphysique* sparked the creation of the Philadelphia Avant-Garde Studies Consortium (PASC), a nonprofit formed in 2015 to cultivate a network of educational and cultural institutions and associated scholars, artists, curators, and collectors who combine expertise and resources to foster the advanced study of avant-garde movements and promote related special collections, exhibitions, and performances in the greater Philadelphia area and Delaware Valley region. As part of this work, a growing collection of pataphysical materials now resides at the Kislak Center at the University of Pennsylvania.

We want to offer our profound thanks and deep gratitude to Emily Brewton Schilling and John Heon for their help with the research and editing of this volume. We also would like to thank the James E. Brewton Foundation for its help and support with research and photography for this publication. Last, but not least, we want to thank Ellie Goodman and Jonathan Eburne at Penn State University Press for believing in this project from its inception and bringing this volume to fruition.

Editors' Note

Readers of this volume will note that authors oscillate between the use of 'pataphysics (*avec* apostrophe) and pataphysics (*sans* apostrophe). Though Jarry himself rarely used it, in *Exploits and Opinions of Dr. Faustroll, Pataphysician*, he writes that the "actual orthography" of 'pataphysics should include the apostrophe "so as to avoid a simple pun."[1] While, as many critics have pointed out, the apostrophe does nothing to avoid any of the many possible puns to which the term is subject, it is commonly used in the noun form and is beloved for its eccentric flair and inherent protest to being placed in an alphabetized dictionary. We have thus asked the authors in this volume to follow the recommendation published by the *Collège de 'Pataphysique* in 1965: "Only the word Pataphysics referring substantially and in conformity with the texts of Jarry, to the Science of Imaginary Solutions as such, is entitled to the apostrophe. It is merely tolerated that in certain cases it be granted, *ad conventientiam*, that the substantive used *in genere* take the apostrophe; in most cases, it is better to refrain. The adjective does not take the apostrophe."[2] Thus, in this volume 'pataphysics refers to Jarry's "science of imaginary solutions," and pataphysics to the delightfully various ways in which artists and writers have conducted experiments in its name.

Notes

1. Alfred Jarry, *Exploits and Opinions of Dr. Faustroll, Pataphysician (A Neo-Scientific Novel)* (1911), trans. Simon Watson Taylor (Boston: Exact Change, 1996), 21.
2. Irénée-Louis Sandomir, "The Apostrophe in Pataphysics," trans. Antony Melville, in *The True, the Good, the Beautiful: An Elementary Chrestomathy of 'Pataphysics* (London: Printed Head, 1965), 87.

Introduction

"Unrolled by the Saliva and Teeth of the Water"

Katie L. Price

In 1960, the absinthe-colored cover of the *Evergreen Review* asked the question "What Is 'Pataphysics?" Now, more than sixty years later, a more appropriate question might be "*Why* has 'pataphysics—a 'science' invented in the 1880s by Alfred Jarry (1873–1907) and his schoolmates to mock their incompetent physics teacher—persisted as a mode of jocoserious artistic production into the twenty-first century?" Pataphysics has maintained a near constant presence through modernism, postmodernism, and into contemporary experimental practices, capturing the imagination of writers, artists, thinkers, and musicians as diverse as Marcel Duchamp, the Baroness Elsa von Freytag-Loringhoven, James Joyce, Samuel Beckett, John Cage, Asger Jorn, Man Ray, the Beatles, Joan Miró, Jean Genet, Jean Baudrillard, Thomas Chimes, Christian Bök, Amy Catanzano, and William Kentridge.[1] Despite only being acknowledged as a word by the *Oxford English Dictionary* in June 2005,[2] pataphysics has been a platform and medium for persistent intellectual, poetic, conceptual, and artistic experimentation for more than a century. Why? To answer these and other questions, we must first turn to its origins.

Alfred Jarry: Pataphysical Origins

Fin de siècle author, artist, and puppeteer Alfred Jarry lived "a pataphysical life."[3] It was short—he died of tuberculosis aggravated by alcoholism at the age of thirty-four—but explosively creative. Jarry cultivated a life of profound ridiculousness, a project he approached with the utmost seriousness. He kept a pet owl, lived on the second-and-a-half floor of a Paris apartment building,[4] wore bicyclists' clothing for almost all occasions, was known to "pronounce mute 'e"s in everyday conversation,"[5] and referred to his bicycle as "that which rolls" and the wind as "that which blows." He was famously fond of absinthe, which he would often drink in massive quantities with the express purpose of inducing hallucinations. The oft-cited culmination of Jarry's commitment to a life of absurdity was his deathbed request for a toothpick.[6] These idiosyncrasies permeated Jarry's existence. He cultivated a systematic resistance to normalcy, rendering the quotidian preposterous and the preposterous quotidian. Clichéd but true for Jarry: life was his art, and art was his life.

Jarry's "science" had an inauspicious birth. During his time at the Lycée de Rennes from 1881 to 1891, he and his classmates coined the term "'pataphysics" to distinguish physics *as such* from the physics nonsensically taught to them by their notoriously incompetent and buffoonish teacher, Félix-Frédéric Hébert. Hébert became the main character in a series of comical poems, stories, and plays written and performed by the boys, appearing alternatively as Père Heb, P.H., or Père Eb. That sophomoric invention eventually transformed into the literary work for which Jarry is best known: *Ubu Roi* (1896). A caricature more than a character, the play's eponymous protagonist boasts three mismatched teeth, a retractable ear, an immense belly,[7] and an insatiable, infantile ego. On December 6, 1896, the play famously caused a riot on its opening night with its very first word, when the corpulent title character bellowed "Merdre!" (the French word for "shit" with an extra *r*), a thinly veiled expletive that symbolically threw excrement at the audience, in equal measure eliciting outraged protests and uproarious laughter of approval. Though the play opened and closed the same night, the scandal of it catapulted the play and its author into notoriety. It has been cited as the birth of absurdist theatre and even, for some, of French modernism and the avant-garde in general. But while the Ubu plays[8] made Jarry famous in France, it is his neo-scientific novel, *Exploits and Opinions of Dr. Faustroll, Pataphysician* (1911), that has had the most lasting and wide-ranging impact on artistic practices of the last century.

Although the Ubu plays and *Faustroll* can be seen as complements, they should more accurately be seen as rivals. After the enormous *succès de scandale* of *Ubu Roi*, Jarry often felt trapped by his own creation—typecast, as it were. He was famous for creating Ubu and, to some extent, for playing the part of Ubu in the cafés and salons of Paris. Yet in his lifetime he was able to publish only short excerpts of *Faustroll*—by far his most philosophical and formally ambitious literary work—and they were largely ignored. *Faustroll* was not published in full until four years after his death; Jarry never got to hear Guillaume Apollinaire call it "the most important publication of 1911."[9] If Jarry were alive today, he might be happily shocked to learn that many leading scholars now acknowledge that *Faustroll* was his real magnum opus. Alastair Brotchie, whose biography of Jarry is the most comprehensive portrait of the author in English, observes that "while the 'public' identified Jarry with Ubu, Jarry identified himself with Faustroll," and he stresses that "*Faustroll* should be seen as a representation of Jarry's present life *in its totality*."[10] 'Pataphysics was Jarry's lifelong work, and *Faustroll* was its fullest expression.

The elevation of 'pataphysics from an adolescent joke to a term of comic-aesthetic and philosophical import worthy of a lifelong (and, indeed, century-long) commitment was due, at least in part, to Jarry's time studying with Henri Bergson from 1891 to 1893 at the Lycée Henri IV in Paris. Jarry deeply admired Bergson and was engrossed by his lectures, but disagreed with him about one key concept: epiphenomenalism, which posited that consciousness itself might be understood as an "accidental side effect of the state of the brain."[11] While Bergson rejected this notion, Jarry was fascinated by the idea that consciousness itself could be a mere accident. Emphasizing how important this philosophical break with Bergson was for Jarry, Brotchie even goes so far as to say that 'pataphysics itself might be understood as an epiphenomenon of Jarry's attendance at Bergson's lectures.[12] *Faustroll* further attests to the term's significance for Jarry. A reference to epiphenomenalism precedes the two most famous definitions of 'pataphysics in the novel, suggesting that the concept is crucial, perhaps even prerequisite, to an understanding of 'pataphysics: if consciousness itself is accidental, then 'pataphysics sets as its enterprise the cultivation of a ludic reality.

While Jarry had originally planned to publish a treatise on 'pataphysics in order to fully flesh out his jocoserious philosophy of art and life, his decision to ultimately write a "neo-scientific novel" on the topic is revealing—suggesting that the terms of the term itself must reside in fiction. Defining 'pataphysics through a novel allowed Jarry to blur the lines between fiction and nonfiction, literature and science, nonsense and philosophy. The novel situates the "science" in the realm of the imaginary and speculative while also making tantalizing use of actual scientific and mathematical theories. *Faustroll* adeptly integrates the real and the imaginary in ways that make us question each: "real science" starts to sound absurd, while Jarry's "imaginary solutions" start to sound plausible. The novel form allows Jarry to embody and enact the complex, paradoxical aspects of 'pataphysics rather than elucidate them.

In order to understand *Faustroll*'s importance for Jarry's own conception of 'pataphysics and for the various pataphysicians after him, an overview of key plot points and main characters will be helpful. The primary narrative involves Faustroll's mock-Odyssean voyage "from Paris to Paris" by sieve, a twelve-meter-long copper-mesh skiff that floats on water by surface tension.[13] His travel companions include his first mate, Bosse-de-Nage, a hydrocephalic baboon whose only words are "ha ha," and Panmuphle, a bailiff who had been sent to collect overdue rent from Faustroll and functions both as a frame-tale narrator and an ironic connection to the rational, "real" world. Faustroll's two comic foils—which represent, respectively, buffoonery and seriousness, lawlessness and the law, instinctual reactions and intellectual responses—act together to personify what Faustroll (and Jarry) reject: the notion that mutually exclusive opposites cannot coexist. In the text, Faustroll is both; 1 + 1 = 3. Along the three characters' journey, they visit fourteen "equivalent"[14] islands, each corresponding to a different artistic figure, including, among others, Aubrey Beardsley, Paul Valéry, Paul Gauguin, Henri Rousseau, and Stéphane Mallarmé. In this series of deliriously hilarious vignettes, Jarry paints a composite portrait of avant-garde Paris and his own psychosocial cityscape. By naming these figures, Jarry simultaneously invites a variety of artists into his pataphysical universe and suggests that the practice of pataphysics should and *does* extend outside the world of the book and into the real.

The novel consists of eight books, each with multiple subchapters, the titles of which echo those found in philosophical treatises. Book 2, "Elements of Pataphysics," opens with a chapter titled "Definition," from which the most widely quoted definitions of 'pataphysics are taken: "DEFINITION. *Pataphysics is the science of imaginary solutions, which symbolically attributes the properties of objects, described by their virtuality, to their lineaments*" (22). Hardly a clear definition to begin with, the novel further complicates things by almost immediately offering even more definitions, including "the science of that which is superinduced upon metaphysics," "the science of the particular," and that which "will examine the laws governing exceptions, and will explain the universe supplementary to this one" (21). Furthermore, the chapter ends with a reference to "the irreverence of the common herd whose instinct sums up the adepts of the science of pataphysics in the following phrase:" (24). Like the famous colon at the end of Ezra Pound's "Canto I,"[15] Jarry's colon acts as a frame for what follows, so that the rest of the novel becomes, comically, "the phrase" that sums up 'pataphysics. The novel thus explodes the single-sentence definition by offering multiple definitions, and formally expanding the definitional task both backward (by naming the entire chapter "Definition," itself being only one "element" of 'pataphysics) and forward (by ending the chapter with a colon that suggests the definitional exercise continues). 'Pataphysics is thus rendered not *in*definable (as is often asserted) but rather *infinitely* definable. Pataphysics is not a science of lack, but of excess, not of foreclosure but of possibility, and, from its origins, includes an invitation to readers to continue its comically rigorous investigation of the absurd.

In book 7, Faustroll sinks his sieve and drowns himself, which is described as "mak[ing] the gesture of dying" (97). Following pataphysical logic, Faustroll is not dead as such, but rather translated to "ethernity," a truly pataphysical realm that is completely outside of time and space. From ethernity, Faustroll offers, in a final pataphysical flourish, a geometrical proof of God's existence that leads him to the solution "$\infty - 0 - a + a + 0 = \infty$" (111–14).[16] The novel concludes, without apology or equivocation, "Therefore, *definitively*: / GOD IS THE TANGENTIAL POINT BETWEEN

ZERO AND INFINITY. Pataphysics is *the* science." (114). Jarry asserts, in his signature deadpan manner, that 'pataphysics could prove what philosophers had tried but failed to prove for centuries: the existence of God. Of course, Jarry has proved nothing at all except, perhaps, that language can render visible in the imagination a mathematical impossibility (a tangential point) while also making a certain kind of poetic sense. As Roger Shattuck notes, "Beneath the double talk and ellipsis, [pataphysics] . . . seems to mean that the virtual or imaginary nature of things as glimpsed by the heightened vision of poetry or science or love can be seized and lived as real."[17] Reinforcing the gesture of the definitional colon, the text's terminal ellipses, in effect, hands the pen to the reader, inviting them to practice pataphysical science into ethernity. It should come as no surprise then, that while Jarry called this a "neo-scientific novel," readers have taken it as a guidebook to pataphysics that includes permission to carry out experiments in its name.

It is to *how* pataphysics has "unrolled" from its origins in Jarry's texts into the contemporary moment that this collection turns its critical attention. *'Pataphysics Unrolled* provides evidence that the prophesy at the heart of what is arguably the most important sentence of Jarry's most important work, and this volume's epigraph, came true:

> And behold, the wallpaper of Faustroll's body was unrolled by the saliva and teeth of the water.
>
> Like a musical score, all art and all science were written in the curves of the limbs of the ultrasexagenarian ephebe, and their progression to an infinite degree was prophesied therein. (99)

By describing "the wallpaper of Faustroll's body"—which should be understood to be the text of *Faustroll* itself—as "unrolled by the *saliva* and *teeth* of the water" (my emphasis), Jarry alludes to textual rumination: a chewing on of the text that releases its full flavor and provides sustenance to the reader. With a hyperbolic, mock-religious tone, the lines both prophesize and invoke the continuation of pataphysical enterprises; they put the roll in *Faustroll*. Jarry's provocation has been answered: artists and thinkers have digested the text, and it has fueled over a century of experimentation in an astounding range of fields and disciplines, in both avant-garde and popular art forms.[18] The claim to "all art and all science" being contained in *Faustroll* should not imply that the novel was comprehensive, but rather that pataphysics—as a mode of aesthetic inquiry—has the capacity to reveal all art and all science (conscious and unconscious, real and imaginary, past and future) as it moves through time and space. By suggesting the text is "like a musical score," Jarry further implies that the text is meant to be *played*: interpreted and performed. In practice, then, pataphysics is more of a verb than a noun—denoting an orientation and approach rather than any particular style or mode. Its insistence on situational interventions that fuse rationality and irrationality, procedure and chance, humor and seriousness, has worked to keep it relevant as a technique that pushes against stagnation in ways of thinking through productive critique (creation). If part of pataphysics' enterprise is to use imagination to invent new realities, then it is perhaps no surprise that real life has imitated literature: pataphysics continued after Jarry's death as *Faustroll* continued after Faustroll's.

Faustroll was written seven years before Albert Einstein published his theory of special relativity in 1905, and Jarry showed a remarkable ability to artistically anticipate scientific discoveries, especially the concept of the space-time continuum and the perspective-dependent nature of space and time. Jarry's image of the "wallpaper of Faustroll's body" becoming a scroll as it "unrolls" through history provides an apt metaphor. When one reads a scroll, one can only see part of the text at any particular time; despite the fact that the text continues (both backward and forward), one can never experience the whole of it at once. When thought of as a scroll, the history of pataphysics represents a different understanding of time and literary history in which past, present, and future can be moved through, unrolled and rerolled—in effect, rendering the scroll its own kind of time machine.[19] This book considers Jarry's legacy as such a scroll—showing the continuous (though not necessarily linear) flow of pataphysical ideas from today to Jarry and before. Faustroll's body is still being "written" as artists, writers, scientists, philosophers, and computer programmers conduct new pataphysical research, play new artistic-intellectual games, and design new pataphysical technologies. As such, Dr. Faustroll goes beyond a figure representing Alfred Jarry and his idiosyncratic pseudoscience to become the embodiment of an artistic-scientific energy, a continually unrolling force that creates and reveals alternative realities as it moves through time and space.

Pataphysics After Jarry

In 1948, a group of Paris intellectuals formed the *Collège de 'Pataphysique* as a parodically formal collective to further explore "*the* science." With Dr. Faustroll as the "Inamovable Curator," Marcel Duchamp as a "Grand Satrap," and such prominent members as Boris Vian, Max Ernst, Raymond Queneau, Man Ray, Jean Dubuffet, Groucho Marx, and Eugène Ionesco, the *Collège* was notoriously esoteric and insular, especially before its "disoccultation" in 2001. Over the years, it has produced a number of publications, but until 2001 these publications circulated clandestinely among its members and friends, a practice that cultivated the *Collège*'s reputation as a secret society producing secret knowledge.[20] Adding to the sense of mystery is the *Collège*'s use of idiosyncratic spellings (*phynance* for finance), dates (preferring the pataphysical calendar), and concepts with uniquely pataphysical connotations (clinamen, antinomy, syzygy). While the *Collège* has certainly been the most important "pataphysical institution" (an intentional contradiction in terms) in maintaining the legacy of pataphysical inquiry, this volume focuses primarily on artists and scholars who have worked with pataphysical ideas but have not been members.[21] The *Collège* has helped to create a lineage of pataphysical artists and thinkers by publishing works, preserving documents and ephemera, and keeping the comedic energy alive, but it does not dictate who or how one could play at pataphysics.[22] While the *Collège* has maintained a largely French and European membership[23] the Ouvroir de Littérature Potentielle (known by the acronym Oulipo)—a subcommittee of the *Collège* that literally translates to "workshop of potential literature"—has proliferated internationally and spawned its own offshoots.

Founded in 1960 by François Le Lionnais and Raymond Queneau, the Oulipo consists of mathematicians and writers whose primary concern has been to research (*anoulipism*) and create (*synthoulipism*) forms and constraints with which literature has been or could be written. The theoretical issues surrounding potential literature are complex, and many members of the Oulipo, both past and present, disagree on how precisely these works should be executed and for what purpose. For example, some argue that the creation of formulas for potential literature should be their main focus, while others insist that constraints must be illustrated, or even exhausted. Regardless of which side of the debate one falls on, the Oulipo's efforts to create "recurrent literature" is linked to 'pataphysics' investment in systematic, procedural, and exhaustive experimentation grounded in jocoserious constraints: "We will thus classify under the heading of 'recurrent literature' any text that contains, explicitly or implicitly, generative rules that invite the reader (or the teller, or the singer) to pursue the production of the text to infinity (or until the exhaustion of interest or attention)."[24] While the Oulipo's origins in the *Collège* is not always acknowledged, its desire to continue pataphysical research (re: creative writing) into infinity comes directly from *Faustroll*'s imperative to continue, to go on, to keep up the joke.[25]

While these two groups, based largely in France, continued the pataphysical enterprise strategically, pataphysics' influence began to take root in a more diffuse manner internationally. The publication of Roger Shattuck's *The Banquet Years: The Origins of the Avant-Garde in France, 1885 to World War I* (1955), the 1960 special issue of the *Evergreen Review*, and other translations of Jarry's work into English gave Anglophone artists and thinkers an opportunity to explore pataphysics outside the context of coterie groups such as the *Collège* or Oulipo. These publications coincided with a general growing interest in countercultures in the United States, with which Jarry's hallucinatory, raunchy, and antiestablishment ideas resonated. A black-humor aesthetic in literature and the visual arts also made American audiences receptive to Jarry. The Theatre of the Absurd—and particularly works by Samuel Beckett, Eugène Ionesco, and Edward Albee—popular in the United States during the 1950s and 1960s, was deeply influenced by Jarry's work, although relatively few realized this at the time. Through all of these developments, American and European forms of pataphysics were continuing to cross-pollinate each other. Perhaps nothing represents the transatlantic presence of pataphysics more than the establishment of a comprehensive Marcel Duchamp collection at the Philadelphia Museum of Art in 1954, which grew into a pilgrimage site for many of the avant-garde in the 1950s and 1960s. Philadelphia continued to be a locus of pataphysical experimentation, most notably through the painter Thomas Chimes and "Graffiti Pataphysic" artist James E. Brewton, a largely forgotten but crucial artist for the ways that his work illustrated transatlantic pataphysical experimentation through his connections with CoBrA artists.[26] As a whole, pataphysics presented an opportunity for American artists of the 1950s and 1960s to further link their work to European lineages while also establishing their own voices.

In Canada, pataphysics was also percolating. The Toronto Research Group (TRG)[27]—the name given to the collaborations between poets bpNichol and Steve McCaffery between 1973 and 1981—explored pataphysical creative-research methodologies that merged mysticism and mathematics, speech and writing, the conceptual and the material. As a result of their work, they coined the term Canadian "Pataphysics.[28] In 1981, *Open Letter* published a special issue on Canadian "Pataphysics, followed by an issue on Millennial Pataphysics in 1997, showcasing how pataphysical practice had continued to evolve in the Canadian literary avant-garde. The issues cemented the link between a pataphysical past and a conceptual future in Canadian literature. While *Open Letter* validated pataphysical literature from a more academic perspective, it was through small literary publications that pataphysical literature thrived, including such works as bpNichol's *Catalogue of the "Pataphysical Hardware Company* (1985), which included "everything for your imaginary needs"; John Riddell's *How to Grow Your Own Lightbulbs* (1997); and Gary Barwin's *Anus Porcupine Eyebrow* (2009), which reads letters and punctuation as icons to produce a series of visual-verbal poems. Also of note were the activities of the Institute of Linguistic Onto-Genetics. Founded in 1981 by Michael Dean, the (imaginary) institute produced several publications and held three events—a 1981 symposium at which Dean offered the keynote as his alter-ego Aldo Breun, an "Un Fair" that never occurred but was documented as if it had in 1984, and *L'Affaire Pataphysique*, an event in 1985 at which attendees visited booths to pay for pataphysical performances by artists in persona.[29]

Part of the allure of Jarry's "science" from midcentury, when his works were translated into English, to the present has been its resonance with modern and postmodern philosophers and theorists, including Henri Bergson, Martin Heidegger, Friedrich Nietzsche, Jacques Lacan, and Gilles Deleuze,[30] as well as its exploration of modern scientific concepts that, in retrospect, can be seen as precursors to string theory, quantum mechanics, and—as Jim Hendler and Andrew Hugill explore in their chapter—quantum computing. Jarry's reading of Nietzsche—discussed by both John Heon and Jean-Michel Rabaté in their respective chapters—was a watershed moment for him. Nietzsche's central principles, especially that meaning is multiple and that philosophy should be a "gay science," helped Jarry to formulate his own expansions of the concept of 'pataphysics as comic aesthetics.[31] The realization that there is not a single source of truth, knowledge, or logic, but rather multiple perspective-dependent truths, competing types of knowledge, and alternative forms of logic began to coalesce with Jarry and his associates, and expanded on a massive scale during the coming decades. For Jarry and many modernists, new scientific discoveries and technologies were making visible the vital role of perspective. They revealed that the world was not a single, stable universe, but a relativistic multiverse in which common sense and direct sensory perception told us only a tiny fraction about what else was at work in the physical world. More general concepts of polysemy and polyphony marked many fields in the early twentieth century, and later burgeoned in the works of Jacques Derrida, Roland Barthes, Jacques Lacan, Michel Foucault, and Gilles Deleuze, whose rise to prominence helped to further broaden the exploration of pataphysical ideas in the second half of the twentieth century. Jarry, like Lacan and Derrida after him, illustrated the importance of play within language and the arts as a way of coming to understand and experience these less-apparent truths. Jarry put polysemic play into play, as it were, bringing it into what would come to be the most influential circles of avant-garde art and thought. While Jarry was not the only figure involved, he was certainly one of the most important and earliest—a truly seminal voice that shaped art and thought throughout the twentieth and twenty-first centuries.

Unrolling 'Pataphysics

Building on the strengths of recent scholarly contributions,[32] *'Pataphysics Unrolled* collects critical and creative essays that, together, present a previously untold account of how and why pataphysical experimentation has persisted from its origins in late nineteenth-century France into the contemporary moment. Touching on fields from literature to art, architecture to technology, and environmental science to education, the volume reveals how pataphysics has evolved *in practice* across decades and across disciplines. Given how influential pataphysics has become, this volume is necessarily incomplete; it is illustrative rather than comprehensive. While we want to acknowledge the rich histories of groups such as the *Collège de 'Pataphysique* and the Oulipo, this volume's primary purpose is to elucidate an *un*authorized history—one that includes experimental poets, popular musicians, environmental scientists, speculative architects, and computer programmers who have explored pataphysical ideas and methodologies outside these groups. Are their exploits "true" to Jarry's original texts? Are their opinions about pataphysics "right"? Pataphysicians would not ask these questions, for their answers exist on a metaphysical plane. But what the essays here do show is how—through application, experimentation, and interpretation—pataphysics has continued to offer a methodology for using imagination to systematically reconceive our realities.

But we must be careful not to call anything that is experimental, weird, or anti-rational pataphysical; while pataphysics resists rational and stable definitions, to call anything experimental pataphysical would dull the term's critical bite. It is indeed true that a strict pataphysician might argue—in tone equally serious and tongue-in-cheek—everything is, of course, ultimately pataphysical; pataphysics is, after all, "*the* science." But rather than posit one definition of what could or could not be considered pataphysical, this volume chooses to show a variety of ways in which the term has been applied and understood. For example, Ted Hiebert counts Marina Abramović as a pataphysician for the ways in which her work manipulates human perceptions of time, and Orchid Tierney finds pataphysical principles in UnderAcademy, an unaccredited anti-degree institution that mocks the rise of massive open online courses (MOOCs). Some of our authors might disagree as to what would "count" or "not count" as pataphysical, but none of our authors uses it as a catchall. Rather, they each, in their own way, develop rigorous and thoughtful uses of the term and its associated concepts.

Jarry's work was radically interdisciplinary and anti-doctrinal, and this volume reflects that spirit. The essays in *'Pataphysics Unrolled* differ widely in methodology, style, and even genre. Their organizational structure within this volume creates disciplinary and temporal dissonance, a tension we hope preserves a sense of discovery and surprise as one moves through the chapters. One of the productive paradoxes of pataphysics is that it is a concept that undermines concepts, a system of thought that undermines systems of thought and categories of knowledge. 'Pataphysics sprang from irreverence toward academic authority, and this volume ends with a speculation that pataphysics might help us find our way out of neoliberal educational models that have made some schools seem more like businesses. Following an academic gospel of pataphysics is anathema to the spirit of pataphysics, and restrictions on approaches to or uses of it are exactly what Jarry would have abhorred. We therefore emphasize playful exploration over strict adherence to academic norms, serendipitous connections over straight paths of influence, and genre-bending over genre-adhering. The authors gathered here represent how artists, writers, and critics have been animated by 'pataphysics, but not controlled by it. We see the bringing together of authors of diverse ages, disciplinary and academic training, and professional positions as a strength of the volume.

Like *Faustroll*, *'Pataphysics Unrolled* takes readers on a journey to several distinct but interconnected islands of creativity and thought. By doing so, it acts as a corrective to the relative critical neglect that pataphysics has suffered and lays the groundwork for establishing a theory of diverse pataphysical practices. Pataphysics has spread rhizomatically throughout twentieth- and twenty-first-century art and thought in both unexpected and more expected ways. Essays in this collection have a more-or-less gravitational pull toward each other and Jarry's work. Some return us to foundational Jarry texts, finding new avenues for exploration (Rabaté, Heon), while others question the multiple ways artists claim "influence" (McCaffery, O'Dair). Some examine pataphysics' avant-garde trajectories (Hansen, Décimo, Dworkin), while others expound on their own pataphysical practices (McDowell, Dickinson, Hugill and Hendler). The essays—like pataphysics itself—challenge seemingly fundamental distinctions between high and low culture, the serious and the comic, the arts and the sciences, and critical and creative writing.

The first section, "'And Behold, the Wallpaper of Faustroll's Body': Jarry's Pataphysical Invitation" offers readings of Jarry's texts and shows how they influenced modernism and eventually sparked the formation of the *Collège de 'Pataphysique* and Oulipo. John Heon's essay begins the volume and serves to orient readers to 'pataphysics through a reading of *Faustroll* that highlights its complex interplay of humor and psychopathology. Positioning Jarry alongside Bergson, Nietzsche, and Freud as one of the great modern thinkers of comedy, philosophy, and psychology, Heon's essay offers close readings of some of *Faustroll*'s most hilariously hallucinogenic passages and connects them to a broad range of figures, from Rabelais to Goethe to Foucault to Cixous. Jean-Michel Rabaté's essay on "pataphallics" analyzes the psychosexual aspects of Jarry's novels *Messaline: Roman de l'ancienne Rome* (1901) and *Le Surmâle: Roman moderne* (1902). While later instantiations of pataphysics tend not to be explicitly sexual, Rabaté's reading asks us to reconsider the relationship between pataphysics and sexuality and the significant impact Jarry had on French modernism. Critical accounts of pataphysics too often jump from the publication of *Faustroll* in 1911 to the founding of the *Collège* in 1948. Catherine Hansen's essay offers new insight into the years leading up to and surrounding the *Collège*'s founding. Bringing to light the pataphysical activities and sympathies of Noël Arnaud, Boris Rybak, and the Main à Plume group, not to mention André Breton's surrealists, Hansen asserts the importance of acknowledging a "wartime pataphysics"—one situated in the wider sociocultural contexts of myth-making and myth-busting at the onset of the Cold War. Marc Décimo, as translated from the French by Anne M. Mulhall, offers insight into the antics of the *Collège de 'Pataphysique* by examining the publications and photographs that reveal Duchamp's material relationship with the institution. Craig Dworkin examines the technique of "definitional literature" pioneered by Stefan Themerson and developed by the

Oulipo, with special attention to the experiments of Georges Perec and Marcel Bénabou. Interrogating the metaphors of "machine" and "engine" as they relate to textual production, Dworkin queries the relationship between the two and the consequences of their divergent ideologies for conceptual writing.

"'Like a Musical Score, All Art and All Science': Pataphysics After Jarry and Beyond the *Collège*" brings together essays that showcase pataphysical experimentation across disciplines by artists who interpret Jarry's ideas somewhat more liberally than those in the first section. Michael R. Taylor locates Jarry's influence in Philadelphia and his profound impact on not only Duchamp but also James E. Brewton and Thomas Chimes. The essay is particularly remarkable for its treatment of Brewton, an artist whose works have been largely forgotten yet represent a significant connection between postwar American art and radical European avant-garde groups such as CoBrA and the Situationist Internationale, through which Brewton discovered pataphysics and brought the ideas back to the United States. Steve McCaffery offers an insider's perspective on Canadian "Pataphysics[33] and bpNichol's most pataphysical work, *Probable Systems*. Pairing this with a reading of the pataphysical influences on American Ed Dorn's *Gunslinger*—which manifests to markedly different effects—works to showcase the wide range of possibilities as they relate to pataphysical influence in North American literature. Expanding on a 2014 article written for online music publication Pitchfork,[34] Marcus O'Dair surveys cult bands and popular musicians who have drawn on pataphysics for inspiration, revealing an astonishing range of influence—from the Beatles and Frank Zappa to Captain Beefheart and the Residents—and provocatively wonders if pataphysics might be found more easily in music that doesn't claim the moniker. Ted Hiebert also examines unconscious pataphysicians: contemporary artists whose art practices can productively be understood as pataphysical despite claiming no direct connection. Reading together Marina Abramović's groundbreaking *The Artist Is Present*, Andrew Buckles's *Why Wait?*, Rirkrit Tiravanija's *Untitled 1992 (Free)*, Doug Jarvis's *Minding the Belly Brain*, Sophie Calle's *Take Care of Yourself*, and Tetsushi Higashino's *Observation Diary of a Hydroponic Nose Hair*, Hiebert examines a contemporary interest in slowing time and stretching everyday activities in ways that render the artworks time machines.

"'Written in the Curves of the Limbs': Pataphysical Criticism" looks at the ways scholars have turned to pataphysics to rethink their critical practices. Jerome McGann, Johanna Drucker, and Brandon Walsh detail how pataphysics was fundamental to conceiving their work at the Speculative Computing Lab at the University of Virginia, when digital humanities was forming as a field of study. Jarry reacted against a reductive form of scientific positivism popularized in the late nineteenth and early twentieth centuries, and here we see pataphysics reappear as a tool to critique technological positivism. McGann shares critical experiments from the

Lab and beyond that creatively explore the work of Swinburne, Lautréamont, and Poe. Drucker revisits her "patacritical demon," an ultimately imaginary platform that would be able to find the anomalies, exceptions, and derivatives in literary texts, accounting for human interpretation. For Drucker, cultivating a pataphysical approach to digital humanities was crucial in preserving the "human" in humanities, and maintaining a form of critical play that kept literary objects from losing their subjectivity (i.e., capacity for interpretation). Walsh explores Prism, an application that builds on the work of Drucker and McGann to crowdsource individual interpretations and visualize imagined collaborative readings of literary texts. Poet-critic Charles Bernstein's farce-essay-manifesto recasts the history of American experimental poetics as the "history of pataquerical struggles," proclaiming the need for a "bent studies" of the truly inchoate, provisional, and ideologically impure. At the end, readers are invited to write in their feedback on the chapter and ponder the question: "Did this essay solve your problem?" Hint: it didn't.

"'Progression to an Infinite Degree Was Prophesied Therein': Pataphysics' Possible Futures" collects essays that examine truly contemporary pataphysical practices and, we hope, suggest avenues for future pataphysical exploration. Seth McDowell stretches pataphysical principles into the world of architectural design and engineering, envisioning cities that turn problems into solutions: a city solves its excessive trash problem by transforming it into "blubber" that becomes the city's own landscape; a city comprised solely of highways is able to solve its economic crisis; and a city installs "privy pods" that act as public restrooms and fueling stations for hydro-scooters, thereby freeing it of its reliance on fossil fuels. Adam Dickinson also uses pataphysics to consider our current environmental crisis, though from a very different perspective. Dickinson develops a theory of "metabolic poetics" in order to understand the ways various poets, including himself,[35] have made legible the otherwise inscrutable biological writing being performed on our bodies, without our consent, by toxic chemicals in our environment. In doing so, Dickinson explores the potential of pataphysics as a form of ecopoetic inquiry to help us understand the Anthropocene. Andrew Hugill and Jim Hendler focus on pataphysics' uncanny relationship with computing, including a discussion of the creation of a pataphysical search engine that provides users with unexpected (though not chance) results, and a sneak peek at what is to come: namely, quantum computers—a technology that might, they argue, be able to save technology from itself. The volume ends with a return to where pataphysics began: as a way to mock academic claims to authority. Orchid Tierney looks at how digital mock-academies use pataphysical methods as a way out of restrictive modes of being and knowledge production, and posits that, in the world of the neoliberal university, pataphysical colleges offer a vital supplement to formal institutions of higher learning.

One of the major premises of *'Pataphysics Unrolled* is that it is time to take the comedic intervention of pataphysics seriously. The playful yet consequential impact of pataphysics—its contribution to modernism and its afterlives—can only be truly appreciated through sustained treatments of the writers, artists, philosophers, and critics who have been inspired and shaped by Jarry's ideas. From the establishment of long-lasting institutions such as the *Collège de 'Pataphysique* to bpNichol's short-lived "Pataphysical Hardware Company, to the Musée Patamécanique (which may or may not exist in Rhode Island),[36] to Tania O'Donnell's recent faculty award–winning thesis show at the Pennsylvania Academy of the Fine Arts (PAFA),[37] the guiding principles of pataphysics—its fusion of science and art, humor and philosophy, play and inquiry—have fueled the imaginations of artists and writers for over a century. To return to the question that began this introduction, pataphysics has flourished for more than a century, in part, because of simple inertia. Jarry put 'pataphysics into motion, and it has continued to unroll, not yet having met any force strong enough to stop it. In other words, pataphysics has staying power precisely because it doesn't stay in one place for long. In its insistence that the act of *creation* is the most defiant tool we have to critique, reimagine, and reconfigure a world that "is the way it is," perhaps by accident, pataphysics can be applied to almost any way of knowing as a way to explode its most basic, and probably unacknowledged, assumptions. Pataphysics, I would argue, can be studied in the past but can only be lived in the present. To be a pataphysician, one must constantly replace the accidental/prior consciousness in which they find themselves with a consciously creative/new one. As Hiebert writes, "The real challenge of setting sail in a sieve is that of keeping the water from seeping in; it requires a constant attention to the act of bailing out the boat in order to maintain a precarious balance at the intersection of imminent submersion and pataphysical buoyancy."[38]

As the wallpaper of Faustroll's body unrolls into the future, what will pataphysics "be" in another two, twenty, or two hundred years? I don't know, but I hope it will.

Notes

I would like to thank Craig Dworkin, John Heon, Emily Brewton Schilling, and Michael Taylor for reading versions of this introduction and providing helpful feedback. I would also like to thank the anonymous readers who provided insight and encouragement. More personally, I would like to thank Leah Benedict for companionship, Rachel Banner for friendship, and Joseph DeVitis for partnership; this would not exist without you.

1. These names could have easily been replaced by other "equivalent" names. For a book-length study of the *many* individuals, groups, and movements that were influenced by 'pataphysics, see Andrew Hugill, *'Pataphysics: A Useless Guide* (Cambridge, MA: MIT Press, 2012).

2. *Oxford English Dictionary*, s.v. "Pataphysics, *n.*," accessed December 15, 2020, https://www.oed.com/.

3. Alastair Brotchie, *Alfred Jarry: A Pataphysical Life* (Cambridge, MA: MIT Press, 2011).

4. His height (Jarry was about 5'2") allowed him to live in such an apartment, though his head would sometimes scrape the low ceiling, causing plaster dust to fall on him. Catalog item no. 61 of bpNichols's Pataphysical Hardware Company is "Plaster de Paris," a bag of talcum powder packaged to read "For those nights you can't remember / NOW people will believe that you, like Alfred Jarry, live in the low-ceilinged room of your choice when they see the dust of ceilings atop your duff." For an image and description, see Brian Dedora, "L'Affaire Pataphysique, Toronto, 1985," part 1, Dispatches from the Poetry Wars, October 6, 2017, https://www.dispatchespoetrywars.com/documents/laffaire-pataphysique.

5. Alfred Jarry, *Adventures in 'Pataphysics: Collected Works I*, ed. Paul Edwards, trans. Paul Edwards and Antony Melville (London: Atlas Press, 2001), 13.

6. Brotchie, *Alfred Jarry*, 358.

7. A belly so big and singular in appetite, in fact, that it required the invention of its own term: *gidouille*.

8. *Ubu Roi* is only one of three Ubu plays. The others are *Ubu Cocu* and *Ubu Enchaîné*. All three are published together in English as *The Ubu Plays*, trans. Cyril Connelly and Simon Watson Taylor (New York: Grove Press, 1969).

9. Cited in Roger Shattuck's introduction to *Exploits and Opinions of Dr. Faustroll, Pataphysician (A Neo-Scientific Novel)* (1911), by Alfred Jarry, trans. Simon Watson Taylor (Boston: Exact Change, 1996), x.

10. Brotchie, *Alfred Jarry*, 228–29 (Brotchie's emphasis).

11. Ibid., 31.

12. Ibid., 29.

13. Jarry, *Faustroll*, 15 (hereafter cited parenthetically in the text).

14. Jarry often played with notions of equivalence and difference, asserting simultaneously that books could be equivalent (*livres pairs*) and that, when examined closely, things that appear similar are not (A ≠ A). For more on his *livres pairs*, see Ben Fisher's *The Pataphysician's Library: An Exploration of Alfred Jarry's livres pairs* (Liverpool, UK: Liverpool University Press, 2001).

15. Ezra Pound, *The Cantos* (1934; repr., New York: New Directions, 1996), 5.

16. John Heon's essay playfully suggests that the eighth and last book of *Faustroll* may, in fact, just be an ∞ writ vertically.

17. Roger Shattuck, introduction to Jarry, *Faustroll*, ix.

18. See, especially, Marcus O'Dair's essay, which shows Jarry's influence on popular music.

19. Jarry was fascinated by the concept of time machines, and the Oulipo's concept of "plagiarism by anticipation" supports this pataphysical approach to time and literary history.

20. Currently, its website allows for some publication downloads and accepts donations that come with subscriptions to publications, illustrating that the *Collège* is opening up its once-closed doors.

21. A notable exception to this is Marc Décimo's essay on Marcel Duchamp and his direct involvement with the *Collège*. Dworkin's essay, too, focuses on the *Collège*, though indirectly through the Oulipo. Décimo and Hugill are both *Collège* members.

22. While 'pataphysics was circulating in esoteric circles, Jarry's works, and in particular his Ubu legacy, had large followings, and the French cult of Jarry expanded far beyond the *Collège*.

23. While technically true, the *Collège* has itself inspired a number of international pataphysical colleges. Hugill, for example, is also a member of De Nederlandse Academie voor 'Patafysica, and the Académie québécoise de la 'pataphysique. A map of pataphysical institutes across the globe can be found at https://www.patakosmos.com/.

24. Warren F. Motte, Jr., *Oulipo: A Primer of Potential Literature* (Normal, IL: Dalkey Archive, 1998), 109.

25. Craig Dworkin theorizes the practice of "definitional literature" and its origins in 'pataphysics in his contribution to this volume.

26. Michael Taylor's chapter in this volume takes a close look at this history with a focus on the work of James E. Brewton, which has only been recently rediscovered. His essay is the first work of criticism on the artist, and the first to publish Brewton images since the early 1970s. These images—Brewton's

Self-Portrait, Portrait of Asger Jorn, Ubu Becomes King, Ubu's Military Mind, Sunrise, Graffiti Pataphysic, Alfred Jarry, Patatarget, and *Alfred Jarry in Paris*—have never before been reproduced in color in print.

27. For more on the TRG, see Steve McCaffery and bpNichol, eds., *Rational Geomancy: The Kids of the Book Machine—The Collected Research Reports of the Toronto Research Group, 1973–1982* (Vancouver: Talonbooks, 1992).

28. Canadian ''Pataphysics adds an apostrophe to 'pataphysics, denoting "a shift from elision to quotation." The TRG continues, "If 'Pataphysics (according to Jarry) is 'the science of imaginary solutions' and thereby the source of answers to questions never posed, then ''Pataphysics (diacriticized via the open quotation of a double elision) will be 'the literature of all imaginary sciences'" (ibid. 301–2).

29. Brian Dedora offers an overview of the many performances at this event in "L'Affaire Pataphysique, Toronto, 1985," parts 1 and 2, both published on the Dispatches from the Poetry Wars website on October 6, 2017, and January 19, 2018, respectively: https://www.dispatchespoetrywars.com/documents/laffaire-pataphysique/ and https://www.dispatchespoetrywars.com/documents/laffaire-pataphysique-toronto-1985-part-2-2. McCaffery also discusses this event in his essay.

30. See, for example, Gilles Deleuze, "An Unrecognized Precursor to Heidegger: Alfred Jarry," in *Essays Critical and Clinical*, trans. Daniel W. Smith and Michael A. Greco (Minneapolis: University of Minnesota Press, 1997), 91–98; Todd Dufresne, "Derrida, Jarry, Nietzsche: Introducing a Deconstructive Pataphysics, Contra Heidegger," *re: post* 1 (1993): 26–33; or Stephen Barker, "Canon-Fodder: Nietzsche, Jarry, Derrida (The Play of Discourse and the Discourse of Play)," *Journal of Dramatic Theory and Criticism* 4, no. 1 (Fall 1989): 69–83.

31. Conversely, Jarry himself helped to bring Nietzsche into greater prominence in France through translations of his works and discussion of them in avant-garde circles.

32. This book would not have been possible without the groundwork laid by Christian Bök's *'Pataphysics: The Poetics of an Imaginary Science* (Evanston, IL: Northwestern University Press, 2001); Brotchie's *Alfred Jarry*; and Hugill's *'Pataphysics*, which have all made overdue and vital contributions to the study of pataphysics for Anglophone readers.

33. For more on Canadian ''Pataphysics, see *Open Letter: Canadian ''Pataphysics* 4, nos. 6–7 (Winter 1980–81), *Rampike: La ''Pataphysique* 5, no. 2 (1986), and *Open Letter: Millennial 'Pataphysics* 7 (Winter 1997).

34. Marcus O'Dair, "'Pataphysics: Your Favorite Cult Artist's Favorite Pseudoscience," Pitchfork, October 21, 2014, https://pitchfork.com/features/article/9527-pataphysics-your-favorite-cult-artists-favorite-pseudoscience.

35. Most notable in his recent *Anatomic* (Toronto: Coach House, 2018), a book that involved chemical and microbial testing on his body.

36. See https://www.museepata.org/.

37. *Presence*, the first annual thesis exhibition for PAFA's Low-Residency MFA program, opened on August 9, 2017. Tania O'Donnell received the faculty award for her exhibition, which included the thirteen-panel installation piece *Machines & Machinations, 6 Crumbs* (featuring the video *Falling into Spiral Thinking—Hare Origin* Stories) and three sculptures: *Machine to Trigger Waves of Powerful Emotion (3 Wheeled with Spring Vacuum Attachment), Ubu Appurtenance,* and *Petite Conscience Box*. Her more recent work, much of which is similarly informed by pataphysics, can be viewed at https://www.taniaodonnell.art/.

38. Quoted from his contribution to this volume.

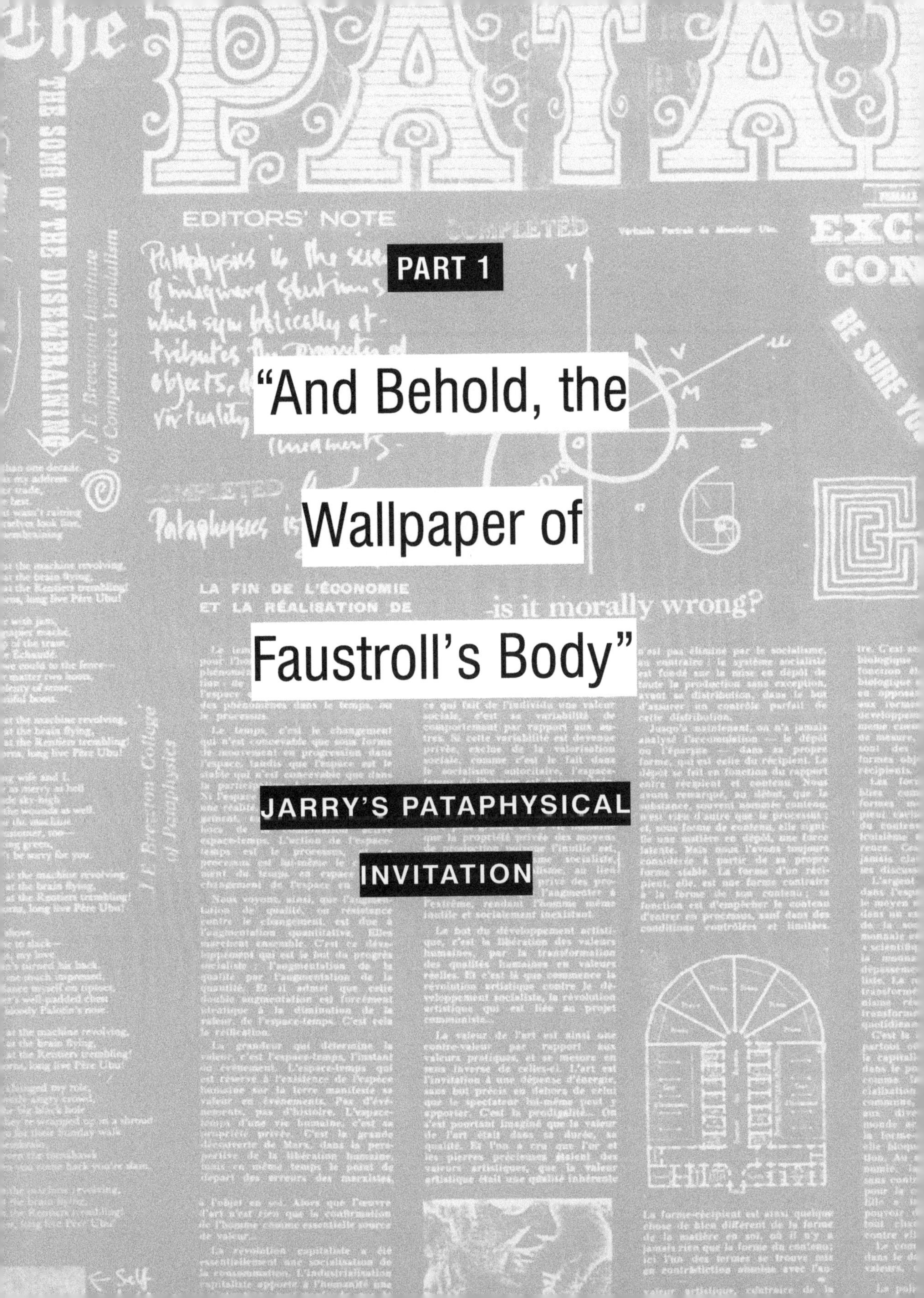

PART 1

"And Behold, the Wallpaper of Faustroll's Body"

JARRY'S PATAPHYSICAL INVITATION

Chapter 1

Twisted *Witz*

Experiments in Psychopathology and Humor by Dr. Faustroll and His Pataphysical Progeny

John Heon

> It is in these impatient spirits that a veritable delight in madness erupts because madness has such a cheerful tempo.
>
> —Friedrich Nietzsche, *The Gay Science*

> The psychiatric expert can only be Ubu himself.
>
> —Michel Foucault, *Abnormal*

Friedrich Nietzsche, founder of "la gaya scienza,"[1] would have been delighted to know that the tempo indication for the overture of the founding theatrical work of pataphysics, *Ubu Roi*, was "gaîment."[2] Indeed, a cheerful tempo of rational madness pervades Alfred Jarry's oeuvre, as it did his life, both of which were devoted to creating his own "fröhliche Wissenschaft." Perusing the fifth edition of the *Diagnostic and Statistical Manual of Mental Disorders* (*DSM-5*), one could find a nice fit for Jarry in several psychopathological boxes: schizophrenia, obsessive-compulsive disorder, alcoholism, bipolar disorder, suicidality, and Tourette's syndrome, to name a few. He probably would have taken pride in those diagnoses—as he did in the diagnosis of "precocious imbecility"[3] that released him from military service—and then scoured the *DSM-5* in an attempt to cultivate even more of the scientifically recognized symptoms of insanity. In fact, much of Jarry's existence was devoted to an extended psychological experiment on himself, an enactment of Arthur Rimbaud's Dionysian dictum that the artist must become a seer through "a long, immense, and reasoned *derangement* of *all the senses*."[4] It was an experiment exploring the limits of consciousness via mock-epic, Surmâlean feats of physical, chemical, and intellectual endurance, with the ultimate experimental results being not only Jarry's novels and plays but also the comic performance art of his life. T. S. Eliot, in his introduction to Paul Valéry's *The Art of Poetry*, asserted that for Valéry, and modern artists as a whole, "the 'cool scientist' is an alternative, rather than the antithesis to the 'disheveled madman': a different mask for the same actor."[5] Jarry, friend and colleague of Valéry, embodied this alternation of masks more fully than any other artist of his time, revealing its inherently comic nature and aesthetic possibilities.

While elements of these ludic, artistic-scientific investigations of madness mark all of Jarry's works, none examines them with greater depth, seriousness, and salubriously sick humor than his 1911 *Exploits and Opinions of Dr. Faustroll, Pataphysician (A Neo-Scientific Novel)*—a title that conveys both its intellectual ambition and puckish playfulness. Although Jarry was and still is best known for his play *Ubu Roi* (1896) and often played the role of Ubu in public, he saw *Faustroll* as his greatest artistic achievement and was far more akin to Dr. Faustroll than Père Ubu in real life.[6] *Faustroll* was also a precursor to some of the greatest modernist and postmodernist works in literature and the visual arts, many of which share its humor noir aesthetic, encyclopedic range, stream-of-consciousness form, and oscillation between rationality and absurdity. As Andrew Hugill states, "The substance of pataphysics is a deeply serious humor,"[7] and this applies to *Faustroll* more than any other work by Jarry. It is a decidedly "jocoserious" book, written decades before Joyce coined that term and Duchamp called for art with "humor that . . . added a note of . . . seriousness."[8] Guillaume Apollinaire, who declared *Faustroll* the most important publication of 1911, encapsulated the profound impact of Jarry's comic aesthetics: "It is thanks to Alfred Jarry that humor has arisen from the lower regions in which previously it had been mired, and now furnishes the poet with an entirely original lyricism."[9] In many respects, Jarry's writings epitomized the core characteristics of avant-garde comic aesthetics. Not only was he included in Breton's *Anthology of Black Humor* (1939),[10] but Jarry was influential on many others (Duchamp, Dalí, Picabia, Apollinaire, Picasso, Arp, et al.).[11] Through its jocoserious juxtaposition of the voices of madness and scientific rationality, Jarry's work as a whole, and *Faustroll* in particular, opened up new realms of both form and content that have proven to be some of the most enduring elements of avant-garde art and thought. At the heart of *Faustroll*'s quintessential modernity and postmodernity is a "psycho-comical opposition engine": the Apollonian examination of the Dionysian and the Dionysian subversion of the Apollonian. Through this interplay of opposites, each driving and intensifying the other, the novel challenges standard definitions of science and art, reality and imagination, and sanity and insanity with a multidimensional humor that reflects the shifting states of the human psyche.

Like Jarry himself, Dr. Faustroll can be seen as a case study of psychopathology. He is a suicidal, homicidal, alcoholic, homeless man who claims to telepathically communicate with dead scientists and displays textbook megalomania in proclamations such as "'I am God.'"[12] His appearance projects the exuberant eccentricity of a lunatic, from his sea-green mustachios to his "tiny little gray boots with even layers of dust preserved on them at great expense" and his right index finger piled with "emerald and topaz rings right up to the fingernail," held in place by "a linchpin made of molybdenum, screwed into the bone of the ungual phalanx, through the fingernail" (7–8). Other characters also manifest colorful forms of psycho-behavioral dysfunction and devoutly practice the systematic "*derangement* of *all the senses*." The narrator for most of the novel, the bailiff Panmuphle, is at least temporarily insane (deeply inebriated during the voyage), and Dr. Faustroll's cabin boy, Bosse-de-Nage, a dog-faced baboon "less cyno- than hydrocephalous," is so cognitively impaired (or wise) that he is capable of only one utterance: "Ha ha" (27). Moreover, the various inhabitants they encounter on their sieve-skiff voyage to the "isles" of Paris exhibit a broad spectrum of bizarre behaviors and hallucinatory worldviews; they frequently engage in the consumption of mind-altering substances, which Faustroll partakes of enthusiastically—reflecting Jarry's own consumption of astonishing quantities of alcohol, sometimes augmented by ether. In short, *Faustroll* is the consummate Dionysian tale, the apotheosis of comic psychological instability and narrative unreliability.

Jarry adds historical resonance to the book's Dionysian madness theme by explicitly employing the motif of the *Narrenschiff*, or ship of fools, which is particularly prominent in works of one of Jarry's most important models, François Rabelais:[13] "Il s'agit d'un voyage de Paris á Paris, par mer, dans la pure tradition rabelaisenne."[14] As Foucault discusses in the "Stultifera Navis" chapter of *Madness and Civilization*, this motif reflected the Medieval-Renaissance practice of putting the mentally ill on ships, which had the triple function of "curing," confining, and exhibiting them for the entertainment of the sane. Jarry, however, effects a comic inversion of this "psychiatric treatment." Dr. Faustroll, the mad scientist-captain of the ship of fools, takes the representative of law and rationality, Panmuphle, prisoner—first hurling him into his wine-and-spirits-filled cellar, and then shackling him to the skiff and forcing him to row in a state that Panmuphle describes as "drunk as I was and ready to believe anything" (31). The novel reverses the expected spectacle of madness: the "insane" man laughs at the confined "sane" man who has come "in the name of Law and Justice" (9) and yet has immediately been made mad with alcohol. In many respects, *Faustroll* resurrects the Medieval-Renaissance role of the sacred or wise fool (and the "gay physician") that Rabelais used throughout his work. As Foucault explains, from the late Middle Ages into the Renaissance and beyond, "the character of the Madman . . . is no longer simply a ridiculous and familiar silhouette in the wings; he stands center stage as the guardian of truth. . . . The madman is comedy to the second degree, the deception of deception."[15] Dr. Faustroll is psychopathological comedy to the second degree, one who constantly unmasks the true folly of slavish devotion to rationalism and the unquestioning acceptance of scientific authority—especially its definitions of mental illness.

Throughout *Faustroll*, Jarry comically destabilizes the notion that sanity and scientific reason are synonymous by undermining the certainty of scientific knowledge and the reliability of supposedly objective observation by having Dr. Faustroll present "science" that is the product of madness or hallucination. As Matthieu Gosztola asserts, Jarry deliberately generates further epistemological confusion because he often parodies scientific discourse by using scientific terminology "avec une excessive et souvent fallacieuse complexité."[16] This "excessive and often fallacious complexity" is, of course, part of Jarry's general satirization of the voice and tone of scientific authority, but it is also a test of and warning to the reader: "Don't think it's true just because it sounds scientific." Gerald Gillespie states, "Jarry . . . realizes that modern science, by spawning absurdity, has unexpectedly released a profound source of artistic energy. It is again possible to embark on Faustian explorations because absurdity ends the paralysis of banal reality and liberates poetic imagination."[17] Conversely, Jarry demonstrated that Dionysian madness and poetically absurd humor could help liberate the scientific imagination and shatter the stereotype of the dull, pedantic, rationalist scientist—or, for that matter, the tragic "mad scientist," such as Dr. Frankenstein, Dr. Moreau, or Dr. Faust. One of the more striking examples of Dr. Faustroll's ostensibly deranged scientific imagination and of Jarry's proclivity for playing with notions of real and spurious science is the surgical procedure Dr. Faustroll performs on Bosse-de-Nage (a comic inversion of the horrors of H. G. Wells's *The Island of Dr. Moreau*):

> The red and blue callosity which they sport on their buttocks, was . . . displaced by Faustroll, by means of some strange medication, and grafted onto his cheeks, azurine on one, scarlet on the other, so that his flat face was a tricolor. (27)[18]

Only the maddest of mad scientists could dream up something so bizarre and cruel—which, of course, is part of what makes this creation of the cheekiest of cheeky monkeys so hilarious. The novel challenges the reader not to laugh at the mad scientist and his unfortunate experimental subject—and perhaps at themselves for feeling guilty about laughing at the depiction of the surgical abuse of a mentally defective animal by a demented "doctor."

While the novel explores the transgressive humor of Dr. Faustroll's rational insanity, it also draws the reader toward psychological instability. Shattuck states that "[Jarry] pushed his sense of the comic into the realm where laughter is mixed with apprehension for ourselves."[19] The idea that the book is at least on one level designed to induce madness in the reader is suggested by its very first words. *Faustroll* opens with an epigraph from the Upanishads that gives a clear indication of the comic parallels he is drawing between the reading and interpretation of his "neo-scientific novel," with its eight books,[20] and the reading and interpretation of the "octophilic" Hindu scriptures: "'There are eight abodes, eight places of sight, eight deities, and eight Purushas. Whoever understands those Purushas in their division, and again in their union, has overcome the world. I ask thee about the Purusha in the Upanishads. And thou explain not him to me, thy head will fall off.' S'akalya knew him not, so his head fell off. Moreover robbers took away his bones, mistaking them for something else."

In other words, if one does not understand all eight books of *Faustroll* in their division and union, one will "lose one's head," go insane. But perhaps this is a good thing and Jarry has deliberately set up this impossible task of interpretation for the reader; one is *supposed* to crack up, lose one's mind, laugh one's head off—or all of the above. Julien Schuh has argued that one of the effects of the book is the induction of a "hermeneutic paranoia," a compulsion to be constantly searching for hidden signs, symbols, and allusions: "Il faut le conduire à voir des signes partout, à interpréter le moindre aspect du texte, à soupçonner du sens sous chaque parcelle de l'œuvre."[21] The process of reading Jarry is blissful and utterly disconcerting: one is immersed in an ocean of endless meaning and interconnection, from the theological, to the philosophical, scientific, alchemical, musical, heraldic, mathematical, art historical, and literary.[22] There is another equal but opposite paranoia at work as well: one must always be alert to the possibility of the interpretive bomb of the joke, pun, or ironic tone that reverses stable, serious meaning and points to the possibility that all of this apparent interconnection is just an illusion, a prank, or *blague*. Hence, the text induces "anti-hermeneutic paranoia," too; the reader can be driven crazy by the possibility of a *lack* of meaning and connection in the text. Perhaps Jarry wanted any reader who attempted to logically master the text to feel as drunk as Panmuphle: "ready to believe anything" or nothing—or both.

Understanding Dr. Faustroll's comic psychopathology and destabilization of scientific authority requires understanding how far beyond Ubu he is as an artistic creation. Although the Ubu plays humorously address conceptions of sanity and insanity, there are several major differences between them and *Faustroll*, and between Dr. Faustroll and Père Ubu. Ubu is a rather unidimensional comic character, and the Ubu plays are essentially farcical sketches, especially compared to *Faustroll*, a "strange, scientifico-lyrico-philosophical elucubration,"[23] with its dense, symbolist prose-poetry and its proto-modernist, stream-of-consciousness flood of imagery. Moreover, Ubu is the personification of what Jarry despised and satirized: the stupid, rapacious, power-mad dictator; whereas Faustroll was very close to what Jarry was: deeply learned and rational but also profoundly artistic and irrational, a mind and body constantly oscillating between Apollo and Dionysus. From a humor-theory perspective, there are also radical differences between the two characters, and this is related to the differences between the forms of comedy they manifest. Ubu is the embodiment of the Bergsonian definition of the comic, "laughable in exact proportion as [he] reminds us of a mere machine,"[24] with his robotic repetition of "Merdre!" and "Par ma chandelle verte!"[25] and compulsive eating and defecating. He is a virtual automaton, the epitome of the Bergsonian encrustation of the rigid and artificial on that which should be flexible and organic, whereas Dr. Faustroll is much more complex. He is far more Nietzschean, Freudian, and Rabelaisian in his humor; he is witty, ironic, and poetic, and yet capable of sudden shifts to the grotesque or slapstick. Likewise, the pataphysics of Ubu is very different from that of Dr. Faustroll. Ubu's pataphysics is largely a mockery of conventional science,[26] whereas Dr. Faustroll's 'pataphysics is a jocoserious exploration of science and the multiple levels of artistic and philosophical meaning it can reveal. We laugh *at* Ubu's pataphysics; we laugh *with* Dr. Faustroll's 'pataphysics and ponder the truths behind its absurdities.

The contrast between Jarry's portrayals of the two characters' psychopathologies is equally striking. Ubu is insane, but in a simple, clownish, mechanical way, repeatedly manifesting his puerility and aggression through Tourettic outbursts and sudden violence. Dr. Faustroll's insanity, however, is a deliberately conjured and contemplated state of mind, a celebration of the multiplicity of consciousness possible through great intelligence, knowledge, and artistic-scientific imagination, a consciousness that is "aberrant" in that it is so far beyond the average in its erudition and vision. When Foucault asserts that "the psychological expert can only be Ubu himself," he is referring to the "penal-psychiatric Ubu,"[27] the ridiculous, robotic nature of scientific authority in certain legal-medical contexts, especially the courtroom, where reductive either-or determinations of insanity are presented by expert witnesses. Ubu is, in effect, the Bergsonian parody of the self-important, narrow-minded scientist, the technocrat-automaton who lacks perspective, humor, and breadth of knowledge. Dr. Faustroll, by contrast, is the scientific and psychological expert (and self-mocking, self-analyzing patient/subject) who embodies the artistic depth, nuanced analysis, comic self-awareness, and wide-ranging intellect of a truly insightful psychiatrist. As such, Dr. Faustroll completely upends "penal-psychiatric" standards of expertise by making madness not only healthy, but a sign of heightened consciousness and intellectual-artistic vigor.

The broader scientific, aesthetic, and philosophical contexts of Jarry's humorous explorations of psychopathology in *Faustroll* are vital for comprehending the book and Jarry himself. They not only link him to many of his immediate contemporaries in Paris, from Mallarmé to Valéry, Gauguin, Rousseau, Picasso, Apollinaire, and the like, but also to wider circles of artists and thinkers from the late nineteenth and early twentieth centuries, such as Duchamp, Man Ray, Ernst, Dalí, Joyce, Stein, Barnes, Artaud, Ionesco, and Beckett, all of whom had profound influence on later modernist and postmodernist art and theory, particularly their focus on the psychological and the comic.[28] Three theoretical thinkers stand out in their relevance to Jarry and his conceptions of humor, psychopathology, and the nature of the psyche as a whole: Henri Bergson, Sigmund Freud, and Friedrich Nietzsche. It is noteworthy that the birth of *Faustroll* (completed in 1898)[29] took place when Bergson's *Laughter* (1900) and Freud's *Jokes and Their Relation to the Unconscious* (1905) were still in embryo. In many respects, *Faustroll* anticipates several of the essential insights that Bergson and Freud would present in their theories about humor and the human psyche.

In the case of Bergson, there was a direct exchange of ideas that preceded the composition of *Faustroll* and the publication of *Laughter*. Jarry took courses with Bergson between 1891 and 1893 at the Lycée Henri IV, and he was a very powerful early influence: "[Jarry] later wrote that Bergson's lectures were 'precious above all others,'" and "followed these lectures for two years, and . . . transcribed them almost word for word" in "more than 700 pages of close writing."[30] Jarry said Bergson presented his early ideas about the comic at Henri IV, working them out in the classroom years before he published them: "He later recalled that Bergson, 'in our presence—we adolescents just awakening to the serious—improvised his theory of humor.'"[31] Jarry heard his first rigorous intellectual discussion of humor in Bergson's lectures, and although he disagreed with him on some points, Bergson was one of the central sources Jarry drew from in the development of his comic literary style. Jarry is also likely to have encountered William James's concept of stream of consciousness during the same general period, given that James was a close friend of Bergson and famous in French intellectual circles.[32] Regardless of the degree of James's direct influence, *Faustroll* is arguably the first full-fledged, modernist, stream-of-consciousness novel, and much of its humor stems from its revelation of the incongruous thoughts, images, words, sensations, and desires constantly flowing through the mind.

While Jarry had a deep engagement with Bergson, he almost certainly had little or no direct knowledge of Freud before writing *Faustroll*; Freud was in Vienna and had not published much that had reached Paris circles. There are, however, significant indirect links:

Freud's Oedipal theories were at their earliest stage of formation at this time, and as yet unpublished, but Jarry's accounts of extreme mental states in *Absolute Love* (1899) are based upon his extensive readings of the same French psychologists, such as Pierre Janet and Jean-Martin Charcot, who significantly influenced Freud.[33]

Perhaps no single statement better illustrates the fundamental role of humor in modern theory, literature, and art than Freud's assertion that "joke-work and dream-work must, at least in some essential respect, be identical," an equivalency he based on his discovery of "the wit [*Witz*] of all unconscious processes."[34] In many ways, Jarry had been investigating the mechanisms of joke-work and dream-work artistically before they existed theoretically and scientifically, but he twisted *Witz* inside out. Opening up the mind for examination via Ubu, Dr. Faustroll, and other characters through their puns, jokes, pranks, and delirious visions, he humorously erased the lines between the conscious and unconscious, reality and dream, the repressed and the expressed. As Shattuck states, "Jarry's humor may, rather, be regarded as a psychological refusal to repress distasteful things."[35] He explains, "Jarry's practice fully illustrates the 'scientific' nature of humor. 'Laughter,' Jarry wrote, 'is born out of the discovery of the contradictory.' He was not clowning, merely; he was observing a relentless method."[36] Jarry was taking the id on stage and onto the printed page before anyone knew the term, and one of the earmarks of his humor is that his characters repress nothing, a technique that would be carried over into the comic aesthetics of Dada, surrealism, and many subsequent movements. In several ways, Jarry's writings and life were precursors to "the immersive, flamboyantly desublimatory objects, poems, and promenades of the Baroness,"[37] the *merdre*-obsessed black humor of William Burroughs's novels, and the buffo grotesquerie of Mike Kelley's performances. Jarry, in effect, uncorked the bottle of the unconscious, drank deeply, and then passed it to generations of artists after him.

Brotchie makes a statement about *Absolute Love* in relation to Freud that could apply to all of Jarry's works, but especially *Faustroll*: "Ironically, the text has resisted Freudian interpretation precisely because it is so overt and exhibits little in the way of inhibition or sublimation."[38] Freud's ideas about repression in dreams and jokes seem to be both anticipated and defied by Jarry's constant revelations of what is normally repressed. Like Gilles Deleuze and Félix Guattari's *Anti-Oedipus*, *Faustroll* is both an homage to and a mockery of Freudian rationalism and systematic thought of all kinds. Dr. Faustroll is evidence that Jarry believed, like Deleuze and Guattari, that "a schizophrenic out for a walk is a better model than a neurotic lying on the analyst's couch. A breath of fresh air, a relationship with the outside world."[39] Dr. Faustroll, out for a stroll/land-sailing voyage around Paris, plays the schizophrenic, cultivating and celebrating his "madness," flouting all laws and rules, and transcending science. Like Hélène Cixous's Medusa, his mission is "to blow up the law, to break up the 'truth' with laughter,"[40] especially the law and accepted truth of the science of psychopathology.[41] Through his constant oscillation between the voices of Apollo and Dionysus, Dr. Faustroll generates a humor of polyphonic heterogeneity that subverts adherence to any single theory: "The schizophrenic passes from one code to the other, . . . deliberately *scrambles all the codes*, by quickly shifting from one to another."[42] And yet, Jarry is not anti-rational (or anti-Freudian ante-Freud), but rather, he sees the need to balance the rational with the irrational, to leaven the Apollonian with the Dionysian.

Nietzsche, the ur-Apollonian-Dionysian, was central to Deleuze and Guattari's critique of Freud, and he was also one of the most crucial figures in the comic aesthetics of Jarry, although his influence is often unrecognized or underestimated.[43] Nietzsche's work was very well known to Jarry and his contemporaries, and in contrast to Bergson's, most if not all of Nietzsche's work was available to Jarry before he wrote *Faustroll*.[44] There are "many resonances with pataphysics in Nietzsche's philosophy,"[45] and there is much evidence of Nietzsche's direct and indirect effect on Jarry and his circles.[46] Carol Diethe writes, "In the literature of the French avant-garde the influence of Nietzsche was already manifest in the absurdist plays of Alfred Jarry, notably *Ubu Roi*," and she adds that "members of the avant-garde such as Jarry . . . were receptive to Nietzsche's iconoclasm."[47] Ben Fisher notes, "Jarry remarked at the end of his life that one of his Rennes schoolteachers, M. Bourdon, had introduced him to Nietzsche even before French translations were available."[48] There is more evidence of Jarry's engagement with Nietzschean ideas via the journals he read and was published in: "Symbolist reviews were instrumental in promoting Nietzsche in France, including the publications most closely associated with the contemporary auteurs pairs, the *Mercure de France* and the *Revue Blanche*; Paul Valéry featured among those who published work on Nietzsche."[49] In fact, the *Mercure*, the journal that promoted Jarry's work more than any other, also published the complete works of Nietzsche, translated by Henri Albert.[50] In addition, Fisher sees various elements of Nietzsche's thought in Jarry and the avant-garde in general: "The new appeal of the *Übermensch* for Jarry's artistic generation is its association in Nietzsche with a worldview that could be regarded as sympathetic to anarchist thought and literary practice. In particular we should note the concepts of *Sklavenmoral* (slave morality) and *Umwertung aller Werte* (inversion of all values)."[51] Although the Ubu plays certainly show the influence of some of these Nietzschean concepts, *Faustroll* is a much deeper, more systematic inverter of all values, whether in science, morality, or culture.

While *Sklavenmoral* and *Umwertung aller Werte* are significant elements of Jarry's work, Nietzsche's radical reconfiguration of philosophy into a "gaya scienza," a "fröhliche Wissenschaft" pertains most directly to Jarry and the avant-garde as a whole. This, however, is often overlooked. Hugill is among the few who have recognized the importance of the Nietzschean ludic in Jarry's work, and he sees the influence of *The Gay Science* in particular, with its "evocation of an archaic Provençal tradition of knight-poets who quested for knowledge through an exuberant poetry and a playful approach to life."[52] In all his major works, Nietzsche repeatedly emphasizes the need to bring laughter, play, and an overarching comic perspective to philosophy, art, and life; in short, to bring the Dionysian into dialogue with the Apollonian: "I know of no other way of dealing with great tasks than that of *play*: this is, as a sign of greatness, an essential precondition."[53] In his mock-biblical *Zarathustra*, he proclaimed, "Laughter I have pronounced holy: you higher men, *learn*—to laugh!"[54] In *The Gay Science* he posited laughter as an essential philosophical method, asserting that one should "laugh at oneself as one would have to laugh in order to laugh *out of the whole truth*."[55] He also highlighted this in the epigraph to the book: "I laugh at every master who does not laugh at himself." Through this self-directed laughter, one could effect a *Selbstüberwindung* (self-overcoming), cure the nausea of *ressentiment*, and comprehend "the eternal comedy of existence."[56] Jarry's transformations of the tragedies of *Faust* and *Macbeth* into jocoserious comedies can be seen as artistic affirmations of Nietzsche's proclamation of the power of the comic vision: "Who among you can laugh and be elevated at the same time? Whoever climbs the highest mountains laughs at all tragic plays and tragic seriousness."[57] Similarly, Nietzsche's statement in *Beyond Good and Evil*, that "the higher man must prick up his ears . . . whenever a buffoon without shame or scientific satyr, speaks out in his presence,"[58] seems to have been perfectly incarnated in Dr. Faustroll, who is not only a clownish scientist but also quite decidedly a satyr: "From his groin down to his feet, in contrast, he was sheathed in a satyric black fur, for he was man to an improper degree" (7). Although Jarry might not have had these specific lines in mind, it is clear that he absorbed and utilized Nietzsche's Dionysian-Apollonian voice, imagery, and symbolism.

This comic inversion of the values of seriousness, sobriety, and conventional sanity is the guiding principle of Jarry's approach to the sciences, particularly psychology. The word pataphysics naturally draws more attention to Jarry's ludic engagement with physics, but, as indicated above, he was equally engaged with psychology, and this corresponds with Nietzsche's repeated assertion of the importance of psychology to philosophy and the arts. In several major works, Nietzsche referred to himself as a psychologist or psycho-physiologist,[59] placing psychology at the center of modern science: "Psychology shall again be recognized as the queen of the sciences, to serve and prepare for which the other sciences exist. For psychology is now once again the road to the fundamental problems."[60] The primacy of psychology for Nietzsche and the modern era as a whole is understandable because it is the science that is most inherently interdisciplinary, subjective, and even artistic. It is no accident that Freud, Jung, James, Bergson, and others created bodies of work that were hybrids of science, literature, art, mythology, philosophy, and linguistics. It was an age of interdisciplinarity, and psychology was a natural locus of that cross-pollination.

Given this intellectual context, *Faustroll* can be read as a psychological case study through which Jarry performs a comic inversion of psychological values, effecting a *Selbstüberwindung* through self-directed laughter. This "patapsychology" is not irrationalism; like Nietzsche, Jarry converts psychology into a *gaya scienza*. Jarry extends psychology beyond its officially sanctioned limits, twisting *Witz*, the stream of consciousness, and the science of the mind as a whole into new forms and putting them to new uses. Jarry's patapsychological method is demonstrated with particularly dark comic force at the very beginning of the novel in a scene that would have been fascinating to Nietzsche, Freud, and Bergson, not to mention Samuel Beckett and Bruce Nauman.[61] Near the end of "Concerning the Habits and Bearing of Dr. Faustroll," we see Jarry's protagonist/alter ego behaving in a way that would prove him by all legal-psychiatric standards to be *non compos mentis*: "By way of a tie, he passed around his neck the ceremonial ribbon of the Great Strumpot. . . . He hanged himself by this ribbon on a specially constructed gibbet, procrastinating for a few quarter-hours between the choice of the two asphyxiating make-ups called *white hanged man* and *blue hanged man*. And, after cutting himself down, he put on a solar topee" (8; Jarry's emphasis). In contrast to the *Sturm und Drang* of Werther's suicide or Faust's contemplation of suicide in the opening of Act I, Dr. Faustroll's "suicide" in the opening of the novel is a mockery of the very idea of the dramatic, tragic suicide: it is suicide as buffoonish theatrical performance and scientific asphyxiation experiment. Jarry "laughs at all tragic plays and all tragic seriousness" and challenges his reader to do the same, to laugh the most taboo laughter, to laugh at tragedy precisely because, in Nietzsche's words, "again and again the human race will decree. . . . 'There is something at which it is absolutely forbidden henceforth to laugh.'"[62] Just as Jarry parodied Shakespeare's *Macbeth* in *Ubu Roi*, he parodied Goethe's *Faust* in *Faustroll*. Dr. Faustroll, whose name opens up at least three possible puns,[63] is a patapsychological *Umwertung* of the "Faust role," and this is crucial to the interpretation of the book as a whole and its humor of psychopathology.

Jarry's comic inversion of the Faust role can be seen, at least in part, as an artistic response to the Faust obsession of his times. Many prominent writers of late nineteenth- and early twentieth-century Europe created versions of the Faust story, from Paul Valéry's *Mon Faust*, to Thomas Mann's *Dr. Faustus*, and George Bernard Shaw's *Man and Superman*. Furthermore, Jarry was a great admirer of Christian Dietrich Grabbe's works, including *Scherz, Satire, Ironie, und Tiefere Bedeutung* (*Jokes, Satire, Irony, and Deeper Meaning*), which he translated into French and is one of Dr. Faustroll's "equivalent books."[64] Gillespie observes that the European

Faust fascination was especially strong in France: "The vogue of Goethe reached an apogee in France during the Symbolist period from about 1880 to the outbreak of the Great War; translations and interpretations of his *Faust* abounded."[65] Gillespie sees Jarry's reconfiguration of the Faust character and story as designed "to highlight the artistic logic behind the new incarnation of Faust, whom Jarry reconceives not as the by definition incomplete Goethean quester but as the complete alternative and exception to the ordinary world."[66] I would add that the primary method by which Jarry creates this "exception to the ordinary" is the comic inversion of the psychopathological nature of Faust. Jarry takes the Faust role and turns it on its head through his patapsychological method of "rational madness"; however, this does not reduce it to a mere parody, but rather expands and deepens it.

Jarry's comic reconfiguration of *Faust* again connects his work to Nietzsche. In *The Gay Science*, Nietzsche posited—in the aphorism "On moral enlightenment"—that "one has to talk the Germans out of their Mephistopheles, and their Faust as well. These are two moral prejudices against the value of knowledge."[67] Jarry responds to these moral prejudices by creating a single character that is both Faust and Mephisto. Faust is leavened and completed through a *comic* insanity that employs and yet transcends both rationality and irrationality, science and nonsense, right and wrong, good and evil. The ability to be one's own inverse, one's comic *Doppelgänger*, to laugh at oneself as Mephisto laughs at Faust (and as Faust ultimately laughs at Mephisto), is embodied by Dr. Faustroll. The differences between the psychopathology of Faust and Dr. Faustroll merit further examination. Goethe's Dr. Faust, the polymath-rationalist scientist-scholar, falls into suicidal despair while he considers his fruitless attempt at intellectual mastery through the systematic pursuit of knowledge. As he contemplates drinking a cup of poison, he says to himself, "I have pursued, alas, philosophy, jurisprudence, and medicine, and, help me God, theology,"[68] indicating that all these efforts were futile. Pure rationality has failed him, left him rudderless and sinking in a sea of nihilism. By contrast, Dr. Faustroll is always amused, content, and curious, even in the midst of his own "insanity" or "death." He is constantly discovering, moving forward into a new world, fascinated, inquisitive; his intellectual explorations are a source of joy and wonder; even death is just another pataphysical transformation, a translation through space, time, and cerebration. Through his patapsychological *Umwertung* of Faust's suicidality, Jarry shows how Dr. Faust's true sin, his deepest tragic flaw: he lacks a comic perspective on himself; he is an Apollonian intellectual narcissist. For Dr. Faust, the failure of intellect, the inability of the rational mind to conquer all, to be perfect (godlike), is psychologically devastating. Jarry laughs at the fact that Dr. Faust cannot laugh at himself. In effect, Dr. Faustroll's twisted *Witz* of patapsychology provides a therapeutic treatment, perhaps even a cure, for the obsessive Apollonian rationality of Dr. Faust and his various literary and real-life counterparts who suffer from FSNPD (Faustian Scientific-Narcissistic Personality Disorder).

As *Faustroll* progresses, it becomes more Dionysian, exhibiting an increasingly polyphonic, stream-of-consciousness style similar to the *Walpurgisnacht* of Goethe's *Faust* and the "Circe" episode of Joyce's *Ulysses* (itself modeled on Goethe's *Walpurgisnacht*). The Rabelaisian/Odyssean *Narrenschiff* journey of Book Three, "From Paris to Paris by Sea, or the Belgian Family Robinson," is essentially a series of hallucinations, or what would be considered hallucinations, in conventional reality. It is driven by an ever-escalating intake of alcohol and other mind-altering substances by Dr. Faustroll, Panmuphle, Bosse-de-Nage, and the various literary and artistic "lunatics" they meet. Scientific terminology is often used to create bizarre, humorously incongruous images and to heighten the hallucinatory nature of the "experiences," conjuring up surrealism two decades before it existed: "The island is like soft coral, amoeboid and protoplasmic: its trees closely resemble the gesture of snails making horns at us" (41). There is also much classic Dionysian imagery. In the chapter dedicated to Stéphane Mallarmé, we learn of "the isolation of two prismatic trinities of Pan pipes," which elicits "the hairy curiosity of the fauns and the rosy bloom of the nymphs" who are "aroused from their reverie by this mellifluous creation" (48). In the chapter dedicated to Rachilde, the imagery takes on a Dionysian-*Walpurgisnacht* character that is dramatic, but the drama is comically deflated: "The philters were drunk joyfully through the reeds of Panpipes, and when little women were laid out on the red-hot couches, Bosse-de-Nage thought the time had come to bring matters to a point: 'Ha ha!' he declared in summary fashion" (61). The further the narrative progresses, the more hallucinatory, disjointed, and fragmented it becomes; in short, the novel starts to go insane, to "crack up." Daniel Accursi considers hallucination to be a key psychological characteristic of Jarry's work, especially in its discontinuity, its rupture of the linear thinking of normal consciousness: "À la continuité de la contemplation s'oppose la discontinuité de l'hallucination. L'hallucination est dans son essence syncope, coupure, blessure instantanée, coup de poignard. . . . Objet à peine paru que disparu. Apparition. Disparition instantanée."[69] Indeed, much of *Faustroll* operates on the principle of rupture and discontinuity, and much of the modern science it presents can seem like a hallucination, a rupture of "normal" reality by the abnormal.

Appropriately, the chapter "Drink" in Book Four, "Cephalorgy," marks the beginning of the movement toward the "gâiment," Dionysian-psychopathological crescendo of the novel. In this "orgy of the head," Dr. Faustroll figuratively dissects and devours his own mind—and to great comic effect. "Drink," like much of book 4, is pure Rabelais, with Faustroll demonstrating Gargantuan capacities, draining an endless series of hectoliter cups of wine served to him on a conveyor belt by Visited, the daughter of Marine Bishop Mendacious (the Bishop himself drinks only “fresh water and rat’s piss” [65]). Visited soon thereafter dies during a Surmâle-like sexual experiment with Faustroll: “She did not survive the frequency of Priapus” (proving he is “man to an extraordinary degree”) (88). Appropriately, this drinking binge leads Dr. Faustroll to his most lucid and detailed discussion of psychopathology, one in which he performs a self-analysis of what triggers his insanity. It is, in many respects, the culmination of all of his explorations of humor and madness, and seems to anticipate Freud:

> And Faustroll interrupted the frivolity of the conversation with an important speech. Doctor Faustroll commenced: “I do not believe that an unconscious murder is therefore necessarily motiveless: it is not generated by any command emanating from us and has no link with the precedent phenomenon of our ego, but it certainly follows an external order, it is within the order of external phenomena, and it has a cause that is perceptible by the senses and is therefore significant.” (68)

He presents this in the hyperrational tone of the detached scientist who is utterly certain of cause-effect logic—and it is no coincidence that Faustroll “cephalorgically” examines his own head in the chapter titled “Capitally.” Then, of course, comes the psychopathological punchline that undermines any rationality: “I have never had a desire to kill except after seeing a *horse’s head*, which has become for me a sign, or an order, or more precisely a signal, like the down-turned thumb in the arena, that the time has come to strike the blow; and lest you should smile, I shall explain to you that there are doubtless several reasons for this’” (68–69; Jarry’s emphasis).

After a long series of ludicrously “logical” explanations for why the horse’s head makes him homicidally insane, Dr. Faustroll observes that Bishop Mendacious has unhooked a sign in the form of a horse’s head from a butcher’s shop, “and Faustroll was overtaken again by insanity” (73). His ensuing crime, is, of course, simultaneously disturbing and hilarious: “But Faustroll crouched over the baboon, spreading his four limbs out on the ground and strangling him from behind. Bosse-de-Nage made a sign that he wished to speak, and, when the doctor had released the grip of his fingers, said in two words: ‘Ha ha!’ and these were the last two words he uttered” (73).[70] This particular “Ha ha!” is especially significant, given that it comes at the end of one of Dr. Faustroll’s longest speeches and right after one of the most dramatically psychopathological moments in the narrative. Bosse-de-Nage’s primary function, established early in the novel, is to be Dr. Faustroll’s fool, his idiot-savant court jester: “This character will prove very useful during the course of this book, to punctuate some of its overlong speeches: in the manner of Victor Hugo . . . and Plato in various passages” (27). Only the water-headed baboon is wise enough to see when the book is in danger of taking itself too seriously, and he proves that Jarry, like Nietzsche, would “laugh at every master who does not laugh at himself.”[71] Jarry reinforces the comic inversion of the psychopathological tragedy by following this horrifying scene with the chapter "Concerning Some Further and More Evident Meanings of the Words, 'Ha Ha.'" Moreover, Bosse-de-Nage is later resurrected by a "subfumigation" that Dr. Faustroll performs.

The psychopathological climax of the book comes when Dr. Faustroll sinks his skiff with himself and Panmuphle aboard—thus committing a murder-"suicide."[72] Rimbaud, author of one of the "equivalent books," seems to prefigure this inebriated self-sinking in "The Drunken Boat," in which he writes, "O, let my keel burst! O, let me go into the sea!" He follows this with a line that would delight both Jarry and Foucault: "No longer can I . . . swim under the terrible eyes of prison ships."[73] Upon scraping away the paraffin that ensures the external impermeability of his sieve-skiff, Dr. Faustroll sinks, and once submerged, he "joined his palms in an attitude of praying or swimming, in the manner of daily devotion," and "thus did Doctor Faustroll make the gesture of dying, at the age of sixty-three" (97). When he "dies," he reveals that he is also, literally, a "Faust roll": "And behold, the wallpaper of Faustroll's body was unrolled by the saliva and teeth of the water. Like a musical score, all art and all science were written in the curves of the limbs of the ultrasexagenarian ephebe, and their progression to an infinite degree was prophesized therein" (99). The new Faust roll/role is to embody not only "all art and all science," much as Goethe did in his time, but also to take over the basic spiritual functions of conventional religion—the very functions that had been undermined by much modern art and science. Moreover, it comically reverses what is generally considered the clearest sign of a profoundly unhealthy mind, suicide, and turns it into a tongue-in-cheek experiment. In Dr. Faustroll's patapsychological hands, suicide is not the mortal sin of Catholicism nor the ultimate sign of psychopathology; rather, it is an artistic, comic transformation. In effect, Jarry kills the tragedy of *Selbstmord* with humor; he laughs suicide to death.

One of the novel's last and most Dionysian acts of twisted *Witz* occurs when Faustroll, in "ethernity" after death, uses his Apollonian scientific knowledge to enlist the help of Maxwell's Demon to resurrect himself. In proper Dionysian-Christian-Hindu fashion, Dr. Faustroll dies in order to be reborn. His insane science and pious apostasy continue to the very end of the book and culminate in the mathematical "proof" of the definition of God. Faustroll derives the equation "$\infty - 0 - a + a + 0 = \infty$" (114),[74] which, through patapsychological logic, allows him to conclude, "Therefore, *definitively*: GOD IS THE TANGENTIAL POINT BETWEEN ZERO AND INFINITY. Pataphysics is *the* science . . ." (114; Jarry's emphasis and ellipsis). The megalomaniac scientist who proclaimed, "'I am God,'" would, of course, claim the ability to create a geometric/algebraic definition of God. If a psychiatrist were given these writings by a patient, they would surely suggest mental illness, with their delusions of grandeur, specious yet self-convinced logic, and absurd evidence. Undoubtedly, this would be exactly what Jarry would have wanted. Through Dr. Faustroll, Jarry proved *definitively* that "the 'cool scientist' is an alternative, rather than the antithesis to the 'disheveled madman': a different mask for the same actor."[75] For Jarry, the constant comic alternation of these Apollonian and Dionysian masks was like the action of the twinned pistons of an engine or, more aptly, the pedals of a bicycle: the downstroke of one drove the upstroke of the other. Together, they generated the *witzig* energy that propelled his Faustrollian-Surmâlean perpetual-motion machine, laughing into the future to shape both modernity and ethernity.

Notes

1. Friedrich Nietzsche, *The Gay Science*, 2nd ed. (1887), trans. Walter Kaufmann (New York: Vintage, 1974). Nietzsche's subtitle for the second edition of *The Gay Science* (1887) was "la gaya scienza."

2. This was the tempo chosen by Jarry's colleague and friend, composer Claude Terrasse, who wrote the music for *Ubu Roi* and other Jarry works. The use of French rather than the traditional Italian for a tempo indicates that the choice was quite deliberate; Terrasse, and likely Jarry himself, wanted "gaîment," not "allegro." Chapter 23 of *Faustroll*, "The Ringing Isle," is a pataphysical portrait of Terrasse.

3. Roger Shattuck, *The Banquet Years: The Origins of the Avant-Garde in France, 1885 to World War I* (1955; repr., New York: Vintage Books, 1968), 198.

4. Arthur Rimbaud, letter to Paul Demeny (May 15, 1871), in *Rimbaud: Complete Works, Selected Letters*, trans. Wallace Fowlie (Chicago: University of Chicago Press, 1966), 306–7 (Rimbaud's emphasis).

5. T. S. Eliot, introduction to *The Art of Poetry*, by Paul Valéry, trans. Denise Folliot (New York: Pantheon, 1958), xix.

6. Alastair Brotchie, *Alfred Jarry: A Pataphysical Life* (Cambridge, MA: MIT Press, 2011), 228–29.

7. Andrew Hugill, *'Pataphysics: A Useless Guide* (Cambridge, MA: MIT Press, 2012), xviii.

8. Calvin Tompkins, *Duchamp: A Biography* (New York: Henry Holt, 1996), 51.

9. Quoted in Brotchie, *Alfred Jarry*, 170.

10. André Breton, *Anthology of Black Humor* (1939), trans. Mark Polizzotti (San Francisco: City Lights, 1997). In the introduction to the Jarry selection, Breton referred to Père Ubu as "the magisterial incarnation of the Nietzchean-Freudian id that designates the totality of unknown, unconscious, repressed energies" (212).

11. Furthermore, many in the anthology were also depicted or alluded to in *Faustroll* (Rimbaud, Nietzsche, Poe, Baudelaire, Grabbe, Lautréamont, et al.).

12. Alfred Jarry, *Exploits and Opinions of Doctor Faustroll, Pataphysician (A Neo-Scientific Novel)* (1911), trans. Simon Watson Taylor (Boston: Exact Change, 1996), 37 (hereafter cited parenthetically in the text).

13. In *Madness and Civilization: A History of Insanity in the Age of Reason* (1965), trans. Richard Howard (New York: Random House, 1988), Michel Foucault presents Rabelais's works as well as Sebastian Brandt's poem *Das Narrenschiff*, Erasmus's *In Praise of Folly*, and Hieronymus Bosch's *The Cure of Madness and the Ship of Fools* as prime examples of the Narrenschiff motif. Rabelais's works, like Rimbaud's, are among Faustroll's "equivalent books."

14. Sylvain-Christian David, *Alfred Jarry, le secret des origines* (Paris: Presses Universitaires de France, 2003), 102.

15. Foucault, *Madness and Civilization*, 14.

16. Matthieu Gosztola, *Alfred Jarry, critique littéraire et sciences à l'aube du XXe siècle* (Paris: Editions du Cygne, 2013), 38.

17. Gerald Gillespie, *Echoland: Readings from Humanism to Postmodernism* (Brussels: Peter Lang, 2006), 216.

18. In Wells's *The Island of Dr. Moreau* (1896), the mad scientist protagonist, Dr.

Moreau, grafts animal body parts from one animal to another and from animals to humans.

19. Roger Shattuck, introduction to Jarry, *Faustroll*, xv.

20. The number eight returns in a visual/typographical pun that closes the novel: the lemniscate, ∞, the mathematical sign for infinity, is, of course, an 8 reoriented from the vertical to the horizontal.

21. Julien Schuh, *Alfred Jarry, le colin-maillard cérébral* (Paris: Honoré Champion, 2014), 557.

22. Interestingly, science itself has been seen as akin to psychopathology; as Lacan states, "Scientific discourse and the hysteric's discourse have *almost* the same structure" (Lacan's emphasis). Quoted in Jean-Michel Rabaté, *The Future of Theory* (Oxford, UK: Blackwell, 2002), 18.

23. Alfred Jarry, *The Supermale* (1902), trans. Ralph Gladstone and Barbara Wright (1964; repr., Cambridge, MA: Exact Change, 1999), 92.

24. Henri Bergson, *Laughter* (1900), trans. Wylie Sypher, in *Comedy*, ed. Wylie Sypher (Garden City, NY: Doubleday, 1956), 79.

25. Alfred Jarry, *Ubu Rex* (1896), trans. Cyril Connolly and Simon Watson Taylor, in *The Ubu Plays* (New York: Grove Weidenfeld, 1969), 5.

26. All the Ubu plays satirize Ubu's risible lack of scientific knowledge.

27. Michel Foucault, *Abnormal: Lectures at the Collège de France, 1974–1975*, trans. Graham Burchell (London: Verso, 2003), 35–36.

28. For examinations of the multiple prominent avant-garde figures Jarry influenced both directly and indirectly, see Shattuck, *Banquet Years*; and Hugill, *'Pataphysics*.

29. The year Faustroll was "born" at the age of sixty-three, when "the 20th century was [−2] years old" (7).

30. Brotchie, *Alfred Jarry*, 29.

31. Ibid., 177.

32. See Jaime Nubiola, "The Reception of William James in Continental Europe," *European Journal of Pragmatism and American Philosophy* 3, no. 1 (2009): 79.

33. Brotchie, *Alfred Jarry*, 238–39.

34. Sigmund Freud, *Jokes and Their Relation to the Unconscious* (1905), trans. James Strachey (New York: W. W. Norton, 1960), 205, 173.

35. Shattuck, *Banquet Years*, 248.

36. Ibid., 238.

37. Amelia Jones, *Irrational Modernism: A Neurasthenic History of New York Dada* (Cambridge: MIT Press, 2004), 126.

38. Brotchie, *Alfred Jarry*, 239.

39. Gilles Deleuze and Felix Guattari, *Anti-Oedipus: Capitalism and Schizophrenia* (1972), trans. Robert Hurley, Mark Seem, and Helen R. Lane (Minneapolis: University of Minnesota Press, 1983), 2.

40. Hélène Cixous, "The Laugh of the Medusa," trans. Keith Cohen and Paula Cohen (1976), in *The Critical Tradition: Classic Texts and Contemporary Trends*, ed. David H. Richter (New York: St. Martin's Press, 1989), 1099.

41. As Deleuze and Guattari observe, Freud did not like working with schizophrenics because they were almost impervious to analysis; indeed, if Jarry could have been analyzed by Freud, one could only imagine how amusing it would have been for Jarry—and how frustrating for Freud.

42. Deleuze and Guattari, *Anti-Oedipus*, 15 (Deleuze and Guattari's emphasis).

43. Alan D. Schrift, *Poststructuralism and Critical Theory's Second Generation* (Chicago: University of Chicago Press, 2010), 19.

44. Ibid. Nietzsche's works were published in France as early as 1877, and the final volume of his complete works translated into French was published by the Mercure in 1909.

45. Hugill, *'Pataphysics*, 200.

46. The influence of Nietzsche on modernists' aesthetics, especially their comic orientation, extended well beyond Jarry's immediate times. In New York Dada in particular, "the importance of Nietzsche is impossible to overestimate." Francis M. Naumann, "New York Dada: Style with a Smile," in *Making Mischief*, ed. Francis Naumann and Beth Venn (New York: Abrams, 1996), 14.

47. Carol Diethe, *Historical Dictionary of Nietzscheanism*, 3rd ed. (London: Scarecrow Press, 2013), 35.

48. Fisher, *Pataphysician's Library*, 531.

49. Ibid., 187.

50. Schrift, *Poststructuralism*, 19.

51. Fisher, *Pataphysician's Library*, 188.

52. Hugill, *'Pataphysics*, 200.

53. Friedrich Nietzsche, *Ecce Homo* (1888), trans. R. J. Hollingdale (New York: Penguin, 1979), 67.

54. Friedrich Nietzsche, *Thus Spoke Zarathustra* (1884–85), trans. Walter Kaufmann (New York: Penguin, 1978), 121 (Nietzsche's emphasis).

55. Nietzsche, *Gay Science*, 66 (Nietzsche's emphasis). Like Rabelais, Nietzsche saw that "laughter has a deep philosophical meaning, it is one of the essential forms of truth concerning the world as a whole, concerning history and man." Mikhail Bakhtin, *Rabelais and His World* (1965), trans. Helene Iswolsky (Bloomington: Indiana University Press, 1984).

56. Nietzsche, *Gay Science*, 74–75.

57. Nietzsche, *Thus Spoke Zarathustra*, 40–41.

58. Friedrich Nietzsche, *Beyond Good and Evil* (1886), trans. R. J. Hollingdale (New York: Penguin, 1973), 58.

59. For a detailed analysis of Nietzsche's engagement with psychology, see my PhD dissertation, "The Dionysia of Science: Humor, Rational Madness, and Comic Experimental Methods in the Works of Bruce Nauman and Thomas Pynchon" (University of Pennsylvania, 2008), 89–94.

60. Nietzsche, *Beyond Good and Evil*, 54.

61. As indicated by Beckett's comic contemplation of suicide by hanging in *Waiting for Godot* and Nauman's cartoonishly macabre neon sculpture *Hanged Man*.

62. Nietzsche, *Gay Science*, 75.

63. As Shattuck and others have discussed, the name "Faustroll" can be interpreted as "Faust troll," because Jarry played the part of a troll in Henrik Ibsen's *Peer Gynt*, and this connection to Ibsen is important, but the other puns in the name are crucial: "Faust role," and "Faust roll." As the culmination of his Faustian role, Faustroll, at the end of the book, literally takes on the form of a roll/scroll, on which is written "all art and all science." Most likely, Jarry intended to bring all three puns into play.

64. Jarry, *Faustroll*, 11. It is quite likely that Jarry also read Grabbe's *Don Juan and Faust*.

65. Gillespie, *Echoland*, 211.

66. Ibid., 221.

67. Nietzsche, *Gay Science*, 203.

68. Johann Wolfgang Goethe, *Faust: A Tragedy* (1832), trans. Walter Arndt, ed. Cyrus Hamlin (New York: W. W. Norton, 2001), 12.

69. Daniel Accursi, *Merdre* (Paris: Presses Universitaires de France, 2000), 40.

70. James Brewton, an American artist active primarily in the 1960s in America and Europe, was fascinated with Jarry and created an aesthetic he called "Graffiti Pataphysic." One of Brewton's obsessions was a still photo from the pulp film *The Sands of the Kalahari*, in which a man strangles a baboon. Given that Brewton included the final equation from the last chapter of *Faustroll* in his studies for other works, it is highly likely that he read the book and quite possible that he associated the photo with Faustroll's throttling of Bosse-de-Nage. If nothing else, we can state with confidence that baboon-strangling imagery is not common—even in modern and postmodern art.

71. Nietzsche, *Gay Science*, epigraph.

72. We learn that Dr. Faustroll does not, in fact, die, but is rather translated into "ethernity."

73. Arthur Rimbaud, "The Drunken Ship" (1871), in *Rimbaud: Complete Works, Selected Letters*, trans. Wallace Fowlie (Chicago: University of Chicago Press, 1966), 120.

74. This equation later appears in some of artist James Brewton's works (see above).

75. Eliot, introduction to *Art of Poetry*, xix.

Chapter 2

Pataphallics in Jarry's Novels

Jean-Michel Rabaté

The most visible experimenter in French modernism was Alfred Jarry, one of the exuberant avant-gardists who had been touched by the spirit of Friedrich Nietzsche. Jarry's main invention was to bring to bear Nietzsche's ethical revolution to the sexual domain. This led him to rewrite Nietzsche's *Übermensch*, aka Zarathustra, as a hyper-phallic "Supermale." Nietzsche's rhetoric of violence also found an expression in Jarry's delirious Ubu plays. Altogether, one can say that he was able to graft late symbolism onto a specific variation on intellectual and artistic anarchism. I will take my point of departure in two novels, *Messalina* and *The Supermale*, that, once they are read together, can be seen to contain the seeds of a later French modernism.

Jarry had been lucky with his teachers, and he paid homage to them, including the unfortunate "Père Hébert," the ridiculous and rotund science teacher who was to be monumentalized in the savage parody of Père Ubu. In Paris, however, it was none other than Henri Bergson who introduced Jarry to his philosophy of time and intuition in 1893. And even earlier, in 1889, while a high-school student in Rennes, Jarry was introduced to the thought of Nietzsche by his philosophy teacher Benjamin Bourdon. Bourdon had just returned from Germany, where he had worked with Wilhelm Wundt on experimental psychology. While teaching in Rennes, he would complete a dissertation then published as *The Expression of Emotions and Tendencies in Language*.[1] Bourdon followed Wundt in linking Darwinian expressive universals visible in animals and humans, and a "popular psychology" stressing features of simplicity, intensity, stylization, and emotional empathy.[2] Wundt's psychology insisted on the pregnancy of formulaic patterns applied to basic gestures. Gestures could be constructed by turning an initial emotion into a "formula." This term later led Aby Warburg to coin his famous expression of "Pathosformel" (formula of pathos).

Jarry's creation of Ubu as a terrifying puppet, a schoolboy's bogeyman condensing the laughable power of adults, their omnipotence experienced as random and pathetic displays of violent sadism by children, owes a lot to Wundt and Bourdon's psychology of emotions. The barely caricatured figure of Bourdon appears as Ubu's "Conscience"—easily identifiable because of his mannerism, the regular interjection of "et ainsi de suite" in all his sentences—in *Ubu Cocu*. It is astonishing to think that Bourdon introduced French high school students to untranslated works of Nietzsche eleven years before the philosopher's demise. Bourdon would "explain" Nietzsche, as Jarry writes in memories of his youth.[3] In 1893, the future poet Léon-Paul Fargue, Jarry's close friend, onetime lover, and soon bitter enemy, wrote to Jarry from Germany, confessing that he wished that Bergson could talk more about Nietzsche; if he did, his lectures would truly be beyond good and evil![4] Soon, Jarry blended Nietzsche's self-proclaimed persona of the "Anti-Christ" with Bergson's theory of intuition in his "pataphysical" or "anarchist" version of *César-Antéchrist*. King Ubu appears for the first time in *César-Antéchrist*, published in several installments in 1894.[5]

Besides being a cultural anarchist tending to nihilism as well as a gifted literary provocateur, Jarry was a fervent disciple of Stéphane Mallarmé. Mallarmé congratulated him on the success of *Ubu Roi*, and then wrote to the young writer several times. When Mallarmé died in 1898, Jarry attended the funeral. His moving obituary evoked the "island of Ptyx" as a homage to the most esoteric and obscure sonnet in "X."[6] Jarry was a living bridge between late symbolism and early futurism. Filippo Tommaso Marinetti, a futurist rarely linked to symbolism, was impressed by the Ubu plays. He met Jarry several times. In 1906, Jarry thanked Marinetti for sending him *Roi Bombance*, a proto-futurist play inspired by the Ubu cycle.[7]

The two linked novels *Messaline: Roman de l'ancienne Rome* (1901) and *Le Surmâle: Roman moderne* (1902) are founded on a parallel: while the former takes imperial Rome as its setting, the latter is situated in the future. *Le Surmâle* takes place, by a neat inversion of numbers, in 1920. If we notice the subtle ways in which the future and the past are intertwined, we can conclude that the conditions are gathered for the creation of French modernism. This idea is confirmed by the subtitle, which, strangely enough, was not translated in the English version: *The Supermale: A Modern Novel*.[8] Jarry flaunts the novel's modernity because it recycles the other novel's reconstructed past. Modernity finds its emblems in a profusion of real and fantastic machines; we encounter bicycles, locomotives, fast cars, phonographs, and dynamos; at the end, a terrifying machine-to-inspire-love explodes and kills the hero. Beyond these obvious differences, in fact, *The Supermale*'s plot is quite similar to that of *Messalina*, for in both novels the main character seeks a paroxystic sexual pleasure and dies after having beaten world records in sex-making. The feminine half of the diptych is situated in the histories of the debaucheries of the Roman emperors, whose piquant vignettes had been narrated by Suetonius and Tacitus. The future of 1920 is marked both by American inventors and by delirious machines. Jarry's central conceit presupposes an almost total identification of technology with sexuality. In both novels, sexual excess leads to new wisdom, but it flirts so much with the Absolute that it leads to an explosive and apocalyptic demise.

Jarry's modernism is thus constituted by splicing the "modern" text of *The Supermale* with *Messalina*, a historical novel more evocative of Gustave Flaubert's *Salammbô* than the Ubu plays. Both novels display narrative techniques that are daringly innovative; this is perhaps more visible in *The Supermale*. The two main "events" of the plot—a bicycle race of ten thousand miles won by the hero, André Marcueil, against a racing locomotive and a team of five cyclists fueled by "perpetual-motion-food"; and the sexual contest in which Marcueil, disguised as an Indian, has sex for a whole day before reaching the sum of eighty-two orgasms—are narrated by several filters like the voice of a journalistic report, and the account provided by a doctor recording the sexual prowess while speculating on God and pataphysics, the pseudoscience invented by Faustroll, another character of Jarry's.

The Supermale is a modernist novel because it keeps rewriting the past in the present. Even though it is shot through with science-fictional speculations about a futurist intermixing of men and machines, it harks back to Roman antiquity. Indeed, Marcueil's wish to make love indefinitely is based on a specific reading of a Latin poem. His curiosity has been aroused when he looked at the notorious passage about Messalina in Juvenal's *Satires*. Juvenal evokes the scene that most young high school students would try to translate. When the Emperor Claudius had fallen asleep, Messalina would disguise herself as a prostitute and go to a brothel in order to sleep with as many customers as possible. She would be the last to leave, and would do so reluctantly, "her taut sex still burning, inflamed with lust." Then she would repair to the Emperor's bed.[9]

Like Jarry, Marcueil is both an athlete and a fine Latinist. The point of departure for his sexual fantasies is a curious word used in a famous Latin poem. He focuses on the adjective "rigidae" used by Juvenal to depict the empress Messalina's insatiable sexual appetite (*Supermale*, 30):

> adhuc ardens rigidae tentigine vulvae,
> Et lassata viris nec dum satiate recessit.[10]

This is the epigraph for *Messalina*,[11] which is not translated—those who do not know Latin need to follow Marcueil's gloss in the third chapter of *The Supermale* (29–31). Marcueil explains to the doctor and the general that lines 128–30 of Juvenal's sixth satire present us a woman "still ardent," but he refuses to translate more. A Latinist can reconstruct the sense. Messalina leaves her "cell" in the "House of Happiness," her brothel in Suburra, feeling "still ardent with the tension of her rigid vulva, and tired of men but not satiated yet." The events evoked in the first chapter of *Messalina* become the object of a heated discussion in *The Supermale*.

The doctor reduces Messalina to a pathological case of nymphomania, and then mentions all at once hysteria, priapism and satyriasis (*Supermale*, 32). Defending her, Marcueil states that "the only real women are Messalinas" (30). He assures his listeners that her case proves that men can also experience what women know (i.e., ithyphallicism): "There is no reason why there should not be produced in men, once a certain figure is reached, the very same physiological phenomenon as in Messalina" (31). In short, men and women are entitled to experience shattering, absolute, and overwhelming paroxysms of sexual "jouissance." When the doctor expresses skepticism facing this literalist interpretation of "rigidi tentigo veretri" (the rigid tension of the penis), Marcueil complicates his position by asserting that the line was an interpolation that he retranslates: "still ardent or kept ardent by the tension of her rigid vulva" (30).

The vertigo experienced by Marcueil hinges around a web made up of classical texts and infinite series. He is as fascinated by the fact that women carry all their ova in their organs (he believes that the number is eighteen million), as by the fact that Messalina's repeated sexual congress should have induced in her a state of sexual "rigidity." The conceit of the novel is that "this manifestation becomes permanent, and even more pronounced, as one moves beyond the limits of human strength toward numerical infinity; and that it is consequently advantageous to pass beyond as rapidly as is possible, or if you prefer, as is conceivable" (31). The ithyphallic fantasy of the novel plays on infinite numbers thanks to which one will reach an immortality beyond excess, because excess has become the norm.

Marcueil asserts, "It is possible that a man capable of making love indefinitely might experience no difficulty in doing anything else indefinitely" (34). The absurd boast that would transform the "Supermale" into a literal "Spermale" triggers the ire of the doctor, who accuses him of not being scientific, of wallowing "in the department of the impossible" (34). Against common sense, Marcueil assumes that sexual excess will lead to a superhuman transformation of women and men into rigid, turgid, ever-ready phalluses. He gladly endorses his station in the department of the Impossible. This futurist fantasy has an exact counterpart in Messalina's quest, for her deepest wish is to be united with Phales, the god of erect phalluses. Phales, she thinks, has fled her brothel, to her immense despair: "A sputtering: Messalina saw, quite distinctly, the flight of the god in a strident clatter of unfurled wings" (*Messalina*, 13).

Messalina keeps invoking the god of phalluses as Pan, Priapus, Phallus, Phales, Love—the various names of her multifaceted god. A passage describes its emblem in a way that would have attracted Sigmund Freud's attention, precisely because he was writing about the "Thing" (*das Ding*) in his unpublished "Project for a Scientific Psychology." Freud attempted to pinpoint the irreducible exteriority or intractable otherness of libidinal objects that cannot be processed by consciousness.[12] In the novel, this is also called, quite symptomatically, the "Thing" (*la chose*): "But the Thing is more monstrous, strange and enticing, for it has meaning. / This divine emblem, the great Phallus carved from a fig-tree, is nailed to the lintel like a night-owl to a barn-door, or a god to the pediment of a temple" (*Messalina*, 10). If one could only catch and keep the priapic "Thing," one would feel an endless immersion in love. This outpouring of "jouissance" is compared to the union of the Emperor and his whore: "A man is the husband of Messalina during the moment of love, and then for as long as he is able to live an uninterrupted series of such moments" (10–11). This sentence generates the entire narrative and the first sentence of *The Supermale*: "The act of love is of no importance, since it can be performed indefinitely" (3). In the end, what happens is the reverse: The act of love is of supreme importance because it can be performed indefinitely.

Why such a parallel debasement and exaltation? *Messalina* provides a clue of what is at stake by showing one of the rare positive characters as Claudius. Although he is weak, a cuckold, and a stutterer, he keeps on writing poetry and playing with dice. Jarry heaps allusions to Mallarmé's "ancient master" who loses himself in abstruse calculations in *Un coup de dés jamais n'abolira le hasard*. Indeed, when by a curious bigamy Messalina marries her lover, the virile Silius, a Roman consul, the only obstacle to their sexual bliss comes when he discovers one of Claudius's dice in the bed where they just had sex: "Silius searched, fumbled feverishly [. . .] and captured what was it that was causing his discomfort—had an insect bitten him? / Livid, angular, crystalline, sharp, senile, obscene, naked to the bone. / A die" (*Messalina*, 56–57). The diminutive die is "that thing" (57) preventing Messalina from loving him "absolutely." Because of this tiny obstacle, Silius can never possess the phallic "Thing." When he grasps this, he screams all of a sudden, quite surprisingly, "MESSALINA IS VIRGIN!" (57). How can this be, given her record of more than twenty-five lovers per night? It all becomes clearer if we see Messalina as a Mallarméan heroine like Hérodiade, who in *Igitur* stands for Salome, a name evoking castration or beheading. However, this time a Christian Virgin is not far.

Mallarmé's Hérodiade had obtained the decapitation of the prophet John in the same way as Messalina manipulates Claudius, who forces Asiaticus to commit suicide although he is innocent. The impure Messalina announces the Christian saint Messalina mentioned in the fanciful *Almanach* of Père Ubu for the month of January 1901. Next to "Décervelage" (debraining, the punishment meted out for the nobles under King Ubu's despotic rule), given for January 1, we find "Saint Messalina" who is presented as the patron saint for January 23.[13] The Christian meaning of the "Real Presence" refers to the Eucharist, a symbol endowed with the reality of divine presence in Catholic rituals. In conformity with the logic elaborated at the end of *L'Amour absolu*, which redoubles a Mallarméan logic of abolition, the divine absolute kills those who experience it. The only chance of surviving the encounter with excessive "jouissance" will have to be mediated through art.

The outcome of Messalina's relentless quest for the "real presence" of her phallic god will, of course, cause her death. It comes ineluctably at the end, because Claudius finally sees her in all her horror. He reluctantly condemns her to death, but she welcomes the centurion's sword: in her delirium, she mistakes it for an ivory phallus and wants to be penetrated by it. She falls in front of the soldier, and when he plunges the weapon into her naked breast, she exclaims, "O how you are a god, PHALES! Phalès, I knew nothing of love; I knew all men but you are the first Immortal I have loved! Phalès, at last, and so late!" (*Messalina*, 69). The centurion has to assert that his sword is a blade, not his penis; she keeps asking Phalès to take her away, and thus dies—of love. As she dies, the god Phalès vanishes: the great Pan of the ancient phallic cults has gone for good.

In this fin de siècle fantasy of "Liebe und Tod," the ithyphallicism sought by Messalina and Marcueil betrays a hyperbolic fantasy of bisexual enjoyment. Jarry's pataphysics depicts men and women as having the possibility of attaining a superhuman energy and sexual bliss, even if their ultimate erection always spells out death. At the last minute, Messalina gazes at her own reflection in the sword that will dispatch her. The phallus is a mirror but also a sharp stake, as those used for impalement. By a loaded Latin pun, the "phallus" turns into "palus" (stake), an association made explicit in *Cesar-Antichrist*: "The Templar: Uprooted phallus, do not bounce around so much. / Fasce: Tail [*pal*] or head [Jarry puns on "Pile ou face"], reflection of my master, in you I gaze at my reflection. . . . Phallus perpendicular to the smile of the Ithyphallic in your laterality."[14] Jarry's own ithyphallicism was not devoid of humor. When Guillaume Apollinaire visited the small apartment in which Jarry lived (the rooms had been divided, the ceiling lowered, thus only a small man like Jarry could stand upright in it), he saw a huge stone phallus made in Japan, a gift of the painter Félicien Rops. As all the objects in the room looked diminutive, Jarry retorted to a visiting lady who had asked playfully whether the object was a plaster cast of his organ: "No, this is a reduction."[15]

Jarry's mixture of laughter and tragedy, his compound of heresy and saintliness, would tap an old doctrine that James Joyce applied to the making of *Finnegans Wake*, that of the unity of the opposites. Joy and sadness combine to heighten each other. Fasce continues, "Axiom and principle of identical contraries, the pataphysician, clinging to your ears and retractable wings, flying fish, is the dwarf climax of the giant, beyond all metaphysics; thanks to you, it is the Antichrist and God too, horse of the Spirit, Less-in-More, Less-that-is-More, cinematics of the zero remaining in the eyes, infinite polyhedron. . . . You are the owl, Sex and Spirit, hermaphrodite, you create and destroy."[16] A similar pun on a lethal phallus underpins several scenes in *Messalina.* At one point, Messalina wonders why she cannot find any "lingam or ithyphallus silhouetting its tall pale" (32) when she visits the stately garden of Asiaticus. The recurrent phallicization of the objects of desire derives from an obvious wish to compensate for the wobbly nature of emotions. Feminine sexuality is bound with a hard and rigid pole. It is from such a vantage point that one can then jump into infinity, as we see at the end of *Absolute Love*, when we are introduced to "the right to lie." The sex or gender of lies is feminine, we learn.[17] Truth is to be found in a masculine God; however, God would prostitute himself if he gave access to the truth he embodies. The way out of this contradiction is to affirm human desire: "Human truth is what man wants: a *desire.* / The Truth of God is what he *creates.* / When one is neither one nor the other—Emmanuel—*one's* Truth is *the creation of one's desire.*"[18]

Jarry would have agreed with Freud's contention that libido, all libido, is male; if a feminine pole is necessary for the transmutation into an infinite power to affect, this pole will be firmly controlled. The love scenes between Marcueil and the young Ellen in *The Supermale* are curiously fraught with tension, marked by aggression. After Marcueil's exertions make Ellen reach the fatidic number of eighty-two orgasms, she appears rather hostile to Marcueil instead of being thankful. Ellen comments dryly, "That wasn't the least bit funny." Then, suddenly, she tries to blind him with her hatpin, and Marcueil needs to hypnotize her to prevent this attack (104–5). When he believes (wrongly, it turns out) that Ellen, exhausted, is dead, Marcueil expresses immense tenderness conveyed in a love poem that he recites on her inert body, concluding with "I adore her." In fact, she has just passed out; the lyrical profession of love was triggered by a "love machine," which explodes and kills Marcueil. With these anarchic and self-destructive machines, we enter the world of futurist modernism. Jarry singlehandedly invented both Italian futurism and the desiring (and bachelor) machines popularized by Gilles Deleuze and Pierre-Félix Guattari.

The best essay on Jarry's philosophy was written by Deleuze. Deleuze was uniquely equipped to grasp the links between Jarry's anarchism and Martin Heidegger's meditation on the disappearance of Being and the domination of technology. Technology is the modern danger, but a form of salvation can come from it: "The bicycle is not a simple machine, but the simplest model of a Machine appropriate to the times. . . . The Bicycle, with its chains and its gears, is the essence of technology: it envelops and develops, it brings about the great turning of the earth. The bicycle is the frame, like Heidegger's 'fourfold.'"[19] What Deleuze does not say, because he was reluctant to use Freudian terms, is that Jarry's textual and allegorical Bicycle connects desiring subjects with the ontology of the drive. Jarry calls up the specific

Freudian term of "Trieb," which should not be confused with "instinct" even under its form of "death drive." Freud saw in the drive a general force accounting for the upsurge of erotic energy in human beings. He defined it in 1915 according to its force, source, object, and aim. Jarry anticipated Freud's later invention of the "death drive" as Thanatos, an ultimate allegory in which Jacques Lacan saw the model for the structure of all drives. Jarry's particular hardness, intensity, and eccentricity derive from his intimate familiarity with a death drive whose increased speed he was hoping to harness and that he magnified until it reached infinity.

An identical symbol of infinity is also hidden in the speeding bicycle drafted by Marcel Duchamp in 1914. Duchamp idolized Jarry, and his visual works are full of references to him. His mysteriously titled *Avoir l'apprenti dans le soleil* (Having the apprentice in the sun) represents a man pedaling up a slope toward the sun, sketched on yellowing music paper. Inverting the common expression of "avoir le soleil dans l'œil" (to be blinded by the sun), Duchamp evokes Jarry's cyclist, Marcueil. His title also puns on "à voir: l'empreinte dans le sol" and "avoir la pente dans le soleil" ("to be seen: the imprint in the ground" and "to have the slope in the sun"). A speeding "apprentice," a learner sublimely fighting against a sun blinding him, was Duchamp's oblique homage to Jarry, a notoriously fierce cyclist: We learn in our "apprentissage" by toiling upward and fighting against a paternal and domineering sun.

But there is more in this title, since it conceals a clear spoonerism. If we invert the letters, we get something like "Le soleil apprend-il à voir dedans?" (Does the sun teach us to see within?). This falsely naïve questions rejects the reduction of art to retinal domination, opening it up to the conceptual. Indeed, there is more to "see" than what we perceive there is to see out there in the world. Art should push "viewers" to see the invisible as well, whether it be a pure concept or the void. Art and literature should make us think, above all. Like the wheels of Duchamp's bicycle, Jarry's novels can be seen as two interlocked cycles, forming thus a diptych of sexual excess. The "novel of ancient Rome" and the "modern novel" are combined like two wheels spinning together; by reading, rereading, and pedaling, readers create a lemniscate, the symbol of infinity. If sexual excess leads to a superhuman transformation of women and men into rigid phalluses, textual excess ushers in the pathos of the new. The frantic ithyphallicism sought by Messalina and Marcueil would recycle Nietzsche's religious parody in *Zarathustra* while pointing to the future. Here, Jarry seems to herald Georges Bataille's principle of the "accursed share,"[20] that "part maudite" in which he finds an anti-economy of pure waste, an excess going beyond the limits of modernism or modernity.

Notes

This chapter is a revised excerpt from Jean-Michel Rabaté, "'Hard' Modernism: Alfred Jarry," in *The Pathos of Distance: Affects of the Moderns* (New York: Bloomsbury, 2016), 37–50.

1. Benjamin B. Bourdon, *L'Expression des émotions et des tendances dans le langage* (Paris: Felix Alcan, 1892).

2. Wilhelm Wundt, *Elements of Folk Psychology* (1900), trans. Edward Leroy Schaub (Project Gutenberg, 2013), 59–64.

3. Alfred Jarry, *Œuvres complètes*, ed. Michel Arrivé et al., 3 vols. (Paris: Gallimard, Bibliothèque de la Pléiade, 1972–88), 3:53.

4. Léon-Paul Fargue to Alfred Jarry, May 5, 1893, https://alfredjarry.wordpress.com/1893/05/05/leon-paul-fargue-a-alfred-jarry-jai-recu-ta-lettre-avec-joie/.

5. Jarry, *Œuvres complètes*, 1:271–332. César-Antéchrist says, "I am the infinite Intuition" (1:330).

6. Jarry, *Œuvres complètes*, 1:685–86. See also Marieke Dubbelboer, *The Subversive Poetics of Alfred Jarry: Abusing Culture in the "Almanachs du Pere Ubu"* (London: Legenda, 2012), 35–37.

7. Jarry, *Œuvres complètes*, 3:635–36.

8. Alfred Jarry, *The Supermale* (1902), trans. Ralph Gladstone and Barbara Wright (Cambridge, MA: Exact Change, 1999) (hereafter cited parenthetically in the text).

9. Juvenal, "Satire VI: Don't Marry," in *The Satires*, trans. A. S. Kline (Poetry in Translation, 2011), https://www.poetryintranslation.com/PITBR/Latin/JuvenalSatires6.php.

10. Jarry, *Œuvres complètes*, 2:75.

11. Alfred Jarry, *Messalina: A Novel of Imperial Rome* (1901), trans. John Harman (London: Atlas Press, 1985), 9 (hereafter cited parenthetically in the text).

12. Sigmund Freud, "Project for a Scientific Psychology" (1895), in *The Invention of Psychoanalysis: Letters to Wilhelm Fliess, Drafts and Notes, 1887–1902*, trans. Eric Mosbacher and James Strachey (New York: Basic Books, 1977), 441.

13. Jarry, *Œuvres complètes*, 1:575.

14. Ibid., 1:289.

15. Guillaume Apollinaire, "Feu Jarry" (1909), in *Œuvres en prose complètes*, ed. Pierre Caizergues and Michel Décaudin (Paris: Gallimard, Bibliothèque de la Pléiade, 1991), 2:1040.

16. Jarry, *Œuvres complètes*, 1:289–90.

17. Ibid., 1:949.

18. Ibid., 1:950.

19. Gilles Deleuze, "An Unrecognized Precursor to Heidegger: Alfred Jarry," in *Essays Critical and Clinical*, trans. Daniel W. Smith and Michael A. Greco (Minneapolis: University of Minnesota Press, 1997), 93.

20. See the Wikipedia entry on Georges Bataille's complex concept of the "accursed share," last modified March 2, 2021, 14:16, https://en.wikipedia.org/wiki/The_Accursed_Share.

Chapter 3

Wartime Pataphysics

Postwar Surrealism, the Main à Plume Group, and Boris Rybak's Intraphysics

Catherine Hansen

Pataphysics—according to the poet Christian Bök—is rooted in both the irrationalism that is shared by symbolism, Dada, and surrealism, and the sur-rationalism of those who call for a "poetic appropriation of science," a category from which he emphatically excludes surrealists. Surrealists, in calling instead for a "poetic emancipation from science," stand for the "aesthetic mysticism of modernity." In a more recent work, by Andrew Hugill, converts are shown to be driven into the arms of the *Collège de 'Pataphysique* by surrealism's unfortunate "drift into mysticism."[1] In also citing, however, the surrealists' ostensible "interest in Stalin," Hugill comes somewhat closer to the truth. In fact, the myth of surrealism's turn to mysticism after the Second World War was invented largely by critics of this movement amid the dogmatically Marxist-Leninist intellectual and cultural establishment in immediate-postwar France, and has tended uncritically to be repeated ever since.

As historian Tony Judt emphasizes, at the time France had "the second-largest Communist party in the free world . . . and one of the most Stalinized."[2] The sphere of public and artistic debate was riven by an "angry Manichaeanism" in which no middle ground could be tolerated or even conceived between unwavering support of the party and craven reactionism. André Breton, as a very vocal critic of Stalinist excesses at home and abroad, became something of a lightning rod in this charged environment. Attacks on him frequently took the form of allegations of mysticism, a word that often functioned as shorthand for failure to get with the Communist program.

This essay argues that Breton's postwar surrealist movement, rather than turning to mysticism (or to Stalinism), was actually attempting something else entirely: to reinvent itself in a pataphysical mode. Such an attempt had already been made by a wartime para-surrealist group calling itself La Main à Plume (1941–44), and particularly by one of its members, the poet, essayist, pianist, and research biologist Boris Rybak, who imagined a science of imaginary solutions he called "intraphysics." Rybak's hybrid science is used here as a lens to examine how, in wartime and after, surrealists and emerging pataphysicians alike responded to the same historical pressures, in a fraught intellectual atmosphere where questions of constraint and ideology (conscious or unconscious), myth and dogma, imaginary solutions and final solutions, weighed heavily.

In 1942, while still in exile in the United States, André Breton composed two texts that proved hugely divisive among his erstwhile followers, many of whom had joined or were about to join the Communist Party. First there was the talk he gave at Yale, "Situation du surréalisme entre les deux guerres," where he encouraged a new, youthful generation of surrealists not only to keep working toward social justice but also to keep alive "the appetite for a universal knowledge to be rediscovered," regardless of the relatively shortsighted demands of political parties.[3] Even more scandalous was what he did in his *Prolégomènes à un troisième manifeste du surréalisme ou non*: under the name of "les Grands Transparents," Breton weaves a story around mysterious higher beings that are to humans what the latter might be to mites and mayflies, camouflaged from their limited senses. The fiction of the "Grands Transparents" serves both to relativize the human world and to deepen it: it relegates political struggles, party lines, and limited imaginations to their proper place, but also lends a face and a mind—terrifying or benevolent—to the mysterious workings of chance, history, and fate.[4]

Could the outraged critics of *Prolégomènes* have been entirely unaware that they were dealing here with a heuristic-didactic fiction, a tactical hypothesis, a "construction poétique" of the kind Breton had once called for in the pages of *Le Surréalisme au service de la révolution*?[5] Yet Breton anticipates the hostile, willfully unnuanced reception his text received in Paris—accusations of "mysticisme" in particular[6]—and vigorously defends surrealism's decision to speak on behalf of a steadfast "minority" that answers nay to every unanimous vote and crosses every party line. He defines the movement's task in the postwar era—to borrow a phrase from the pataphysicians—as "minoritaire par vocation."[7] Breton also responds to anticipated criticisms by defending surrealism's right to maintain its own "system of coordinates" and its own "instruments of knowledge," according to circumstance.

Who, he adds, would tell a carpenter that hammers are fundamentally unacceptable, since they cannot be used to saw planks? Breton's point echoes one made by Raoul Ubac in a 1943 article for (future Oulipian) Jean Lescure's journal *Messages*, on the possibility of redirecting "l'expérience mystique" away from the supernatural and occult and treating its methods of knowledge and its mental "states" as tools, as disposable use-values rather than as truth-values.[8] Here occult sciences, such as they are, find themselves subject to a pataphysical "principle of equivalence"; as far as both Ubac and Breton are concerned, one tool is as good as another if it works for present purposes. Ubac, however—a member of the Main à Plume group—was soon ruthlessly excommunicated from it, on the grounds of "mysticism."

The international surrealist exhibition of 1947 at Galerie Maeght, Paris, designed and organized by Breton and Marcel Duchamp—and devoted to the theme of myth—is frequently taken as evidence for the scholarly-historical commonplace about surrealism's "turn" to myth and mysticism after the war, according to which the movement volte-faces in a kind of half-defiant, half-traumatized escapism toward a magical fairyland. Once again, however, the myth of the "turn to myth" owes largely to a prevailing early Cold War Manichaeanism that drew certain strict lines in the sand—for example, between scientific, materialist, and revolutionary thought and idealist-metaphysical, reactionary thought. The postwar Bretonians' interest in metaphors and tool-concepts derived from magic, mythic, and mystical traditions was also in firm continuity with prewar surrealist theory and practice. What did in fact characterize this postwar moment in surrealist history was this: the "minor" form of thinking, reasoning, and creating defended by Breton was forced, in response to prevailing pressures and criticisms, to redefine and rename itself, and became increasingly aware of itself, as "myth." In the immediate postwar period, in other words, "myth" became a surrealist catchall term for everything heretical with respect to the status quo, Communist or otherwise, and came to represent the possibility of revolutionary action and thought outside of party politics. Myth remained a slippery terrain, however, as the Bretonians acknowledged—for in the form of ideology, political or otherwise, it could also become a trap.

Many of the essays in the 1947 Galerie Maeght exhibition catalog share what one could loosely call a Lucretian vision of nature—in reference to Lucretius's atomic physics in *De rerum natura*, along with his doctrine of the clinamen (or "swerve") later picked up and modified by Alfred Jarry and afterward by the *Collège de 'Pataphysique* and the Oulipo. In such a vision, language, social reality, and everything else is composed of building blocks or atoms that, for all the apparent solidity of their existing arrangements, can always be recomposed or recollaged: this is the task of the surrealist "myth"-maker. Pierre Demarne, for example, in his catalog essay "Suranalogie et pollen de surréalité," evokes a timeless and "astounding domain" of forms, a "crucible of the possible" where history is replaced by a series of "combinations" of formal elements and impulses, infinite but theoretically repeatable. Surrealism's task (its "métascience du *comme*") must be continually to seek and to provoke new "combinations," and systematically and rigorously to explore their implications.[9]

The catalog contributors and organizers of the exhibition also share a deep interest in what they call "analogical" thought, allied to the necessarily "open" rationalism of modern-day science and to the "open realism" that surrealism must champion.[10] Breton writes in 1948 that analogy in its surrealist meaning makes the mind apprehend "the interdependence of two objects of thought located on different planes, between which thought's logical operations cannot cast any bridge and indeed oppose themselves a priori to any such act of bridging."[11] The only limit to surrealist analogical thought is an individual's desire and ability to see or construct such bridges, and not any principle of verisimilitude or categorical system of similarity and difference. Surrealist analogy is also a dialectical tool, since (according to one catalog writer) it recognizes the Hegelian principle that "if a thing possesses a certain group of attributes, it must also possess the group of attributes contradictory to these," making dialectics a "doctrine of equivalence" and founding surrealism itself on the principle that "reality is entirely constructed upon the principle of equivalence."[12]

In the sense that any two entities might, at any swerve-like pretext, be taken as equivalent, surrealist analogical thought is *clinamenic* thought, and also—to use another of pataphysics' "three declensions of the exceptional"—*syzygial* thought.[13] Syzygy, in pataphysics, is that which "finds a way to equate things to each other in a system that values the norm of difference." It is an attempt literally to "imagine the incompossible," to assume its possibility and to extrapolate from it.[14] And since the syzygial alignment of celestial bodies, as in the original definition of the word, also comprises "the idea of a chance encounter,"[15] syzygy is not unallied to clinamen: a sudden deviance or detour from what is or seems determined in advance. Clinamen is about escaping a "system"; surrealists' revolutionary sensibilities might be gratified by its definition as "the smallest possible aberration that can make the greatest possible difference."[16] One might even put forward that the classical surrealist poetic principle of juxtaposing unlike things, for the purpose of producing a "shock [which tends] to establish a new conceptual order,"[17] places syzygy and clinamen, those two pataphysical terms par excellence, at the heart of the surrealist project.

As far as the exceptional goes, and the laws governing exceptions, one of the most powerful doctrines of postwar French Stalinist Communism was that there is no such thing as exception. Economic relations of inequality, and the realities of class struggle, as expressed and translated in one's social-cultural context, inform and determine one's every act and thought whether one knows it or not. To ignore or flee these realities is uncritically and unwittingly to reproduce them.

This was an idea shared on general lines by many in the surrealist milieu during and after the war, particularly by members of the Main à Plume group. Main à Plume member Christian Dotremont, for example, writes that what we think of as our inalienable human liberties are all blighted by sociocultural tics, moth-eaten myths, unexamined beliefs—unconscious constraints, in short. He explains that what one experiences as "interior liberty" actually does no more than add "a few bars to [one's] cage."[18] Main à Plume member Noël Arnaud (later a member of a Stalinist "revolutionary-surrealist" splinter group, then a pataphysician, and finally an Oulipian, in turn) explains that the same principle holds good for both social and artistic activity: what appears to be personal choice is actually necessity in disguise—an affirmation of the status quo.[19]

One here recalls the Oulipo's famous critique of surrealism: that the absolute freedom of expression the latter seeks is no more than a slavery to laws—unconscious constraints—of which it is ignorant.[20] One purpose of the Oulipian formal constraint will be to free artistic imagination and creation from such unconscious (social, historical, autobiographical, stylistic) constraints and from necessities disguised as freedoms, replacing them with paradoxically liberating and conscious constraint. In the same way, Main à Plume, with its preference for mechanism- or chance-based creative procedures ("the mechanism is master," as Arnaud exults)[21] wishes to replace unconscious unfreedom with a conscious unfreedom that paradoxically reverses itself into ultimate freedom. Arnaud explains that what might appear in the guise of arbitrary necessity—the intervention of blind mechanism, the incursions of chance—is actually the highest freedom, an exalted forgetting of whatever temporary configurations status quo reality has seen fit to form.

This paradoxical logic of exception resonates with certain founding documents of the *Collège de 'Pataphysique*, and brings the pataphysical "imaginary solution" close to the postwar surrealist understanding of myth. The 1948 "Inaugural Harangue" of Irénée-Louis Sandomir, for example, sweeping its gaze over all that has been done and thought during and after the Second World War, finds nothing to disrupt its "universal and impeccable Pataphysical Harmony." The world itself, "in all its breadth," *is* the *Collège*—only that it fails to recognize itself as such. What distinguishes the *Collège* from the rest of the world, in short, is simply that it practices pataphysics consciously.[22] In Sandomir's 1956 *Testament*, similarly, there is nothing in the world but pataphysics, nothing but imaginary solutions. One either consciously manipulates and invents imaginary solutions, or one is unwittingly subject to them. Moreover, says Sandomir, "it is no less true to say that imaginary solutions have all the efficacy of supposedly real solutions. They move things; they move men."[23]

In the months leading up to the 1947 exhibition, the surrealists are seeking to create myths that recognize themselves as such. And if "myths" are—as Breton and his group believe—nothing other than the constitutive matter of the social, cultural, and political world, then to work with and within myth, whether benign and familiar or outré, is to reshape this very matter. Poetry, the imagination, desire, all the great surrealist forces, are all mythic: which is to say that they make and remake the armature of ideas, beliefs, and fictions that humans live by. Georges Bataille, in his contribution to the 1947 exhibition catalog, describes a world made of myths that are all equally insubstantial and equally powerful. For Bataille myths are (to borrow the words of Julien Torma) façades of façades, behind which there is nothing: they live their ephemeral lives in an immense "void" of whose substance they partake.[24] But since all is empty, all is permitted, and myths, with their "pale transparency of the possible," have strong currents and countercurrents, like "rivers under the sea."[25]

A 2008 *Collège de 'Pataphysique* publication describes the founding event of the *Collège* in May 1948 at Adrienne Monnier's Paris bookshop, Maison des amis des livres, "by a small circle of erudite types for whom the 'restrictions' of the time were not solely dietary"—explaining, significantly, that "not everyone could be satisfied by Stalino-humanist engagement or patriotic purges."[26] It is true that the postwar surrealist movement in its successes and travails, and the *Collège* in its founding years, were deeply dismissive of each other when they crossed paths, and their respective programs of action were hardly in accord. The *Collège* founders, after all, also set firmly aside "the stammerings of surrealistico-marxist phraseology."[27] However, it must again be recognized that the two groups—surrealists and pataphysicians—were responding to the same exasperating, Manichaean, "Stalino-humanist" milieu, where words like myth and mysticism were treated as weapons in a culture war and the atmosphere was hostile to imaginary solutions of any kind. For this reason, their strategies and attitudes were often more congruent than not. And as it will become particularly clear amid the wartime surrealist Main à Plume group, both surrealism and pataphysics, during and after the war, sought to formulate and demonstrate a new "gay science" that might step light as air over the social, political, and quotidian stumbling blocks set before it.

For Main à Plume, the word "science" should be taken quite seriously, albeit idiosyncratically. Group member Jacques Bureau, for example, calls for a systematic recourse to magic—"but an *extended* magic," he specifies, "that could be easily integrated into a *complete* Physics."[28] This "extended" magic would be a science of nature that strives to incorporate its own margins—all the exceptions, all the strange and residual phenomena that are typically ignored in order to create and maintain methodological and epistemological coherence. For Bureau, this would amount to a return to the "Middle Ages" of science, to a sort of high-yielding epistemological anarchy. Group member Jean-François Chabrun feels, similarly, that he and the others are something like laboratory technicians of thought;[29] Main à Plumer Gérard de Sède, going further, feels that poetry will eventually be replaced by science, and that the "utopian" surrealism of the past should cede to a scientific surrealism, surpassing and replacing even the "open rationalism" attempted by the likes of Breton and dissident surrealist Roger Caillois.[30] Group member Marcel Mariën awaits the elevation of poetry to a new "science expérimentale," the "stupefying intrusion of the discipline of the sciences called exact into a domain devoted for evermore . . . to vagaries, to tics, to the miserable enslavements of the worker to the matter that he works."[31] The real difference for Mariën is that—amid the general call for a reappropriation, redefinition, and revitalization of science in the postwar advent of the jet age and the atomic age—the victory over the "blind forces of matter" that science represents will be aligned, in the new experimental-poetic science, with the "world proletarian revolution." Surrealism must become a mode of "expérience" (meaning both an experimental and an experiential science) that addresses and détourns these very "blind forces," which include the social, cultural, productive, and material determinants, and the inertia of the status quo, against which the Communist Party (for Mariën representing "action" and "efficacité") also struggles.[32]

Before further exploring this notion of a poetic science as it took shape in the group, it is necessary to contextualize it in the group's broader climate of ideas. Many of the members of Main à Plume hailed from amid the prewar surrealists in France and Belgium, though many were too young to have had the chance to participate. Some, after their involvement in the French Resistance, later joined or rejoined Breton's group after the war. Others, after their group disbanded in 1944, devoted themselves to attacking Breton in the name of Communist ideals, while still others went on to found other groups and movements. Some did all three. Isolated in wartime Paris, the last they had heard on how to properly think and behave as a surrealist was before Breton and many others left the continent for the duration of the war. They were pulled between two opposing tendencies: first, to hold the flame of surrealism aloft through the hell and high water of the Occupation, staying faithful to Bretonian orthodoxy and avoiding all heretical deviations; and second, as beacons of its truth and becoming, to allow surrealism room to grow and to strike out in new directions. As founding member Chabrun comments, prewar surrealism "lifts and crushes us at once."[33] In the meantime, the group had to face the worst of conditions for maintaining an active surrealist group, under the threat of exposure, arrest, interrogation, even death, though they were still able to publish relatively frequently.[34] With the end of hostilities in Europe, the group fell apart almost immediately, almost as if wartime secrecy and solidarity were what had kept them together.

From the outset Main à Plume's goal was to breathe new life into the surrealist movement by rethinking collectivity, whether as collective aesthesis, poiesis, or praxis. Chabrun felt that the group's greatest innovation was to have formed "a perfectly homogeneous nucleus" of "workers of thought" who had left behind any sense of personal or intellectual property.[35] The artistic impersonality he and the others desired was grounded in what they saw as the impersonality of language, often conceived as unexplored combinatorial potentiality. The particular sort of *merveilleux* unique to language was its sly revelation, to use Breton's words, of "all sorts of new ways of recombining itself," in its "infinite whispering behind and before us."[36] At its deepest level, the powers of language merged with those of the unconscious and of chance. The Main à Plume group treats chance—as with automatism from the beginning of the surrealist movement—as a mode of access to all that lies beyond individual will or subjective self-expression in the act of creation. Chance governs a complex poetics of the impersonal.

But one of the richest aspects of Main à Plume's theory and practice is its work on objects. In the wake of the "surrealist object," which reached its peak just before the war, Main à Plume carried out vigorous experimentation on what could be called "textualities" of objects and "objectualities" of texts. The group sought, for example, a "language of objects" that would allow objects to be read and in a sense to write, "trac[ing] their poem upon the world."[37] Bureau speaks of a new language literally *made of objects*, "which emerges neither from grammar nor from manuals of physics"; Dotremont believes that certain combinations of objects should be directly mappable onto the rules of language: there are pairs of objects that are synonyms and antonyms (sugar and saccharine, sugar and salt), homonyms (two forty-five-year-old Parisian dentists), and clichés (a mantel and a vase).[38] It was as if there were some imponderable, infra-thin space between the two domains, where objects could be written and words held in the hand. The group's intense concern with "objectivation" (Arnaud writes that the group's raison d'être is its "extravagant will to objectivation")[39] is largely focused on this material/verbal between-space.

"Objectivation" is the process by which what is merely imagined becomes material; or by which what is not yet materially imaginable is made so; or by which something enters a collective discourse or system of social significance and acts therein. It is the concrete construction and literal reification of what once were only myths and imaginary solutions, enabled by a new species of material textuality "beyond the laws of language."[40] Main à Plume also experiments, along these lines, with what one can only call an Oulipianism of the object, in which they collectively impose arbitrary (but freeing) constraints on objects—"false" situations, strange uses, inappropriate interrogations—imagining that doing so makes these objects, like words or like Lucretian atoms, rewritable or recombinatory.[41] The hope is that such activity, carried out collectively, might culminate in a massive "Poem by No One, written on the world by the ensemble of things in it, for the use of all beings."[42]

In the Main à Plume group's speculative materialism—for this is what it all amounts to—a systematic and passionate suppression of subjective expressivity (of the "subjectivité du poète") is believed to catalyze a combinatorial-Oulipian rewriting of the material world. The group is fiercely opposed to the idea that what exists, exists necessarily. Like the "new objectivity" championed by the poet Yves Bonnefoy around the same time (Bonnefoy contributed to the 1947 surrealist catalog and exhibition), this speculative materialism strives to confound the real with the possible—just as for the ultimate pataphysician, "the imaginary and the real are indistinguishable and . . . for him it suffices to think of worlds for them to be."[43] The veritable object, obscured both by the abstractions and equations of physics and by the subjectivity of the poet, can now see a triumphal return: "the vanishing of the physical object, the apparition of the surrealist object: in this ceaseless game of communicating vessels between science and poetry is founded the true materialism."[44]

It is in this context of ambitious theorizing and hybrid experimentation that Main à Plume member Boris Rybak's contributions to the group's oeuvre should be read, specifically his invention of "intraphysics." Rybak (1923–2003), along with contributing to the group's publications, helped to forge many of the false papers that kept these publications and their authors afloat. In the summer of 1943 in occupied Paris, with the Romanian surrealist painter Jacques Hérold, Rybak created a slew of such imaginary solutions, including "certificates of civil status, birth certificates, police records, identity cards, marriage certificates, baptism certificates and even *Ausweisen*."[45]

Already around this time, before the group began to fall apart over its political and ideological differences, Rybak was wary of the Stalinist influences and positions propagated by certain members. By early 1944—the year he published his "Intraphysics" essay, a glowing article on Hérold, a number of poems, and a sketch toward a "Géométrie et structure des moustaches"[46]—Rybak was among those disconcerted to see that almost the entire group had declared its unconditional loyalty to the French Communist Party. At a May 9, 1944, meeting at Arnaud's home, Hérold was accused of attempting to justify his failure to join the others by pointing to the "revolutionary" formal qualities of his painting; Rybak was also attacked for his political "abstentionism." Gérard de Sède, although inspired by the young Rybak's research and interests, nevertheless held him to account, telling him that his recognition that "science or art are revolutionary not by the mere proletarian *form* that one gives them, but by their very *essence*, is already to have attained a level of revolutionary consciousness high enough to have no excuse for practical political abstentionism."[47] Rybak angrily retorted that de Sède looked ridiculous giving lessons in revolutionary praxis while personally benefiting from Rybak's efforts as a forger. A week later Rybak himself called a group meeting to address what appeared to be a Stalinist takeover of the group and to help it recover its equilibrium. This and other efforts failed, and Rybak among others left Main à Plume and went his own way.

Rybak earned his doctorate in natural sciences by 1954, and immediately began making strides in the fields of open-heart surgery and the mechanisms of the heart, robotic surgery, and radiosurgery.[48] Between 1955 and 1958 he was also resident science writer for *Les Lettres nouvelles*, a journal founded in 1953 by Maurice Nadeau, an erstwhile Communist and surrealist collaborator, and Maurice Saillet, one of the founders of the *Collège de 'Pataphysique*. *Les Lettres nouvelles* published Yves Bonnefoy and Jacques Prévert, future Oulipian and pataphysician François Caradec, Egyptian surrealist Georges Henein and Beirut surrealists Georges Schéhadé, Salah Stétié, and Gabriel Bounoure, dissident surrealist Michel Leiris, and none other than Emmanuel Peillet—guiding light of the early *Collège*, writing both as Jean-Hugues Sainmont and as himself. But while in early 1953 almost every issue of *Lettres* features texts, sometimes more than one, by Peillet and/or Saillet (not to mention Alfred Jarry), by 1955 neither name appears any longer.

Rybak's articles begin showing up in *Lettres* shortly after this apparent changing of the guard. One of these essays, titled "L'Objet perdu" (1957), is a tender look back on the surrealist cult of the object and of chance.[49] The human being, in this essay, is a paradoxical alloy of "underlying bestiality and emergent consciousness." It is a living thing that, pretending to observe and pronounce upon life, is confused by its own words and myths, conditioned and molded by the very things it most dismisses. It fails to see that even the things it holds eternal, like love and death, are subject to evolutionary forces greater and deeper than it. Yet subtending even these deeper forces is pure blind chance: "All is chance. . . . I see only chance guided by necessity and the latter ordered by chance."[50] Thus the *inconnu* and the *insolite* await one at every step, littering one's path with things, events, and phenomena stranger than any surrealist invention. Trapped within our own limits, "our 'open sesames,' echoing at all the walls, lose themselves in the infinite murmuring of time, and man, orphaned even by his hopes, led by an inexorable and blind evolutionary force, holds fast to his neighbor, holds fast to his objects, holds fast to his memories."[51]

For all our hapless ignorance, Rybak continues, our scientists as well as our poets do know how to construct time machines—"very concrete machines for exploring time." The scientists have discovered carbon-14 and uranium-thorium dating; they can measure the temperature of the Devonian seas; they can track the climates of past ice ages. The poets in turn know that the *inconnu*, whether quotidian or of past eras, passes through the finest empirical nets, and that the affective resonance of things in the past can only be recovered by poetic means. Both kinds of time machine, however—scientific and poetic—must be recognized as imaginary solutions. As Rybak explains, "there is an osmosis between each of us and our human, animal, vegetal, and objectual environment,"[52] such that we can only echo and reiterate this environment even in imagining and re-creating others. Seeking the past and the unknown, what we keep finding is the present and the known.

Like "L'Objet perdu," Rybak's 1943 essay "Introduction au surréalisme scientifique ou naissance de l'intraphysique" does not mention pataphysics outright. In fact, a footnote toward the end cites René Daumal's 1929 "La Pataphysique et la révélation du rire," in particular its lines on absurdity and irreducibility, but cuts these short to leave out the word "pataphysique."[53] The subject of this sharp, sardonic, verbally playful essay might, in any case, better be called *pœtaphysics*, since it mostly concerns the potential conjoining or reconjoining of the disciplines of poetry and physics. At once anti-utilitarian and eminently practical, poetry and physics are disciplines of "the most real . . . total reality" as opposed to the prevailing "hyporéalité." At the same time they are both public and "social" disciplines that tend toward an ultimate "libération de l'homme." Finally, both the physicist and the poet "doubt nothing" and affirm everything. Everything is equivalent before their enthusiasm; neither in any way resembles the inveterate "pyrrhonists" of Dada.[54] In this, one recalls Sandomir's 1956 *Testament*: "None is more positive than the Pataphysician: . . . he is ready to greet and gather all with the same geniality."[55]

Rybak's intraphysics is, of course—along with a reimagining of Jarryan 'pataphysics—an attempt to imagine a new surrealism, to renew the movement from within. His ambition is to move from a "sentimental and more or less individualist surrealism" to a "methodical, ideologically intransigent, active, scientific surrealism." This intransigence has little to do with that characteristic of the Stalinists: Rybak dismisses the red-flag-waving Louis Aragon in the same breath as he does "mysticism" and "positivism."

Scientific surrealism is a "synthetic" discipline in that it proceeds by way of "constructive dissociation"—which is to say, by treating the smooth and uniform surface of status quo reality as, in fact, a fragile and arbitrary agglomeration of units that can be de- and recomposed.[56] In fact, Rybak anticipates what I have called the "Lucretian" combinatorialism—or, more aptly for this historical moment, the atomicism—of the 1947 surrealist exhibition. He quotes, for example, the geologist Raymond Furon: "It is very probable that all the simple elements that we know are only provisional atomic states whose duration of life is enough that we consider them as fixed and stable entities."[57] Intraphysics is also well within the lines of the surrealist glorification of *Poésie* as a social-constructive force rather than a literary pursuit, and within its simultaneously anti-positivist and anti-metaphysical position (to the transcendental, Rybak writes, he answers with the "cissendental"). Finally, intraphysics draws from and participates in the surrealist cult of the object. It studies "the immanent nature of objects," the "interactions and . . . intimate connections between objects."[58]

But how, specifically, can the practice of intraphysics be recognized? Rybak explains that the intraphysicist concerns himself not only with that which is, has been, and will be, but also creates ideas with irrational content that he then dissects; he studies *what might have been*, that is, not only the hypothetical and its probable determinants . . . but also the imaged concretization of the unimaginable. Doting mother, intraphysics observes the *games* of her "monsters."[59]

Rybak gives several vivid examples of this type of activity. Take, he says, a piece of wood. To recognize it *as* a piece of wood and not some other thing is knowledge of the "first degree." To recognize the wood as pine, demonstrating a modicum of education, is knowledge of the second degree. To recognize the practical properties and uses of pine, demonstrating technical competence, is knowledge of the third degree. To give the tree its scientific name and to distinguish it by its reproductive processes is knowledge of the fourth degree: scientific. To ask, with deep anguish and intensity, why indeed this piece of wood is a piece of wood is metaphysics (which has no degree.) And the stage after metaphysics? "To take a piece of wood and a piece of iron and find their continuity, and from there seek to transform one into the other, that is intraphysics."[60] Intraphysics, in other words, is a heuristic but rigorous science of unauthorized equivalence, of reckless analogy.

Intraphysics can also be practiced, quite literally, in a laboratory: Rybak describes what he calls the creation of "surrealist animals" (or "automatic animals") by technicians in the field of experimental embryology who carry out centrifuge experiments on fertilized eggs. Rybak finds intraphysics in merogony—the generation of embryos from egg fragments—and in the mechanisms of heteromorphic regeneration.[61] Regardless of how one feels about mad-scientist surrealists taking up gene-splicing instead of image-splicing, the point is that intraphysics is intended to be both conceptual and concrete—equally at home on a written page and in a petri dish. And since Rybak is a surrealist, his intraphysical pataphysics also nurtures an ambition to change the world; its disjunctions and conjunctions have an ultimately revolutionary purpose.

For all its wild originality, intraphysics was a clear expression of its zeitgeist. After the Main à Plume group ceased to exist, its successors continued imagining new surrealisms as well as new worlds supplementary to this one. In the case, for example, of former Main à Plumers Noël Arnaud, Christian Dotremont, and their friends, an unstable equilibrium between revolutionary intransigence and surrealist/pataphysical experimental openness subsided into a rather unpleasant form of Stalinism, at least for a time. Struggling to reconcile an unconditional loyalty to the Parti communiste français—which they felt to be their only real option—with stubbornly lingering surrealist impulses, they formed the short-lived and unviably hybrid "Surréalistes-Révolutionnaires" group in 1947–48, and proceeded to attack Breton and his 1947 exhibition. However, in order to sustain this monstrous fusion, what they were forced to fall back on was pataphysics.

Dotremont, dismissively recalling his revolutionary-surrealist days, characterized the group's ultra-serious efforts as "pata-pensée."[62] As a matter of fact, one of the first things the revolutionary-surrealists did was to produce an alternative "Patalog" to replace the 1947 surrealist exhibition catalog. The front cover of their *Patalogue officiel de l'Exposition internationale du surréalisme* pretends to reveal (among other things, and in awful taste) that Marcel Duchamp's famous latex-breast cover for the original catalog is actually part of a larger image in which Breton, done up as an Orientalistically stylized dancer, parades with his single breast across a stage. A number of pastiches follow, bitter but playful (irrepressibly so, even amid the *langue de bois* the group otherwise affected): some of which create sententious links between the "mysticism" of the exhibition and the recently implemented Marshall Plan, in which the United States under Truman both supplied material aid to, and assured its economic influence in, Western Europe. Pataphysics was very much in the air, in other words, and the authors of the *Patalogue* found a useful oppositional energy in Jarry's illustrious prefix—a year before the founding of the *Collège*, and five years before Arnaud joined it.

As the revolutionary-surrealists lost steam, ultimately rejected by the party whose favor they had sought, the *Collège de 'Pataphysique* was only getting started. But even before the May 1948 bookshop meeting, the *Collège* founders, old schoolmates, had contributed to or worked together in various journals. These included *L'Etudiant socialiste: Organe mensuel de l'Association générale des étudiants socialistes* (1926–37; Peillet was a frequent contributor); the wartime *Le Rouge et le bleu: Revue de la pensée socialiste française* (banned in August 1942; Peillet may have been an editor);[63] and *Essais et combats: Organe mensuel de la Fédération nationale des étudiants socialistes*. The arch-pataphysician Peillet was editor in chief of this last from January 1938 to January 1939, contributed texts under the name "Faustroll," and included a "Gestes et opinions" rubric. The wartime pataphysics, the (perhaps) socialist pataphysics, and the triumphantly imperturbable postwar pataphysics of the founders of the *Collège* were all born in the same crucible as Arnaud et alia's Stalinist pataphysics, Main à Plume's speculative materialist pataphysics, Breton's mythical pataphysics, and the mad biologist Boris Rybak's pœtaphysics.

Notes

1. See Christian Bök, *'Pataphysics: The Poetics of an Imaginary Science* (Evanston, IL: Northwestern University Press, 2002), 12; and Andrew Hugill, *'Pataphysics: A Useless Guide* (Cambridge, MA: MIT Press, 2012), 128.

2. Indeed, Judt continues, "there was something almost ludicrously imitative about the P[arti] C[ommuniste] F[rançais]'s practices in those years." Those inevitably marginalized from party politics were accused of "deviations" ranging from Titoism to nationalism to Gaullism to Trotskyism to general indiscipline. Tony Judt, *Past Imperfect: French Intellectuals, 1944–1956* (Berkeley: University of California Press, 1992), 111. Ongoing public debates often gave rise to

rather startling remarks: Jean-Paul Sartre, for example, writes that it is wrong "to speak out against injustice in a Communist state" for to do so would be to provide ammunition against "what is *in the long run* the cause of justice itself" (123).

3. André Breton, "Situation du surréalisme entre les deux guerres: Discours aux étudiants français de l'Université de Yale, 10 décembre 1942," in *Œuvres complètes*, ed. Etienne-Alain Hubert et al., 3 vols. (Paris: Gallimard, 1999), 3:716–18 (my translation). Breton writes that no party, "ce parti fût-il à vos yeux celui de la liberté," should be permitted to obstruct the search for a new knowledge and a new language.

4. For the "Grands Transparents" see Breton, *Prolégomènes à un troisième manifeste du surréalisme ou non* (1942), in *Œuvres complètes*, 3:3–14.

5. See "L'Objet fantôme," in *Le Surréalisme au service de la révolution* 3 (1931): 20. Such "poetic constructions" serve as a warning to those who, forgetting the fragility and arbitrariness of human knowledge, pretend to know everything, "la bible d'une main et Lénine de l'autre" (Breton, *Œuvres complètes*, 3:7).

6. Breton, *Œuvres complètes*, 3:8–9: Nothing prevents me, he writes, "de laisser mon esprit vagabonder, sans prendre garde aux accusations de mysticisme dont on ne me fera pas grâce."

7. Quoted by pataphysician Thieri Foulc in "Jean Dubuffet," in *Le Cercle des pataphysiciens*, by the *Collège de 'Pataphysique*, Inédit 544 (Paris: Mille et une nuits, 2010), n.p.

8. For an account of the "incident Ubac," see Michel Fauré, *Histoire du surréalisme sous l'Occupation* (Paris: La Table Ronde, 1982).

9. Pierre Demarne, "Suranalogie et pollen de surréalité," in *Le Surréalisme en 1947*, ed. André Breton and Marcel Duchamp (Paris: Pierre à feu, Galerie Maeght, 1947), 49 (my translation). See also Jules Monnerot, who deals with numbers instead of combinations. For human beings, audible frequencies and visible colors correspond to fixed figures; beyond these limits one finds "l'échelle mathématiquement concevable de tout ce qui n'est pas perçu." Thus what one calls the real world is the function of a series of limits, or a series of imposed "choices" on a number line of possible frequencies along which reality is transmitted. In line with Breton's "Grands Transparents," the surrealist imagination must maintain itself in the awareness that other "real worlds" along the number line exist, and that human attention habitually "centrifuges" them; thus the surrealist imagination becomes a point of "rupture," transgressing limits. Jules Monnerot, "Contre la peur d'imaginer," in Breton and Duchamp, *Le Surréalisme en 1947*, 52.

10. André Breton, "Limites non-frontières du surréalisme" (1937), in *La Clé des champs* (Paris: Jean-Jacques Pauvert, 1967), 18.

11. André Breton, *Signe ascendant* (Paris: Gallimard: 1968), 9 (my translation). The London-based surrealist Stuart Inman writes that while surrealist analogy deals indeed with "the relevant likeness in unlike things," analogy most importantly permits one to "see things, not just as reason or power demands that it is, but as desire demands that it should or could be. Analogy is meaning linked to non-identity." Stuart Inman, "Analogy," in *The Overflowering Milkmaid with Curved Feet*, by the London Surrealist Group (self-pub., 2012), unpaginated.

12. Arpad Mezei, "Liberté du langage," in Breton and Duchamp, *Le Surréalisme en 1947*, 60–61 (my translation).

13. Bök, *'Pataphysics*, 31.

14. Ibid., 11 and 41, relying both on the classic Jarryan passages on the term and on various pataphysicians' and theorists' interpretive layerings.

15. Hugill, *'Pataphysics*, 14.

16. Bök, *'Pataphysics*, 45. (This translation quoted in Hugill, *'Pataphysics*, 15–16.) *De rerum natura* has it that, were atoms not to swerve, "down they would fall . . . through the unbottomed void; / And then collisions ne'er could be . . . / Among the primal elements; and thus / Nature would never have created aught." The clinamen thus places the chance *rencontre* at the foundation of the creation of matter, making it a principle of objectivation and objectification, and moreover linking it to human freedom. If "primordial seeds" did not swerve to "sunder the covenants of fate," whence would come the free will "whereby we step right forward where desire / Leads each

man on"? Lucretius, *On the Nature of Things*, trans. William Ellery Leonard (Mineola, NY: Dover, 2004), 42–43.

17. Jean-François Chabrun, "Naissance de l'homme-objet" (1941), in *La Main à Plume: Anthologie du surréalisme sous l'Occupation*, ed. Anne Vernay and Richard Walter (Paris: Éditions Syllepse, 2008), 56 (my translation). This principle of juxtaposition is encapsulated for surrealists in a passage from the Comte de Lautréamont's *Les Chants de Maldoror* (Paris: Balitout, Questroy et Cie, 1868–69): "comme la rencontre fortuite sur une table de dissection d'une machine à coudre et d'un parapluie" (canto 6, strophe 1). The surrealist concept of objective chance might also be considered a pataphysically sustained dialogue between desire (and/or the conscious or unconscious vagaries of a given individual), and the laws and exceptions, anomalies, and startling regularities governing worlds and planets.

18. Christian Dotremont, "Vie de l'objet" (1944), in Vernay and Walter, *Main à Plume*, 240 (my translation).

19. Noël Arnaud, "Crier = créer," in the 1943 Main à Plume publication *Le Surréalisme encore et toujours*, 28. Arnaud joined the *Collège de 'Pataphysique* in 1952 and the Oulipo in the sixties, after a brief stint with the Surréalistes-Révolutionnaires (1947–48).

20. For Raymond Queneau's early version of the Oulipian critique of surrealism, see "Qu'est-ce que l'art?," *Volontés* 3 (February 20, 1938): 1–6. The classic Marxist take on surrealism is similar: the movement had no business speculating on the occult workings of the mind (for example) when the latter was "conditioned by innumerable social factors all of which would be changed by the revolution." Robert Short, paraphrasing Pierre Naville, in "The Politics of Surrealism, 1920–36," in *Surrealism, Politics and Culture*, ed. Raymond Spiteri and Donald LaCoss (Burlington, VT: Ashgate, 2003), 25.

21. Arnaud, "Crier = créer," 28.

22. See http://claude.ognois.pagesperso-orange.fr/ubu01.htm#Harangue%20inaugurale, accessed April 29, 2021.

23. Irénée-Louis Sandomir, *Testament de Sa Feue Magnificence le Docteur I. L. Sandomir* (Patakosmos Press Open Access, 2014), 4 (my translation). Or as political theorist and law professor Bernard Harcourt just as pithily puts it, "What we come to believe—so often, in reality, mere fictions and myths—takes on the character of truth and has real effects, tangible effects on our social and political condition. These beliefs, these human fabrications, are they simply illusions? Are they fantasies? . . . Thinkers have proposed a range of theories and methods to emancipate us from these figments of our imagination. They have offered genealogies and archaeologies, psychoanalysis, *Ideologiekritik*, poststructuralism, and deconstruction . . . [but] their central point continues to resonate loudly today: our collective imagination has real effects on our social condition and on our politics." Bernard Harcourt, "On the American Paradox of *Laissez-Faire* and Mass Incarceration," *Harvard Law Review Forum* 54 (2012): 1.

24. See Torma's letter to René Daumal in response to the latter's 1928 essay "La Pataphysique et la révélation du rire": "Or le propre de la 'Pataphysique est d'être une façade qui n'est que façade sans rien derrière." Quoted in Ruy Launoir, *Clefs pour la 'pataphysique* (Paris: Seghers, 1969), 179.

25. Bataille writes "comme les fleuves dans la mer." Georges Bataille, "L'Absence de mythe," in Breton and Duchamp, *Le Surréalisme en 1947*, 65 (my translation).

26. *Le Cercle des pataphysiciens*, "Introduction," n.p. (my translation).

27. Quoting here, according to the editors, from the *Cahiers du Collège*, no. 19 (March 1955): n.p. (my translation).

28. Jacques Bureau, "Morale des mots et des objets," in Vernay and Walter, *Main à Plume*, 66 (my translation).

29. Jean-François Chabrun, "Situation de la poésie," in La Main à Plume, *Le Surréalisme encore et toujours*, 3–6.

30. Gérard de Sède, "Objectivité théorique et objectivité lyrique," in Vernay and Walter, *Main à Plume*, 174–78.

31. Marcel Mariën, "Géographie de la lumière," in the short-lived *Le Salut public* (June 1945) after the official dissolution of Main à Plume. In Marcel Mariën, *L'Activité surréaliste en Belgique, 1924–1950* (Brussels: Lebeer-Hassmann, 1979), 352 (my translation). He is quoting the Belgian surrealist Paul Nougé's text "L'Expérience souveraine."

32. Breton's movement was not of course opposed to this sort of alliance between

surrealist and Communist desiderata. He states in a 1946 interview with Jean Duché, for example, that "tout progrès scientifique accompli dans le cadre d'une structure sociale défectueuse ne fait que travailler contre l'homme, que contribuer à aggraver sa condition." However, if science is to make any "progress" at all, "la connaissance scientifique de la nature ne saurait avoir de prix qu'à la condition que le *contact* avec la nature par les voies poétiques et . . . mythiques puisse être rétabli." Breton, *Œuvres complètes*, 3:597.

33. Jean-François Chabrun, "Naissance de l'homme-objet," in Vernay and Walter, *Main à Plume*, 56 (my translation).

34. Censorship and surveillance were not as much a problem in occupied Paris as they were in the "zone libre," and it was easier to get around German regulations than it was to get print authorizations from the Vichy authorities. But historian of surrealism Gérard Durozoi still comments, "Les membres de la Main à Plume y usèrent des faibles moyens qui restaient à leur disposition, ils durent ruser quotidiennement, tant pour vivre que pour publier, ils furent amenés à prendre des risques très réels." Gérard Durozoi, "Les Audaces de la Main à Plume," in Vernay and Walter, *Main à Plume*, 6.

35. Jean-François Chabrun, "La Situation poétique," in La Main à Plume, *Le Surréalisme encore et toujours*, 5 (my translation).

36. André Breton, "Le Merveilleux contre le mystère" (1936), in *Œuvres complètes*, 3:67; and André Breton, "Le Message automatique" (1933), in *Œuvres complètes*, 2:387 (both my translation).

37. See Bureau, "Morale des mots et des objets," 66; and Arnaud, "Crier = créer," 29 (my translation).

38. For Bureau, see "Morale des mots et des objets," 66; for Dotremont, see "Vie de l'objet," 246 (both my translation).

39. Noël Arnaud, "L'Avenir du surréalisme," in Vernay and Walter, *Main à Plume*, 280 (my translation).

40. Quoting again from Bureau, "Morale des mots et des objets," 66 (my translation).

41. Here is Bureau again: "Les techniques, je devrais dire les tactiques, dont l'emploi peut se montrer fertile, sont diverses . . . toutes paraissent dériver de la nécessité *d'observer la réaction de l'objet placé dans une situation fausse* vis-à-vis d'un autre objet, ou notre réaction devant un objet placé dans une situation fausse vis-à-vis de nous." He recalls, for example, a group game that consisted of describing "comment leur paraissait devoir être utilisé pour des fins amoureuses un très insolite parallélépipède gainé de noir (un assez ancien appareil de photo)" (65–66).

42. Ibid., 67 (my translation).

43. Jean-Hugues Sainmont, presentation of Alfred Jarry's "Commentaire pour server à la construction pratique de la Machine à explorer le Temps," in *Cahiers du Collège* 2 (September 22, 1950): 10 (my translation).

44. Yves Bonnefoy, "La Nouvelle objectivité," *La Révolution la nuit* 1 (1946): n.p. (my translation). The first number of the *La Révolution la nuit* magazine, put out by the group of the same name, was dedicated to Main à Plume, though Bonnefoy was not a part of the latter.

45. Fauré, *Histoire du surréalisme*, 330 (my translation).

46. Ibid., 326.

47. Ibid., 401 (my translation).

48. Rybak himself describes the greatest scientific discoveries of his career as deeply intertwined: his work on the fundamental mechanisms of contractile automatism in the human heart leads to a study of the "sons linguistiques" underlying these mechanisms—a "phonétique analogique ventilatoire" measurable using a special ventilometer. This in turn leads to the discovery of a "code lingual (au cours d'une énonciation verbale, la surface dorsale de la langue se marque de fins canaux de morphologie spécifique . . . cet air codé agit selon son impédance acoustique sur le microphone et donne sa form à l'oscillogramme) . . . le code lingual est le seul code propre à l'Homme, qui ajoute au code génétique. *C'est le Verbe.*" The pataphysical air of these discoveries is likely unintended, but striking nonetheless. See introductory page of http://www.boris-rybak.fr/, accessed April 30, 2015. On the lingual code, see Boris Rybak, "Demonstration echographique du code lingual," *Cahiers d'anthropologie et biométrie humaine* 1–2 (1996): 219–22.

49. "L'Objet perdu," reprinted in Boris Rybak, *Anachroniques* (Paris: Gallimard, 1962), first appeared in *Les Lettres nouvelles* 53 (1957).

50. Rybak, *Anachroniques*, 58 (my translation).

51. Ibid., 59 (my translation).

52. Ibid., 65 (my translation). Rybak's "very concrete machines for exploring time" evokes the first lines of Alfred Jarry's time-travel manual, "Commentaires pour servir à la construction pratique de la machine à voyager dans le temps" (1899).

53. René Daumal, "La Pataphysique et la révélation du rire," *Bifur* 2 (July 25, 1929), reprinted in *L'Évidence absurde: Essais et notes*, I (1926–1934) (Paris: Gallimard, 1972). The original passage reads as follows: "Et, par *la réduction à l'absurde*, procédé proprement pataphysique, dessine le cercle vicieux de la science tout en lui échappant. En résumé: l'irréductible est absurde. Réduisons donc à l'absurde pour prouver l'évidence" (93). Daumal writes in the same essay that pataphysics is specifically the science of the "particular and the irreducible" (83). Rybak himself never became involved in the *Collège*. However, Rybak's name appears in a publication of the Société des Amis d'Alfred Jarry, along with Arnaud's, in June 1980 (*L'Etoile-Absinthe: 5-6ème Tournée*), in a note on the election of an administrative counsel; and in the meeting archives of the Oulipo from August 1986 (see Camille Bloomfield, "L'Oulipo: Histoire et sociologie" [PhD diss., Université de Paris VIII, 2011]), 89. Rybak also glancingly mentions pataphysics in a 1982 essay titled "Physique et biologie," in *La Pensée physique contemporaine*, ed. Simon Diner, Daniel Fargue, and Georges Lochak (Hiersac: Augustin Fresnel, 1982), 294; and in his book *Vers un nouvel entendement* (Paris: Denoël, 1973), 163.

54. Boris Rybak, "Introduction au surréalisme scientifique ou naissance de l'intraphysique," in Vernay and Walter, *Main à Plume*, 162–64 (all quotations from this essay, my translation).

55. Sandomir, *Testament de Sa Feue Magnificence*, 3 (my translation).

56. Rybak, "Introduction au surréalisme," 160–61. In terms of continuity with prewar surrealism, Rybak also places intraphysics in a direct lineage with the method of "paranoia-critique" first developed by Salvador Dalí (162). For attempts to renew or rewrite surrealism, see also the journal *84* founded by the writer and poet Henri Thomas, an early close friend of Peillet and a close witness of the "protohistory" of the *Collège de 'Pataphysique*. For all its critique of surrealism, the magazine remained in sympathetic dialogue with it, and its "manifesto" appeared in *Combat* (July 1949), which was soon to become an unofficial but frequent venue for Breton's surrealists. Philippe Blondeau, "Henri Thomas, André Dhôtel et l'aventure de 84," in *Henri Thomas: L'Ecriture du secret*, ed. Patrice Bougon and Marc Dambre (Seyssel: Champ Vallon, 2007), 219–21.

57. Rybak, "Introduction au surréalisme," 163.

58. Ibid., 160–61.

59. Ibid., 161–62.

60. Ibid., 164.

61. For heteromorphic regeneration, see for example Richard Goss, *Principles of Regeneration* (New York: Academic Press, 1969), 95: "In the walking stick, for example, an antenna may be replaced by a leg, especially when amputated proximally. In crustaceans, mandibles have been known to grow in place of antennae, and antennae may sometimes regenerate from amputated eyestalks." Rybak also cites the work of Hans Spemann and Hilde Mangold on the "primary embryonic organizer." To quote from a recent biology textbook, "Spemann and Mangold . . . did an experiment that produced momentous results: they transplanted the dorsal lip of the blastopore. When this small piece of tissue was transplanted into the presumptive belly area of another gastrula, it stimulated a second site of gastrulation, and a second whole embryo formed belly to belly with the original embryo." William K. Purves et al., *Life: The Science of Biology*, 7th ed. (Sunderland, MA: Sinauer Associates, 2004), 417.

62. Françoise Lalande, *Christian Dotremont, l'inventeur de Cobra: Une biographie* (Paris: Editions Stock, 1998), 82–86.

63. For this latter, and for speculations about editorship, see Luc Autret, "Le roman à l'aune de l'amitié," in Bougon and Dambre, *Henri Thomas*, 199.

Chapter 4

Marcel Duchamp and the *Collège de 'Pataphysique*

Marc Décimo
Translated by Anne M. Mulhall

The *Collège de 'Pataphysique*—"a learned and useless research society"—was founded in Paris at 7 rue de l'Odéon, near La Maison des amis des livres, a bookshop run by the author and publisher Adrienne Monnier (1892–1955). Although she is perhaps most well known for publishing the French translation of James Joyce's *Ulysses*, Monnier also established a lending library and organized public lectures where she hosted many artists, writers, and cultural figures. On 22 Palotin 75 of the Pataphysical Era (May 11, 1948, vulgate),[1] His Magnificence Doctor Irénée-Louis Sandomir and Jean-Hugues Sainmont established the *Collège de 'Pataphysique* to commemorate the fiftieth anniversary of the partial publication, in the *Mercure de France* gazette, of *Gestes et opinions du docteur Faustroll, pataphysicien: Roman néo-scientifique*, later translated as *Exploits and Opinions of Doctor Faustroll, Pataphysician.*

The statutes of the *Collège* were signed by His Magnificence on 1 Décervelage 76 (December 29, 1948, vulgate), and cosigned by Mélanie Le Plumet, Jean-Hugues Sainmont, and Oktav Votka. While the *Collège* was principally inspired by the life and works of Alfred Jarry (1873–1907), it was more than just a typical author's "society of friends." The *Collège*'s activities continue to this day, both publicly and privately. They take the form of various "epiphanies," such as reunions, performances, lectures, and exhibitions, as well as the publication of reviews, such as the quarterly *Viridis Candela* (The green candle). Their periodical is divided into series under the titles: *Cahiers, Dossiers, Subsidia Pataphysica, Organographes, Monitoires, L'Expectateur, Carnets, Le Correspondancier*, and *Le Publicateur*.

In 1986, the novelist Henri Thomas (1912–1993) had no choice but to imagine a prehistory of the *Collège* in his work *Une saison volée*. Today, however, its history is much better known. Several works have set themselves the task of documenting that history, among them, in 2000, *Les très riches heures du Collège de 'Pataphysique* and *Les très riches heures du Collège de 'Pataphysique: Documents intimes*, the latter of which was published separately and especially for the *Collège* Optimates and members. In 2008, the Subcommittee of the Great Outdoors published *Le Cercle des pataphysiciens: Collège de 'Pataphysique* and, in the same year, Ruy Launoir produced *Gestes et opinions de quelques Pataphysiciens illustres: Emmanuel Peillet, Jean-Hugues Sainmont, Latis, etc.*, with a preface by Gayot. Finally, in 2014, Paul Gayot published *Du Collège au Collège par l'Occultation.*[2]

Duchamp at the *Collège*

Marcel Duchamp entered the *Collège* on 24 Tatane 79 (August 6, 1952, vulgate). He was assigned to the "Subcommittee of Forms and Graces" to deal with rules, formalities, exceptions, exemptions, and liberalities, but also to the "Subcommittee of Glory and Protuberances," which was concerned not only with the plastic arts, but with benefits, curves, seductions, and ticklings of every kind. The "Subcommittee of Glory and Protuberances" was both a sociological and a medical organism, able to diagnose illnesses and to dispense recipes for astringents and emollients scientifically proven by the S[ub]-C[ommission] of Imaginary Solutions and the Subcommittee of Probabilities.[3] Alexina "Teeny" Duchamp, the artist's second wife,[4] was enrolled in a private capacity on 7 Clinamen 100 (March 29, 1973, vulgate). She paid an honorific phynance[5] and received its publications free of charge.

On 22 Palotin 80 (May 11, 1953, vulgate), His Magnificence Doctor I.-L. Sandomir, the chief administrator of the *Collège*, signed the most important promotion of his reign. He decided to elevate Marcel Duchamp to the Satrapy, a distinction given to figures—predominantly human, although not exclusively—who were close to the *Collège*. Duchamp thus qualified as an "Entity."[6] Also elevated to the dignity of Optimate alongside Duchamp were Camille Renault, the Attignatien Sculptor, whose work today would be categorized as "outsider" art; Max Ernst, Official Painter to H. M. the Imperator (who qualified for the promotion because of a tableau he painted in 1923, *Ubu Imperator*);[7] the Marx Brothers, Economists and Sociologists; Madame of the Fourth Republic, woman of the world; Jacques Prévert, Manufacturer ("Les Petit plats dans les grands," among other things); Ergé, Dog of the Above, a Hungarian Briard of the Pusztas Region and a "Certified Expert in

Catachresis"; Boris Vian, Knacker of the Highest Class; His Serene Highness, Khan of the Uygher Tartars; Pascal Pia, Amateur; and Baron Mollet, Feudal Lord.[8] The body of Satraps symbolizes the freedom of the *Collège*; it is "not subject to any rule, nor does it impart any . . . it meets only when it is appropriate, and no one person is considered indispensable, nor is any teaching or activity."[9] This proposition, which gave him a statutory release from all duties, suited Duchamp perfectly.

On March 16, 1962, following the recommendation of H. M. Simon Watson Taylor (1923–2005), the seventy-five-year-old Duchamp was chosen as "foreign correspondent" of the Workshop of Potential Literature, the subcommittee of the *Collège* known as Oulipo.[10] Duchamp only ever attended one meeting of the Oulipo, on June 25, 1965.[11]

One of the many ways in which Duchamp showed his interest in the *Collège* was by acquiring all of its publications, which were seemingly gifted to him. A list of publications in Duchamp's possession can be found in my book *La Bibliothèque de Marcel Duchamp, peut-être*, and it goes without saying that we can find Jarry's works in his library.[12] Among notable works was an otherwise banal edition of *Ubu Roi*, which had a sumptuous binding made by Duchamp's longtime American companion Mary Reynolds (1891–1950), based on a sketch he produced in 1934. The book plates were made in the form of a U, with the binding edge in the form of a B, thereby spelling out UBU (color plate 1).[13]

Marcel Duchamp and *Viridis Candela*

What can we find out about Duchamp from these *Collège* publications? And where, in these texts, does he make his mark? The publications often reported on events that had been organized around his work, or pieces that had been published about it. *Cahier* 19, for example, references an article published in January 1955 in *La Parisienne* (no. 24), although without specifying either the title, "Vie de Marcel Duchamp," or the author, Henri-Pierre Roché, who was Duchamp's friend and a collector of his works. Today Roché is chiefly recognized for two novels, *Jules et Jim*, published in 1953, and *Deux Anglaises et le continent*, published in 1956, both of which were adapted for the cinema by François Truffaut.[14] Roché's article recounts Duchamp's many encounters in New York, notably with the pataphysicians Eugène Ionesco, Edgard Varèse, Noël Arnaud, and Watson Taylor.[15] In the same issue, Marie-Louise Aulard, the Regent of Social and Culinary Sciences, as well as of the Subcommittee of Peremptions, jumped headfirst into a critique of the exhibition *Surrealist Intrusion in the Enchanters' Domain*, held at the D'Arcy Galleries in New York from November 28, 1960, to January 14, 1961. The criticisms directed at Duchamp are virulent. He is accused of urging Salvador Dalí to exhibit the religious work *La Madone Sixtine* (The Sistine

Madonna), and of receiving an invitation to the opening in the first place.[16] Elsewhere, in the subsequent edition of the *Dossiers*, it is specified that the Regent Aulard had previously wished to submit a draft of her article to the Most Hon. Duchamp "in order to avoid, according to the rules of the *Collège*, any inaccuracies in the reported facts." It was His Magnificence Simon Watson Taylor who undertook to submit the text. Duchamp responded to him from his vacation in Cadaquès, on June 11, 1961, vulgate:

> Dear Watson Taylor,
> I received the draft of the forthcoming article.
> There are no facts in error, and the entire conformist/subversive dissertation is heavily perfumed with pataphysics.
> —a detail in the title: is it the subcommittee of PEREmptions or the subcommittee of PREEmptions?
> Kind Regards,
> Marcel Duchamp.[17]

In 1958, when the Regent Simon Watson Taylor, Proveditor-Delegate, wanted to translate *Faustroll* into English, he consulted Duchamp.[18] The stakes were high, as it is in *Faustroll*, book 2, where the fundamental definitions—or the "Elements of Pataphysics"—can be found.[19] The project was successful, and, in 1965, Watson Taylor and the Proveditor-General Roger Shattuck published *The Selected Works* of Jarry with Grove Press in New York. Watson Taylor's autographed dedication on Duchamp's copy says much about his affection for the artist:

> This [*sic* for the typos that follow] first exemplar of this book of Science, hot off the press eight weeks prior to its publication date, is reserved for Marcel Duchamp, the chief pataphysician of our times (and of all others, in accordance with the "values of equivalence" promulgated by the inventor of our Science).
> Pataffectionate Respects (*Homages*) from Simon Watson Taylor (vulg. January 1965 AD).[20]

As the "great discoverer" of Raymond Roussel and Jean-Pierre Brisset, Duchamp had already offered advice to André Breton's close friend Jean Schuster in 1955. Schuster wished to reedit the work of Brisset, who was considered an "outsider" in the literary field. Elected "Prince of Thinkers" in 1912 on account of his oeuvre, Brisset had wanted to prove, mostly through puns, the Batrachian origins of humanity. The international phonological signifiers [koa] or [kwa] for Brisset suggested "coa!" (the cry of the frog), "quoi?" (the French for "what?" and as such, the first question), and "coi" (meaning "bafflement" in French). And don't French academics always tend to wear green?

In 1953, when Schuster had written an article on Jean-Pierre Brisset, Duchamp advised him to win the support of the painter and patron of the arts William Copley, and then to seek out Arnold Fawcus, who had founded the Trianon Press in Paris. It was to be a mission in vain.[21] Yet Brisset's "delirious imagination" and his "philological analysis of language—analysis conducted through an incredible system of puns," as Duchamp put it, did not fail to attract the attention of the *Collège*, which in turn celebrated "Jean-Pierre Brisset, Philologist," on 25 Haha (October 30, vulgate), among the saints in its Pataphysical Calendar. They all had a shared sensibility.[22] Duchamp also likely contributed to an extraordinary binding produced by Mary Reynolds for a rare work of Brisset's, *La Science de Dieu ou la création de l'homme* (1900).[23] The piece is today preserved at the Ryerson and Burnham Library of Chicago. Made of green calfskin, the binding is decorated with the skin of the "bufo," or common toad. An incision on the lower abdominal region of the toad skin reveals a phallus (color plate 2). This detail is significant, as it illustrates precisely Brisset's thesis of how the supposed evolution of the frog into the sexed human being is betrayed in the French language. The question "Qu'est-ce que c'est?" (What is that?) might be picked up by the more seasoned listener as "Que sexe est?" (What is sex?).

It is no surprise therefore to find the Regent of the *Collège*, along with certain Satraps (Michel Leiris, Jean Ferry, and François Caradec), taking an early interest in Raymond Roussel, another eccentric writer fetishized by Duchamp. Within Duchamp's library, we find not only Roussel's texts, but also studies published about him by the *Collège*.[24] We may recall that Duchamp, along with Gabrielle Buffet-Picabia and Guillaume Apollinaire, attended a performance of Roussel's *Impressions d'Afrique*, and it left a permanent mark on him.[25]

Simon Watson Taylor also wrote an article, from a pataphysical viewpoint, on the opening of the New York Museum of Modern Art (MoMA) exhibition *The Art of Assemblage*, curated by William C. Seitz, and the related symposium held in October 1961. There, the Most Hon. Duchamp presented his views in "À propos des readymade" (Apropos of readymades).[26] The original dactylography was given to Watson Taylor by the Most Hon. Duchamp at the close of the ceremony.[27] A photograph was attached, showing Shattuck, Duchamp and Watson Taylor, which I will revisit below. The journal then recalls the "Patamostra" organized by the Regent Arturo Schwarz, Duchamp's dealer, in Milan in 1963, with an attached photograph showing Duchamp and Schwarz in Milan in June 1962.[28] In the same edition, Schwarz published an article entitled "Jeux de mots."[29]

The journal also reports on the 1963 retrospective organized in Pasadena by Walter Hopps (1932–2005), another member of the *Collège*, and on the catalog *By or of Marcel Duchamp or Rrose Sélavy*.[30] Finally, a short piece announced exhibitions at the Cordier and Ekstrom Gallery, New York, beginning on January 14, 1965,[31] and also at the Tate Gallery in London in 1966.[32]

Marcel Duchamp's Appearances at the *Collège*

They are very rare, and all the more precious because of that. They punctuate the life of the *Collège*. They are of two types, which are often conjoined: epistolary and photographic.

Epistolary

On 14 Haha 89 (October 19, 1961, vulgate), the Most Serene Shattuck and Watson Taylor, and the Most Hon. Duchamp sent a postcard from New York for the eighty-fourth birthday of His Magnificence, "Baron" Jean Mollet (1877–1964), which had been sumptuously celebrated in Paris.[33] Of course, the editors of *Les très riches heures du Collège de 'Pataphysique* didn't fail to include this unique and brilliant document in their collection.[34] The "Baron," who had known Jarry and was also close to Apollinaire, was elected Satrap on May 11, 1953, vulgate. He was then elected Vice-Curator of the *Collège* by Raymond Queneau on May 10, 1959, vulgate,[35] and has remained one of the *Collège*'s most eminent figures.

To congratulate His Magnificence Opach on his election as Vice-Curator (which occurred because of the passing of "Baron" Mollet), Duchamp sent a telegram from his vacation in Cadaquès. It was addressed to the Most Hon. Dubuffet, Sole Voter, who had brought together a number of Optimates at his home for the occasion:

> SORRY TO PHYSICALLY MISS THE PATAPHYSICAL ASSOCIATION GREETING THE NEW SUPREME LEADER MARCEL DUCHAMP S.[36]

Concerning this election, Ruy Launoir, the biographer of Emmanuel Peillet and some of his other assumed heteronyms, also transcribed a snippet of a letter from Latis[37] to another Satrap of the *Collège*, most likely Pascal Pia:

> By sending his transcendent vote, Duchamp took the trouble, (he doesn't have a way with words), to explain [*pour spliquer*] that the Vice-Curator should be R. Queneau. But at the same time, he votes for him—by vigorously scratching out the three others—as the *sole voter*. He did not, then, as it is commonly understood and as the statutes forbid, cast a vote for himself. Marcel Duchamp is lucky that he is Marcel Duchamp. If I published it, you'd believe it a suave "sélavyté."[38]

Queneau declined the offer. And the sole voter, Jean Dubuffet, was persuaded to vote for Opach.

Duchamp sent a postcard of the Monaco Cactus Garden to the Most Hon. Latis who, as was widely known, had a passion for these plants. No doubt Duchamp had in mind *Subsidia Pataphysica* 2, which had been given over to cacti, and in which his three-minute speech, "À propos des readymade," made at MoMA New York on

October 19, 1961 (vulgate), had just been published. An Anglicist Regent, Antoine Tavera, had been charged with its translation.

Duchamp's presence within the *Collège* can also be seen to be photographic, as explained below.

Photographic

No. 1. It was decided to republish, *in extenso*, the article by the Most Hon. Michel Leiris on Duchamp's *Boîtes-en-valise*, which had been published in reduced form in the *Nouvelle Revue française* in 1936. Three portraits adjoin it: one of the author (Leiris), and two of Duchamp. The first photo of Duchamp is almost contemporaneous with the essay, having been sent the previous year by the artist himself. Here, Duchamp appears in low-angled lighting, holding a pipe in his hand (fig. 4.1). The accompanying handwritten annotation reads "Bien pataphysic à vous. Marcel Duchamp" (Pataphysical greetings to you. Marcel Duchamp).[39]

The second photograph, as has been noted, was taken by Man Ray "around the time of *Bride*." The portrait is described here as a "masterpiece."[40]

4.1. Photograph of the Most. Hon. Duchamp sent to the *Collège* by the artist himself (photographer unknown). Printed in *Subsidia Pataphysica* 6, 10 Sable 96 (December 10, 1969, vulgate), 31.

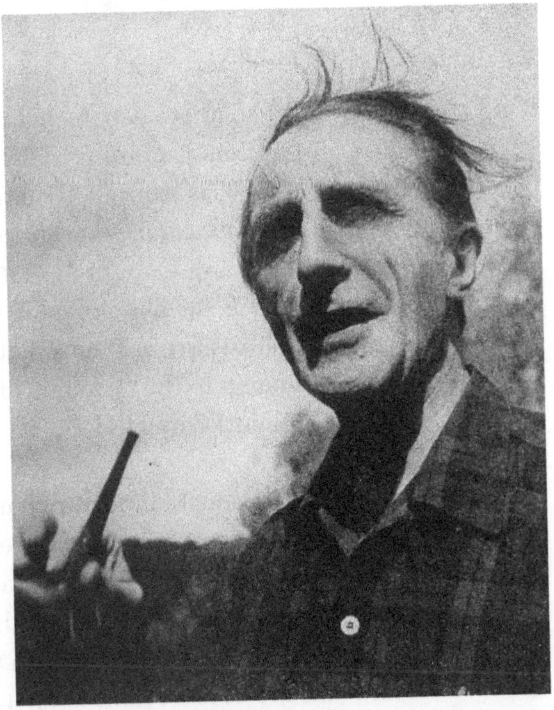

No. 2. In the same number, another photograph can be found under the heading "Celebration."[41] The caption reads, "The Opening of the Marcel Duchamp Exhibition at La Hune."

Any iconographic study of the *Collège* must, of course, state "some of the honours due to the Right Hon. Marcel Duchamp," and testify to other members the importance of the Duchamp exhibition at La Hune bookshop in the heart of Saint-Germain-des-Prés, Paris. The event coincided with the Trianon Press publication of "Robert Lebel's opulent book *Sur Marcel Duchamp*." In order "to give the event an extra sheen," an equivalence—a precious dogma for pataphysicians—was inserted into the publication.[42] This photographic equivalence (fig. 4.2) is indeed worthy of a lengthy panegyric.

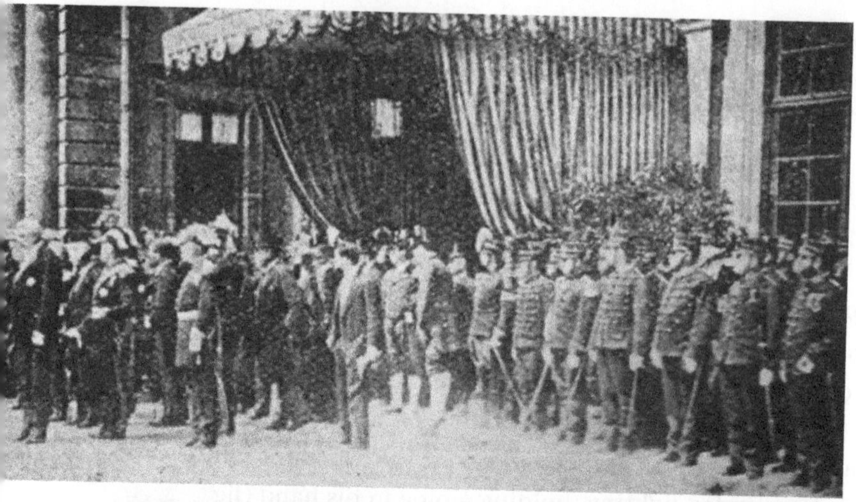

4.2. Photograph printed with the intentionally falsified caption "The Opening of the Marcel Duchamp Exhibition at La Hune Bookshop" in *Dossier* 7, 11 Gidouille 86 (June 25, 1959, vulgate), 94 (photographer unknown).

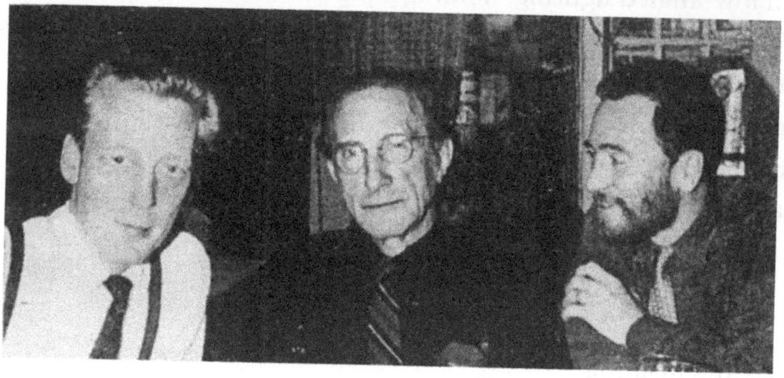

4.3. Photograph of Simon Watson Taylor, Marcel Duchamp, and Roger Shattuck (*left to right*) alleged to have been taken at the opening of H.M.'s grand exhibition at the Pasadena Art Museum and capturing Proveditor-Delegate S. Watson Taylor asking permission of the Most Hon. Marcel Duchamp to consider "Et qui libre?" (photographer unknown). Printed in *Dossiers* 26, 22 Merdre 91 (June 8, 1964, vulg.), 51.

In fact, the photo depicts not the exhibition opening at La Hune, but something else entirely. According to the Most Serene Proveditor Rogator General, Paul Gayot, who was last consulted on this point, the photograph actually comes from *Histoire de Reims depuis les origines jusqu'à nos jours*, published by Georges Boussinesq and Gustave Laurent in 1933.[43]

In that book, the photograph is titled (probably incorrectly) "The Reception of President Félix Faure at Reims Station." President Faure was said to have arrived with great pomp to the unveiling of a statue of Joan of Arc that had been erected in front of Reims Cathedral.

No. 3. An occasional photograph, in which we see Duchamp in conversation with Shattuck and Watson Taylor, can be found in *Dossier* 17 (fig. 4.3). It accompanies an account given by the Regent, Watson Taylor, of MoMA's *The Art of Assemblage* exhibition in 1961. I will return to this photograph below.

No. 4. Dossiers 10–11 of 8 Clinamen 87 (March 30, 1960, vulgate) are largely given over to the Most Hon. Jean Dubuffet. But on page 42, it is stated that the Most Hon.

Duchamp helped to translate, in New York, the English preface of the catalog for the Dubuffet exhibition, held at the Pierre Matisse Gallery from February to March 1952, vulgate. This mention of Duchamp is immediately followed by a photograph of the Most Hons. Duchamp and Dubuffet encircling the Satrapesse Dubuffet at a New York pleasure ground, with a nymph hovering over them.[44]

There should be no need to explain this seemingly trivial photograph, in which both Duchamp and Dubuffet sport false moustaches. It is obviously part of the series of pre- and post-Duchampian images of mustachioed Mona Lisas, or at the very least reminds us of their existence. And there is a lot to say on the fate of the hairy-faced Mona Lisa.[45] Acts of "jocondoclastie," or the creation of iconoclastic variations of the *Mona Lisa*, flourished considerably after 1887, when the "Illustrious Sapeck," Eugène Bataille (1853–1891), added a "cheeky pipe" to the picture (act 1).[46] Then, in 1911, Vincenzo Peruggia stole the da Vinci original from the Louvre (act 2), and, in 1919, Duchamp added a moustache and a goatee to the portrait and gave it the promising, if enigmatic title *L.H.O.O.Q.* (act 3).[47]

The post-Duchampian series of Mona Lisas with moustaches was initiated by Francis Picabia in *391* of March 1920. These versions dispensed with the goatee, and from then on Duchamp repeatedly seized on it as a concept. Thus, the idea of masquerade was still in the air in 1952 when the snapshot of Duchamp and Dubuffet was taken. In 1954, Philippe Halsman photographed *Dalí en Joconde* (Dalí and Duchamp were very close friends).[48] Duchamp returned to it in 1958, again in 1960, and once more in 1965, with the *L.H.O.O.Q. Shaved*, where the Mona Lisa figure was returned to her original hairless appearance.

It is not insignificant, then, that this particular photo of Duchamp and Dubuffet, taken in 1952, was later published in *Viridis Candela* in 1960. Although it fits into the jubilant and fragmented series just described, it is also part of a larger system of multiple portraits taken by Duchamp, either depicting himself or his alter ego, Rrose Sélavy. The rectified hairy portraits of the Mona Lisa, along with these retouched pictures of Duchamp himself, exemplify the jocular spirit that permeated both his life and work.

Duchamp deliberately plays with bovarism, or the human capacity to conceive of things other than as they are. He takes multiple photographs of himself, real and fictional—equivalent categories for him—in order to make sense of his own existence. Although some of the pictures see him adopting a feminine appearance, such as the Rrose Sélavy series in the 1920s, he also appears in a variety of fantasy male guises. He poses shaved with the tonsure (1919), with soap on his head (1925), as an old man (1942), *At the Age of Eighty-Five*, an altered image of Duchamp, or what he imagines he might look like at eighty-five (1945), in profile (1958), and so on. All of these detours into exotic portraiture, all of these fictions where he duplicates himself or projects himself in shadow, essentially enable him to plumb his own depths, and to gain a clearer vision of himself. It is this pared-down work that makes Duchamp who and what he is. His image is never fixed once and for all, but is constantly revitalized through his semiological-photographic life. As reflections, these facets best show what it is that Duchamp is trying to grasp when he talks about likeness and difference as "infrathin," even when it relates to his own selfhood.[49] This may be what Duchamp had in mind when he carried out the *Portrait-miroir*, probably in a fairground booth, in New York in 1917. In this photograph, he appears from five different angles simultaneously, including from behind and in profile.

For Duchamp, the idea of escape—from the self, from his vocation as a painter, from his culture, from European mores, from the French language (from 1915 onward, in discovering Manhattan), from his habits, from his gendered identity (through the Rrose Sélavy photomontage in 1921), from fixed representations (1924), and from his age (1945)—was an essential way of becoming aware of the habitus that imposes itself on and shapes a particular mode of being in the world. These detours through alterity and into other spaces were absolutely necessary for him to dissociate with the social and cultural values that had shaped him, values that Duchamp always experienced negatively as asphyxiating, castrating, and mortifying.[50]

To be entirely oneself, for Duchamp, was to be precisely what others were not. It was to do what others were not doing. It was to be the exception. This is where Marcel Duchamp definitively embodies the pataphysician. For instance, he never aligned himself with patriotism, even at a time when this stance would have been deemed unforgivable. He was not a "poilu," but rather a deserter. Duchamp was not a painter. He did not share the family vocation toward working with pencils, colors, paintbrushes, and turpentine, as had his maternal grandfather (Émile Nicolle), his mother (Lucie Nicolle), his brothers (Jacques Villon and Gaston Duchamp-Villon), his sister (Suzanne Duchamp), or his brother-in-law (Jean Crotti). He was, in other words, an artist defrocked.

When Duchamp called himself a "breather" (*respirateur*), it was a rejection of everything that poisoned him and prevented him from being. He refused to practice a profitable profession in the manner of either his maternal grandfather, who had made a fortune, or his father, who was a notary. He never worked. While his brothers changed their names, he left his intact. While they were artists, he became an anti-artist. Whereas other people *did* things, Duchamp would instead delegate to others the task of getting their hands dirty.

But *doing nothing*, or indeed *doing as little as possible*, also comes to verify the basic premise of pataphysical equivalency. In this sense, the "readymade" is as good as a piece of art that was time-consuming to make. Duchamp says as much in his definition of the "Total Pataphysician," for whom there is no difference in nature or degree between the mind and what it produces, or even between things in general.

In delivering the much-lauded bicycle wheel on the stool, the bottle rack, the dog comb, the urinal, the coatrack, and the hat rack, among others, Duchamp sumptuously illustrates the pataphysical recommendation of the exception (*Faustroll*, book 2). Viewed in this light, the most banal piece of graffiti might equal the most accomplished book, even *Exploits and Opinions of Dr. Faustroll, Pataphysician* itself, and any ordinary cooking pot could be a match for Albrecht Altdorfer's *Nativity* series.[51]

Duchamp himself could never be the same as everyone else. He tended to deviate. In this respect, he took as his guiding principle the concept of "clinamen,"[52] inherited from Epicurus and Lucretius and mentioned by Jarry in book 4, chapter 23, of *Faustroll*. Clinamen, by Lucretius's definition, is the name given to small deviations in the directions of atoms that enable the world to exist and which enable us to think freely as humans.

No. 5. A photograph published in *Dossier* 26, 22 Merdre 91 (June 8, 1964 vulgate), shows Duchamp in a more normative appearance. Here we see Simon Watson Taylor and Duchamp. It is said that at the time of his death Duchamp was reading Alphonse Allais, in the edition that was later republished by the Rgt. François Caradec.[53] Even then, Duchamp was keeping up to date with the affairs of the *Collège*, which had just celebrated Allais by mounting an exhibition at La Hune, the "Germanopratin" bookshop.[54]

An *Hommage à Marcel Duchamp* was made in *Subsidia Pataphysica* 6, published 10 Sable 96 (December 10, 1969, vulgate). It consisted of the title and then three blank pages, a move referencing an exploit of Pierre de Massot, a close associate of Duchamp's who had written a "wonderful" book on the inventor of the readymade. In February 1924, Massot had produced the aptly titled *Wonderful Book: Réflections on rrose sélavy*, a pamphlet of twelve blank pages, each with a header bearing a month of the year in the manner of a diary.[55] As Henri-Pierre Roché later remarked in 1953, "The most beautiful work of Marcel Duchamp is the use of his time."[56] To appreciate the effect, we may note how "reflections," an English word that is francized here, allows us to hear the French "réflexions" (reflections or thoughts) but also "reflets" (reflections of light).

When inscribing his pamphlet, Massot took a quotation from Gertrude Stein. It is drawn from *Next: Life and Letters of Marcel Duchamp*, a text written in 1920 and published in 1922. The quotation reads as follows: "I was looking to see if I could make Marcel out of it but I can't."[57] And following the preface by Stein was an "Introduction" by "a Woman of No Importance" (alluding to the Oscar Wilde play of 1893):

> Far from denying its influence glorying in it on the contrary, P[ierre] de M[assot] determined . . . to write a wonderful book on MARCEL DUCHAMP.

But at each attempt he was overwhelmed by the difficulty of such a task. For, I ought to explain that M has always declared he considers Duchamp the greatest genius he knows.

To speak about the youth, the evolution, the work and especially the life of Marcel Duchamp without blundering! Might not one well hesitate? Anybody would hesitate. The thing is impossible.

We know that the author of "Nu descendant l'escalier" [*sic*] lives on chess and love. The author of this book loves to recall on a Sunday afternoon when he slept in Duchamp's room under the gaze of the King, the queen and the pawns. Black and white move on the chequerboard of life.

After years of hesitation, P. de M. brought me this book. I preface it without the slightest hesitation. It is perfectly idiotic—or idiotically perfect! But since it is my duty to be sincere, I must admit, for the benefit of the reader, that this lazy, naughty little boy said to me the other evening: "Un livre agréable doit toujours être illisible." ["A good book must always be unreadable."][58]

As was usual for publications of the *Collège de 'Pataphysique*, the volume *Subsidia Pataphysica* 6 (December 10, 1969, vulgate) contained photographs that had

4.4. Photograph, cropped to remove Simon Watson Taylor, of the Most Hon. Marcel Duchamp in conversation with H.M. Proeditor-General Roger Shattuck (14 Haha 89 [October 19, 1961, vulgate]). Printed in *Subsidia Pataphysica* 6, 10 Sable 96 (December 10, 1969, vulgate), 30.

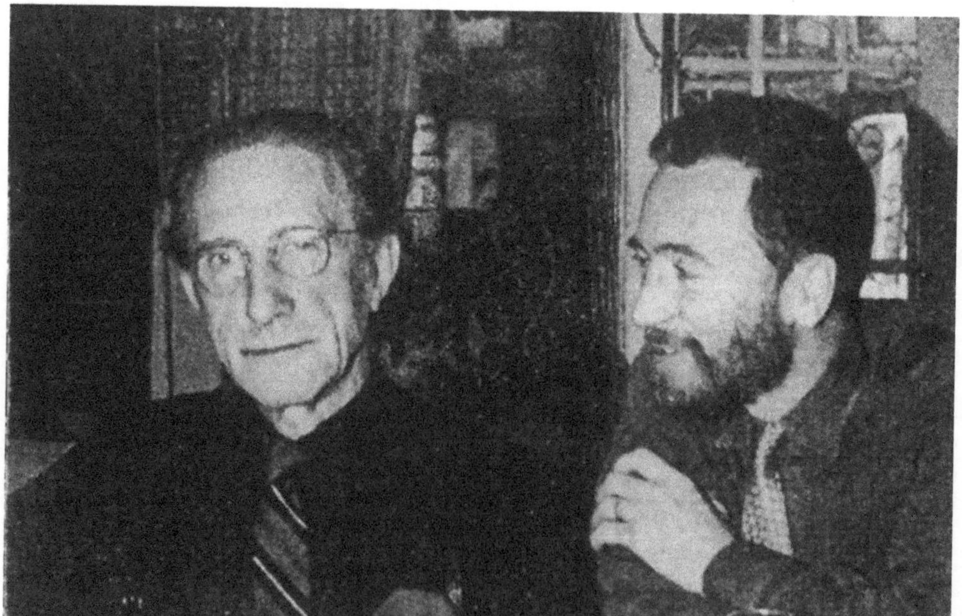

already been published but that were added presumably because the material was rare and precious. This time, however, the triple portrait mentioned above, the one that brought Duchamp, Shattuck, and Simon Watson Taylor together, had been cropped. Curiously, Watson Taylor had now disappeared! (fig. 4.4).

An investigation was required, and it turned out that the photograph in *Dossier* 17 (December 22, 1962, vulgate) had been faked. The finger of blame pointed at someone, but even today we are not sure at whom. It follows that the picture in *Subsidia Pataphysica* 6 may either be the original picture or a doctored one—only the Most Hon. Duchamp could possibly know the whole truth of it.[59] Perhaps this kind of trickery was common practice in Stalinist times. It is also amusing to note that Robert Lebel, who did not actually have a photograph of himself and Marcel Duchamp with André Breton, fashioned one, and then rephotographed it for "authenticity." The picture appeared as an illustration to his article "Marcel Duchamp and André Breton" in the catalog of the exhibition organized by Anne d'Harnoncourt at the Philadelphia Museum of Art in 1973.[60]

Subsidia Pataphysica 6 continued its homage by evoking the sixteen years of Marcel Duchamp's pataphysical life, his "rather notorious . . . great epistolary reserve," and how, even a year before his enrolment into the *Collège*, he was already following its publications. This "mark of attention was for the founders the most valuable incentive: he could not come from any higher position." As the eulogy concludes, "The late Sainmont once said that the approval of Marcel Duchamp was, for a pataphysician, infinitely greater than the Nobel Prize. Clearly, for an Optimate steeped in the Doctrine of Equivalence, this was not merely a figure of speech."

Launoir, who wrote biographies of Peillet, Jean-Hugues Sainmont, and Latis among others, attributed the authorship of this anonymous article to Latis. Latis, Ruy Launoir comments mischievously, "had, it is true, no trouble in writing, or rather not writing, this final note: 'four blank pages [in fact three],' 'that would contrast with the others' and 'be worthy of [Duchamp].'" And Latis added, for the benefit of Paul Gayot who looked after the review at that time, "I can guess what your objection will be, obviously. It's too easy . . . But it shan't happen again!"[61]

And so it came to be.

Notes

1. The Pataphysical Era begins on September 8, 1873, the reported date of Alfred Jarry's birth.

2. See Henri Thomas *Une saison volée* (Paris: Éditions Gallimard, 1986); *Les très riches heures du Collège de 'Pataphysique* (Paris: Fayard, 2000); *Les très riches heures du Collège de 'Pataphysique: Documents intimes* (Paris: Collège de 'Pataphysique, 2000); *Le Cercle des pataphysiciens: Collège de 'Pataphysique* (Paris: Éditions Mille et une nuits, 2008); Ruy Launoir, *Gestes et opinions de quelques Pataphysiciens illustres: Emmanuel Peillet, Jean-Hugues Sainmont, Latis, etc.*

(Paris: L'Hexaèdre, 2008); and Paul Gayot, *Du Collège au Collège par l'Occultation* (Paris: L'Hexaèdre, 2014).

3. *Dossier* 7, 11 Gidouille 86 (June 25, 1959, vulgate), 26–27. This issue also contains an article by Michel Leiris on Duchamp.

4. Duchamp's first wife was Lydie Sarazin-Levassor (1903–1988). Her memoirs were published as *A Marriage in Check: The Heart of the Bride Stripped Bare by Her Bachelor, Even* (Dijon: Les presses du réel, 2007).

5. Jarry's orthography. He embellishes the spelling of superfluous elements to the detriment of the spelling.

6. *Cahier* 11, 25 Merdre 80 (June 11, 1953, vulgate), 51; *Dossier* 28, 22 Merdre 92 (June 8, 1965, vulgate), 35–36.

7. *Ubu Imperator* is today housed at the National Museum of Modern Art at the Centre Pompidou in Paris.

8. *Dossier* 7, 26–27.

9. I.-L. Sandomir, *Statuts du Collège de Pataphysique*, 1948, article 6, section 1.

10. Oulipo was created in 1960 by the Most Hon. Raymond Queneau and King François Le Lionnais, a mathematician and, like his old friend Duchamp, a chess player. See Olivier Salon, "François Le Lionnais, érudit et disparate," in *Ouvroir de littérature potentielle* (Paris: Gallimard-BnF, 2014), 49–55.

11. Marcel Bénabou, "Duchamp à l'Oulipo ou un secret trop bien gardé," in *"Regarde de tous tes yeux, regarde!": L'art "contemporain" de Georges Perec*, ed. Jean-Pierre Salgas (Paris: Joseph K., 2008), 74, published in conjunction with an exhibition of the same title, presented at the Musée des Beaux Arts de Nantes, June 27–October 12, 2008, and the Musée des Beaux Arts de Dole, November 21, 2008–February 21, 2009.

12. Marc Décimo, "Marcel Duchamp et le *Collège de 'Pataphysique*," in *La Bibliothèque de Marcel Duchamp, peut-être* (Dijon: Les presses du réel, coll. Relectures, 2002), 121–22.

13. Ibid., 15, 17; Hugh Edwards, *Surrealism and Its Affinities: The Mary Reynolds Collection* (Chicago: Art Institute of Chicago, 1956), 84. See also the Ryerson and Burnham Libraries pages on the Art Institute of Chicago's website, https://www.artic.edu/library/. See also Marc Décimo, "Bibliothèques supposées, bibliothèques mentales, connaissances diffuses: La pratique anartistique de Marcel Duchamp," in *Les bibliothèques d'artistes (XX–XXIe siècles)*, ed. F. Levaillant, D. Gamboni, and J.-R. Bouiller (Paris: Presses de l'université Paris-Sorbonne, 2010), 397–404.

14. *Cahier* 19, 4 Clinamen 82 (March 26, 1955, vulgate), 76.

15. *Dossier* 14, 9 Clinamen 88 (March 31, 1961, vulgate), 73–74.

16. On this affair, see Marc Décimo, *Les Jocondes à moustaches* (Dijon: Les presses du réel, coll. Hétéroclites, 2014), 175–77; and Marie-Louise Aulard, "Sous-Commission des Péremptions: Le Surréalisme prend un nouveau tournant grâce au T.S. Marcel Duchamp," *Dossier* 14, 73–74, reprinted in *Étant donné Marcel Duchamp*, no. 5 (2004): 48–51.

17. *Dossier* 15, 15 Gidouille 88 (June 29, 1961, vulgate), 71.

18. *Dossier* 4, 1st Tatane 85 (July 14, 1958, vulgate), 47.

19. The commentary on the whole text kept members of the *Collège* occupied for decades. The annotated edition of *Faustroll* was published in the review, and as a full annotated volume in 1985 and again in 2010.

20. Décimo, "Marcel Duchamp et le *Collège*," 122.

21. Brisset's *Œuvres complètes* has since been reedited (Dijon: Les presses du réel, coll. L'écart absolu, 2001).

22. Marcel Duchamp, *Duchamp du signe: Écrits*, ed. Michel Sanouillet with Elmer Peterson (Paris: Flammarion, coll. Champs, 1976), 173.

23. Marc Décimo, *L'esprit de la modernité révelé par quelques traits pataphysiques—ou le Brisset facile* (Dijon: Les presses du réel, 2009), 90–91.

24. Décimo, "Marcel Duchamp et le *Collège*," 143–44.

25. Marcel Duchamp, *Entretiens avec Pierre Cabanne* (Paris: Somogy, 1995), 42.

26. "La Science à New York," *Dossier* 17, 22 Sable 89 (December 22, 1962, vulgate), 87–88 (photographs). The piece was reproduced in *Subsidia Pataphysica* 6, 10 Sable 96 (December 10, 1966, vulgate), 87–88.

27. *Subsidia Pataphysica* 2, 29 Tatane 93 (August 11, 1966, vulgate).

28. *Dossier* 25, 9 Pédale 91 (March 3, 1964, vulgate), 6 and 10.

29. Ibid., 14–16.

30. *Dossier* 26, 22 Merdre 91 (June 8, 1964, vulgate), 51.

31. *Dossier* 27, 21 Décervelage 92 (January 18, 1965, vulgate), 127.

32. *Subsidia Pataphysica* 2, 14.

33. *Dossier* 17, 61.

34. *Les très riches heures du Collège de 'Pataphysique*, 89.

35. *Dossier* 7, given over for the most part to the "Election of His Magnificence Baron Mollet"; Subcommittee of Pope Marcel, *Album mémorial en souvenir de Sa Magnificence le Baron Mollet, Vice-Curateur du Collège* (*Collège de 'Pataphysique*, coll. "Élyséenne," 11 Décervelage 92 [January 8, 1965, vulgate]).

36. *Subsidia Pataphysica* 1, 29 Sable 93 (December 28, 1965, vulgate), 22.

37. Latis was one of several pseudonyms used by Emmanuel Peillet, and the name under which he was a founding member of the Oulipo.

38. Launoir, *Gestes et opinions*, 288–89. By choosing the word "sélavyté" here, Latis makes a pun by incorporating a reference to Marcel Duchamp's female alter ego, Rrose Sélavy, mentioned below.

39. *Dossier* 7, 75–79.

40. Ibid. These images were reprised in *Subsidia Pataphysica* 6, 30–31. The photos that follow, curiously enough, did not appear there.

41. Ibid., 94.

42. Ibid.

43. The Most Serene Proveditor Rogator General Paul Gayot, postcard to the author, 20 Pédale 138 (March 22, 2010, vulgate). See Georges Boussinesq and Gustave Laurent, *Histoire de Reims depuis les origines jusqu'à nos jours*, 2 vols. (Reims: Matot-Braine, 1933), 2:837.

44. For reproductions of this photograph and related others, see Décimo, *Jocondes à moustaches*, 160–61.

45. Ibid.

46. Ernest Coquelin, *Le Rire* (Paris: Ollendorf, 1887), 5.

47. When spoken quickly, with the letters elided, *L.H.O.O.Q.* sounds something like "Elle a chaud au cul," or, in English, "She is hot in the ass." The caption is another instance of Duchamp's witty play with words and images.

48. F. Joseph-Lowery has analyzed the relationship that Dalí had with *L.H.O.O.Q.* in "Duchamp à la merci de Dalí," in *Marcel Duchamp et l'érotisme*, ed. Marc Décimo (Dijon: Les presses du réel, coll. L'écart absolu, 2008), 223–36. See also *Étant donné Marcel Duchamp*, no. 5 (2003).

49. "Quand la fumée de tabac sent aussi de la bouche qui l'exhale, les deux odeurs s'épousent par inframince." Duchamp, *Duchamp du signe*, 274.

50. The historical, social, and affective reasons why Duchamp was forced to adopt such an approach are analyzed in Marc Décimo, *Marcel Duchamp mis à nu: À propos du processus créatif* (Dijon: Les presses du réel, coll. L'écart absolu, 2004). What is evident is that "the incident" of 1912—when his brothers came *en habits* and asked him to withdraw his canvas *Nu descendant un escalier no. 2* from an exhibition at the Salon des Indépendants, an occurrence that Duchamp said had actually made his blood run cold—was merely epiphenomenal, and triggered by a much longer process.

51. *Opus pataphysicum: Testament de Sa Feue Magnificence le Docteur I. L. Sandomir* (Éditions du *Collège de 'Pataphysique*), 15 Clinamen 86 (March 6, 1959, vulgate), 138.

52. H. M. Oktav Votka gives an enlightened commentary on this in *Cahier* no. 22/23, 22 Palotin 83 (11 May 1956, vulgate), 105–6.

53. Décimo, *La Bibliothèque de Marcel Duchamp*, 85.

54. *Catalogue de l'exposition Allais du centenaire magnifiquement visible à la Hune à Saint-Germain-des-Prés*, Haha and As 82 (October–November 1955, vulgate).

55. A French version of this almanac was translated in 2000 by Marie Viat and was made available only to subscribers of the review *Étant donné Marcel Duchamp*. The original version was faithfully reproduced in *Étant donné Marcel Duchamp*, no. 2 (1999): 97–120.

56. Henri-Pierre Roché, "Souvenirs sur Marcel Duchamp," *La Nouvelle Revue française*, June 1953, reprinted in both Robert Lebel, *Sur Marcel Duchamp* (Paris: Trianon Press, 1959) and Henri-Pierre Roché, *Écrits sur l'art* (Marseille: André Dimanche Éditeur, 1998), 211.

57. Gertrude Stein, *Geography and Plays* (Boston: Four Seas Company, 1922).

58. Pierre de Massot, *The Wonderful Book*, in *Étant donné Marcel Duchamp*, no. 2 (2000): 106.

59. Paul Gayot, letter to the author, 27 Pédale 138 (March 21, 2011, vulgate), and since confirmed by Ruy Launoir in *Gestes et opinions*: "This silent tribute was accompanied by a photograph reproducing a picture that had been previously published in *Dossier* 17 (page 87); a picture of three people, truncated, in the pure tradition of Stalin's 'Commissariat of the Archive.' It is true that the first photo was itself a montage, where a third figure was added" (314).

60. The catalog was reprinted in 1989. The article was also translated into French by Monique Fong for *Étant donné Marcel Duchamp*, no. 7 (2006). The trick is revealed on page 66.

61. Launoir, *Gestes et opinions*, 314.

Chapter 5

The Potential Energy of Texts $[\Delta U = -P\Delta V]$

Craig Dworkin

Un dictionnaire commencerait à partir du moment où
il ne donnerait plus le sens mais les besognes des mots

A dictionary would begin the moment it no longer
gave the meaning of words, but their labors.
—Georges Bataille, "L'informe"

In Stefan Themerson's novel *Bayamus and the Theatre of Semantic Poetry*, the exasperated narrator vents his frustration with the linguistic abstractions of modernism's avant-garde. "I had been fed up," he declares, with "ezrapoundafskinian jazz plus joyce plus dadamerz plus homespun rachmaninoff glossitis."[1] Concurring with an anti-Cratylian Renaissance nominalism that "a rose, called by any other name, smells as sweet," he then counters the ethnopoetic transcriptions, neologisms, and portmanteaux flaunted by sound-poetry with "lots of diction, good avant-garde Diderot dictionary defined diction" (67). Rather than freeing words of "their semantic weight and letting them loose on the ear-drums," the narrator instead attempts to increase its meaningful mass, "enlarging their weight, spreading it on to a wider cognitive and affective spectrum" (68). By way of demonstration, he distributes the "semantic mass" of Li Po's poem "Drinking Under the Moon" with a metaphrastic transformation. The line "the wine among the flowers," for example, becomes "the fermented grape-juice among the reproductive parts of seed-plants" (69). This procedure similarly amplifies the swooning sigh of the poem's climactic conclusion—"drunk, we are united"—into a garrulous congeries. Ostensibly equivalent in meaning, Themerson's enumeration breaks the satisfied spell of Li Po's languorously triumphant closure with its superfluity: "having the fermented grape-juice in our stomach / absorbing it into our cerebro-spinal fluid / paralyzing various parts of our nervous system with it / speaking thickly / unable to maintain equilibrium / our vision blurred and double / we get merged with one another cognitively and affectively" (72). Themerson's narrator continues to expatiate the poem before wreaking the same expansive ruin on the xenophobic ballad "Taffy Was a Welshman." Perhaps simply delighting in the distortion of a once-familiar nursery rhyme, perhaps taking a cue from the homonymous sweetmeat's metaphoric ability to be stretched to great lengths, and perhaps playing on the centuries-old stereotype of the Welsh as "loquacious dissemblers" speaking an unintelligible language in place of proper English, Themerson's narrator loquaciously dissembles and distends the original verse.[2]

Before offering these illustrative examples, however, he opens his lecture at the "Theater of Semantic Poetry" with figures that hint at the ultimate failure of the very procedure they seek to justify. Each word, he explains, "should have one and only one meaning. . . . They should be washed clean of all those diverse aureolas which depend on the condition of the market" (65). By way of examples, he offers *war* and *snow*, words he feels to be especially liable to inexact, subjective understanding. To avoid idiosyncratic interpretations shaded by personal experience, he proposes replacing *war* with "the open conflict between nations, or active international hostility carried on by force of arms," and *snow* with "multishaped crystals, belonging to hexagonal systems, formed by slow freezing of water water-vapour" (65).[3] Readers who recall Carl von Clausewitz' famous description of the cognitive weather common to the uncertain terrain of the field of battle can see the link between the three seemingly random terms. Clausewitz's forecast for "das Gebiet der Ungewißheit" (the territory of uncertainty)[4] calls for fog, where even the density of that mist is itself uncertain: "Nebel einer mehr oder weniger großen Ungewißheit" (fog of a greater or lesser extent).[5] From "diverse aureolas" to the fog of war, to "vapour," these atmospheric conditions of low visibility all render outlines indistinct and suggest a nebulous lack of focus. In other words, they figure the exact opposite of *definition*: precisely what Themerson's orator is after and precisely what is lost in his surfeit of semantic dilatation. Simultaneously invoking the two principal denotations of his key word—the exact statement of what a word means and the sharp rendering of a visual form or outline—Themerson emphasizes the polysemy that will ultimately doom his semantic enterprise.[6]

That same semantic play, however, offered hope to two writers who saw a use for the inherent slippages of metaphrastic translation. Themerson anticipatorily plagiarized what the Oulipo would come to call "littérature définitionnelle" (definitional literature), a practice first proposed by Raymond Queneau.[7] However, whereas Themerson's semantic poetry displaced each word by only one remove, the Oulipo imagined an infinite regress of displaced definitions, each of which provided further words for further definitional relief. Marcel Bénabou explains the rule as follows: "Dans un énoncé donné, on remplace chaque vocable signifiant (substantif, adjectif, verbe, adverbe) par une de ses définitions dans un dictionnaire donné; on réitère l'opération sur le nouvel énoncé obtenu, et ainsi de suite." (In a given statement, one replaces each significant word [noun, adjective, verb, adverb] by one of its definitions from a given dictionary; the operation is repeated on the new sentence thus obtained, and so on.)[8] René Étiemble was perhaps the first to recognize the poetic potential of such a procedure, opining that "remplacé par la définition qu'en donnerait un dictionnaire ingénu, chaque mot de prose vulgaire devient semence poétique" (replaced by the definition given by an ingenious dictionary, every word of vulgar prose becomes the seed of poetry).[9] Those seeds were cultivated most carefully by Georges Perec and Marcel Bénabou, who exploited and encouraged the tendency toward divergent drift in substituted definitions. As the *Oulipo Compendium* explains, "the goal of differentiation in Definitional Literature is consummated in a complementary method" known as "littérature semo-définitionnelle" (semo-definitional literature, or LSD), a variation that Perec and Bénabou also referred to as the "production automatique de littérature française" (automatic production of French literature, or PALF for short), underscoring a valence of automatization and mechanization that—as we will see—serves as a litmus test for whether readers understand the failure of their literary production as necessary or avoidable.

In Bénabou and Perec's apotheosis, two quite different sentences were to be translated into their dictionary-definition equivalents, and the process was to be repeated—transforming the sense with each successive substituting iteration. Moreover, the inevitable drifts, connotative allowances, and small margins of semantic play inherent in the dictionary's denotations were precisely what permitted Bénabou to "hypothesize, not without a certain audacity, that the results obtained will eventually, inevitably, coincide."[10]

Not without a certain audacity, he and Perec set out to equate "prolétaires de tous les pays, unissez-vous!" (workers of the world, unite!) and "le presbytère n'a rien perdu de son charme, ni le jardin de son éclat" (the presbytery has lost none of its charm, nor the garden its sparkle). It was to be their calling card to the Oulipo, gaining them membership in the young organization, even though they never succeeded in coaxing those sentences toward much evidence of a semantic convergence.[11]

Bénabou blamed the failure on his own negligent laziness, but, as David Bellos suggests, Perec may have been haunted by the thought that they had in fact proven the two sentences belonged to fundamentally different, incompatibly alien languages.[12] From the beginning, the direct imperative of the communist rallying cry and the refined observation—with its balanced correlative conjunctions, gentility, and recherché vocabulary—evince obvious stylistic differences; nonetheless, they might still have been drawn from the same discourse (one in which, for example, the speaker of the former would want to dismantle the privileged ecclesiastic architectures of the latter). Bénabou and Perec's failure to link them, however, could have further proven that the sentences come not just from different subject positions, but from radically incomprehensible ones. They may have demonstrated, in other words, that the sentences do not, in Ludwig Wittgenstein's terms, participate in the same *Sprachspiel* (language game). Or, as he summarized in a memorable shorthand, "Wenn ein Löwe sprechen könnte, wir könnten ihn nicht verstehen." (If a lion could talk, we would still not understand him).[13]

Whatever the case, the inability to stop the semantic proliferation once and for all in a single, master sentence had been predicted by Michel Foucault at precisely the same moment as Perec's experiments with semo-definitional literature. Foucault proclaimed:

> Pour la première fois peut-être dans la culture occidentale se découvre cette dimension absolument ouverte d'un langage qui ne peut plus s'arrêter, parce que, jamais enclos dans une parole définitive, il n'énoncera sa vérité que dans un discours futur, tout entier consacré à dire ce qu'il aura dit; mais ce discours lui-même ne détient pas le pouvoir de s'arrêter sur soi, et ce qu'il dit, il l'enferme comme une promesse, léguée encore à un autre discours . . .
>
> Perhaps for the first time in Western culture one finds completely laid bare the aspect of a language that cannot stop itself, because it is never enclosed in a definitive statement; it announces its truth only in some future discourse entirely devoted to what it *will have* said. But even this future discourse itself does not have the power to halt the progression, and what it says is enclosed within it like a promise, a bequest to yet another discourse . . .[14]

Or, in short, "le langage a en lui-même son principe intérieur de prolifération" (language contains its own inner principle of proliferation).[15] Decades earlier, Antonin Artaud had phrased a similar sentiment, in a statement related to Michel Leiris's experiments with tracing subversive and subterranean passages through dictionaries:

> Voici maintenant le seul usage auquel puisse servir désormais le langage, un moyen de folie, d'élimination de la pensée, de rupture, le dédale des

déraisons et non pas un DICTIONNAIRE où tels cuistres des environs de la Seine canalisent leurs rétrécissements personnels.

From now on language has only one use: as a means for madness, for elimination of thought, for rupture, as the unicursal labyrinth of insanity, not a *dictionary* where certain left-bank pedants channel their spiritual strictures.[16]

P.A.L.F. short-circuits Artaud's dichotomy by using the pedant's dictionary *as* a means for madness, leveraging a *rétrécissement personnel* (personal constraint) against the coherence of expressive thought. Arthur Rimbaud triangulates Foucault's meaning and Artaud's madness with his famous call for the "dérèglement de tous les sens," which translates equally to "the disruption of all meaning" and "the derangement of the senses."[17] Foucault would call this the "face à face de la poésie et de la folie" (the standoff of poetry and madness): on the one hand, a poetics in which the play of well-defined distinctions masks a language of resemblances; on the other hand, the insane erasure of those signs under the burden of similitude—"la folie d'écrire—le jeu insensé" (this insane game of writing), as Maurice Blanchot quotes Stéphane Mallarmé.[18] Adhering to the rules of their senseless game, Perec and Bénabou follow that spiraling labyrinth of Artaudian rupture, hopeful that they are not merely going in circles but moving ever closer, like Ubu's *gidouille*, to the convergence of "prolétaires de tous les pays, unissez-vous!" and "le presbytère n'a rien perdu de son charme, ni le jardin de son éclat."

Those two germinal sentences, however stylistically distinct and ultimately unresolvable, are both far from incidental. Something of the revolutionary political spirit of communism carries over to the optimistic experimentalism of the poetic project, which shares the same fundamental goal as the *Manifeste du Parti communiste*: to unite (one can almost hear Perec and Bénabou urging "Paroles de tous les mots, unissez-vous!"). Though less well-known, the source of the other seed sentence is also significant. David Bellos, inexplicably, attributes the line about the presbytery to Mallarmé, though it originates in George Sand's second "Letter to Marcie" and comes to Perec—who would quote it again in *Vie: Mode d'emploi*—by way of its reprise in Gaston Leroux's locked-room detective novel *Le Mystère de la chambre jaune* (*The Mystery of the Yellow Room*), one of the serial "extraordinary adventures of Joseph Rouletabille, Reporter," a genre fiction probably better known in France than his international hit *Le Fantôme de l'opéra*.[19] In Leroux's *roman policier*, the talismanic sentence functions as a kind of secret code. Both a mystery in itself and the clue to solving the book's primary mystery, it works for the eponymous reporter (and amateur detective) as a sort of *open sesame* password, allowing for the passage from one level of architectural and narrative enclosure to another, even as the characters who utter it cannot fathom what the sentence itself means.

With its paradoxical requirement that a chamber be hermetically sequestered and its threshold necessarily crossed, the locked-room mystery is a narrative version of a philosophical problem: a closed system that must try to account for itself. The various exercises in definitional literature pose a linguistic variant of this same problem; they can be seen as extrapolations of the realization that words in a dictionary only point to other words, which are also in the same dictionary, gesturing toward other words, and so on, ad infinitum. "On peut en effet considérer la chaîne des définitions comme le discours autonome que le langage tient sur lui-même" (One could, in effect, consider the concatenation of definitions as the autonomous conversation that language holds with itself), as Bénabou puts it, explaining elsewhere, "Le langage tourne en rond et fonctionne en circuit clos" (Language runs in a circle, operating in a closed circuit).[20] With those implications of growth and activity, made explicit in Bénabou's sense that when used for semantic poetry "le dictionnaire devient un être vivant" (the dictionary becomes a living being), his statements recall Foucault's claim that "le langage a en lui-même son principe intérieur de prolifération." This may be what Perec was acknowledging when he conceded, in the preamble to the LSD notebooks, "on ne commande au langage qu'en lui obéissant" (one can only control language by obeying it).[21] Moreover, these pronouncements sound like linguistic versions of what the physics professor in Leroux's novel intends to read before the Academy of Sciences. The professor, father of the victim, has written a sensational paper on his new theory: *The Dissociation of Matter*, a "théorie destinée à ébranler sur sa base toute la science officielle qui repose depuis si longtemps sur le principe: rien ne se perd, rien ne se crée" (theory destined to shake the foundations of all official science, which has so long been based on the famous principle that nothing is lost and nothing is created).[22] Antoine-Laurent de Lavoisier's maxim, quoted in part by the professor, concludes that "everything transforms."[23] Perec and Bénabou might well have had Lavoisier in mind as their sentences continually transformed, all the while adhering to a law of conservation for semantics.

Leroux's hero explains his procedure as if he were describing Perec standing before his battery of dictionaries: "Je ne fais que transcrire des faits sur lesquels une documentation exceptionnelle me permet d'apporter une lumière nouvelle." (I do nothing more than transcribe certain facts on which some exceptional documents in my possession enable me to throw a new light.)[24] Competing with a rival detective (the criminal himself, as it turns out), the hero and his nemesis represent two different theories of deductive methodology, and the difference between them hinges on the hermeneutic, and even the epistemological, viability of a closed system: whether anything may be legitimately "s'ajouter aux constatations matérielles faites" (added to the material facts so far established) and whether significance should be given exclusively to the "signes extérieurs" (external signs) of a crime.[25] Indeed, the reporter's *coup-de-théâtre* discourse on method and the virtues of being methodical rhyme nicely with Bénabou and Perec's own modus operandi of philological tracking through the dictionary toward a shared convergence. Rouletabille explains that the course of his investigation led him to follow a series of footprints, each obviously related but each also slightly different from the next, gradually diverging in their paths but ultimately leading back to the same, identical spot: the scene of the crime. Leroux then repeats the basic contours of this scene when he describes the two detectives (not unlike the two collaborating poets) following two sets of parallel boot prints until they lead back to the same location. One set of prints was evidently made by a rough, hobnailed worker's boot, while the other indicates a more elegant, neatly symmetrical pair of footwear: the perfect figures for the contrasting quotations from Marx and Sand, selected by Bénabou and Perec, respectively.

Le Mystère de la chambre jaune further reveals itself to be a relevant intertext on account of its paradoxical foregrounding of both an ineluctable logical telos as well as a series of distracting, diverting, nonsensical aporiae. On the one hand, the plot follows from a crime that must, by the end of the novel, have a solution discoverable by deductive reasoning, while on the other hand that plot's maladroit execution litters the story with illogical leaps and implausible coincidences. The novel veers from transparency to deceit, moving between the twin poles of its adherence to, and its simultaneous failure in, the genre of the detective story (one hesitates to be unkind, but Leroux was such a bad writer the surrealists took him as a hero of irrationality, an absurdist *avant la lettre*). Beyond delighting in the novel's general preposterousness, the surrealists would come to learn specific literary lessons from the gaps and decoys produced by Leroux's multiplication of "manufactured evidence and false trails."[26] Moreover, as Jonathan Eburne has described the poetics of Leroux's novel, "the imposition of logic is as mechanical, and indeed as solipsistic, as the 'sensational machines' of [Raymond] Roussel's photographic writing." Indeed, the machine was the figure singled out by Philippe Soupault as the hallmark of Leroux's interest to the avant-garde: an ironic relation to the rote formulae of the detective-story genre that permit "the transformation of positivist description into a kind of killing machine."[27] Not coincidentally, the two antipodes of telos and aporia—which ramify at the levels of both Leroux's plot (the deceptive, murderous trick of the criminal and ensnaring trap of the amateur detective) and his stylistic execution of that plot within its ostensible genre (the dogged necessity of a logical conclusion arrived at by deductive reasoning)—are precisely what define the discursive uses of the engine and the figure of the machine itself.

Most obviously, *machine* and *engine* connote analytic reasoning and analytic purpose. Beyond referring to any kind of complicated mechanism with moving parts, *engine* specifically denotes a calculating machine, as in Charles Babbage's early nineteenth-century proto-computer, which was referred to as a "difference engine" or "analytical engine." Today, accordingly, the word also means "a piece of hardware or software with a specific computational function; a program module which performs a particular kind of operation."[28] The earliest definitions for *engine*, however, suggest a chain that slips toward something quite different: from "ingenuity; artfulness; and disposition" to "cunning, trickery: a plot, a snare, a wile." These connotations reinforce the deceptive, false, illusionistic theatricality of "stage machinery" and the prevalent early modern uses of "machine" associated with the theater and the means of its deceptive tricks. In short, they suggest *machinations*, in the sense that also haunts the early, now obsolete senses of the word *machine*, an early synonym with *engine* in the sense of an "engine of war" or a "siege engine": a military device for circumventing the constraints of fortifications. This militarized, anti-architectural association of *engine* and *machine* goes as far back as postclassical Latin, and so all of these registers, one should note, obtain in French as well. Continuing from these senses of deceit and danger, *machine*, in the Elizabethan period and throughout the seventeenth century primarily denoted "a scheme or plot," the word was used as a transitive verb meaning "to contrive or plot the death or downfall of a person; to plot *against* a person." So Eburne's characterization of Soupault's interest in "a kind of killing machine" marks a philological redundancy by naming a kind of machining machine. In fact, the early idiomatic senses and stereotyped uses of *engine* are all iniquitously negative as well: *evil engine*, *false engine*, *malengine* (meaning an "evil machination, ill intent; fraud, deceit, guile" as the pedantic dictionary explains). So the word carries both the senses of craft and crafty, of devising and deviousness, schemes and scheming—*calculating*, in both senses of that word. The verb form corroborates: "to engine" means "to trick or deceive; to ensnare." In summary, before becoming computers and algorithmic programs, engines are instruments of war, instruments of torture, instruments of entrapment: nets, snares, decoys—gins, in a sense that derives aphetically from the Old French *engin*. These senses are all obviously relevant to both the story and the method of a crime novel like *Le Mystère de la chambre jaune*, with its backstory of a criminal plot, followed by the narrative account of the detectives' attempt to entrap the culprit in turn—both of which constitute the plot of the author who further plots against inquisitive readers who might discover it too soon.

These senses of *engine* and *machine* are also relevant to definitional literature, which "on peut opérer . . . de la façon la plus mécanique" (one can operate in the most mechanical way), and to PALF in particular, with its identification of a "production automatique," as well as to the frequent description of procedural poetics as "text engines" or "writing machines."[29] More broadly, when American artist Sol LeWitt explains conceptual art by stating that "the idea becomes a machine that makes the art," the future of conceptual art and writing opens out along two diametric paths depending on how the rhetorical figure of the machine and the ghosts of its history are understood.[30] LeWitt, not coincidentally, describes conceptual art in distinctly pataphysical terms with his pronouncement that "irrational thoughts should be followed absolutely and logically."[31] His signature white open cubes, in their various mathematical permutations and series, provide a prime example; whatever their scale, the relative dimensions of the cubes always strictly adhere, with an absurd precision, to a meaningless architectural ratio of 1:8.5 (that is, the open space between the edges of a cube is 8.5 times the width of each edge). LeWitt elaborates on this imaginary solution: "As with the white color, the 8.5:1 ratio was an arbitrary decision, but once it had been decided upon, it was always used."[32] The pataphysical underpinnings of LeWitt's practice have been largely ignored, but Rosalind Krauss picks up on the primacy of that assertion and comes all the way to the verge of identifying its pataphysical tenets without ever quite mentioning Alfred Jarry's name explicitly. With an echo of Jarry's definition of 'pataphysics as the "science of imaginary solutions," Krauss reads LeWitt's open cubes and line drawings, alongside Samuel Beckett's permutational syntax, as the answer to a false problem:

> It is the ironical presence of the false "problem" that gives to this outburst of skill its special emotional tenor, its sense of its own absolute detachment from a world of purpose and necessity, its sense of being suspended before the immense spectacle of the irrational.
>
> For LeWitt's generation a false and pious irrationality was seen uniformly as the enemy of art. . . . It was an extraordinary decade in which objects proliferated in a seemingly endless and obsessional chain, each one answering the other—a chain in which everything linked to everything else, but nothing was referential. To get inside the systems of this work, whether LeWitt's or Judd's or Morris's, is precisely to enter a world without a center, a world of substitutions and transpositions nowhere legitimated by the revelations of a transcendental subject.[33]

Krauss's recognition of the tension in postwar art between irrational procedures and deodorized surfaces is astute, but I quote at length to juxtapose her machinic description of that art with the writing of definitional literature, in which language (to recall Foucault's description) cannot stop itself. Like the artworks she outlines, the words of Bénabou and Perec's project are motivated in endless and obsessional chains, each answering the next with their series of denotative equivalences, until each new sentence has coupled a chain of inclusive linkages in which nothing is referential beyond the horizon of the dictionary's lemmata. The twin facets of this seemingly endless movement are the very poles that have defined the modern conception of the machine, with its double-edged promise and threat. On one side, that movement is relentless, focused and single-minded, but the obverse is dizzyingly eccentric ("a world without a center"); similarly, the procedure of definitional literature is relentlessly determined, but each stage of its results is subsequently shunted by further transpositions and substitutions: a perpetual motion machine that is also something of a Rube Goldberg contraption. Accordingly, incessant persistence and inevitable diversions, the two paths that fork from LeWitt's pataphysical art, are the same that follow from his assertion that "the idea becomes a machine that makes the art," because they figure the two models of the idea of the machine itself.

On the one hand, the machine would seem to offer the perfect figure for rule-following: mindless repetition; uniform regularity; analytical perfection; ceaseless effort; and efficient, single-minded telos. Or, as Ludwig Wittgenstein puts it more abstractly:

> Die Maschine (ihr Bau) als Symbol fur ihre Wirkungsweise: Die Maschine—könnte ich zuerst sagen—scheint ihre Wirkungsweise schon in sich zu haben. Was Heiß das?—Indem wir die Maschine kennen, scheint alles Übrige, nämlich die (Bewegungen), welche sie machen wird, schon ganz bestimmt zu sein.
>
> The machine as symbolizing its action: the action of a machine—I might say at first—seems to be there in it from the start. What does that mean?—If we know the machine, everything else, that is its movement, seems to be already completely determined.[34]

This symbolization would be true for *engine* as well, with its etymological ties to the Latin *ingenium* (an inherent quality or character), or what "scheint ihre Wirkungsweise schon in sich zu haben" (seems to be there in it from the start). On the other hand, however, as Wittgenstein goes on to note:

> Wir reden so, als könnten sich diese Teile nur so bewegen, als könnten sie nichts anderes tun. Wie ist es—vergessen—wir also die Möglichkeit, daß sie sich biegen, abbrechen, schmelzen, ete.? Ja; wir denken in vielen Fällen gar nicht daran.
>
> We talk as if these parts could only move in this one way, as if they could not do anything else. How is this—do we forget the possibility of their bending, breaking off, melting, and so on? Yes; in many cases we don't think of that at all.[35]

These two aspects of the machine—its ineluctable, relentless repetition and its propensity toward inevitable error and erratic failure—are nicely narrativized in one of the vignettes that make up John Cage's lecture, *Indeterminacy: New Aspects of Form in Instrumental and Electronic Music*, written just as Perec was beginning his investigations into the automatic production of French literature:

> One evening I was walking along Hollywood Boulevard, nothing much to do. I stopped and looked in the window of a stationary shop. A mechanized pen was suspended in space in such a way that, as a mechanized roll of paper passed by it, the pen went through the motions of the same penmanship exercises I had learned as a child in the third grade. Centrally placed in the window was an advertisement explaining the mechanical reasons for the perfection of the operation of the suspended mechanical pen. I was fascinated, for everything was going wrong. Then pen was tearing the paper to shreds and splattering ink all over the window and on the advertisement, which, nevertheless, remained legible.[36]

The opening catachresis signals the punning spirit of Cage's seemingly sincere, naïve recollection. By stopping, he becomes like the pen and paper in the window in front of him: both "suspended in space" and "stationary," with the stationery, ironically, in frantic motion. "Suspended before the immense spectacle of the irrational" and fascinated by the scene of a literalized *écriture automatique*, Cage then mechanically reiterates the words *mechanized* and *mechanical*, echoing four times in a single sentence and spoiling his prose with excessive repetition. But that repetition allows him to enact as well as to describe the writing process he observes (a process that is itself an excessive repetition of the drills that taught him to write in the first place). Behind its anecdotal tone, Cage's writing of the scene of writing is carefully performative.

His sketch also foregrounds one of the key tropes of the modern machinal imagination. Since the nineteenth century, wonder at the machine's feats of repetition have been bought at the cost of a fear that it might not stop, and Cage offers a tame and comical version of the Victorian paranoia that the same machines that seemed to work so tirelessly—propelled by hidden, hermetically contained internal processes of combustion—might never stop working at all, resulting in runaway trains, steam-engine explosions, and the specter of unstoppable automaton juggernauts.[37] Cage's scene of inscription describes a decidedly modern understanding of writing not merely on account of its underscored mechanization and opaque materiality, but because it exhibits a particularly modern conception of the machine. As Michel Serres has argued, the ideology of machines in the seventeenth and eighteenth centuries, when mechanical devices were understood primarily as tools for transferring and transforming external forces, ceded to a nineteenth-century imagination of the motor as an engine with internal powers of its own, circulating with a theoretical continuity by exploiting differences within thermodynamic systems and consuming pre-stocked stores of fuel.[38] The textual mechanism of Perec's definitional procedure, accordingly, operates as a specifically modern engine by locating its motivation internally. As Bénabou explains, PALF "supprime les critères extérieurs au langage et les remplace par des contraintes internes au langage" (suppresses the external criteria of language in favor of internal linguistic constraints).[39] He continues, clarifying that "la définition même de l'automatisme implique que l'on fait un effort par soi-même" (the very definition of automatism implies that something labors diligently under its own steam) to such a degree that "l'automatisme suppose une construction rigoreuse qui porte en soi le principe de son mouvement" (automatism requires a rigorous construction that carries in itself the principle of its own movement).[40] Animated by its own internal powers, motivated by the dynamic alternation between contiguity and continuity and the reservoir of the dictionary's accumulated semantic fuel, "le dictionnaire devient un être vivant, puisque s'opère ainsi le passage du contigu au continu" (the dictionary becomes a living being, since it operates by moving from adjacent to incessant).[41] Foucault, as we have seen, similarly locates an engine-like agency in language itself, with its own inner principle of proliferation: "Paroles trouvent sans cesse leur pouvoir d'étrangeté et la ressource de leur contestation" (Words ceaselessly renew their power of strangeness and the stores of their contestation).[42] That movement, for Serres, arises from both material and semiotic changes of state: "Ce qui produit le mouvement, c'est la différence dans l'état des choses, et c'est le calcul des signes" (Movement is effected by differences in the state of things and by the calculus of signs).[43] In Serres's analysis, all motors are the mechanical elaboration of some differential, and they operate through the dynamic tensions between difference and equivalence.[44] In definitional literature, the calculus of signs moves between identity and incompatibility, motivating the textual engine by means of the potential energy generated by the gap between reversible equivalence (the semantic conversion presumed by the exchange of a word for its denotation) and entropic difference (the drift and play of connotative imprecision; homonymic ruptures; the wandering stray from idiomatic syntax).

In the passage from *Indeterminacy*, Cage confesses that he delights in what is "going wrong," but going wrong—as Wittgenstein reminds us—is in fact part of the proper operation of machines. Recalling one of T. E. Hulme's fragments, in which he proclaims "the grit in the machine" to be "the fundamental element of the machine," Gilles Deleuze and Félix Guattari similarly theorize that not only does "le détraquement fait partie du fonctionnement même" (breaking down become part of the very functioning) of machines, but that malfunction is in fact the essential element of the machine: "c'est *pour* fonctionner qu'une machine . . . doit *ne pas fonctionner* bien" (*in order* to operate, a machine must *malfunction*).[45] And here is where we can begin to see the further convergence of the concept of the machine and the concept of 'pataphysics. For Jarry, the notion of the clinamen—a chance, atelic disruption—became a key tenet of his pataphysical doctrine. Jarry's *terme de métier* derives from a Lucretian understanding of the machinal pre-Socratic universe, in which:

> corpora cum deorsum rectum per inane feruntur
> ponderibus propriis, incerto tempora ferme
> incertisque locis spatio depellere paulum
>
> bodies are carried downward by their own weight in a straight line directly through the void, at unforeseeable moments and in unpredictable places they swerve a bit.[46]

In Serres's analysis, this atomism already contains the seeds of "la fin des différences motrices" (the twilight of mechanical machines) and a brave new modern world of entropy and turbulence.[47] That non-laminar turbulence, initiated by the clinamen's minimal disruption of the atoms' vertical fall and playing out in the unmappable eddies of fluid mechanics, transforms noise into a new order of signification, generating meaning from the interplay of coherence and chaos:

> Il y va du grand nombre et du clinamen, voilà tout. Le bruit de chute d'eau, dans le hasard dansant des myriades, et cette inclination, de haut en bas, qui fait le mouvement. Et qui produit le sens, parce qu'elle est le sens du mouvement, dans la foule des signes.
>
> There is the vast data set and the clinamen, that's all. The noise of the cascade, in the spray's chance dance of myriad droplets, and that inclinaison, from high to low, which produces movement. And which makes meaning—because it is the meaning of movement—in the crush of signs.[48]

Lucretius describes, in essence, an abstract model of the machine on two counts: a perpetually generating structure of difference (void and matter, laminar and non-laminar flow, uniformity and singularity, determinism and stochastics, linear monotony and Brownian white noise) in which the diametric differentials are themselves exactly what we have seen to be the defining characteristics of the figure of the machine: uniform repetitive perfection and the inevitable malfunctioning derangement of its parts "bending" and "breaking off." The machine of Lucretian nature contrasts the endless repetition of the uniform rain of prime atoms, perfectly alike in their linear plumb, with the disruption wrought by the occasional errant swerve—inevitable but unpredictable—of an outlier breaking off and bending from the orthogonal for no predictable or externally motivated cause. Bénabou understood that swerve to be "précisément cet aspect qui faisait tout l'intérêt, à nos yeux, de la méthode" (precisely the most interesting aspect, to my mind, of the definitional method), because the unpredictable errancy "introduisait, dans le jeu trop bien réglé des définitions, la possibilité d'une légère dérive. Ce qui n'est pas sans rappeler le principe du *clinamen*" (introduces, into the too-tightly regulated play of definition, the possibility of a slight drift, which is reminiscent of the principle of the *clinamen*).[49] It is the persistence of that clinamenatic drift, I would submit, which keeps the Oulipo—with its roots in the *Collège de 'Pataphysique*—from becoming a too-perfect parody of itself.

That becoming, at the same time, is both the mechanism and history of pataphysics: an unrolling that is simultaneously the essence and legacy of Faustroll's science. The "as if" at the heart of pataphysical logic inserts a potential energy at the level of grammar and it invites the speculation of what follows from its initial supposition, of the post hoc playing out of consequences from initial, imaginary, exceptional conditions. The invitation and permission to follow through—to carry on, as if—is what allowed, and perhaps destined, the Oulipo to follow from the *Collège de 'Pataphysique*. That succession occurred because the Oulipo imagined the absurdity of 'pataphysics with just enough seriousness. My own essay, accordingly, has been made possible by the same potential energies: taking seriously the literary absurdities of the Oulipo. I hope its own earnest seriousness will be furthered—with a properly absurd literary imagination—in turn.

Notes

1. Stefan Themerson, *Bayamus and the Theatre of Semantic Poetry* (London: Gaberbocchus Press, 1965), 67 (hereafter cited parenthetically in the text).

2. The bigoted phrase is from A. A. Gill, "Smile—You're on Cameo Camera," *Sunday Times*, September 28, 1997, quoted in Jeremy Paxman, *The English: A Portrait of a People* (Woodstock, NY: Overlook, 1998), 40. Christina Luckyj notes, "Renaissance dramatists often used Welsh as the prototype of an unintelligible language." John Webster, *The White Devil*, ed. Christina Luckyj, 3rd ed. (London: Methuen, 2008), 59n39.

3. With negligible alterations, the definitions for *war* occurs in H. C. Wyld, ed., *The Universal Dictionary of the English Language* (London: Routledge & Kegan Paul, 1932), 1375; the definition for *snow* occurs in Wilhelm Kôersner, *Praktik handbok för alla utarbetad af sakkunniga personer* (Stockholm: Fahlcrantz, 1886), 186.

4. Unless otherwise noted, all translations are mine.

5. Carl von Clausewitz, *Vom Kriege* (Berlin: Dümmler, 1905), 38.

6. *Oxford English Dictionary*, 2nd ed. (1989), s.v. "definition."

7. Sylvie Cassayre, *Les fleurs bleues de Raymond Queneau* (Paris: Editions du Temps, 1999), 10.

8. Marcel Bénabou and Paul Fournel, eds., *Anthologie de l'OuLiPo* (Paris: Gallimard, 2009), 417.

9. René Etiemble, review of *Exil*, by St. John Perse, *Valeurs: Revue de critique et de littérature* 2 (July 1945): 61, reprinted in *Hygiène des lettres*, vol. 4, *Poètes ou Faiseurs* (Paris: Gallimard, 1966), 147.

10. Marcel Bénabou, *Presbytère et prolétaires: Le dossier P.A.L.F.*, Cahiers Georges Perec 3 (Paris: Éditions de limon, 1989), 17.

11. Jacques Roubaud interviewed by Marcella Durand, *BOMB*, July 1, 2009, https://bombmagazine.org/articles/jacques-roubaud/. The Oulipo was founded on November 24, 1960.

12. David Bellos, *Georges Perec: A Life in Words* (Boston: Godine, 1993), 342.

13. Ludwig Wittgenstein, *Philosophische Untersuchungen / Philosophical Investigations*, rev. 4th ed., ed. P. M. S. Hacker and Joachim Schulte (London: Blackwell, 2009), §327.

14. Michel Foucault, *Les Mots et les choses: Une archéologie des sciences humaines* (Paris: Gallimard, 1966), 56 (ellipses in original).

15. Ibid., 55.

16. Antonin Artaud, *La Révolution surréaliste* 3 (April 1925): 7.

17. Arthur Rimbaud, letter to Paul Demeny (May 15, 1871), in *Œuvres complètes*, ed. Antoine Adam (Paris: Gallimard, 1972), 251.

18. Foucault, *Mots*, 63; Maurice Blanchot, *L'Entretien infini* (Paris: Gallimard, 1969), 622.

19. Bellos, *Georges Perec*, 342; George Sand [Amantine-Lucile-Aurore Dupin], *Œuvres complètes*, rev. ed. (Paris: Perrotin, 1843), 15:179; Georges Perec, *La Vie: Mode d'emploi* (Paris: Hachette, 1978), 382.

20. Bénabou, *Presbytère et prolétaires*, 9.

21. Ibid., 32, 16.

22. Gaston Leroux, *Le Mystère de la chambre jaune* (Paris: Lafitte, 1907), 4.

23. Attributed to Lavoisier, the maxim is a classically modeled ex post facto reduction of his more discursive description of state changes; see Antoine Lavoisier, *Traité élémentaire de chime* (Paris: Cuchet, 1789).

24. Leroux, *Mystère*, 3.

25. Ibid., 6, 93.

26. Jonathan Eburne, *Surrealism and the Art of Crime* (Ithaca, NY: Cornell University Press, 2008), 42.

27. Ibid.

28. Unless noted otherwise, all definitions are drawn from the *Oxford English Dictionary*, 2nd ed. (1989).

29. Oulipo, *La Littérature potentielle (Créations re-créations récréations)* (Paris: Gallimard, 1973), 119; see, for examples, Stephen Bury, "The Text Engine and the Artist's Book," in *At the Turn of the Centuries: The Influence of Early 20th Century Book Arts on Contemporary Artists' Books* (New Haven, CT: Jenny Press, 2010), 10–14; and "Machines in Texts, Texts as Machines," ed. Linda Kleiger Stillman, special issue, *L'esprit créateur* 26, no. 4 (Winter 1986).

30. Sol LeWitt, "Paragraphs on Conceptual Art," *Artforum* 5, no. 10 (June 1967): 79.

31. Sol LeWitt, "Sentences on Conceptual Art," *0 to 9*, no. 5 (January 1969): 3.

32. Irving Sandler, *American Art in the 1960s* (New York: Harper & Row, 1988), 347.

33. Alfred Jarry, *Gestes et opinions du docteur Faustroll, pataphysicien* (Paris: Charpentier, 1911), 31; Rosalind Krauss, "LeWitt in Progress," *October* 6 (Autumn 1978): 60.

34. Wittgenstein, *Philosophische Untersuchungen*, §193.

35. Ibid.

36. John Cage, *A Year from Monday: New Lectures and Writings by John Cage* (Middletown, CT: Wesleyan University Press, 1969), 134.

37. See Julie Wosk, "The Traumas of Transport in Nineteenth-Century Art," in *Breaking Frame: Technology and the Visual Arts in the Nineteenth Century* (New Brunswick, NJ: Rutgers University Press, 1992), 30–66.

38. Michel Serres, *Feu et signaux de brume: Zola* (Paris: Grasset, 1975), 209–10; but see also, more generally, chapter 2, "Moteur et Circulation," 60–128.

39. Bénabou, *Presbytère et prolétaires*, 25.

40. Ibid. 25.

41. Ibid., 32.

42. Foucault, *Mots*, 64.

43. Michel Serres, "Moteurs: Préliminaires aux systèmes généraux," in *Hermes IV: La Distribution* (Paris: Les Éditions de Minuit, 1977), 52.

44. Ibid., 44; cf. especially "Le moteur produisait du mouvement de la rupture d'équilibre à son rétablissement, de la différence à l'égalité" (47).

45. T. E. Hulme, *Selected Writings*, ed. Patrick McGuinness (New York: Routledge, 2003), 24; Gilles Deleuze and Félix Guattari, *Capitalisme et schizophrénie 1: L'Anti-Œdipe*, rev. ed. (Paris: Les Éditions de Minuit, 1973), 39, 177 (emphases in original).

46. Lucretius, *De rerum natura*, trans. W. H. D. Rouse, Loeb Classic Library (Cambridge, MA: Harvard, University Press, 1975), 112.

47. Serres, "Moteurs," 55.

48. Ibid. Cf. Michel Serres, "The Genesis of Sense," in *The Birth of Physics*, trans. Jack Hawkes, ed. David Webb (Manchester, UK: Clinamen Press, 2000), 144–47.

49. Bénabou, *Presbytère et prolétaires*, 11–12.

PART 2

"Like a Musical Score, All Art and All Science"

PATAPHYSICS AFTER JARRY AND BEYOND THE *COLLÈGE*

Chapter 6

Pataphysics in Philadelphia

The Strange Case of James E. Brewton

Michael R. Taylor

Art is the way I live.
—James E. Brewton, *The American Dream-Girl*, 1965

This essay traces the trajectory of the Philadelphia-based artist James E. Brewton's career, from his discharge from military service as a marine sergeant in May 1954 to his death by suicide in May 1967. A fascinating yet under-recognized artist today, James Edward Brewton was born in Toledo, Ohio, on November 4, 1930, and attended his first art classes at the Toledo Art Museum, before enlisting in the United States Marine Corps in 1951 and serving for two years in the Korean War, an experience that made him an outspoken pacifist for the rest of his life. However, the bulk of his artistic training took place after he returned from the Korean War on the USS *General W. H. Gordon*, which arrived in San Francisco on April 20, 1953 (fig. 6.1). In 1954, with funding provided by the GI Bill following his military discharge, Brewton enrolled at Oxford University's Ruskin School of Drawing and Fine Art in England, where his fellow students included the American writer and critic John Updike, then an aspiring cartoonist.[1] In the summer of 1955 Brewton transferred to the Pennsylvania Academy of the Fine Arts in Philadelphia, where he studied with such noted artists and instructors as Hobson Pittman and Franklin

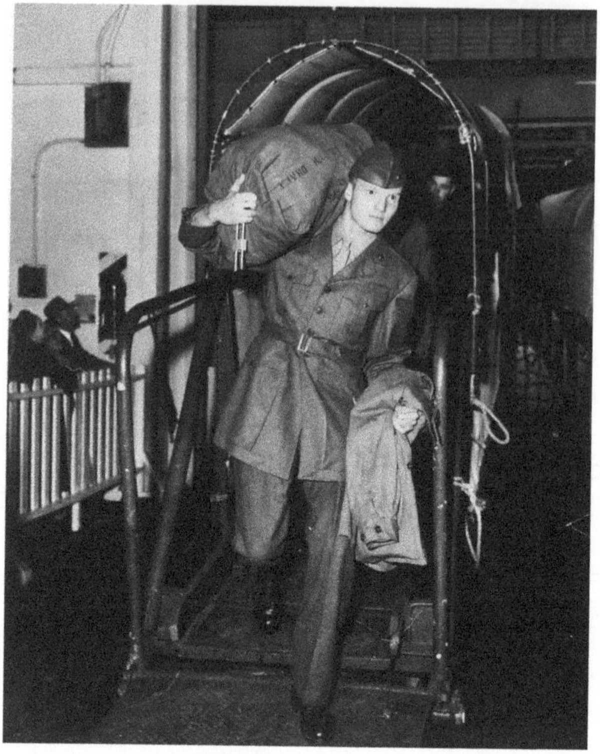

6.1. Sergeant James E. Brewton disembarks the USS *General W. H. Gordon* in San Francisco from Korea. Official Marine Corps photograph taken by Corporal D. A. Soriano on April 20, 1953. Gelatin silver print, 9 ¾ × 7 ¾ in. Private collection. Image courtesy of the James E. Brewton Foundation.

Watkins, before completing his studies in 1958. In the following year Brewton's precocious talent was recognized when his painting *The Suicide of Judas* was awarded the $1,000 J. Henry Scheidt Memorial Prize at the Pennsylvania Academy's 155th Annual Exhibition of American Painting and Sculpture. As Victoria Donohoe, the art critic for the *Philadelphia Evening Bulletin*, duly noted, "The tall, ex-Marine sergeant thus captured—at the age of 28—the same award that William Glackens, Stuart Davis, Hans Hofmann, Ivan Albright, and Charles Burchfield had earned in their maturity."[2]

Brewton's artistic training coincided with the heyday of Abstract Expressionism, when art students were encouraged to create large-scale abstract compositions that built on, but did not add to or extend, the powerful legacy of American painters of the previous generation, such as Franz Kline, Willem de Kooning, and Jackson Pollock, who by the late 1950s had attained a near-heroic status in the American art world. Rather than doom himself to an unfulfilling career as a second-generation Abstract Expressionist painter, Brewton found inspiration in the iconoclastic writings of Alfred Jarry, as mediated through the powerful figure of the polemical Danish artist, writer, and theorist Asger Jorn, who was a key figure in the revival of interest in Jarry and pataphysics after the Second World War.

On June 29, 1962, Brewton sailed to Copenhagen and then traveled by train to visit Jorn's hometown of Silkeborg in the Jutlandic peninsula of Denmark. Accompanied by his partner, the novelist Barbara Holland, then pregnant with his daughter Emily who was born in Denmark on September 10, 1962, Brewton arrived unannounced at the trout farm of the CoBrA painter and ceramicist Erik Nyholm and his wife, Janet, who grew up in Rochester, New York, and attended Swarthmore College. Brewton had enthusiastically discovered the work of the CoBrA group while working at the Print Club (now Print Center) in Philadelphia in the late 1950s to support his studies at the Pennsylvania Academy of the Fine Arts. Knowing of his interest in CoBrA, Brewton's mutual friend, Claire Van Vliet, a fellow artist, printmaker, and founder of the Janus Press, introduced him to Erik and Janet Nyholm when they spent some weeks in Philadelphia around the time Erik had a solo exhibition at the Makler Gallery in January 1962. When the Nyholms returned to Denmark they extended an open invitation to Brewton and Holland to visit their home, which also functioned as an artists' commune. Despite the lack of advance warning about their visit, the young couple was given a warm welcome by the Nyholms and the artistic community of Silkeborg; they rented their own farmhouse, which doubled as a studio, for twelve dollars per month for the next five months, before returning to the United States on November 20, 1962. It was through Erik Nyholm that Brewton met Jorn, and the American artist's paintings from this time, such as *Self-Portrait* (color plate 3), reveal the lessons he learned from the Danish artist.

Prior to Brewton's arrival, Jorn has vociferously rejected what he considered to be the self-absorbed, inward-looking aesthetic of Pollock, de Kooning, and other Abstract Expressionists, as well as the overblown rhetoric of triumphant nationalism that accompanied it, arguing that "the conception of art implicit in 'action painting' reduces art to an act in itself, in which the object, the work of art, is a mere trace, and in which there is no longer any communication with the audience. This is the attitude of the pure creator who does nothing but fulfill himself through the materials for his own pleasure."[3] Seeking to produce artworks that engaged with critical ideas and lived experience, rather than merely express inner feelings, Jorn adopted the artistic strategies of appropriation, irony, and parody.[4]

The impact of Jorn's ideas can be seen in the powerful sensory address of Brewton's subsequent paintings, including the use of bold, broad brushstrokes, vibrant color, and heavy pigmentation, in which the paint was often pressed straight out of the tube and smeared across the canvas in a similar manner to the Danish artist's remarkable paintings of the late 1950s, such as *Letter to My Son* (1956–57). Brewton would later refer to this painting in *Letter to My Daughter*, a 1964 mixed-media composition in which he expressed his love for his two-year-old daughter, Emily. Like Jorn, Brewton was profoundly responsive to the physical properties of oil paint, and the frenetic energy and raw emotional power of his *Self-Portrait* stems from its rejection of the academic traditions that had been so thoroughly ingrained in him at the Ruskin School and Pennsylvania Academy, in line with the artistic de-skilling and refusal of finish and good taste (what Jorn called "artification") that the Danish artist had promoted in the previous two decades through his involvement as an important catalyst within numerous international avant-garde groups. These included CoBrA, a European collective that Jorn cofounded in 1948, whose name originated from the initial letters of the cities that the various artists came from: Copenhagen, Brussels, and Amsterdam; and the Situationist International, a revolutionary cultural organization formed in 1957 by artists, writers, and activists, including Jorn's friend and comrade Guy Debord, that sought to reconstruct modern society through the complete transformation of everyday life.

Unlike the vast majority of American artists of his generation, Brewton had firsthand knowledge of these seminal European art movements through Jorn and Nyholm, and shared their interest in the subversive writings of Alfred Jarry, as well as their commitment to collectivism, their insistence on the political implications of their art-making process, their versatility in different media and use of unorthodox materials, and their rejection of a single, unified approach or style. As Brewton argued in the catalog that accompanied an exhibition of his work at the Galerie AP in Copenhagen in May 1965, "I think style in art is injurious to anyone who likes freedom of movement. The people in Denmark who know my work will find it changed. I would rather innovate than live in the comfort of a manner."[5] This statement echoes similar pronouncements by Jorn and his colleagues in the Situationist International, and underscores the liberating effect of Brewton's exposure to their radical ideas in the early 1960s, including the notion that artists should create *situations* that consisted of constructed encounters and creatively lived moments to agitate and polemicize against the uneven abundance of mass consumption and repressive sterility of the urban environment imposed by the ruling economic and political systems, which in the opinion of Debord, Jorn, and other members of the Situationist International had reduced life to a spectacle.[6]

Brewton's profound admiration for Jorn and his artistic philosophy that art was for everyone and not just the privileged few led him in 1964 to paint his *Portrait of Asger Jorn*, in which the Danish artist is shown with paintbrush and palette in hand and surrounded by sinuous, arabesque designs reminiscent of the art of the Viking era that Jorn greatly admired (color plate 4). The portrait also contains the French phrase "pour tous les hommes" that Brewton would soon adopt, in an English translation, as a slogan in his own artwork after creating a stamp bearing the legend "For All Mankind."

Like many artists who have responded to Jarry's transgressive writings and pataphysical ideas, including Enrico Baj, Victor Brauner, Thomas Chimes, Max Ernst, William Kentridge, Dora Maar, and Joan Miró, Brewton initially found inspiration in the monstrous character of King Ubu, who inspired a number of paintings that he made in the early 1960s.[7] *Ubu Becomes King*, of 1962 (color plate 5), which was painted on a piece of tapestry-like fabric with a preexisting spiral design, reveals the artist's knowledge of Jarry's own graphic representations of King Ubu, including an 1896 woodcut that the French writer entitled *Veritable portrait de Monsieur Ubu*. Jarry's woodcut, which was first reproduced in Paul Fort's monthly review *Le Livre d'art* on April 25, 1896, to accompany the first published edition of *Ubu Roi* in its entirety, created an easily identifiable, almost cartoonlike image of Ubu, who is shown with a strange pointed head and bulbous belly, for which Jarry invented the term *gidouille*. This enormous gut bears the emblem of a nebula-like spiral, which functions as a target or bull's-eye and identifies the insatiable *gidouille* as the source of Ubu's unbridled greed, malice, and stupidity. This woodcut image inspired numerous later manifestations of Ubu, such as Max Ernst's *Ubu Imperator* (1923), in which the pompous ruler takes the form of a blast furnace built of bricks that appears to gyrate like a hollow spinning top, perhaps in mocking reference to the Fascist dictator Benito Mussolini, who had recently usurped power in Italy in Ubu-like fashion.

In *Ubu's Military Mind* (color plate 6), a mixed-media composition on aluminum that Brewton also completed in 1962, the artist drew on his own experience in the United States Marine Corps, which had exposed him to the mind-numbing absurdity of the military's rules and regulations that Jarry had satirized to great effect in the *Ubu* plays and the haunting novel *Days and Nights: A Novel of a Deserter*, published in 1897. When giving voice to the dictatorial character King Ubu, Jarry insisted that his tone always remain clipped and inhumanly pompous, much like the "official" language of the military that Brewton knew so well. In *Ubu's Military Mind*, Ubu defecates a US Army Sharpshooter medal, while Brewton's own Korean War Service Medal with three service stars was placed inside Ubu's distended belly. The inclusion of military medals, numbers, and other insignia in this portrait underscores Brewton's profound antiwar sentiments at this time, as well as his understanding of Jarry's own notions of King Ubu and his voracious *gidouille* as the direct embodiment of the deeply ingrained, unconscious, abject, and libidinal forces that we all carry within us—hence the grotesque, pear-shaped body that gives Ubu the appearance of a giant turd. By equating military service medals with shit, Brewton was clearly aware that the scandalous nature of the *Ubu* plays lay precisely in their appropriation of the base, scatological qualities of folk puppetry, as seen in Ubu's toilet-brush scepter and enormous protruding belly.

Brewton was also interested in Jorn's Scandinavian Institute for Comparative Vandalism, which the Danish artist established in 1961 along with Peter Glob and Werner Jacobsen of the National Museum of Denmark and Holger Arbman of the University of Lund in Sweden. Jorn's stated purpose for the organization was to research and document ten thousand years of Nordic folk art and archeology as an alternative to academic art history, which he believed had unfairly overlooked Scandinavian culture in favor of a slavish devotion to the Western canon. In 1964, back in Philadelphia, Brewton founded the J. E. Brewton Institute of Comparative Vandalism in an effort to bring Jorn's ideas to the United States and apply them through posters, stamps, and publications bearing the organization's grandiloquent title. Brewton's conception of Comparative Vandalism was informed by the graffiti and street culture of Philadelphia,[8] as well as Marcel Duchamp's notorious readymade *L.H.O.O.Q.*, in which the French-born artist altered and transformed a cheap chromolithograph of Leonardo de Vinci's *Mona Lisa* through the addition in pencil of an upturned mustache and rakish goatee. Duchamp completed the work with the deliciously scurrilous inscription "L.H.O.O.Q." in the bottom margin that, when read aloud in French, has the double meaning of "elle a chaud au cul," which can be translated as "she has a hot ass" or, as Duchamp preferred, "there is fire down below."[9] This iconoclastic gesture, carried out in Paris in 1919, a year that commemorated the four-hundredth anniversary of da Vinci's death, reveals Duchamp's irreverent attitude to the canonical traditions of art upheld by such hallowed institutions as the Louvre, where the *Mona Lisa* has hung almost continuously since the museum opened in 1793. Brewton clearly admired *L.H.O.O.Q.* as a forerunner to his own interest in graffiti and comparative vandalism, which may explain why he chose to add the capital letters in yellow paint to one of his posters advertising the J. E. Brewton Institute of Comparative Vandalism.

Brewton's interest in Duchamp's transgressive artworks was no doubt informed by the fact that the Philadelphia Museum of Art houses the largest collection of the artist's work in the world, thanks to the generous bequest in 1954 of the collection of Duchamp's great friends and patrons, Walter and Louise Arensberg. Brewton frequently made reference to Duchamp's radical ideas in his own work, such as the hilarious drawing and related wood construction that he titled *Irony Bored* after the French Dadaist's provocative suggestion in one of his *Green Box* notes that a Rembrandt painting should be used as an ironing board. Brewton also made his own version of Duchamp's *Three Standard Stoppages*—three measuring devices made with chance procedures to challenge the legal and scientific authority of the standard meter in the Pavillon de Breteuil in Sèvres and thus destabilize the very premise of a single unit of measurement—which he deliberately mistitled *Three Stander Stoppages for Wall and Floor*.

In 1962 Jorn refused to represent Denmark at the 1982 Venice Biennale, preferring to work instead on his Scandinavian Institute of Comparative Vandalism project, as well as a series of paintings titled *Modifications*, which were painted over preexisting oil paintings that he found in antique shops and flea markets. These amateur works were chosen for their highly sentimental or kitsch value and then transformed by Jorn's vibrant and, at times, aggressive overpainting, which usually included painterly scrawls suggestive of demonic figures and primeval monsters. Remarkably, Jorn's additions reinvigorated the original works, whose style and content often appeared homogenous and altogether natural when seen alongside or underneath Jorn's painterly daubs, despite the radical differences in technique and brushwork. In the 1962 painting *Faustroll*, for example, an image of a smiling, bearded man appears at the center of the recycled painting, surrounded by monstrous, grinning creatures no doubt intended to invoke the tortured imagination of Dr. Faustroll, Alfred Jarry's pataphysical alter ego.

Ralph Rumney, an English artist and friend and colleague of Jorn in the Situationist International in the late 1950s, has connected works like *Faustroll* with the Situationist notion of *détournement* (or rerouting), which is "a method of changing or modifying either the context or the nature of a presently-existing cultural object so that it acquires a new and higher significance."[10] This statement provides a deeper context in which to understand what at first glance might seem a gratuitous act of vandalism by Jorn against a harmless, Frans Hals–like portrait of a happy-go-lucky gentleman. As a Situationist *détournement*, the preexisting painting can indeed by seen to have acquired "new and higher significance" through the Danish artist's graffiti-like additions, which add an atmosphere of mystery and solemnity to the portrait, as well as the title, which identifies the bearded rogue with the eponymous hero of Alfred Jarry's posthumously published masterpiece. In the catalog essay to his May 1959 exhibition at the Galerie Rive Gauche in Paris, which was written in defense of the perceived vandalism of these found canvases, Jorn declared with a pataphysical logic worthy of Jarry himself: "Be modern, collectors, museums. If you have old paintings do not despair. Retain your memories but détourn them so that they correspond with your era. . . . Painting is over. You might as well finish it off. Détourn. Long live painting."[11]

Brewton employed similar tactics in his own détourned artworks, as seen in a 1964 work called *Sunrise* (color plate 7) in which a recycled image from a magazine of a bikini-clad woman having her breast touched is détourned to become a statement on the sexual revolution of the 1960s. Her half-joyful, half-surprised expression adds a layer of ambiguity to the work, since we have no way of knowing if she slaps the man's face in return for his impromptu action. As with the best of Jorn's détourned paintings, Brewton utilized what he was already given in this work, but added so much of his own personality and humor—including his blue "Graffiti Pataphysic" stamp that bears an Ubuesque spiral between Brewton's initials—that the result was a highly original work of art. The work utilizes a variety of printing techniques, including offset lithography, screenprinting, and handmade stamps, which led Brewton to invent the term "combine print" to describe its making. Made in 1964, two years after Brewton returned from his first stay in

Denmark, the outrageously funny, sexy, irresponsible, and liberating *Sunrise* speaks to his ambitions to bring the revolutionary ideas he encountered in Silkeborg back to Philadelphia.

Around 1964, Brewton's interest in Jarry's writings shifted from the scatological *Ubu* plays to the realm of pure and boundless imagination presented in the French writer's dauntingly dense masterpiece of antirationalism, *Exploits and Opinions of Dr. Faustroll, Pataphysician.* "Graffiti Pataphysic," which Brewton used as the title of his solo exhibition at Harry Kulkowitz's Kenmore Galleries in Philadelphia, which was on view from February 3 through 17, 1965, drew on Jarry's notion of 'pataphysics as presented in his posthumously published novel, as well as the May–June 1960 issue of the *Evergreen Review*, which was devoted to Jarry and titled "What Is 'Pataphysics?" This seminal issue of the American literary magazine has come to be regarded as one of the most important English-language publications ever devoted to the pint-sized writer's life and work. Although the bulk of the magazine's contents consisted of excerpts from Jarry's writings, the publication also included a carefully argued and informative introduction to pataphysics by the literary scholar Roger Shattuck, titled "Superliminal Note," which included the famous line "Only the comic is serious," which Brewton frequently deployed in his own artist statements, exhibition catalogs, and press releases.[12]

As Asger Jorn enthusiastically commented in the August 1961 issue of the *Internationale Situationniste*, "The honour of presenting Pataphysics to the world belongs to the Americans, by means of a special issue of the *Evergreen Review* which allowed the great pataphysical satraps to speak for themselves."[13] Jorn's essay, titled "La Pataphysique, une religion en formation" (published as a book in English under the title *Pataphysics: A Religion in the Making*), went on to predict that by the twenty-second century Pataphysics would replace Judaism, Christianity, and Islam as the most widespread belief system in the world. Jorn's controversial attempt to understand the religious significance of pataphysics was vehemently criticized by his former colleagues in the Situationist International. Missing Jorn's humor and polemical intent, the Situationists issued a strongly worded statement declaring all religions to be "as risible as each other" and guaranteeing "an equivalent hostility to all religions, even that of science fiction."[14] Brewton clearly sided with Jorn in this dispute, and his subsequent work similarly examines Jarry's pataphysical ideas as the basis of a new religion, albeit a religion of passivity and of pure absence, with its ideas currently understood by a small handful of believers.

Jorn's contentious essay on the religious significance of pataphysics, as well as the "What Is 'Pataphysics?" issue of *Evergreen Review*, helped Brewton to absorb the French writer's invented science of exceptions. Jarry's Rabelaisian, metatextual *Exploits and Opinions of Dr. Faustroll, Pataphysician* was first published in 1911, although a few fragments of the book had appeared in the *Mercure de France* in 1895. In this "neoscientific novel,"[15] Jarry presents a highly imaginative alternative universe where even the most absurd and contradictory propositions can make sense. In direct contrast to the adolescent nihilism, parody, and satire of the *Ubu* plays, *Faustroll* offers a positive vision of the future in which pataphysics will harness the energy of the universe to extend the laws of science and physics and push the possible to the limits of the imaginable, thus anticipating to some extent quantum physics and other scientific developments of the twentieth century.

Other works in the "Graffiti Pataphysic" exhibition, including the exhibition poster (color plate 8), were informed by the liberating example of Jorn's Scandinavian Institute for Comparative Vandalism, which as we have seen was directly inspired by the Danish artist's understanding of Jarry's 'Pataphysics, as well as the remarkable graffiti that Brewton saw in Philadelphia, which held a strong fascination for him in its direct, raw, untutored expression, as well as its outsider status as an unsanctioned, illegal art form. In his artist's statement for his exhibition at the Kenmore Galleries, which took the form of a typed, one-page handout, Brewton also claimed that his interest in graffiti stemmed from its anonymous nature, which made it available for all humankind, as opposed to modern art, which was only available to a privileged few. However, Brewton's defense of graffiti quickly turned into an evocation of Alfred Jarry's pataphysics, hence the title "Graffiti Pataphysic": "Graffiti are found on walls and pavements the world over, scribbled inscriptions or drawings. Pataphysics is the science of the realm beyond metaphysics; or, pataphysics lies as far beyond physics as physics lies beyond addition, in one direction or another. It is the science of imaginary solutions, the science of the particular, of laws governing exceptions. The pataphysician is concerned, not through engagement in an attempt to create human values, but in the manner of a child looking through a kaleidoscope."[16]

Perhaps the most startling work in Brewton's 1965 exhibition was *The Pataphysics Times* (fig. 6.2), which was permanently displayed in the window of the Kenmore Galleries at 122 South Eighteenth Street in Philadelphia, so that it could by easily read by passersby. Using the lost-cost cyanotype printing process that was more commonly used by engineers and architects for blueprints and building plans, Brewton printed *The Pataphysics Times* in an edition of one hundred copies that he then distributed throughout Philadelphia in an act of generosity that underscores his belief in the social nature of the artwork. The single-sheet newspaper was based on a labyrinthine collage of interspliced photographic reproductions, newspaper headlines, advertising slogans, and snippets of found texts clipped from a variety of sources. This transgressive broadsheet can be understood as Brewton's own blueprint for an artistic revolution in Philadelphia based on Jarry's science of imaginary solutions as presented in the posthumously published *Exploits and Opinions of Doctor Faustroll, Pataphysician*.

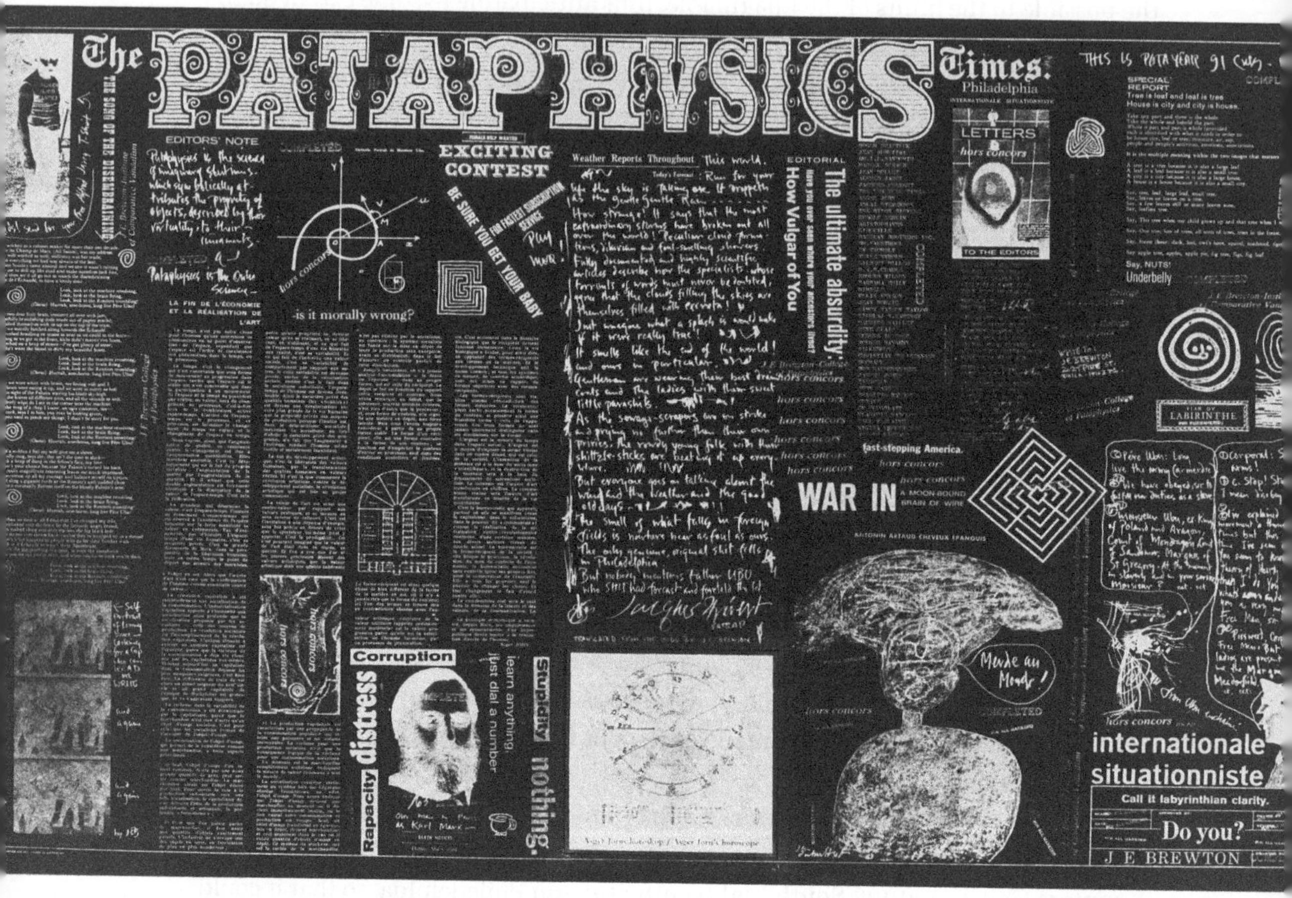

6.2. James E. Brewton, *The Pataphysics Times*, 1964. Cyanotpye, 23 × 35 ½ inches. Virginia Museum of Fine Arts. A. Paul Funkhouser Endowment, 2021.75. Image courtesy of the James E. Brewton Foundation.

Inspired by earlier avant-garde broadsheets, posters, and artists' books from Europe, especially Guy Debord and Asger Jorn's *Fin de Copenhague* (End of Copenhagen or Goodbye to Copenhagen) of 1957, Brewton's cyanotype newspaper represents a humorous synthesis of the rational and the absurd, as seen in the images of Alfred Jarry sporting a T-shirt bearing the slogan "Screw good taste!"; Lenny Bruce trying to find a cop who could read or write; a photograph in the "letters" section of a urinal inspired by Marcel Duchamp's *Fountain*, replete with a spiral design and the stamped words "Hors concors," in reference to the fact that Duchamp's readymade toilet fixture was rejected from the 1917 Society of Independent Artists exhibition; a poem on the tree-leaf relation ("Tree is leaf and leaf is tree") by the Dutch architect Aldo van Eyck;[17] and Jean Dubuffet's portrait of Antonin Artaud shouting "Merde au monde" (Shit to the world). Like a veritable roadmap to pataphysics, the blueprint newspaper contorts external reality through a complete embrace of contradiction and paradox, as seen in Jacques Prévert's weather forecast, which predicted foul-smelling showers and clouds filled with excrement, which would slowly turn into heavy torrents of shit later in the afternoon, especially over the city of Philadelphia. In a delightful pun on ordure, Brewton claimed to have translated Prévert's weather report from "Urdu" and clearly enjoyed the scatological aspect of Jarry's writings and those Satraps who followed in his footsteps.

Following the success of the Kenmore Galleries exhibition—whose visitors included Andy Warhol, who saw *The Pataphysics Times* in the window and stopped in to invite Brewton to the opening of his upcoming exhibition at the Institute of Contemporary Art, Philadelphia, which opened to the public on October 8, 1965—Brewton decided on a whim to return to Denmark and arrived in Copenhagen on February 27, 1965, just in time to surprise Asger Jorn by attending the opening of his retrospective exhibition at the Louisiana Museum of Modern Art in Humlebaek the following evening. The artist also connected with Erik Nyholm again during this visit (fig. 6.3), which lasted until April 9, 1965, and resulted in Brewton's first exhibition in Europe. After showing slides of his work to Arne Plockross, an art dealer from Copenhagen, Brewton was offered a solo exhibition whenever he had made enough new paintings for a show. Brewton replied that if the gallery owner could find him a studio he could make the work in Denmark and thus save on shipping costs from the United States.

With the help of Aage Damgaard, a wealthy industrialist and collector of contemporary art, Brewton was given a studio in Damgard's Angli shirt factory located in Herning in the Jutland peninsula, which Damgaard later converted into the Herning Kunstmuseum (now the Herning Museum of Contemporary Art). Within a matter of weeks Brewton had created enough artworks for his exhibition in Copenhagen and gave Damgaard a work of art as a token of his appreciation. These new works continued the artist's involvement with collage and mixed-media assemblage—made with

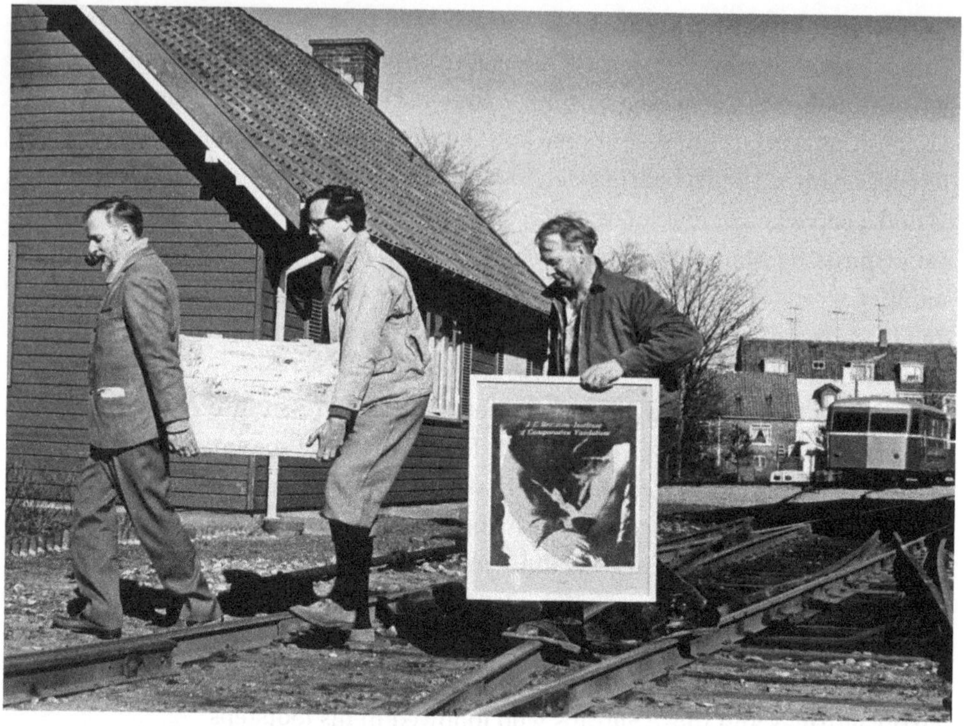

6.3. Ulrik Ross (Danish, born 1939), *Asger Jorn, Jim Brewton, and Erik Nyhold*, spring 1965. Gelatin silver print, dimensions unknown. Museum Jorn, Silkeborg, Denmark. © Donation Jorn, Silkeborg. Used with permission.

assistance from some of the seamstresses at the shirt factory, who helped Brewton by sewing buttons, pleats, seams, shirt fabric, and other items onto his canvases—while others incorporated soft-core pornographic images of lingerie-clad women, often blown up to the point where they were no longer decipherable as pin-ups from adult magazines, but read instead as abstract compositions embellished with words like "Alfred Jarry," "Do not bend," "For All Mankind," "Fragile," "J. E. Brewton College of Pataphysics," "Registered," and "Rush" that the artist added in ink using wood-handled rubber stamps that he had custom-made from stationers and office-supply stores in Philadelphia and brought with him to Denmark.[18]

Brewton's exhibition, titled *The American Dream-Girl: Graffiti Pataphysic*, was on view at the Galerie AP at Ny Adelgade 4 in Copenhagen from May 12 through 26, 1965. Sadly, the artist had returned to the United States one month earlier so therefore had to miss the opening of the only solo exhibition of his work to be held in Europe during his lifetime. Despite his absence, the Galerie AP show nonetheless proved to be a critical and commercial success, with the sales of his work more than paying for the cost of his spur-of-the-moment trip to Denmark. The exhibition's title once again underscores Brewton's obsession at that time with Jarry's concept of pataphysics, as well as his interest in the "American Dream-Girl" of adult magazines and popular culture.[19] In the illustrated catalog that accompanied the exhibition, Brewton declares, that "Pataphysics is the science of imaginary solutions; to the pataphysician only the comic is serious. We can understand the logic of Alfred Jarry's tripod. It had four legs. After all, a tripod with three legs has something missing. Pataphysics is as far beyond metaphysics as metaphysics is beyond physics. It is the science."[20] This statement reveals that Brewton had not only read and absorbed *Exploits and Opinions of Doctor Faustroll, Pataphysician*, but had found a way to apply what he described as its "ineluctable logic" to his own artistic practice.[21] The reference to Jarry's tripod, a wooden cabin-like residence by the Seine at Le Coudray that, according to his friend and patron Rachilde, rested on four masonry pillars and had a wine cellar, for example, is exactly the kind of comically serious pataphysical notion that would fuel Brewton's imagination and creativity for the rest of his all-too-short life.[22] Jarry's idea of further extending frontiers clearly appealed to Brewton, who was fascinated by the author's search for a new reality through humor and a heightened vision informed by science, classical learning, poetry, and, above all, an unfettered imagination that allowed his mind to conjure, for example, a supplementary universe made up entirely of exceptions.

While earlier paintings like *Alfred Jarry* (color plate 9) and *Ubu's Picnic*, which were both completed in 1962, referenced Jorn's swirling painterly abstractions of the CoBrA period, Brewton's subsequent works, including his remarkable broadsheet *The Pataphysics Times*, reveal his maturity as an artist with a singular vision that can no longer be traced back exclusively to recent developments in postwar European painting. The impact of urban graffiti is found in the scratched, scribbled, and scumbled surfaces of his paintings, which also call to mind the work of Cy Twombly, while the subject matter and metallic finish of paintings like *Patatarget* (color plate 10) can also be compared to Jasper Johns's contemporaneous use of target imagery and sculpmetal. Color is kept to a minimum in this work, as if to give the artist's imagination free rein, and it is in this tondo painting, with its exciting vocabulary of esoteric, quasi-scientific imagery, that the influence of Jarry's tongue-in-cheek philosophy of pataphysics is most keenly felt. Works like *Patatarget* reveal the creative excitement at this pivotal moment in the artist's career, when, despite his financial struggles and frequent bouts of depression, Brewton enthusiastically spread the word about pataphysics to his fellow Philadelphians through his paintings, prints, publications, stamps, and slogans. He even planned to launch a Patacomic on April 1, 1965, based on Jarry's *Le Surmale* (*The Supermale*), although its nonappearance suggests that it was probably designed all along as an April Fools' Day joke.

Two years later Brewton's work was included in a group show featuring the work of four Philadelphia-based artists at the Socrates Perakis Art Gallery at 2116 Locust

Street, which opened at 12:10 a.m. on the morning of May 15, 1967. Organized by the American graphic artist Jim McWilliams, who also made the exhibition poster (color plate 11), this show presented the work of Brewton, Thomas Chimes, Paul Anthony Greenwood, and McWilliams. Brewton was almost certainly responsible for the exhibition's grandiose title, *The Society for the Commemoration of Festivals and Fetishes*, which reflects the numerous, official-sounding societies and institutes that the *Collège de 'Pataphysique* and Brewton's friend Asger Jorn had founded across Europe. I also suspect that Brewton may have been behind the idea to have the exhibition open just after midnight, an event that was billed as a "pure party" and attended by hundreds of people. Unfortunately, the opening celebrations were overshadowed by Brewton's suicide four days earlier when, emotionally unstable, financially impoverished, and suffering from spinal problems and alcoholism, he shot himself with the rifle he was issued in the Korean War. The former marine sergeant was just thirty-six years old.

Brewton's suicide on May 11, 1967, from a self-inflicted gunshot wound to the head in his third-floor studio at 718 Pemberton Street, could be read as the ultimate homage to Jarry, akin to the French writer's own self-inflicted demise in a haze of luminiferous ether and alcohol.[23] However, Brewton's death was the result of a lifetime of coping with depression, illness, and poverty, since he refused to teach, believing that a true artist should devote all of his or her available time and energy to making art. This heroic stance often cost him dearly, since his income from the odd jobs that he took on to survive was so meager that he could not pay his rent for months at a stretch. As Harry Kulkowitz, the director of the Kenmore Galleries, succinctly stated at the time, "We feel that Jim was one of the great talents to emerge from Philadelphia institutions (like P.A.F.A.), and his death may be attributed in great measure to the lack of encouragement and subsidy for artists like him."[24] Two memorial exhibitions were held in quick succession, the first at the Peale Galleries of the Pennsylvania Academy of the Fine Arts in 1968, where Brewton's work was shown alongside that of Robert Rauschenberg, and three years later the Kenmore Galleries organized a memorial show in which proceeds from the sale of paintings and works on paper were used to establish the James E. Brewton Student Aid Fund to benefit needy graduates from the Pennsylvania Academy, giving them the sort of financial aid that was unavailable to Brewton during his lifetime.

Brewton's legacy can be felt in the work of another Philadelphia-based artist, Thomas Chimes, whose elaborate metal-box constructions were shown to great critical acclaim in the 1967 *Society for the Commemoration of Festivals and Fetishes* exhibition. Two years earlier, Chimes had been "stopped in his tracks in complete amazement" when he saw a copy of Brewton's *Pataphysics Times* in the window of the Kenmore Galleries during the artist's show there in February 1965.[25] Chimes was intrigued by the blueprint's numerous references to Alfred Jarry, having recently discovered the French author's visionary writings and vitriolic humor through his own issue of the *Evergreen Review*, which had been fortuitously given to him by his brother-in-law in 1964. After viewing the exhibition, Chimes contacted Brewton, who was about to leave for Denmark and so could not meet until the summer of 1965, but their initial encounter sowed the seeds for the exhibition that took place at the Socrates Perakis Gallery two years later, which was intended to launch a pataphysical art movement in Philadelphia. Although Brewton's tragic early death by suicide scuppered their plans, Chimes would return to Jarry and pataphysics in 1973, when he embarked on an extended series of panel portraits inspired by Doctor Faustroll's hallucinatory, Gulliver-like voyages to the imaginary realms of a particular artist, writer, or scientist. These haunting portraits, all of which were based on period photographs and housed in oversized wooden frames, were intended to refer "less to the man it represents than to the ideas he generated,"[26] and secured Chimes's reputation as the leading artist in the city, a position that had previously been held by Brewton, who had "almost singlehandedly changed the whole art scene in Philadelphia," as one friend and supporter later recalled.[27]

Chimes began work on his celebrated series of intimate, sepia-toned panel paintings in the summer of 1973, beginning, appropriately enough, with several portraits of Alfred Jarry (color plate 12), whose unconventional life and radical nonconformism had interested him to the point of obsession for almost a decade. Reminiscent of nineteenth-century daguerreotypes, these panel portraits reveal Chimes's strong feelings of affinity and continuity with avant-garde forebears like Jarry, Guillaume Apollinaire, Antonin Artaud, Joris-Karl Huysmans, Edgar Allan Poe, Arthur Rimbaud, Robert Louis Stevenson, Paul Verlaine, and Oscar Wilde, all of whom he regarded as possessed characters whose work remains as relevant today as when it was first created. Each portrait required Chimes to embark on his own voyage of discovery by completely immersing himself in the writings of, say, Charles Baudelaire, who appears in a 1974 painting from the series (color plate 13). After reading Baudelaire's poetry and criticism, as well as biographies and critical essays on the French writer, Chimes devoted a great deal of the time to selecting the right photograph for the panel portrait, which was intended to encapsulate the world of the subject portrayed through a single moment of his life. Chimes thus employed an emotional objectivity when sifting through the range of photographs of Baudelaire, and I believe that he eventually chose the 1862 *carte-de-visite* photograph by Gaspard-Félix Tournachon Nadar, rather than the slightly earlier and instantly recognizable photograph taken by Étienne Carjat, because he wanted to highlight the romantic appearance and mesmerizing gaze of the influential French poet and art critic.

Chimes selected his source image from the 1969 anthology *Baudelaire: The Artist and His World*, which, along with biographical commentaries by Robert Kopp and a critical essay by George Poulet, was also generously illustrated with photographs, caricatures, and paintings.[28] Many of the other images reproduced in this anthology appear elsewhere in Chimes's work of this time, including the panel portraits of Edgar Allan Poe and an outstanding pencil drawing, which Chimes made in 1975, of Nadar wearing a top hat. Although Nadar was too successful in his paid profession as a photographer to be included in the series himself, his photographs of his peers were used for several of Chimes's panel portraits, including the one of his close friend Baudelaire, standing with one hand in his trouser pocket and the other plunged into his vest like Napoléon Bonaparte in Jacques-Louis David's famous 1812 portrait. Nadar's smoldering image captures the charisma and vitality of the poet-critic, but also hints at his life's struggle and exhaustion through the dark shadow that falls across Baudelaire's face like a curse. Chimes thus chose the photograph that best conveyed the French poet's life in its entirety, as a nineteenth-century man of letters, as well as the misunderstood, romantic bohemian who died of venereal disease just five years later.

Once Chimes had chosen the photograph that would provide the impetus for the portrait, the task of re-creating and translating the image in oil paint on a carefully prepared wood panel began. Working from the photographic reproduction in front of him, the artist would select the appropriate mode of representation to render the individual's likeness, believing that the technique itself would correspond to that particular person. As Chimes later recalled, "In the case of someone like Baudelaire, having read his poetry, read the biographical material on him, I then started painting. I suddenly felt and thought I saw in the painting itself an almost ghostlike, moonlit face that I had used in some of the others. So I dropped this lunar quality in the work at that point and concentrated on the cut of his coat. And there's where the emphasis really is, which not only amused me, but I felt it was saying something significant about Baudelaire himself. So to sum it all up, my approach to these portraits was to use a technique and a way of working that would be appropriate to the individual I was trying to represent."[29]

When completed, each panel portrait was enshrined within an oversized wooden frame resembling those found on the paintings of fellow Philadelphian Thomas Eakins, who taught at the Pennsylvania Academy of the Fine Arts several generations before Chimes and Brewton attended the school. Eakins's frames similarly consisted of flat wooden boards made of chestnut, sometimes almost a foot wide, that were used to establish a great deal of space around his work, while also functioning as directional devices to focus attention on the painting's subject. Chimes's frames similarly situate his work somewhere between a family snapshot and a monumental devotional icon, allowing him to isolate the particular person and home in on their visage. These frames were specially constructed by the artist out of strips of oak, pine, mahogany, or ebony, and were occasionally furnished with a small brass plaque, denoting the subject's name.

As the forty-eight paintings in his panel portrait series attest, Chimes adopted a methodical, obsessive, and highly disciplined approach to his paintings of Jarry and his contemporaries that are very different in style from the more spontaneous, gestural, and expressionist canvases that Brewton made in the previous decade. Brewton had painted portraits of his own pantheon of modern artists, filmmakers, musicians, and writers, including Charles Baudelaire, Alban Berg, Jean Cocteau, Alfred Jarry, Amedeo Modigliani, Edgar Allan Poe, and Arthur Rimbaud, many of whom would later appear in Chimes's series of panel portraits. As is the case for the majority of his mature work, Brewton rejected a unified style in these portraits in favor of a détourned approach to art-making, as seen in his unexpected color choices and rampant artistic borrowings from artists as varied as Vincent van Gogh, Jasper Johns, Asger Jorn, Edvard Munch, Cy Twombly, and Chaïm Soutine, whereas Chimes deliberately restricted his palette to the brown hues and dark varnished sheen found in the paintings of Thomas Eakins for all the panel portraits he made between 1973 and 1978.

Brewton's portraits, which were made intermittently throughout his career, were never planned as a series, as opposed to Chimes's research-based, serial approach to portraiture. Although Brewton often based these portraits on period photographs, the artist used source images to unleash his imagination while working in a frenzy of artistic activity that ensured the finished portrait would be unrecognizable from the photograph that provided its point of departure. This can be seen in Brewton's undated *Portrait of Charles Baudelaire* seated at his writing desk, which was loosely based on the same Nadar photograph that would inform Chimes's portrait in the following decade. Pen in hand and paper at the ready, Baudelaire is shown deep in thought as he contemplates a vase of exuberantly colored flowers, no doubt a reference to the poet's 1857 volume *Les Fleurs du mal*, while, in a brilliant touch, a white bird rises phoenix-like behind the bouquet to enhance the visionary quality of the painting, which can be understood as an effort to create a visual equivalent of the extraordinary imagery of the French writer's poetry. Brewton's rapidly executed portrait of Baudelaire demonstrates that he had no interest in the meticulous craftsmanship that Chimes favored, preferring a direct, spontaneous expression in which the ideas presented were more important than the method of their conveyance.

Other Brewton portraits, such as the jaunty *Alfred Jarry in Paris* (color plate 14), reveal Brewton's unique sense of humor as he détourns a found image of a Victorian-era chimney sweep wearing a top hat and riding a bicycle into an imaginary portrait of Jarry and his signature mode of transport, his Clément Luxe bicycle, as he metaphorically sweeps away the soot, dust, and cobwebs of French literature and ushers in the modern and the new.[30] Despite the major differences in their working practices and creative vision, the Jarry-inspired portrait paintings of Chimes and Brewton, when seen together, comprise a potent visual testament to the enduring power of his literary creations and his frontier-extending concept of pataphysics.

In her review of the 1971 James Brewton memorial show at the Kenmore Galleries, Nessa Forman, the art critic at the *Philadelphia Inquirer*, wrote, "There was an artist who was ahead of his time, who was brilliant, sensitive and nonviolent, who loved his art and just wanted to paint. . . . Ironically, his graffiti paintings and lithographs hold more insight and value for us today than when he painted them. But Brewton knew this would happen. He knew that someday he would make it."[31] Four decades later this prophecy still holds true, yet as I hope to have made clear, in order to grasp the full significance of Brewton's work and ideas one needs to understand the reception of Alfred Jarry's notion of pataphysics among the revolutionary cultural organizations of the postwar avant-garde and the defiant, inspirational example of Asger Jorn, who like a modern Faustroll guided aspiring artists like Brewton on their pataphysical journey.

Notes

The epigraph is drawn James Brewton, *The American Dream-Girl: Graffiti Pataphysic* (Copenhagen: Galerie AP, 1965), James Brewton Archive, Van Pelt Library, University of Pennsylvania, Philadelphia (hereafter cited as James Brewton Archive). I would like to thank the artist's daughter, Emily Brewton Schilling, for sharing this exhibition catalog with me, along with Brewton's artworks, correspondence, passports, photographs, and other archival materials, and for her generous assistance with this essay, which has greatly benefited from her enthusiastic advice and encouragement.

1. John Updike later published a fictional account of his experiences at the highly traditional Ruskin School, which he renamed as the "Constable School." See Updike, "Still Life," *New Yorker*, January 24, 1959, 35–41. Brewton is undoubtedly one of the "four other resentful American veterans" mentioned in the text, who spend their days in dimly lit galleries drawing from dust-covered plaster casts of antique statues (35).

2. Anonymous [Victoria Donohoe], "James Brewton, Posthumously," *Philadelphia Inquirer*, May 28, 1976, James Brewton Archive.

3. Asger Jorn, "Peinture détournée" (*Détourned* painting), in *Vingt peintures modifiées par Asger Jorn*, exhibition catalog (Paris: Galerie Rive Gauche, 1959), n.p. (my translation).

4. For an excellent discussion of Jorn's artistic practice, see Karen Kurczynski, "Ironic Gestures: Asger Jorn, Informel, and Abstract Expressionism" in *Abstract Expressionism: The International Context*, ed. Joan Marter (New Brunswick, NJ: Rutgers University Press, 2007), 108–24.

5. Brewton, *American Dream-Girl*, n.p.

6. For an insightful overview of the fruitful interchange between art, theory and politics among members of the Situationist International, see Peter Wollen, "Bitter Victory: The Art and Politics of the Situationist International," in *On the Passage of a Few People Through a Rather Brief Moment in Time: The Situationist International, 1957–1972*, ed. Elisabeth Sussman (Cambridge, MA: MIT Press; Boston: Institute of Contemporary Art, 1989), 20–61.

7. For more on the artistic response to Jarry's *Ubu Roi*, see Michael R. Taylor, "The Regenerative Legacy of Alfred Jarry's *Ubu Roi*," in *The Puppet Show*, ed. Ingrid Schaffner and Carin Kuoni, exhibition catalog (Philadelphia: Institute of Contemporary Art, University of Pennsylvania, 2008), 61–68.

8. As Sid Sachs has noted, Brewton's interest in graffiti reflects Philadelphia's preeminent role as the first major American city in which aerosol spray paint "bombing" developed, with graffiti appearing on Philadelphia highways as early as 1959, see Sachs, ed. *Invisible City: Philadelphia and the Vernacular Avant-garde*, exhibition catalogue (Philadelphia: Rosenwald-Wolf Gallery at University of the Arts, 2020), 46.

9. Marcel Duchamp, radio interview with Herbert Crehan, broadcast by WBAJ-FM (New York, 1961), published in "Dada," ed. Robert Cowan, special issue, *Evidence* (Toronto), no. 3 (Fall 1961): 37.

10. Ralph Rumney, "Asger Jorn," *Art Monthly* (London), no. 9 (July–August 1977): 19.

11. Jorn, "Peinture détournée," n.p. (my translation).

12. Roger Shattuck, "Superliminal Note," in "What Is Pataphysics?," ed. Roger Shattuck and Simon Watson Taylor, special issue, *Evergreen Review* 4, no. 13 (May–June 1960): 29. Brewton's statement for the pamphlet that accompanied his "Graffiti Pataphysic" exhibition at the Kenmore Galleries in February 1965 included the "Only the comic is serious" line, as well as an entire passage lifted virtually wholesale from Shattuck's introduction: "When asked to fill out in quadruplicate a questionnaire on his political affiliations or sexual habits, [the pataphysician] details a different and equally valid activity on each of the four sheets [Brewton changed this word to 'papers']" (*American Dream-Girl*).

13. Asger Jorn, "La Pataphysique, une religion en formation," *Internationale Situationniste*, no. 6 (August 1961), reprinted in Jorn, *Pataphysics: A Religion in the Making*, trans. Department of Dogma and Theory, London Institute of 'Pataphysics (London: Institute of 'Pataphysics, 2007), 5.

14. Anonymous, "Pataphysics as Apostasy," *Dossier acénonètes du Collège de 'Pataphysique*, no. 17, 22 Sable 89 (December 22, 1961, vulgate), reprinted in Jorn, *Pataphysics*, 11.

15. This was Jarry's subtitle.

16. Brewton, *American Dream-Girl*, n.p.

17. I am thankful to Emily Brewton Schilling for identifying Aldo van Eyck as the author of this text.

18. I am grateful to Emily Brewton Schilling for sharing with me the surviving rubber stamps that Brewton used in his work and correspondence, many of which include the name of the Philadelphia stationery stores that made them: Evans and Convey, 126 South Eleventh Street; Paramount Stationers, 142 North Tenth Street; and H. Dilks, 1613 Sansom Street.

19. Brewton, *American Dream-Girl*, n.p. "This exhibition is an homage to woman," Brewton wrote in the Galerie AP exhibition catalog. "I think the creation of woman was the best idea God ever had, and he must have had lots of them. He was not born of woman so He cannot die. He is the eternal orphan, poor bastard. Woman is part of man, he defeats himself when he tries to make a subject of her, just as nature is not something to make war on for we are a part of it. We must live with ourselves, by ourselves, for ourselves. Being not having. I am in no way negative, and this is a positive observation of the female. As to its worth, time will take care of that as it does all art."

20. Ibid.

21. Ibid.

22. Alastair Brotchie, *Alfred Jarry: A Pataphysical Life* (Cambridge, MA: MIT Press, 2011), 324.

23. It should be noted in this regard that a black-and-white photograph of one of Brewton's lost paintings, *Homage to Alfred Jarry*, that was made around 1964, reveals that it contained the inscription "Suicide by Hallucination," which was the title of Roger Shattuck's chapter on Jarry in *The Banquet Years: The Arts in France, 1885–1918* (London: Faber and Faber, 1955).

24. Harry Kulkowitz, quoted in Dorothy Grafly, "Artist's Suicide Gives Tragic Overtone to Exhibit," *Philadelphia Evening Bulletin*, May 28, 1967, James Brewton Archive.

25. Thomas Chimes, interview with the author, February 28, 2008.

26. Anne d'Harnoncourt, "Thomas Chimes," in *Philadelphia: Three Centuries of American Art*, exhibition catalog (Philadelphia: Philadelphia Museum of Art, 1976), 636.

27. Harry Kulkowitz, quoted in Nessa Forman, "Now That He's Dead, Has His Time

Come?," *Sunday Bulletin* (Philadelphia), April 25, 1971, James Brewton Archive.

28. Georges Poulet and Robert Kopp, eds., *Baudelaire: The Artist and His World*, trans. Robert Allen and James Emmons (Geneva: Editions d'Art Albert Skira, 1969).

29. Thomas Chimes, interview with the author, September 20, 2000.

30. The chimney sweep's broom also recalls Ubu's "unmentionable brush," the toilet brush that serves as his scepter and weapon.

31. Nessa Forman, "Now That He's Dead, Has His Time Come?," *Sunday Bulletin* (Philadelphia), April 25, 1971, James Brewton Archive.

PLATES

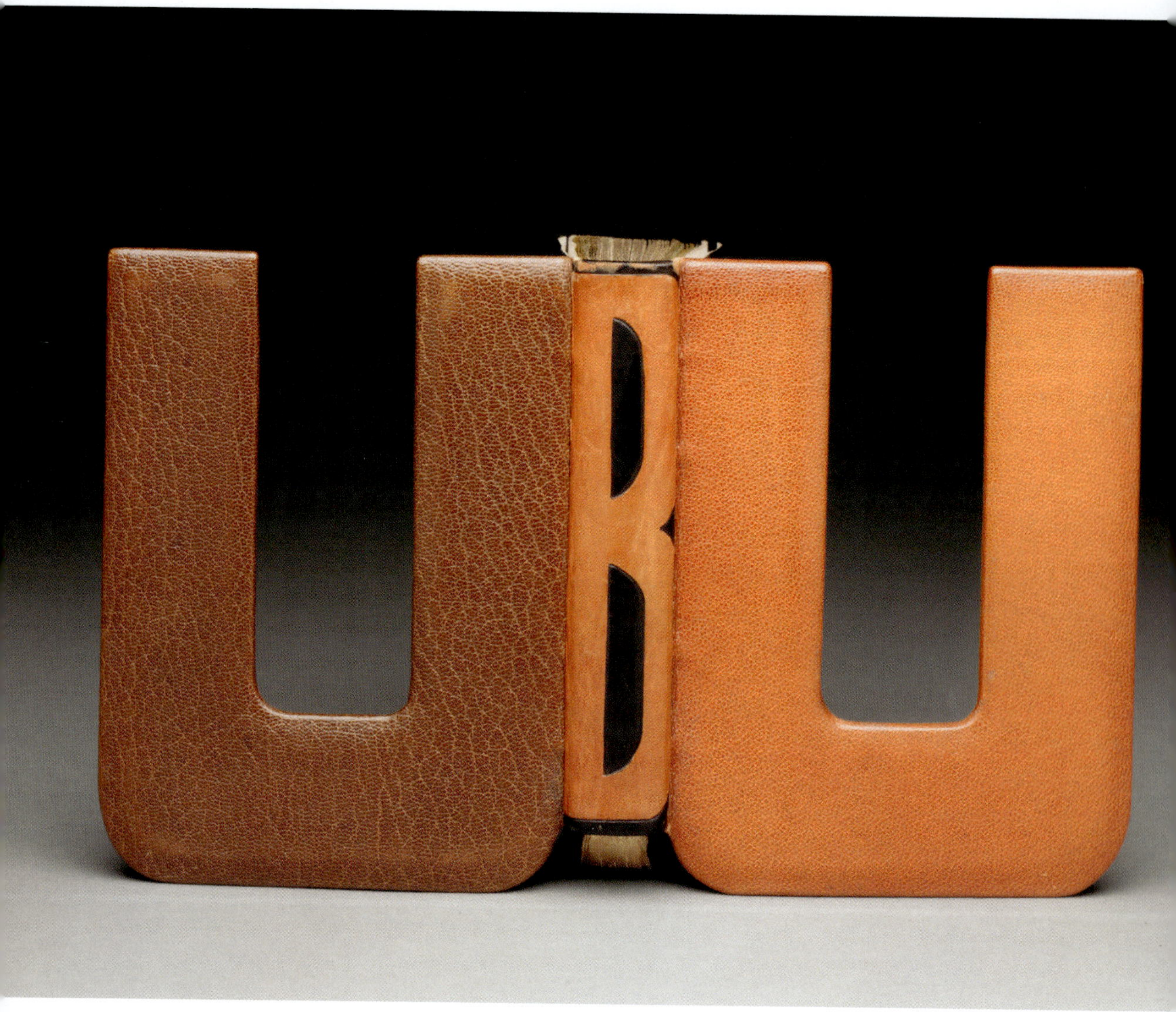

Plate 1. Mary Reynolds, binding for Alfred Jarry, *Ubu Roi: Drame en Cinq Actes* (Paris: Librairie Charpentier et Fasquelle, 1921), 1935. Full tan morocco binding with black silk endleaves, designed by Marcel Duchamp and Mary Reynolds. The Art Institute of Chicago, Mary Reynolds Collection, ref. no. 2019.180.

Plate 2. Mary Reynolds, binding for Pierre Nicolas Brisset, *La Science de Dieu* (Paris: Chamuel, 1900), n.d. Full black calfskin binding with full green calfskin and toadskin onlays on covers. The Art Institute of Chicago, gift of Mr. Frank B. Hubachek, ref. no. 1963.757.

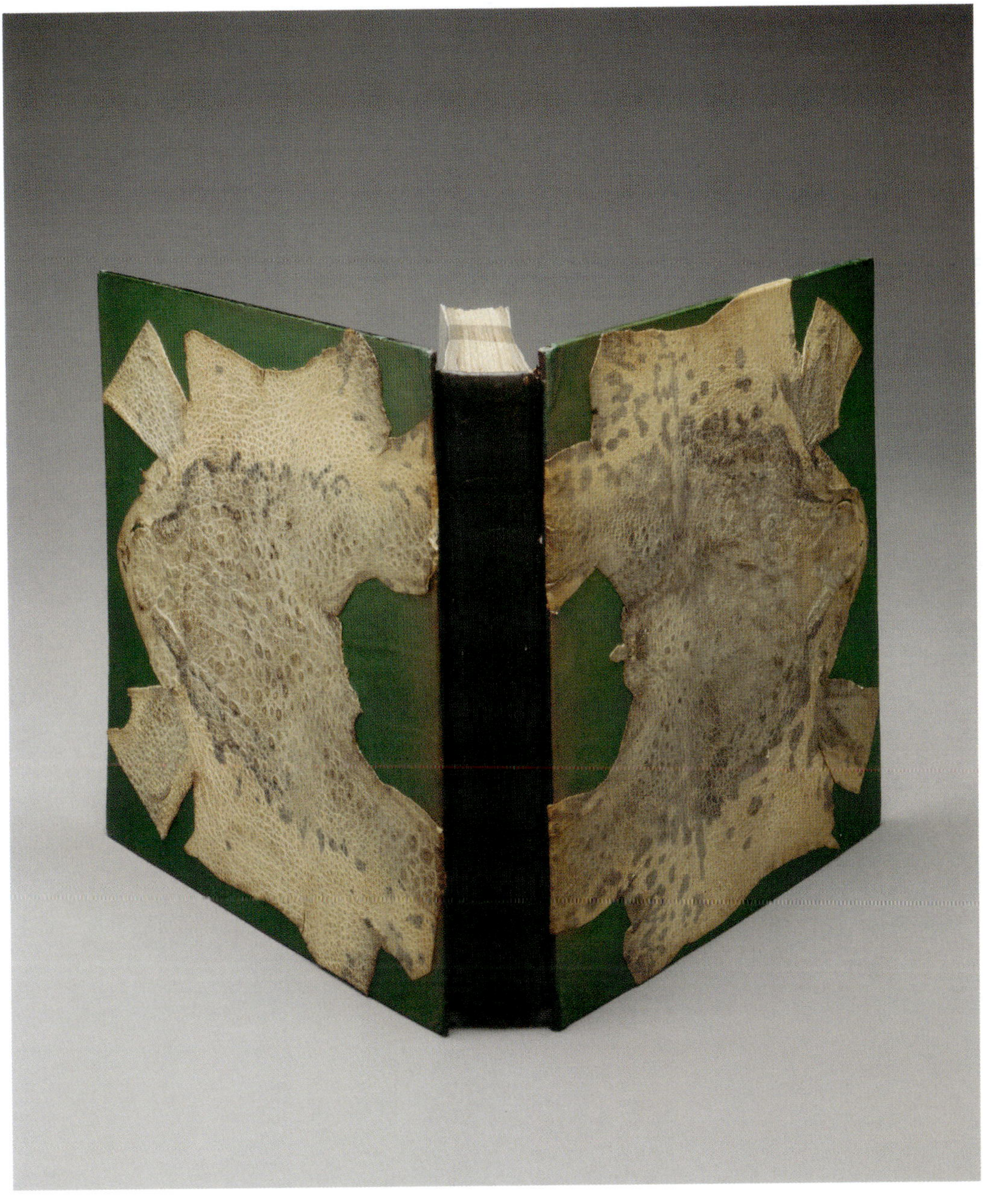

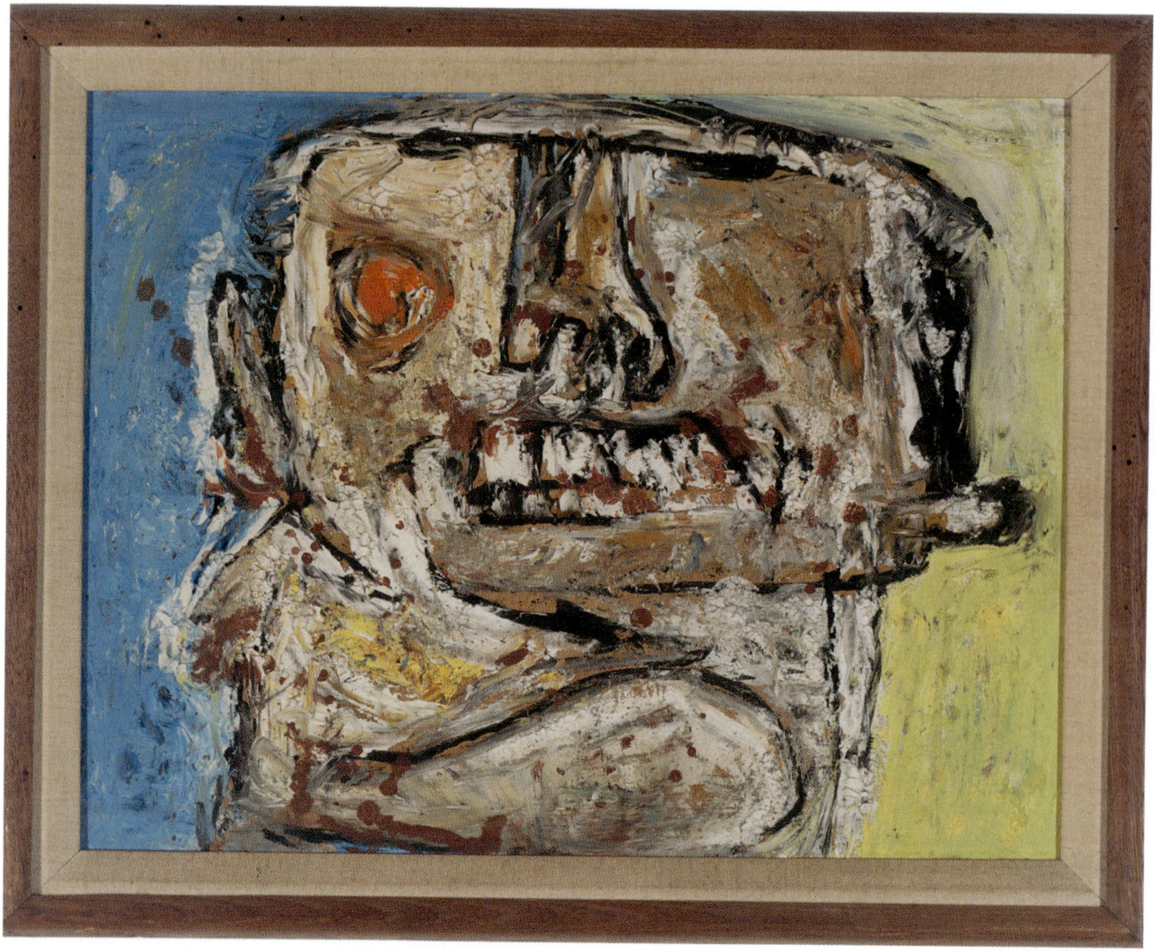

Plate 3. James E. Brewton, *Self-Portrait*, circa 1962. Oil on panel, 17 × 21 inches. Private collection. Image by Elena Bouvier, courtesy of the James E. Brewton Foundation.

Plate 4. James E. Brewton, *Portrait of Asger Jorn*, 1964. Oil on canvas, 51 ½ × 37 ¼ inches. Private collection. Image by Vera Carbo, courtesy of the James E. Brewton Foundation.

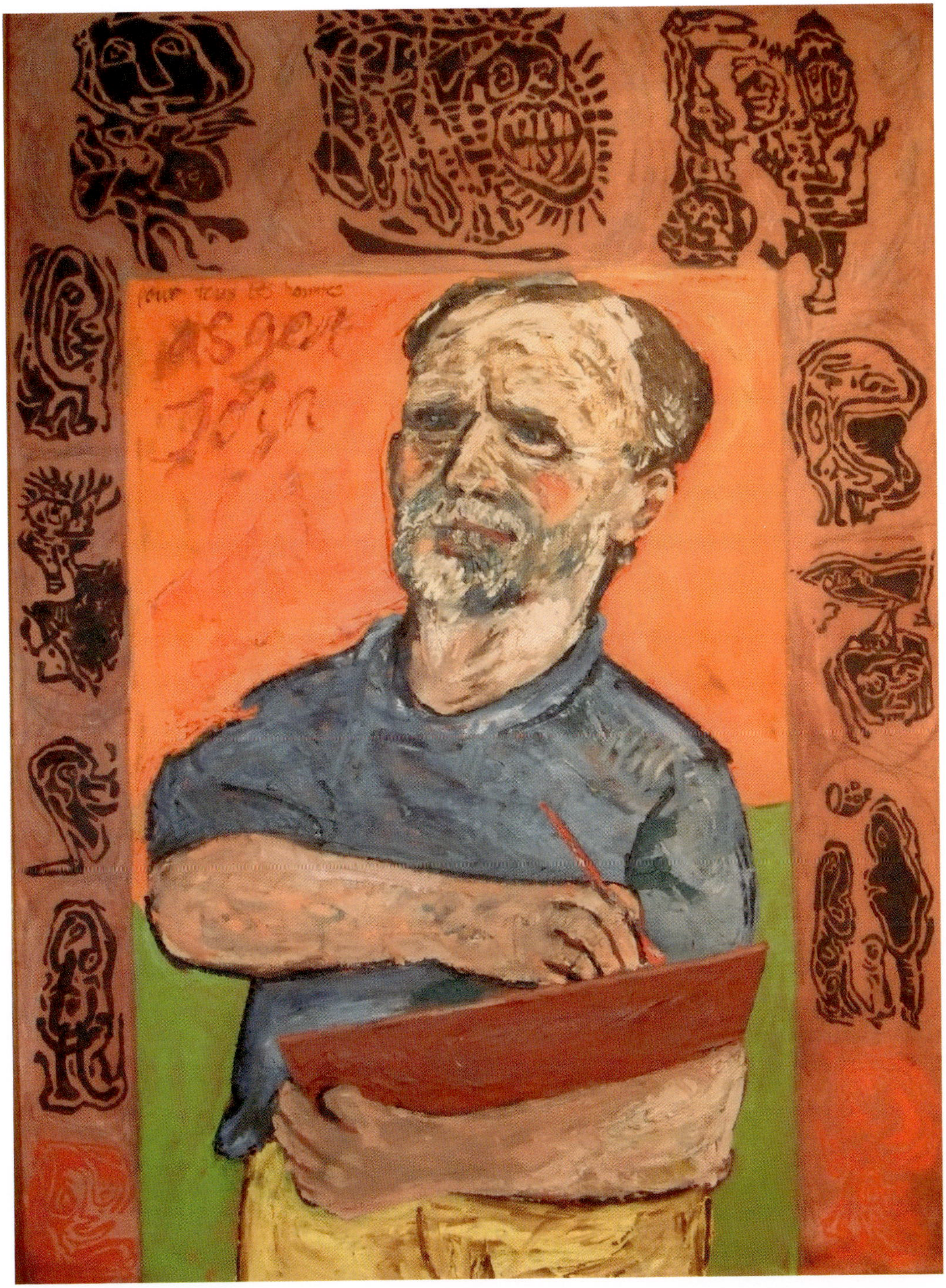

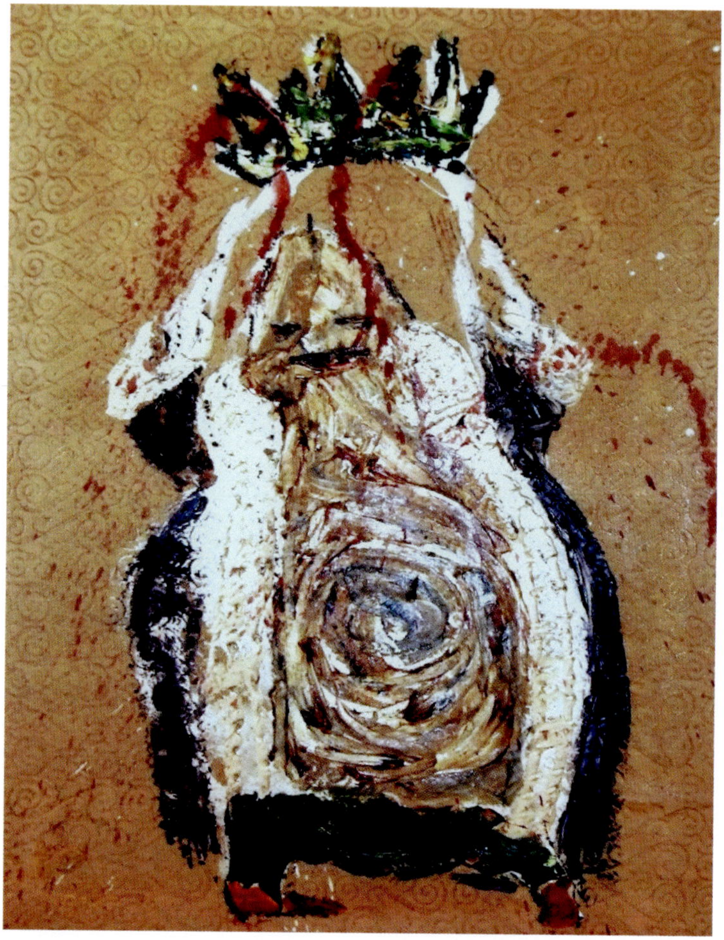

Plate 5. James E. Brewton, *Ubu Becomes King*, 1962. Oil on linen, 45 ½ × 35 ½ inches. Private collection. Image courtesy of the James E. Brewton Foundation.

Plate 6. James E. Brewton, *Ubu's Military Mind*, 1962. Mixed media with military medals on aluminum mounted on plywood, 32 ½ × 14 inches. Private collection. Image by Elena Bouvier, courtesy of the James E. Brewton Foundation.

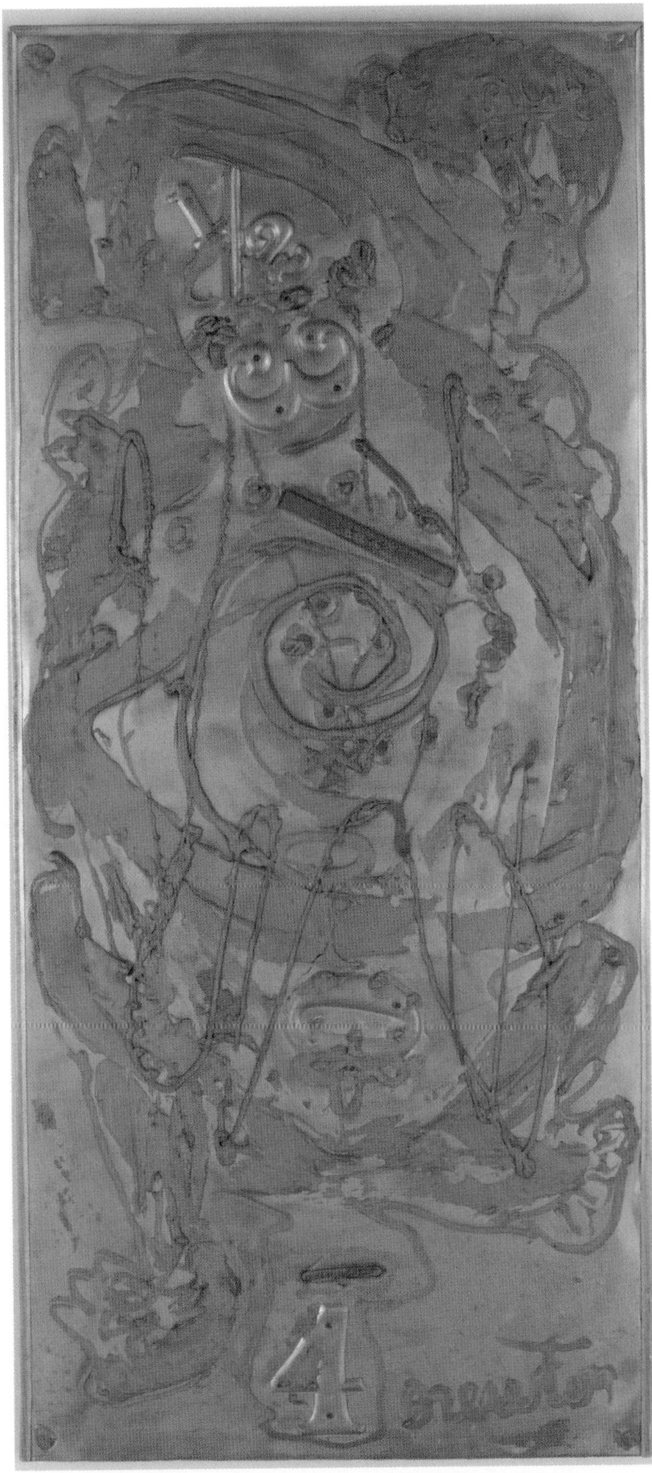
4

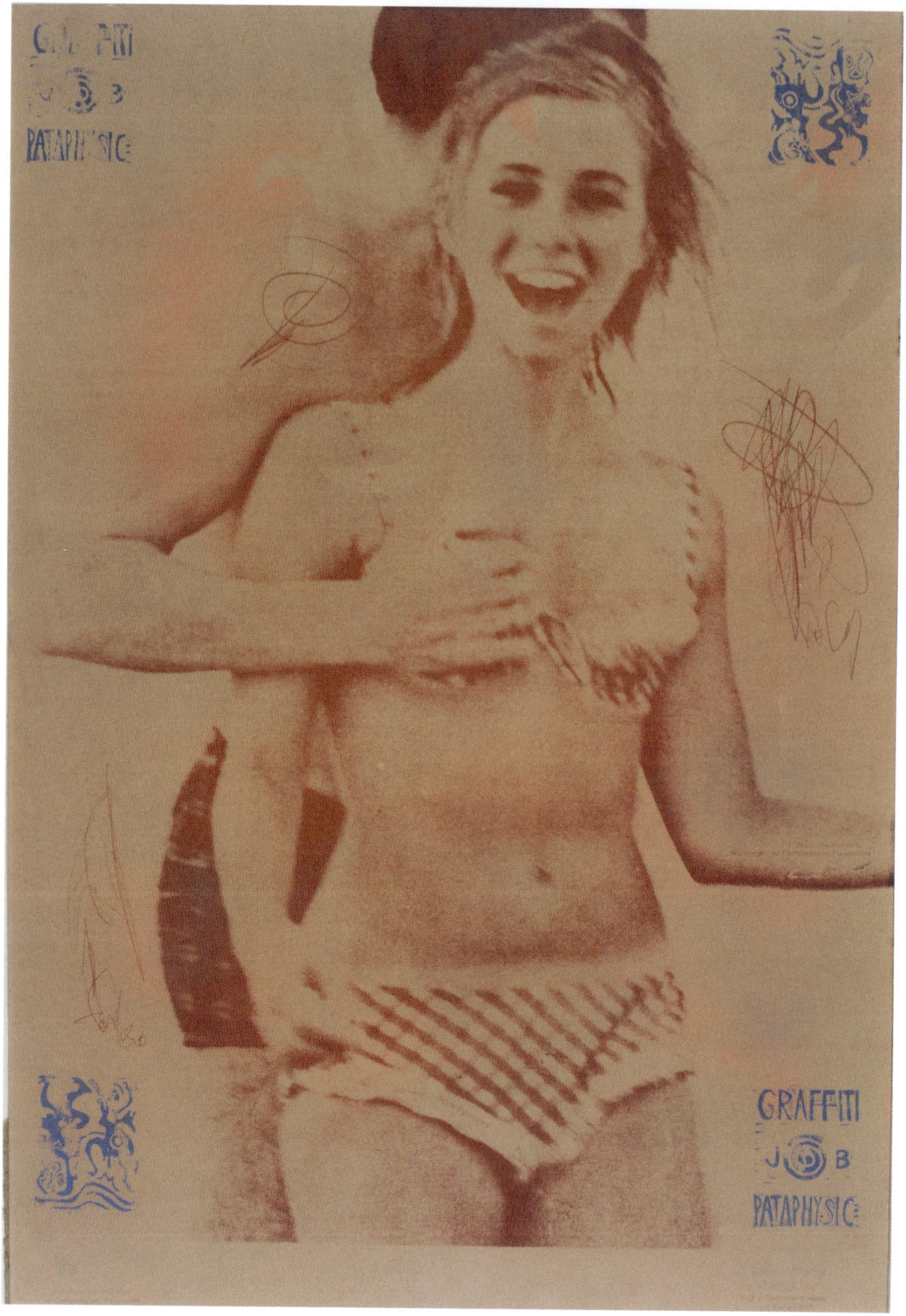
GRAFFITI
J B

Plate 7. James E. Brewton, *Sunrise*, 1964. Combine print with artist's stamps, 37 × 25 inches. Private collection. Image by Elena Bouvier, courtesy of the James E. Brewton Foundation.

Plate 8. James E. Brewton, *Graffiti Pataphysic*, 1965. Offset lithograph, 23 ½ × 15 inches. Exhibition poster, Kenmore Galleries, Philadelphia. Private collection. Image by Elena Bouvier, courtesy of the James E. Brewton Foundation.

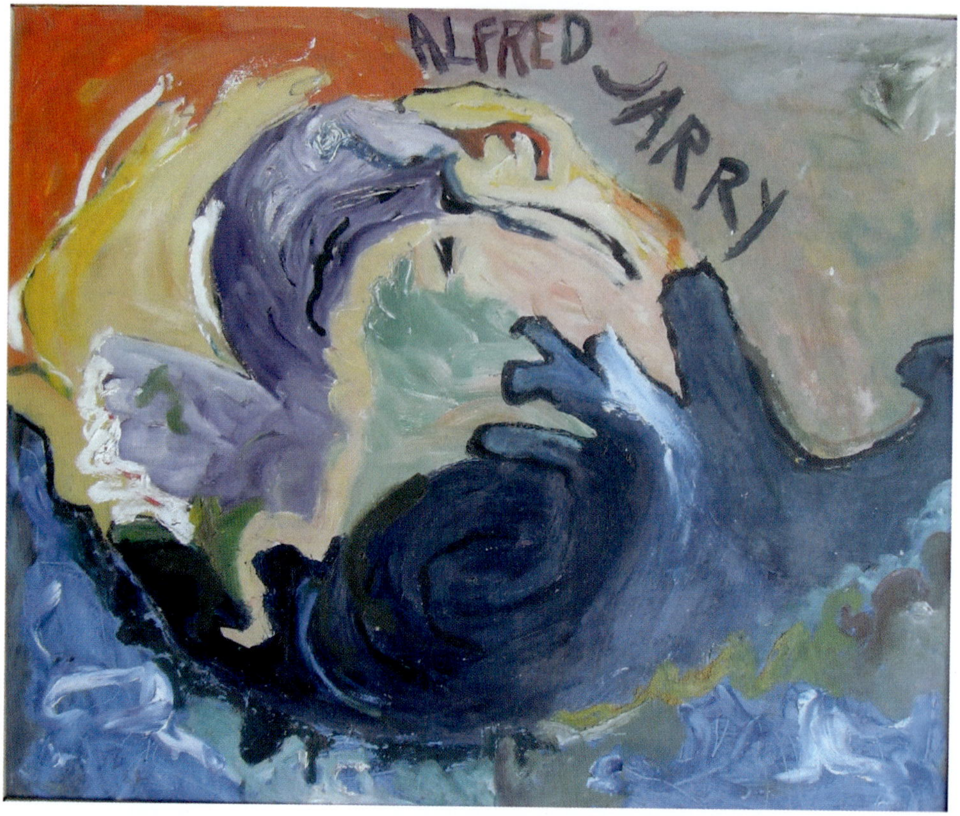

Plate 9. James E. Brewton, *Alfred Jarry*, 1962. Oil on panel, 21 × 25 inches. Private collection. Image courtesy of the James E. Brewton Foundation.

Plate 10. James E. Brewton, *Patatarget*, circa 1964–65. Mixed media on canvas, 34 inches diameter. Private collection. Image courtesy of the James E. Brewton Foundation.

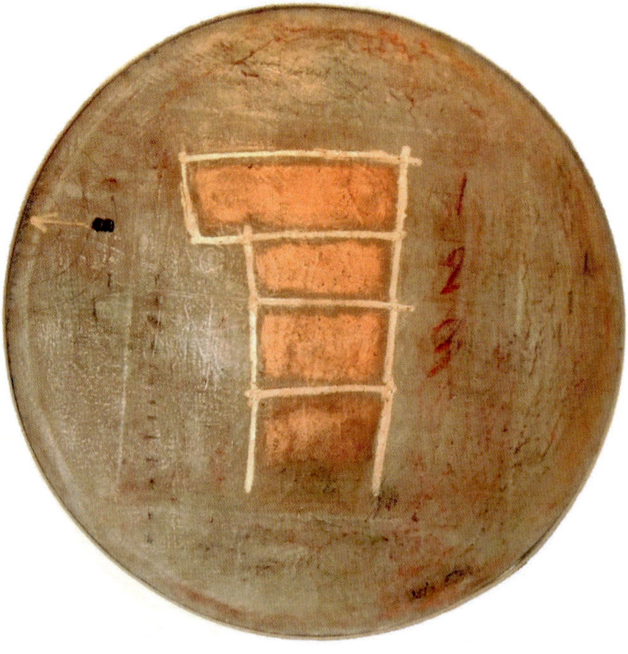

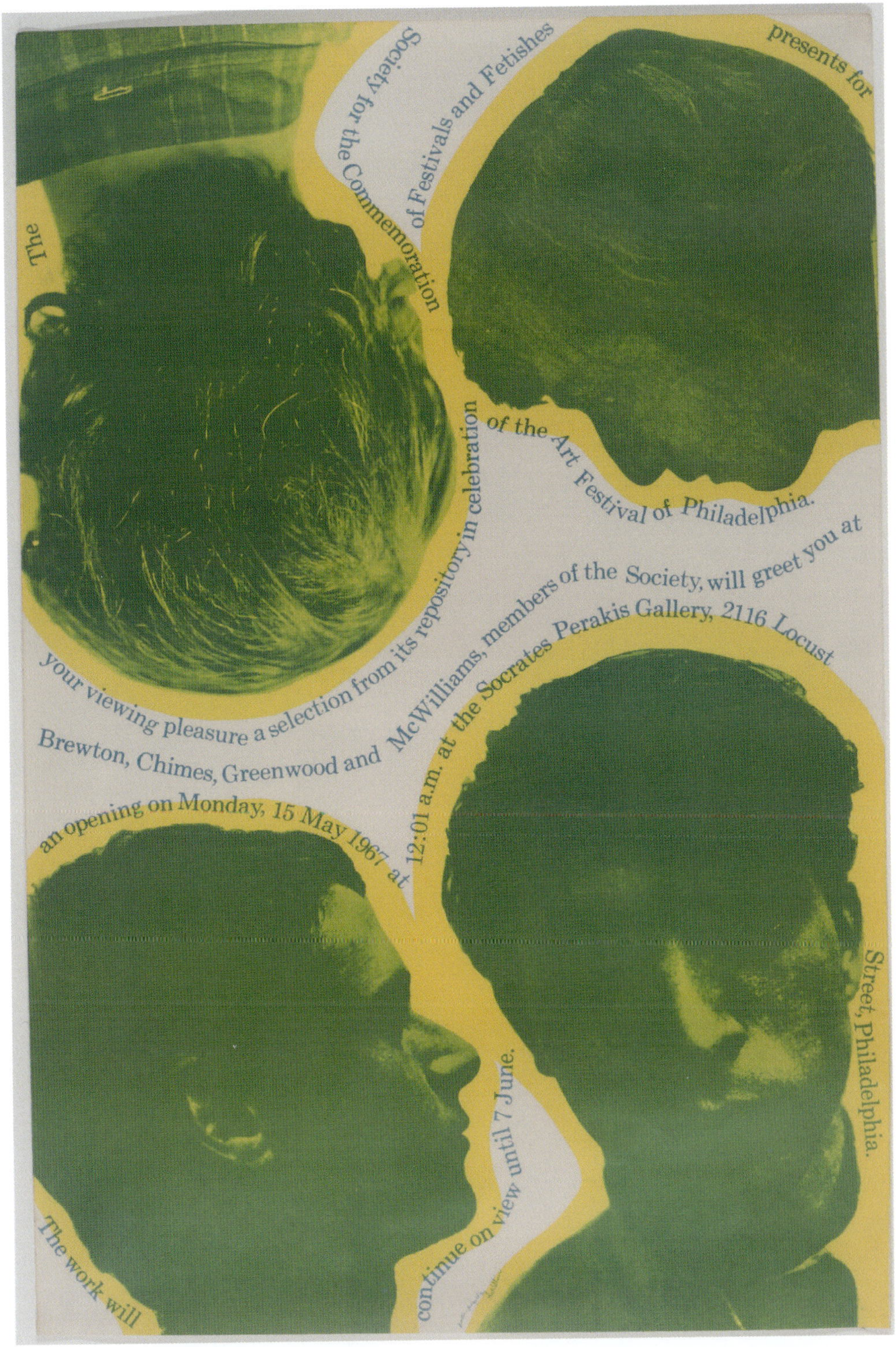

Plate 11. Jim McWilliams, *Society for the Commemoration of Festivals and Fetishes: Brewton, Chimes, Greenwood, and McWilliams*, 1967. Screenprint, 22 $\frac{3}{16}$ × 33 $\frac{7}{8}$ inches. Exhibition poster, Socrates Perakis Gallery, Philadelphia. Private collection. Image by Elena Bouvier, courtesy of the James E. Brewton Foundation.

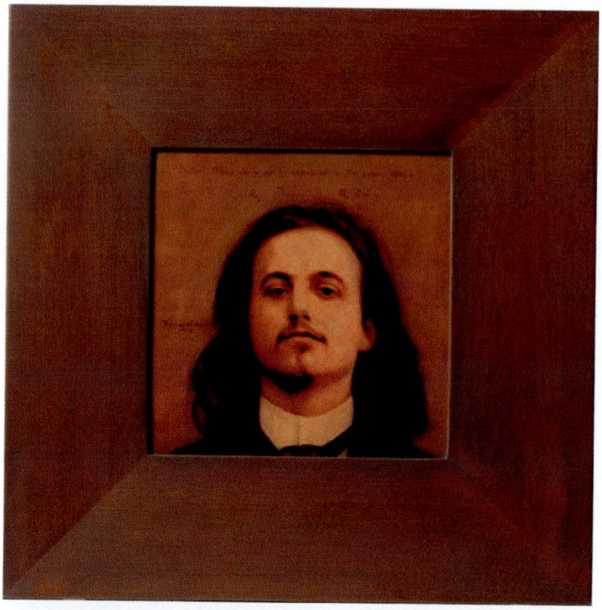

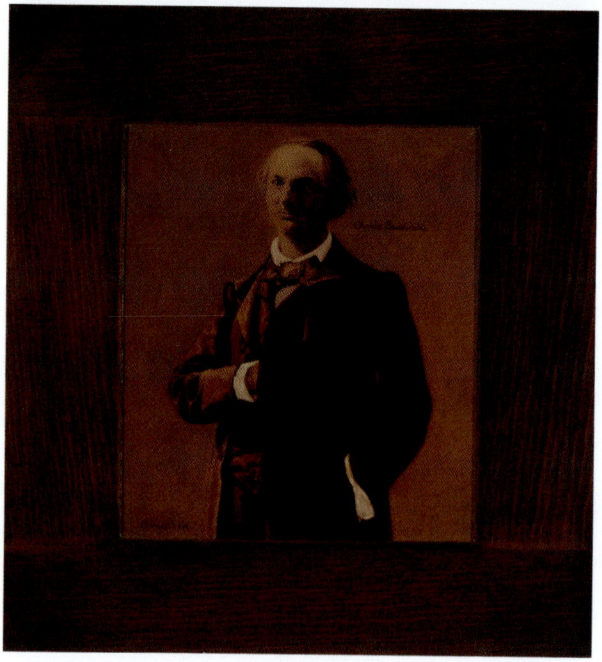

Plate 12. Thomas Chimes, *Alfred Jarry*, 1974. Oil on panel in original artist's frame, 22 ½ × 22 ¼ inches. Philadelphia Museum of Art. Purchased with the Adele Haas Turner and Beatrice Pastorius Turner Memorial Fund, 1975-82-1. © The Estate of Thomas Chimes.

Plate 13. Thomas Chimes, *Charles Baudelaire*, 1974. Oil on canvas in original artist's frame, 19 ⅛ × 17 7/16 inches. Virginia Museum of Fine Arts. Gift of the Estate of Frances and Bayard T. Storey, 2017.433. © The Estate of Thomas Chimes.

Plate 14. James E. Brewton, *Alfred Jarry in Paris*, circa 1966. Cyanotype, 25 × 20 inches. Private collection. Image courtesy of the James E. Brewton Foundation.

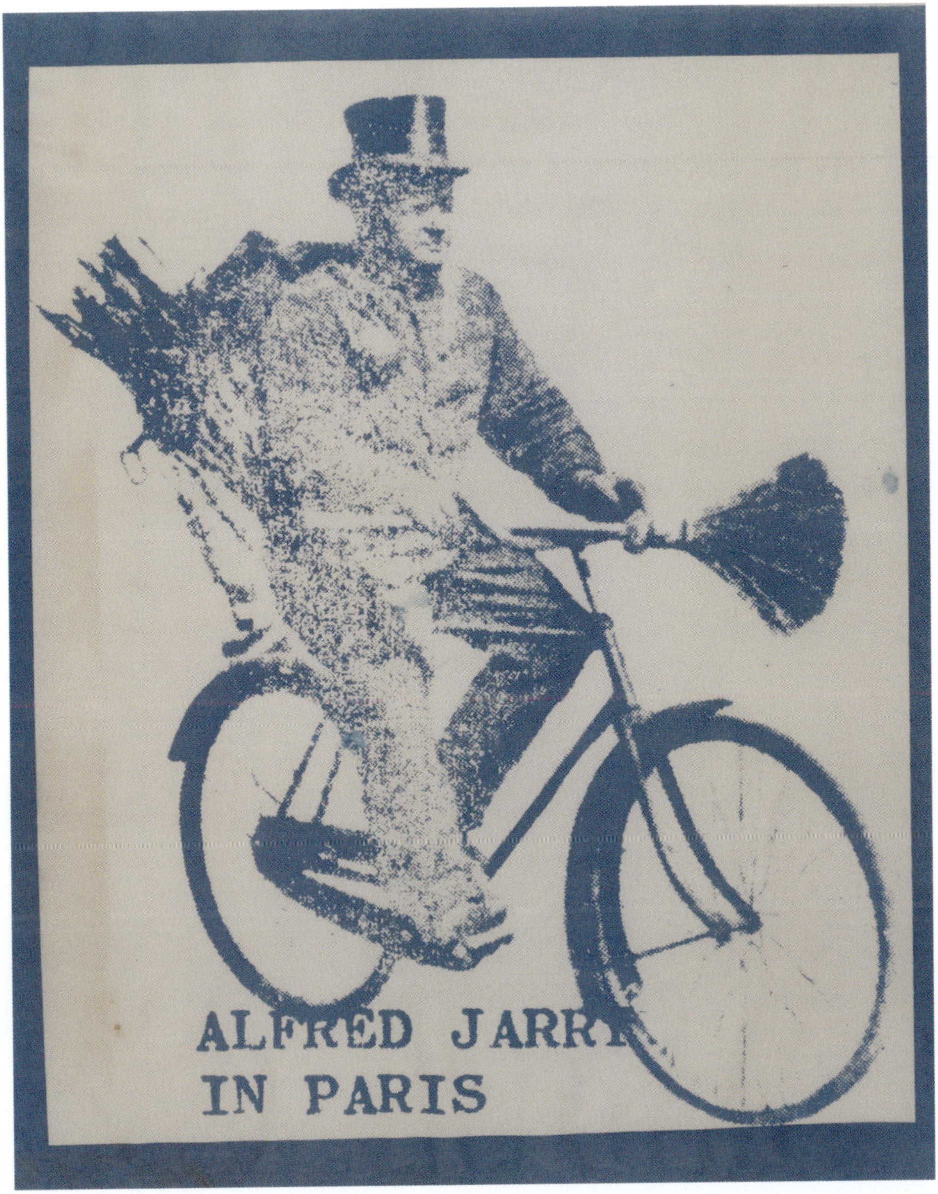
ALFRED JARRY
IN PARIS

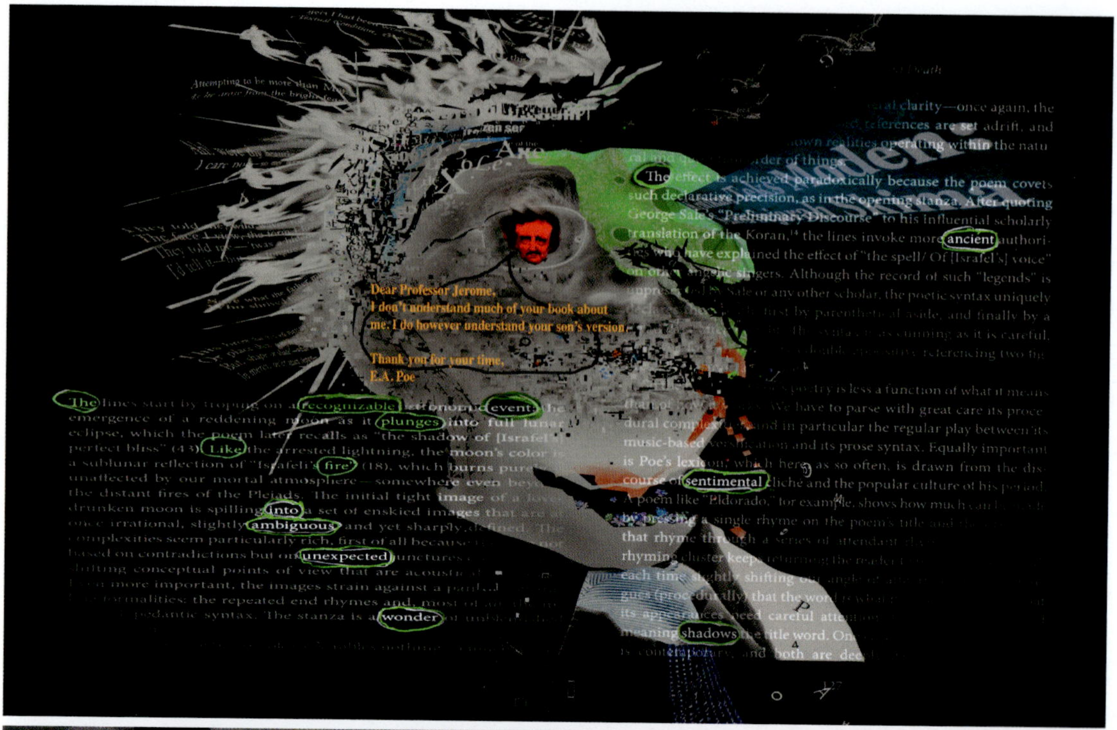

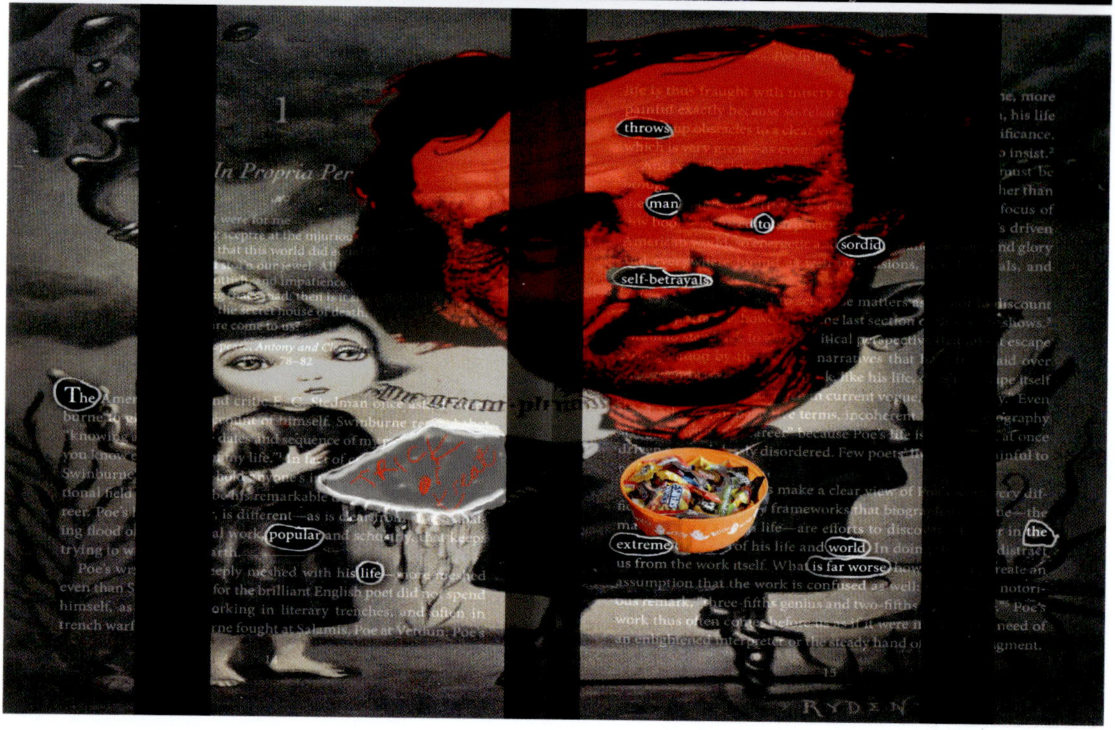

Plate 15. Geoffrey McGann, *Poe and the Professor*, from *ALIEN*, 2015. Privately printed by the artist in Los Angeles. Published with permission of the artist.

Plate 16. Geoffrey McGann, *Poe and the Saintly Child*, from *ALIEN*, 2015. Privately printed by the artist in Los Angeles. Published with permission of the artist.

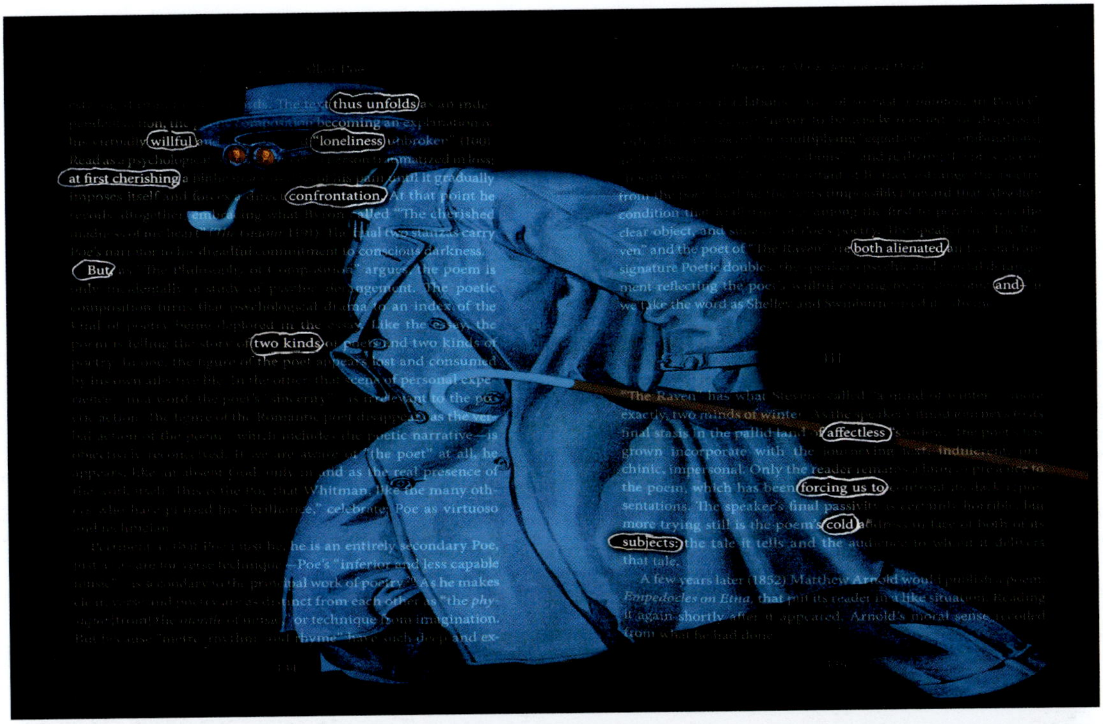

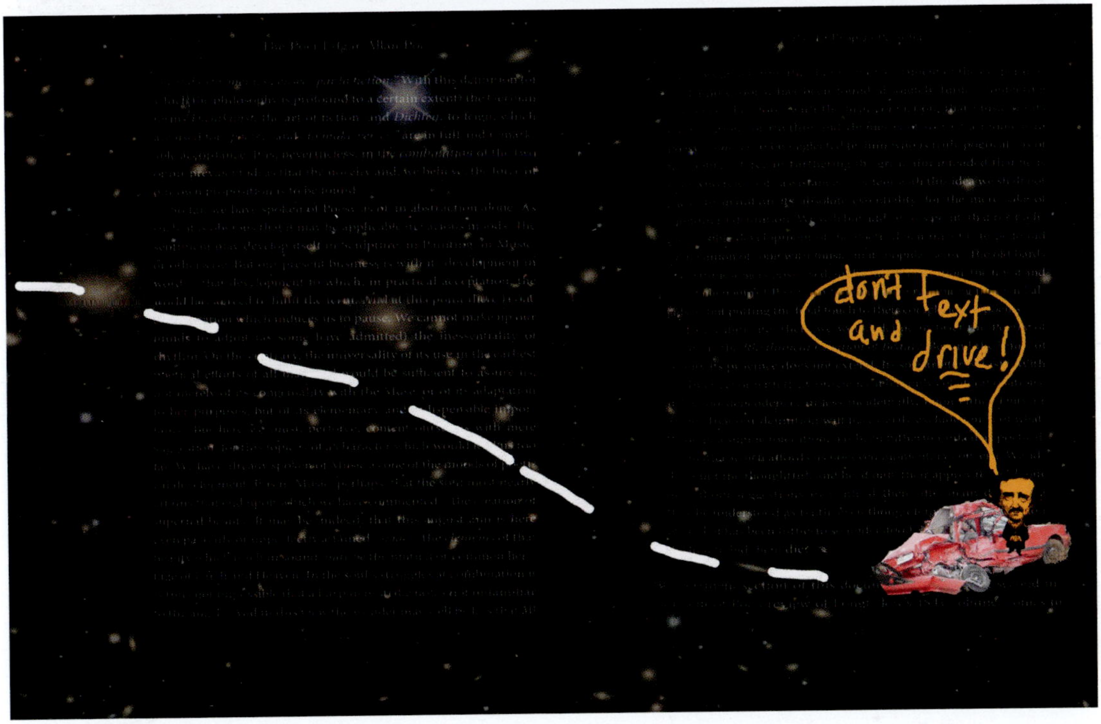

Plate 17. Geoffrey McGann, *Poe/Holmes/Marx*, from *ALIEN*, 2015. Privately printed by the artist in Los Angeles. Published with the permission of the artist.

Plate 18. Geoffrey McGann, *He Drives by Night*, from *ALIEN*, 2015. Privately printed by the artist in Los Angeles. Published with the permission of the artist.

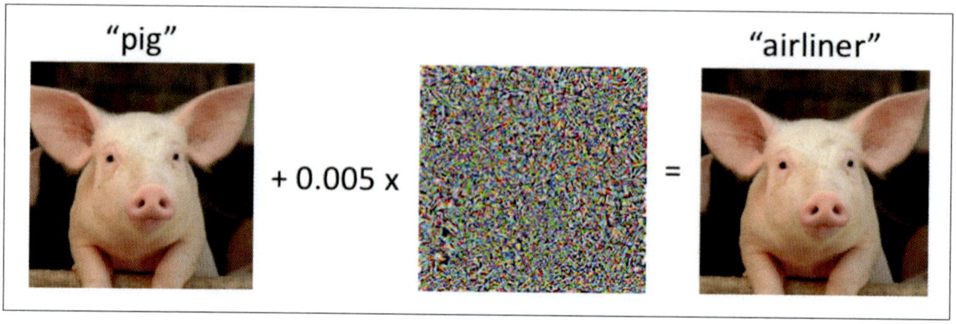

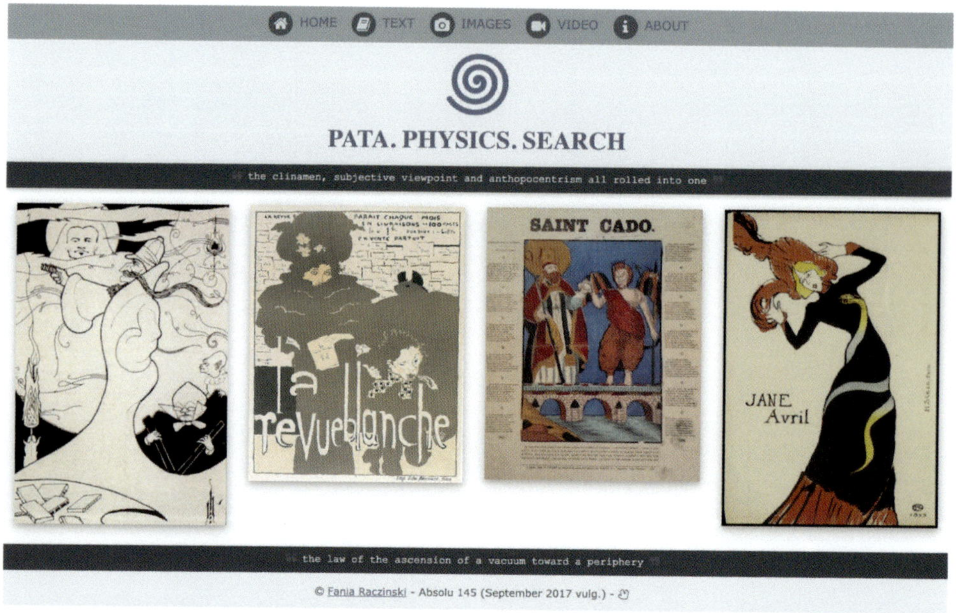

Plate 19. An example of adversarial noise confusing a deep learning system. While to the human eye the two pigs appear identical, a deep learning machine categorizes the one on the left as a pig and the one on the right (with background noise) as an airliner.

Plate 20. Screenshot of pata.physics.wtf, designed by Fania Razcinski as part of her PhD thesis, 2017. The site allows users to do pataphysical searches within one of two corpora (*Faustroll* or Shakespeare). Used with permission.

Chapter 7

Circumstantial Evidence

Pataphysical Inflexions in Edward Dorn's *Gunslinger* and bpNichol's *Probable Systems*

Steve McCaffery

I: Edward Dorn

William Anastasi has gone far in adducing the impact and influence of Alfred Jarry's ideas and writings on the work of both James Joyce and Marcel Duchamp, and this essay attempts to expand that research beyond those two giants of modernism into a more proximate era.[1] Accordingly, and with Faustrollian fortitude, I vouch it: INFLUENCE IS THE EPIPHENOMENON OF COINCIDENCE, and with that point settled I'll continue with what I hope will be a speculative contribution toward a small but important facet within the Anglophone poetic mapping of the late 1960s and 1970s, specifically Edward Dorn and bpNichol as common readers of Alfred Jarry and related pataphysicians. To enter into the speculative is to enter the quintessentially pataphysical domain where the distinction between illusion and reality no longer holds and—if, however, justification were required for this hunting down of influence and coincidence—I need only petition Harold Bloom, the Great Panjandrum of New Haven, and his meditations on the implications of that most famous of atomic phenomena, the *clinamen* or swerve:

> The *clinamen* or swerve . . . is necessarily the central working concept of the theory of Poetic Influence. . . . We must understand that the *clinamen*

stems always from a Pataphysical sense of the arbitrary. . . . Pataphysics proves to be truly accurate; in the world of poets all regularities are indeed "regular exceptions"; the *recurrence* of vision is itself a law governing exceptions. . . . Know each poem by its *clinamen* and you will "know" that poem in a way that will not purchase knowledge by the loss of the poem's power.[2]

In the case of Dorn I'll attempt to interlace a brace of aspirations: first, to demonstrate the pataphysical nature of Dorn's comic pocket epic *Gunslinger* through a pataphysical reading of many of its elements; and second, to attempt to answer the question as to whether Dorn read any texts of Alfred Jarry around the time of *Gunslinger*'s composition (*Gunslinger* appeared serially between 1968 and 1975) and, if so, do we find traces of Jarry's writings in the poem, any anxious or unanxious influence?

Brian McHale places Dorn's *Gunslinger* (what Kyle Waugh aptly terms a "narco-transgenic, serial mock epic of the postatomic American West")[3] in the largely prose tradition of Menippean satire as outlined in Mikhail Bakhtin's *Rabelais and His World*. Accordingly, McHale reads Dorn's epic of the West as a comic poem of carnivalesque humor, replete with logical inversions and delivered in a stylistically heterogeneous manner. McHale offers his own paraphrase of Bakhtin's definition:

> A Menippean text is not a single integral text, but a patchwork of texts, some juxtaposed, some inset in others, belonging to various genres, prose and poetry alike; it possesses not a single consistent style, but a multiplicity of styles, registers, dialects etc.[4]

However, the poem can equally be situated within a pataphysical tradition through its incorporation of many elements evident in Jarry's seminal 1911 neo-scientific novel *Exploits and Opinions of Dr. Faustroll, Pataphysician* and his other writings available to Dorn in English through the 1960s and 1970s.

In a paper sieve of his own imagining, Jarry arrived posthumously translated on the shores of America in the 1950s and 1960s to leave pataphysical plums, ripe for poaching and picking. Indeed, Dorn might well have discovered Jarry's writings and the imaginary science of 'pataphysics through Roger Shattuck's *The Banquet Years*, first published in 1955, with a revised paperback edition following in 1968. Two years later, in 1960, Shattuck's and Simon Watson Taylor's "What Is 'Pataphysics?" appeared as a special edition of the *Evergreen Review* containing English-language selections from *Faustroll*. Coincidences instantly appear. Among the *Evergreen Review*'s preliminary advertisements we find a full-page announcement of Donald M. Allen's *The New American Poetry, 1945–1960* containing Dorn's name among the contributors. Shattuck and Taylor's *Selected Works of Alfred Jarry*, which appeared through Grove Press in 1965, contained a broad selection from Jarry's work, including passages from the Ubu cycle, writings on the theater, poems, essays and speculations (including "How to Construct a Time Machine"), excerpts from his two novels *Days and Nights* and *Messalina,* as well as the entirety of *Faustroll.*

Jarry first introduced the term "pataphysics" in his Ubu cycle (a scatological trinity of marionette plays conceived during his school days in the late 1880s) where he describes its leading character, Pa Ubu, not only as Ex-King of Poland but also as Doctor of Pataphysics, "a branch of science which we have invented and for which a crying need is generally experienced."[5] However, the actual definition of this new branch of science is not delivered in the plays; rather the action and dialog enact it. As the science of the particular, examining the laws that govern exceptions, pataphysics is strictly regulated by two laws: those of the *syzygy* and those of the *clinamen,* both of which pertain to the broad relationship of matter to motion. In its astronomical use, *syzygy* refers to a conjunction or opposition of the systems of two planets in their orbit around a third; in its biological deployment the term denotes the conjunction of two organisms without the loss of identity. *Syzygies* make manifest those momentary oppositions and conjunctions in verbal meanings (as puns and portmanteaux, such as Jarry's famous semantic conjunction of space and time, *ether* and *eternity* in the word "ethernity"). Deriving from ancient Greek particle physics, the term *clinamen* finds mention in book 2 of the first-century Roman poet Lucretius's scientific poem *De rerum natura*:

> so that the mind itself may not be subject
> To inner necessity in what it does—
> And fetch and carry like a captive slave—
> The tiny swerve of atoms plays its part
> At unanticipated times and places[6]

However, the atomic clinamen gains its verbal counterpart when Lucretius famously compares the atomic swerve to the positioning and repositioning of alphabetic letters. For the Roman poet, atoms are to matter what letters are to words. The clinamen, then, marks an atom's deviation from its path, its aberration from a stable flow, and its consequent collision with other atoms to produce a new material formation.[7] Whereas science would work to suppress any deviance from its own regulatory laws, its deterministic logical mechanisms and Cartesian coordinates, pataphysics seeks their proliferation and operates at the very moment and place where *the law is insufficient to prevent the clinamen.* It is thus that we understand Jarry's portmanteau term "ethernity" and the (in)famous neological euphemism that is the first word spoken in Jarry's *Ubu Roi*: "Merdre!" (translated by Connolly as "Pschitt").

The term *syzygy* is explicitly mentioned in the important section of *Gunslinger* where the Slinger explains a spatiotemporal anomaly in his gunfight: the elimination of the draw.

To eliminate the draw
permits an unmatchable Speed
a syzygy which hangs tight
just back of the curtain
of the reality theater
down the street[8]

Further scrutiny of Dorn's poem reveals several syzygies between *Gunslinger* and Jarry's writings, conjunctions of incidents that are sometimes reversed but seemingly manifesting in both the poem's narrative and its linguistic element in a sufficient number to suggest Dorn drew voraciously from Jarry's texts. The theatricality of both writers is undeniable. *Gunslinger* adopts a cartoon semiology where narrative meanderings are fueled by skewed causality (what Dorn himself calls its "marvellous accidentalism" [198]).[9] At the beginning of book 2 Dorn calls the poem a "tapestry," as if underscoring its patent artifice (45). The characters and exploits of Jarry's Ubu and Faustroll, like Dorn's in *Gunslinger*, obey a cartoon semiology and illogical caprice (Faustroll, for example, is sixty-three years old at the time of his birth and never gets older).

Unlike *syzygy*, the word *clinamen* does not appear in *Gunslinger*. However, its presidential operation is felt throughout the poem. Indeed, one can interpret the narrative trajectories of both Dorn's poem and Jarry's neo-scientific novel as a journey or quest enacted through a succession of clinamina. The parallel journeys are worth summarizing.

Evicted from his home on Rue Richer, Faustroll takes up residence in an elongated waterproof sieve of his own construction. He then assembles an atomic trinity to commence his pataphysical meanderings in the sieve-skiff across the dry land of the French metropolis.[10] Faustroll invites René-Isidore Panmuphle (the main narrator and bailiff initially sent to serve a notice of eviction) and the echolalic baboon Bosse-de-Nage. Called by Jarry a "Belgian Family Robinson," they embark on a madcap itinerary of things, places, and episodes that includes the Squitty sea, the land of Lace, the forest of Love, the Amorphous Fragrant isles, the isles of Ptyx, Her (with its Cyclops and crystal swan), Cyril, and the Ringing isles.[11]

This technique of disconnected narrative and short scenarios finds its counterpart in *Gunslinger*. Like Faustroll, the Slinger accumulates a human and animal constellation that undergo a series of divergences marked by numerous episodes and devices along the swerves of the narrative. He first meets the character I (both the narrator and a character and hence the ready subject of boundless *paronomasia* throughout the poem), then successively Cocaine Lil, Claude Levi-Strauss (a "Plugged-In" talking horse), an acid freak named Kool Everything, Dr. Jean Flamboyant (who would not be out of place in Swift's Academy of Projectors in Lagado), and a drifter poet. Collectively they form a terrestrial Pleiades in a micro-macrocosmic, atomic-stellar correspondence, connecting the "inside real" to the "outsidereal" (111). A few other characters join the party, including Portland Bill, Taco Desoxin, and Tonto Pronto from Toronto. The episodes include a gunfight, the discovery of a new, counter-cinematic device, a Hill of Beans coated in rubber, the death of I and I's subsequent rebirth, a genetic louse trap, a speaking barrel, a final battle with Howard Hughes's army of mogollions and single-spacers (through most of which the Slinger sleeps), and finally the Slinger's departure on a timetrain. The poem ends anticlimactically in goodbyes: "Adiós Taco / Goodbye Tonto / and take my greetings / to the lads in Toronto" and a final five lines in Spanish (200). It is as if both authors had abandoned the calculated moves of a chess game for the hazards and *hasards* of a pinball machine. Their trajectory is decidedly nonlinear. Opening in Mesilla on the New Mexican border, the trajectory swerves when Slinger changes his quest from Boston (the purported residence of Howard Hughes and target of his pursuit) to Las Vegas (Hughes's new location).[12] The route takes the party along the Rio Grande, through Truth or Consequences (New Mexico), Cortez (Colorado), and then on to Four Corners Generating Station (near Fruitland, New Mexico), the subject of book 4.[13] This is the Slinger's "map of locations" on which the poem's mutations, dislocations, and surprises are played out (4).

These episodes remark largely terrestrial clinamina, however the swerve equally operates on the level of nomenclature. For example, the "Plugged-In" talking horse named Claude Levi-Strauss is at times called both Horse and Heidegger. The Slinger himself sometimes inclines to "Zlinger" and the poem's archvillain Howard Hughes becomes "Rupert" and "Robart." (The latter is perhaps a slight inclination away from Hughes's actual middle name, Robard.)

Let me now enumerate the coincidences, reversals, and commonalities in *Faustroll* and *Gunslinger*, videlicet:

Dead Letters

Extraterrestrial epistolary phenomena and letters from the dead figure prominently in both *Gunslinger* and *Faustroll.* Book 6, part 36, of the latter concerns a bishop reading a letter from God, and in book 8, part 37, occur two telepathic letters from the deceased Faustroll to Lord Kelvin discussing, among other things, life beyond space and time, and the precise length of a second: "Suddenly, the second was rediscovered in the absolute measure of 9,413 kilometers per mean solar second of the Siemens unit" (*Selected Works*, 250). The first letter further offers a definition of a portmanteau word worthy of the pen of Joyce: "Eternity appears to me in the image of an immobile ether, which consequently is not luminiferous. I should describe luminiferous ether as *circularly* mobile and perishable. And I deduce from Aristotle (*Treatise of the Heavens*) that it is appropriate to write ETHERNITY" (249). The term is Jarry's pataphysical formulation of the doublet that Albert Einstein and quantum physics proved to be ineluctable: the fusion of space and time. In book 2 of *Gunslinger*, after I has become a "living batch" by swallowing the entire fifty gallons of Kool Everything's LSD, the Slinger informs, "we'll send a telegram to Parmenides" (67). Book 3 concludes with a pataphysical gem: a Nightletta from the Secretary to the dead pre-Socratic philosopher is brought by a goggled deliverer dangling from a biplane on "a pure hemp line" (131). The letter is signed by a defunct character in the narrative "i" (having swerved from upper- to lowercase format). In it Dorn offers a species of "Linguatilt" (a term suggestive of the lettristic clinamen). Here is a sample

> REPORT BGX + QUAD III [2D'S—4 C'S] EARTH FOR TRANSMISSION DEEP SECTION REF. "EMISSION POSITION 9" CLEAR PAST HOURS PRESENT TIME ALIEN PLANTATIONS REVERSE SENSE EE GEE ROWS B TO Z DECADE 7 NATION 4 (140)

The parallel between the two dead figures (Faustroll and Parmenides's secretary) communicating with the living by letter is striking to say the least.

Ontological Anomaly

Jarry argues that laws in *strictus senso* are not rules at all but merely "correlations of expectations" in relation to which the anomaly is "the repressed part of a rule which ensures that the rule does not work."[14] Both Faustroll and the Slinger are ontological anomalies that ensure exceptions to the governing ontological laws of human being. The former defies growth and development and never ages, being sixty-three years old at birth and remaining so throughout his life. When Faustroll eventually dies (at the age of sixty-three), he adopts an astral body posthumously. Similarly, the Slinger is not of the human world; he remains anonymous throughout the poem, describing himself as "un semidios" (31) and confessing through his being "extraterrestrial" that he has "no practical sense of smell" (59).

Also, like Faustroll, he enjoys an extraterrestrial connection, moving "between the sun and you" (32). He announces that his departure from the poem will be "along with the tachyon showers / which are by definition faster than light / & faster than prime" (200). Equipped with an extragalactic notebook, he exists within yet beyond mortality and the control of meaning, naming, and description (the triple agents that militate against regimes of fluidity and becoming). As the anonymous Slinger informs, "it is dangerous to be named / and makes you mortal." The mortal too "can be described / the Gunslinger finished, That's all mortality is in fact" (32).

Clinamina

We know Dorn was familiar with a 1971 book by Van Rensselaer Potter, *Bioethics*, whose central thesis argued that human beings are a highly complex set of adaptive systems with intrinsic, essential elements of disorder built into it. One level of disorder is accidental genetic combinations. Potter identifies human novelty (creativity) with disorder. The genetic mutational theme is forcedly advanced by Robert von Hallberg in his essay "The Marvellous Accidentalism."[15] Genetic mutation, however, can be viewed as a sub-aspect of, or a superinducement on, that more archaic rule of declension: the clinamen. An apt example of comic mutation occurs in book 4, when the character Dr. Jean Flamboyant is described as driving "a green 1976 Avocado with a white vinyl top and full hyperbolic clutch" (*Gunslinger*, 166). An analysis of the major clinamen here reveals a swerve from fruit to automobile in the green 1976 avocado nomination, but the character's name, too, deserves pataphysical analysis: it comprises two words that carry a double function, a paronomastic syzygy in fact, with "Jean" (homophonically "gene") and "Flamboyant," a conjunction of both name and adjective.

Puns and Reversibility

Like *Faustroll*, *Gunslinger* effervesces with puns, homonymic humor, linguistic reversibility, and linguistic trapdoors sufficient to establish an authentic linguistic disorder: "Hi! Digger," a scene in a bar becomes a "bas-relief" (25), the poet refers to his guitar as an "absolute" (39), "you're in Beenville, is that a place / of the FLATULENT TENSE" (135), "Been / Bean" (136), "He's so low / he's solo" (167), "Stockholder" (27), "a notion an ocean" (55), the "Lawg" (law and log, i.e., the log[book] of the law) (113), "an appetite for apatite" (100), "aftermath that's post-numeral" (120), "looking all over the Milky Way for a Mars Bar" (124), "zeveral xeiks xilly xally in the xade" (where "x" is pronounced "sh") (179); the more sophisticated Robart's "Mogollones" that plays on "Mogollones," an ancient people, but also on "mogollon," a disordered crowd, as well as on the "mogul" status of Howard Hughes himself; and "austentic," that is, a solution of ferric carbide used in the manufacture of corrosive resistant steel but also a playful allusion to Austin, Texas (186). Examples of reversibility establish a species of palindromic ontology, a canceling reversibility: ".daeha sa kcab emas eht si I ecnis" (since I is the same back as ahead) (56). This reversibility is equally applicable to the names of Lil, "Sllab," and "EMIT NO TIME" (131, 104). *Faustroll* likewise contains a playful proliferation of odd names. "Faustroll" itself is a fusion of Goethe's "Faust" and Henrik Ibsen's "troll" (the possessor of power-knowledge and the cavernous nonhuman); there is a bull named "Shell-Bottom" (*Selected Works*, 215); the dog-faced baboon (which may or may not be a fiction of Faustroll's imagination) is named Bosse-de-Nage; and a bishop's daughter is named "Visited" and "does not survive the frequency of Priapus" (237). Puns and palindromes abound in Jarry's writings, the most famous being Ubu's "MERDRE MERDRE MERDRE M."

Speaking Barrels

Toward the end of act 2, scene 4, of *Ubu Cocu* (*Ubu Cuckolded* in Cyril Connolly's translation), the Palcontents describe the corpulent Ubu as "this barrel that rolls" (*Selected Works*, 38), and scene 5 opens with a statue of Memnon being erected with a barrel serving as its base (38–39). (A little later, in act 4, scene 1, Memnon calls for his barrel and, shortly thereafter, in scene 3, he describes the Conscience of Ubu as "like an empty barrel" [46–47]). The barrel enjoys its epiphenomenal occurrence toward the latter part of *Gunslinger* in the episode of the Speaking Barrel (187).

Machines

Both *Faustroll* and *Gunslinger* involve machines of a pataphysical (i.e., exceptional) nature. Faustroll invents a revolving Painting Machine, called the beast Clinamen, "animated inside by a system of weightless springs [that] followed its own whim in blowing onto the walls' canvas the succession of primary colors ranged according to the tubes of its stomach, like a *pousse-l'amour* in a bar, the lighter colors nearest to the surface" (*Selected Writings*, 238). The shift here from human to machinic agency and the likening of a painting to a cocktail finds a parallel reversal in Dorn's poem in the Literate Projector. Described as "a revolutionary medium," it reverses the material trajectory of cinematic word and image (from screenplay to screen) to filmstrip to word: "when a 35mm strip is put thru it / turns it into a Script / *Instantaneously*! / and projects that—the finished script / onto the white virgin screen." The Projector's potential is truly pataphysical: "it will Invent a whole new literatchure / which was Already There" (76).

Icicles

From his own copy of Rimbaud's *Illuminations*, Faustroll conjures up, into the third dimension, "the icicles hurled by the wind of God into the waters" (*Selected Writings*, 191) to reappear in *Gunslinger* as the subject of Jean Flamboyant's doctoral dissertation: *The Tensile Strength of Last Winter's Icicles* (82).

Talking Animals

Both works involve a talking animal as companion to the protagonist. To compare Bosse-de-Nage with the more human animal presence in *Gunslinger* is to evoke the pataphysical rule of equivalent opposition. Whereas the baboon, like Echo, is committed to repetition, Dorn's equine character is fully sentient and enjoys the gift of the gab. The horse, too, is the subject of volatile nomenclature, variously addressed as Horse, Claude, Claude Lévi-Strauss, and Heidegger. It is tempting to speculate that Dorn saw a pataphysical syzygy in this oppositional conjunction. For as Heidegger was the twentieth-century philosopher committed to the overthrow of metaphysics as first philosophy and its replacement by ontology, so Jarry's imaginary science studies the realms beyond metaphysics, realms less ontological than imaginary. Jarry has Faustroll go to great lengths to elaborate on Bosse-de-Nage's circumscribed vocabulary. After a cursory dismissal of the two *h*s as aspirations "never written in the ancient world," he offers an analysis of A A:

> A juxtaposed to A, with the former obviously equal to the latter, is the formula of the principle of identity; a thing is itself. It is at the same time the most excellent refutation of this very proposition, since the two A's differ in space, when we write them, if not indeed in time, just as two twins are never born together—even when issuing from the obscene hiatus of the mouth of Bosse-de-Nage.
>
> The first A was perhaps congruent to the second, and we will therefore willingly write thus: A = A.
>
> Pronounced quickly enough until the letters become confounded, it is the idea of unity.
>
> Pronounced slowly, it is the idea of duality[.] (*Selected Writings*, 228)

Rather than being a mere clone of the mythic Echo, Bosse-de-Nage enjoys doubly the status of originator and first practitioner of the great spatiotemporal episteme of poststructuralism: Derridean *différance*. As Christian Bök phrases it, "His 'tautological monosyllable' *ha ha* is a laugh track for the sophistry of *différance*, the limit of *différance*, the limit between differing and deferring."[16] In its Faustrollian explication, *ha ha* remarks the principle of duality that becomes the principle of unity when subjected to dromomechanics in the specific domain of enunciation.

Additionally, Dorn would have found an incident with talking horses toward the end of book 7, chapter 35, at the moment of Faustroll's "gesture of dying":

> The great ship Mour-de-Zencle passed like a black iron over an ironing board;
> and the echo of the sixteen horny fingers of the preterite horses whispered KHURMOOKUM beneath the vault's exit, fading away with the soul. (*Selected Writings*, 244)

A reference to a horse's head occurs in book 2 of *Gunslinger*:

> Don't lower the Horse,
> Gunslinger admonished Everything
> He has a pure Head
> It's a rare thing these days. (63)

Was Dorn familiar with Faustroll's savage negative analysis of the horse's head in book 2, chapter 27, and book 3, chapter 16, of *Faustroll*?

> Now, there is nothing in the whole world as ugly as the head of a horse, except perhaps that of a grasshopper, which is almost exactly similar without having the gigantic size of the former. . . . [T]he head alone, although I cannot define any reasons—perhaps because of the simple enormity of its teeth and the abominable rictus natural to it—is for me the sign of all ferocity, or rather the sign of death. (*Selected Writings*, 224–25)

Dorn's horse, however, partakes of a distinctly human existence. Perhaps inspired by a similar conversant *equis*, Mr. Ed, who appeared in a famous television series launched in the early 1960s, Dorn's humanoid horse, Claude Levi-Straus, aka Heidegger, talks, smokes dope, plays cards, drinks, frequents Lil's cathouse, converses, and rides a coach drawn by fellow members of his species.

Guns

Being in part a Western pastiche, Dorn's poem naturally features guns. The Slinger's own gun calls for comment. It is a .44 Colt that shoots "pure information" rather than bullets and describes rather than kills (37). Moreover, as indicated above, the Slinger increases the speed of its delivery by the elimination of the draw. Coincidence: Jarry's *Selected Works* contain his short article on the New Rifle (125–26). Like the Slinger's, his proposal involves an elimination. Where the Slinger eliminates the draw, Jarry eliminates the rifling on the barrel:

> By the mere removal of the rifling of the barrel, the range is brought within a reasonable limit to permit accurate shooting; the gun also becomes more murderous because of its increased caliber. (125)

Time

Gunslinger is famously held to be a protégé's repudiation of his master in the form of a paradigm shift from space to time. Charles Olson, in his first book, *Call Me Ishmael* (1947), boisterously proclaims space to be the central fact of the American psyche:

> I take SPACE to be the central fact to man born in America, from Folsom cave to now. I spell it large because it comes large here. Large, and without mercy. It is geography at bottom, a hell of wide land from the beginning.[17]

In the first two books of *Gunslinger*, Dorn quickly establishes time, not space, as the central quality of the present. The Slinger is a time-traveler with strong bonds to the sun. This is the contemporary condition as Dorn sees it, but it folds back to the pre-Socratics, especially Parmenides. For the Slinger, all times blend into one and the instant supersedes the sequential. Hence, during the gunfight in the Saloon, when the Slinger eliminates the draw, his action is based on pure intention. By eliminating the draw, Slinger collapses time and space into one concentrated, instant action.

Time figures centrally in Jarry's work also, and to understand its nature requires a brief excursion via Henri Bergson's thought. In his first book, *Time and Free Will: An Essay on the Immediate Data of Consciousness* (1889), a work Brotchie believes that Jarry most likely knew, Bergson rejects all established notions of linear, divisible, "clock" time on the ground that they involve spatialization of time.[18] Conventional time, he writes, is "nothing but the ghost of space haunting the reflective consciousness."[19] In their place, Bergson substitutes *durée* (duration), a condition of mental and material fluidity in which both causality and determination are abolished. As Bergson states, "Duration when restored to its original purity, will appear as a wholly qualitative multiplicity, an absolute heterogeneity of elements which pass over into each other."[20] In duration, past and present enter a unity by way of an act of memory—this remarks the "virtual" in Jarry's pataphysical elements, and it is Brotchie's contention that "duration was Bergson's own "imaginary solution" to epistemological problems that will "return philosophy to common sense."[21] Dorn has the Slinger depart in a "timetrain" faster than both the speed of light and prime; he would have found in *Selected Works* "How to Construct a Time Machine," where Jarry also advances the proposal that time might be thought of as the fourth dimension of space (114–21). The machine is so designed as to conserve its contents outside of time, sheltered from all phenomena, isolating duration and permitting temporal reversibility. One of bpNichol's pataphysical inventions is such a machine.

II: bpNichol

In contrast to Dorn, Jarry's influence on the late Canadian poet bpNichol is palpably evident and far from circumstantial. bpNichol was a cofounder of the Canadian College of ''Pataphysics in 1979 and cosignatory (with me, under the moniker of the Toronto Research Group) of the "Introduction-Manifesto" in the special double issue of the magazine *Open Letter* devoted to Canadian ''Pataphysics.[22] The fact that bpNichol was the conceiver and creator of the ''Pataphysical Hardware Company seems an additional endorsement of him as what Christian Bök terms a Canadian "Jarryite." bpNichol became aware of Jarry circa 1960 through the May–June 1960 issue of *Evergreen Review*, and his reflections on pataphysics first emerge in print in his 1984 essay "The 'Pata of Letter Feet, or, the English Written Character as a Medium for Poetry."[23] In it, bpNichol reductively defines "the literature of ''pataphysics" as "serious wit" and additionally erroneously equates "metaphysics" with "ontology" (353). Misprisions apart, bpNichol productively argues for a triple reality in the poetic realm:

> Poetry has its physical reality, its metaphysical reality and its ''pataphysical reality and, in my experience as a writer, it's at the interface between the eye the ear and the mouth, the two suddenly see/hear the real ''pata of poetic feet. (354)

The fusion of eye, ear, and mouth occurs in the phenomenon of notation, that is, "the conscious act of noting things down for the voice . . . instructing the eye on the movement of the tongue for the pleasure of the ear" (354). As well as a coordinated phenomenon, bpNichol's notation is grounded in a thoroughly material poetics in which writing is conceived fundamentally as a scriptive action upon a surface, and it is only a social *doxa* that causes writers to treat it otherwise (as "blank," "white, "8½ × 11") (355). Most importantly, bpNichol's exposure to pataphysics led him into a singular theorization of paranomasia as pataphysical logic. In the essay he elaborates the pataphysical dimension within the single word "notation":

> There is *no* tation the word erases itself. No it doesn't. Well, yes it does but only if i read it that way. And that's not real. Except, of course, that it is real. i can literally point to it—no tation. So i'm pointing to something which is erasing itself even as I point to it. And that's important too because that phenomenon is one of the identifying features of the "pataphysical that even as you say it exists you know it doesn't exist and even as you know it doesn't exist you see that it exists and so on. Thus one is led through a chain of "pataphysical logic where each step cohered only for the length of the transition and then disintegrates, disappears behind you, even as a new, unexpected step it too disappears & you never make it. (354)

Whether bpNichol's pataphysics can be included *strictus senso* in Jarry's definition of 'pataphysics is a moot point. Indeed, bpNichol's logic takes the form of a scissiparity performed at the level of primary articulation, where a separation is simultaneously denied and asserted: "no tation." However, the rhythm of emergence and disappearance, central to bpNichol's ""pataphysical logic," accurately describes the rhythm of the brief chapters in *Faustroll* that take the reader from the Castle Errant by a junk to the Isle of Ptyx, onward to the Isle of Her, the Cyclops, and the Great Swan that is of Crystal, to the Isle of Cyril and the Great Church of Snoutfigs.

Alongside Jarry, bpNichol speaks of René Daumal (1908–1944) as being a pataphysical influence on him. So let me navigate that tributary in a sieve of my own making. A disciple of George Gurdjieff and trained in Sanskrit, Daumal shared a literary temperament close to Gérard de Nerval's and became associated with a nonpartisan surrealism through his editing of *Le Grand Jeu*. However, Shattuck has traced the distinct influence of Jarry's imaginary science on the younger French writer in his introduction to Daumal's unfinished, posthumously published novel, *Mount Analogue*:

> One of [Daumal's] most brilliant demonstrations, called the "Falsehood of Truth," isolates *error* as the principle of creation and existence, for one tiny truth would obliterate the entire universe by its wonder. This advanced sense of cosmic humour has no other name than Jarry's term, pataphysics.[24]

Daumal's remarkable fragment provides ample evidence to substantiate Shattuck's claim. Indeed, *Mount Analogue* is redolent with pataphysical atmospherics. The very name of the book's protagonist, Father Pierre Sogol (like Dorn's "Sllab," arrived at via an obvious pataphysical reversal of Logos), and several other names in the book, suggest the regime of the exception. For example, the vessel carrying them to the mountain-continent is named *The Impossible*; Sogol's cook is called Physics; and members of the expedition include Ivan Lapse, Judith Pancake (an American painter of mountains), Arthur Beaver (a British inventor among other qualities) and Benito Cicoria (a Hegelian tailor). The motley crew seems constructed to conform to the law of the particular, and the quest of the journey itself, Mount Analogue, is a pataphysical exception par excellence. Being larger than any known mountain on the globe and with a base the size of Australia, it remains invisible owing to the curvature of space and the resultant deflection of light rays. Moreover, the mode of approach to the mountain is quintessentially pataphysical and governed by the law of the distinctly egregious:

> To find a way of reaching the island, one must assume the possibility and even the *necessity* of reaching it. The only admissible hypothesis is that the "shell of curvature" which surrounds the island is not absolutely *for everyone*. At a *certain moment* out in a *certain place, certain persons* (those who know how and wish to do so) can enter. (52)

There is a parallel inventiveness of pataphysical endeavor in both *Faustroll* and Daumal's narrative. In chapter 3 Pierre Sogol attempts to measure the power of human thought as an absolute value:

> "This power," Sogol said, "is arithmetical. In reality every thought represents a capacity to grasp the divisions of a whole. Now, numbers are nothing else than the divisions of a unity, which is to say *the division of any whole whatever*. In myself and in others I began to observe how many numbers a man really can conceive, that is to say, can carry in his mind without breaking them down or writing them out; how many successive consequences of a principle he can grasp at once, instantaneously; how any inclusions of species within genus; how many relations of cause to effect, of means to end. And I never found the number to be greater than four." (63)

Among Sogol's "satanic devices" is

> a pen for facile writers which spattered or blotted every five minutes; a tiny portable phonograph, equipped with an earpiece like those on hearing aids and which would cry out at the most unexpected moments: "Who do you think you are?"; a pneumatic cushion [that Sogol calls] "the soft pillow of doubt" and which deflates unexpectedly under the sleeper's head; a mirror whose curvature was designed . . . so as to reflect any human face like a pig's head. (32)

This practical blend of Faustrollian bachelor mechanics and Robinson Crusoe is complemented by Arthur Beaver's own inventiveness; he fabricates, for example, a "portable kitchen garden" connected to an ingenious respiratory mechanism (64).

These devices and inventions are surely one inspiration behind bpNichol's own merchandise offered for sale in his "Pataphysical Hardware Company. Founded in 1944 (the year of bpNichol's birth and, coincidentally, Daumal's death) and first manifesting, complete with printed catalog, in May 1985 as part of the Toronto-hosted *L'Affaire Pataphysique*, the company purported to offer "everything for your imaginary needs." Without a doubt, the "Pataphysical Hardware Company illustrates bpNichol's own pataphysical prankishness at its most ludic. This is immediately evident in the categorization of the products into series: "Speech & Thot," "Hardware," "Concepts," "Reference," "Leisure Living," and even a "Non Series." The catalog lists a total of twenty-seven items (as wells as zero in the Non Series). Items listed for the pataphysically needy include inflatable party bubbles with bespoke phrases printed on them (literal speech balloons), called Thought Balloons; a double-ended pencil; and "A Night on the Town" that comprises a bag full of talcum powder labeled "Plaster de Paris" (alluding no doubt to Jarry's national capital).

However, bpNichol's most pataphysical thinking (as opposed to factured commodities and ideas for commodities) is undoubtedly embodied in his Probable Systems: instantiations—often dazzling—of pataphysical cognition. Many are gathered in two volumes: *zygal: A Book of Mysteries and Translations* (1985) and *Art Facts: A Book of Contexts* (1990); some are not "systems" at all but simply readymade objects recontextualized and renamed à la Duchamp. For example, "Probable Systems 16: a device for measuring the signified," is a water glass with pictures of four animals (a camel, a donkey, a pig, and a hen) on the surface of the glass. Such mass commodities appropriated to pataphysics would not be out of place in either the "Leisure Living" or "Hardware" offerings in the "Pataphysical Hardware Company catalog. Other "systems" read as ludic logic applied to letter sequences within certain words that can be opened to expose hypo-significations. For example, the ending of "probable systems 13: text o' deduction" from 1973:

> if l is on g
> & l is in e
> and since s is in e (as we have already seen)
> & s is on g
> then s & l (- e & e is on g
>
> now since e is one g & f lies between e & g
> then the meaning of the alphabetic sequence 'e f g' becomes clear[25]

Such an application of what I will call "lettristic patalogic," a logic devised to reveal hidden sentences in single words, leads easily into the linguistic insanity that Jean

Jacques Lecercle terms "Brissetism."[26] If f is h and w is h then either I must wish for fish or believe wishing and fishing to be identical.

One of bpNichol's contributions to the Canadian 'Pataphysics issue of *Open Letter* was an early system (Probable System 14) conceived in 1972 and unpublished until this issue (Winter 1980–81). In its skull-melting analyses, "Re-discovery of the 22 letter alphabet. An Archaeological report" exudes the influence not only of Jarry, but also the English mystic Alfred Kallir, whose *Sign and Design: The Psychogenetic Source of the Alphabet* appeared in an English translation in 1961, a copy of which bpNichol is known to have owned. (He lent it to me for a couple of weeks, and I live to regret my returning it to its rightful owner.) bpNichol's obsession with the individual letter is well known, but the reference of the letters' history via Kallir is not. Here's the simple formula italicized: *You look at letters and fiction begins*. In a curious blend of Carl Jung, Cratylus, Hugo, and Daumal, Kallir offers a highly moot and speculative theory on the psychogenetic development of the alphabet from a matrix of primordial signs present in a collective unconscious, that sequentially encode a magic chain of procreative symbols destined to safeguard the human race.[27] The signs themselves derive from a multiplicity of body parts and objects: arm, penis, breast, house, mountain. No doubt bpNichol would have been attracted to Kallir's theory of the pictographic origin of letters, as well to the holistic nature of the speculations that argued for both a graphic and phonic Cratylism (as I will explain). Kallir, however, laminates an elaborate psychosexual narrative on his theory. The first letter "A," for example, has the literal interpretation of a flipped, frontal view of an ox's head, an image of virility that further carries in the horns the pictograph of the male member and all its procreative and inseminatory associations. Similarly, the second letter "B" carries the image of the feminine, the breasts and belly clearly depicted in the double curvilinear shape of the letter; "C" depicts the womb open for impregnation; "D" is the growing womb; "G" the act of penetration. On the later alphabetic characters, Kallir theorizes a link between the letter Y and V, treating the former as a variant of the V; it is similarly seen as a tree symbol and linked to the T shape as an arboreal proto-sign, not to mention to the female genitalia, with both mimographic and mimophonic V, as in cunnilingus, cuneiform. Such analyses bear juxtaposing with Faustroll's extended and profound reflection on the phrase "ha ha" and, in comparison, Kallir's thinking can be readily endorsed as pataphysical.

Many of the earlier Probable Systems are gathered in the 1985 collection *zygal: A Book of Mysteries and Translations*.[28] The first, subtitled "thot probes," dates from late 1970 and comprises five stacked permutations. The first is the most complex:

AR
eAR
ARt

heAR
heARt
heARth
AR[29]

Doubtless the one closest to Jarry's own spirit is Probable Systems 10, "a time machine." After establishing a number of parallel and intersecting time-life time-lines, bpNichol presents two intersecting and one connecting line marked at their terminals as F G and A E respectively; the shorter line connecting the two others is designated at its tips A Z. Then follows a dazzling display of numerical calculations before the following conclusion: "on october 1 1967 R-Z actually traveled forward to august 15 1970 intersecting with F-G at the same time F-G of course traveled into the past to october 1867."[30] bpNichol's "probable systems 4" (dedicated to "James Joyce in his worst bummer") draws heavily on the Jewish mystical practice of Gematria.

faith
= 6 + 1 + 9 + 20 + 8
= 44
= 8 + 15 + 16 + 5
= hope[31]

The operative letter-number equation here is what bpNichol calls "Base Alphabet," where A is assigned a numerical value of 1 through Z with the value of 26. This in itself is a variant on the Kabbalistic and Hebraic practice of assigning letters numerical values, thereby opening up the possibility of a poetical mathematics. Two further examples come from bpNichol's posthumously published 1990 collection *Art Facts: A Book of Contexts*. In Probable Systems 22 "translation (a continuation of PS 11)," which is in part a pataphysical translation of Daumal's 1938 poem "Origine de l'Astronomie," bpNichol makes the proposal that a word can be considered as the complex expression of a single letter.[32] Probable Systems 23 (composed in spring 1975) is either a homage to, or parody of, Noam Chomsky's phrase structure diagrams. The chains operate by way of a sound —> semantic homophonics, as two branches will indicate:

c —> sea —> see—> a c that sees the sea
u —> you —> ewe—> you and your ewe and your u[33]

There are ample intimations in Jarry to ignite bpNichol's fascination with exploring the pataphysics of the single letter, word permutation, letter accretion/removal, and lettristic meditation like the ones above. One will serve as my valedictory example. In book 8, chapter 39, in the "Fragment of the Dialogue upon the Erotic," Ibicrates offers the following analysis of bpNichol's famously favorite letter, H:

The juxtaposition of the two signs of the binary and ternary gives the shape of the letter H, which is Chronos, father of Time and Life, and thus embraces mankind. For the Geometer, these two signs cancel each other out or impregnate each other, and there results simply their progeny, which becomes egg or zero, all the more identical because they are contrary." (*Selected Writings*, 52)

Adios!

Notes

1. See, for instance, William Anastasi, "Jarry in Duchamp" and "Jarry and Joyce" in *William Anastasi's Pataphysical Society: Jarry, Joyce, Duchamp, and Cage*, ed. Aaron Levy and Jean-Michel Rabaté (Philadelphia: Slought Foundation Contemporary Arts, 2005), 32–52.

2. Harold Bloom, *The Anxiety of Influence* (Oxford, UK: Oxford University Press, 1973), 42–43.

3. Edward Dorn, *Abilene! Abilene! A Variorum Edition with Appendices and Commentary*, ed. Kyle Waugh, CUNY Lost and Found Poetics Document Initiative Series 4, no. 2, part 1 (New York: CUNY Press, 2013), 1.

4. Brian McHale, *The Obligation Toward the Difficult Whole: Postmodernist Long Poems* (Tuscaloosa: University of Alabama Press, 2004), 71.

5. Alfred Jarry, *Selected Works of Alfred Jarry*, ed. Roger Shattuck and Simon Watson Taylor (New York: Grove Press, 1965), 27 (hereafter cited parenthetically in the text).

6. Lucretius, *De rerum natura*, trans. W. H. D. Rouse, Loeb Classic Library (Cambridge, MA: Harvard, University Press, 1975), 113.

7. See Alastair Brotchie, *Alfred Jarry: A Pataphysical Life* (Cambridge, MA: MIT Press, 2011), 31. Brotchie traces the origins of pataphysics to Jarry's time as a student in Paris at the Lycée Henri IV, where Henri Bergson was a lecturer. Jarry attended the philosopher's classes on philosophy, fastidiously transcribing the philosopher's often improvisatory and digressive lectures into small green notebooks. Jarry would have been introduced to Lucretius's theory of the atomic clinamen in Bergson's lecture on determinism.

8. Edward Dorn, *Gunslinger* (Durham, NC: Duke University Press, 1989), 30 (hereafter cited parenthetically in the text).

9. See also Robert G. Eisenhauer, *Paradox and Perspicacity: Horizons of Knowledge in the Literary Text* (New York: Peter Lang, 2005), 123. For his part, Eisenhauer describes "marvelous [*sic*] accidentalism" as a condition "where reference or *depth* of reference is uncertain, and representation is subject to abrupt shifts of subtext." The shifts here, of course, are examples of clinamina.

10. This absence of water is dominant at the very opening of *Faustroll* when Faustroll opts to take his sponge bath not in water but in a receptacle filled with two-toned wallpaper painted by Maurice Denis.

11. It might be worth noting that Jarry's *Selected Works* also reprints another "Belgian" topic, "Virgin and Manneken-Pis," the latter being the statue-fountain of a small child urinating into the fountain's basin that Jarry saw in Brussels. In Jarry's pataphysical narrative, "the good Father Prout" plans to convert "by an ingenious system of ducts" all statues of the Virgin and Child into Virgin and Manneken-Pis (129). It is surely Jarry's short episode that is the inspiration behind Duchamp's *Fountain*.

12. It may be a mere coincidence but Mesilla was declared a state monument on September 10, 1967.

13. The coal-fired power plant was built on land leased from the Navajo Nation. It comprised five units and was constructed between 1963 and 1970.

14. Christian Bök, *'Pataphysics the Poetics of an Imaginary Science* (Evanston, IL: Northwestern University Press, 2002), 38.

15. Robert von Hallberg, "The Marvellous Accidentalism," in *Internal Resistances: The Poetry of Edward Dorn*, ed. Donald Wesling (Berkeley: University of California Press, 1985), 45–86.

16. Bök, *'Pataphysics*, 42.

17. Charles Olson, *Call Me Ishmael* (London: Jonathan Cape, 1967), 15.

18. Brotchie, *Alfred Jarry*, 31.

19. Henri Bergson, *Time and Free Will: An Essay on the Immediate Data of Consciousness* (1889), trans. F. L. Pogson (Mineola, NY: Dover Books, 2001), 99.

20. Quoted in Brotchie, *Alfred Jarry*, 31–32.

21. Ibid., 32.

22. "Canadian "Pataphysics," ed. Toronto Research Group, special issue, *Open Letter*, nos. 6–7 (Winter 1980–81).

23. bpNichol, "The 'Pata of Letter Feet, or, the English Written Character as a Medium for Poetry," *Open Letter*, 6th. ser., vol. 6, no. 1 (1985): 79–95, reprinted in bpNichol, *Meanwhile: The Critical Writings of bpNichol*, ed. Roy Miki (Vancouver: Talonbooks, 2002), 353–72 (hereafter cited parenthetically in the text).

24. René Daumal, *Mount Analogue* (1959), trans. Roger Shattuck (San Francisco: City Lights Books, 1968), 9–10 (hereafter cited parenthetically in the text).

25. bpNichol, *zygal: A Book of Mysteries and Translations* (Vancouver: Talonbooks, 1985), 106.

26. See Jean-Jacques Lecercle, *Philosophy Through the Looking Glass* (La Salle, IL: Open Court, 1985).

27. Alfred Kallir, *Sign and Design: The Psychogenetic Source of the Alphabet* (London: J. Clarke, 1961). Kallir's book is notoriously difficult to obtain. However his speculations on the psychogenetic origins of the letter "B" can be found in full in Jed Rasula and Steve McCaffery, eds., *Imagining Language* (Cambridge, MA: MIT Press, 1998), 401–10.

28. *Zygal* published Probable Systems 1 through 10, *art facts* 17 through 26.

29. bpNichol, *zygal*, 31.

30. Ibid., 92.

31. Ibid., 48.

32. See bpNichol, *art facts*, 108. A note at the end informs that it was written over a period of four years (1971–74) with additional research toward a final draft in November 1986.

33. Ibid., 138.

Chapter 8

Beyond "Maxwell's Silver Hammer"

Pataphysics and Popular Music

Marcus O'Dair

The link between Alfred Jarry and popular music might not be immediately apparent. Jarry died in 1907 and, while he did pen a few songs, his reputation is primarily as a writer. Yet, as Andrew Hugill points out, Jarry made numerous references to music; for Hugill, music was part of Jarry's work at all levels.[1] And while pataphysics may have started as a literary phenomenon, it influenced music—as well as cinema, the visual arts, theater, and digital media. A number of popular musicians have made explicit reference to Jarry and pataphysics in their band names, in album and track titles, in lyrics, and in interviews and other public statements. Perhaps most famously, the Beatles referred to pataphysics in their track "Maxwell's Silver Hammer," from *Abbey Road*. Paul McCartney was reportedly inspired to write the song after hearing a BBC broadcast of Jarry's *Ubu Cocu* in 1966, which he described as "the best radio play I had ever heard in my life."[2]

The truth is, however, that "Maxwell's Silver Hammer" is not a particularly pataphysical piece of music. It is the argument of this chapter that the work of those popular musicians who explicitly reference Jarry may not, in fact, be the most indebted to pataphysics. At the same time, I argue that Jarry has had a profound influence on popular music (broadly defined, including not only "pop" but the left field, experimental, and avant-garde, some of which is not very popular at all). This influence can be detected in three main areas: words, music, and performance.

While there is a good deal of scholarship on the influence on popular music of other literary movements such as Romanticism there is little work on the influence on popular music of pataphysical literature. Before analyzing this influence in relation to specific popular musicians including Robert Wyatt, Peter Blegvad, Pere Ubu, Frank Zappa, Captain Beefheart, and the Residents, I first examine those who, like the Beatles, make some direct reference to Jarry and his influence. I then analyze those who, while they do not claim to have been influenced by Jarry, do in fact show signs of his influence in their work. Following the convention that 'pataphysics (with apostrophe) refers to conscious identification with Jarry,[3] we can think of these two groups as popular music 'pataphysicians and popular music pataphysicians. All things may be pataphysical, but few practice 'pataphysics consciously.[4]

Pataphysicians avec Apostrophe: Popular Musicians Who Directly Reference Jarry

As I go on to argue, some artists who claim Jarry's influence have indeed made music that could be considered pataphysical. As with the Beatles, however, this is not always the case. Artists claiming Jarry's influence include those who make references in their very names: the Australian MC and producer Pat Marks, who uses the stage name Pataphysics; the American ambient musician Faustroll; and the French progressive rock band Pataphonie.[5] Other artists claiming Jarry's influence make references in album titles: *Pataphysical Music* by the Institute of High Speed Art; *Pataphysical Graffiti* by Le Sans Culottes; *Ubu* by Yojiro Noda; *Pataphysics* by Koji Marutani; *Clinamen Episteme* by Inquisitor; and *The Sisters of Pataphysics* by Nurse with Wound. Two different acts—the improvisational trio made up of Giovanni Di Domenico, Arve Henriksen, and Tatsuhisa Yamamoto, and the metal act Love Lies Bleeding—have released albums titled *Clinamen*. Finally, there are popular musicians who refer to pataphysics in the names of particular tracks, among them post-punk band the Fall; Japanese trio Mouse on the Keys; Rock in Opposition band Henry Cow; and industrial duo Coil. And this is to cite only those who reference Jarry and pataphysics in their band names and/or track and album titles. Others, such as space-rock band Hawkwind with "Silver Machine," have written songs inspired by Jarry.[6]

In addition to artists who make overt reference to pataphysics in specific tracks or albums, numerous others self-identify as inspired by Jarry in interviews or other published statements: for instance, German electronica band Farmer's Manual; American singer-songwriter Tim Reed, who performs as the Reverend Dr. Fred Lane; Austrian musician and producer Tomoroh Hidari; Norbert Stein, who runs the record label Pata-Music; the artist, writer, and musician Paul D. Miller, better known as DJ Spooky; American singer and composer Karen Mantler; and John White, described by Hugill as almost a composer in residence for the London

Institute of 'Pataphysics. Hugill himself is also a composer—and an avowedly pataphysical one.[7]

In truth, the influence of pataphysics on the artists cited above is not always clear: claims to have been influenced by Jarry may say more about those making the claim than about Jarry himself. As a cited influence, Jarry is appealing in at least three respects. Firstly, Jarry had a proto-rock-star life and early death. Roger Shattuck, for instance, depicts Jarry's short life as a slow "suicide by hallucination"[8] and suggests that Jarry's premature death represented something akin to an act of literary martyrdom.[9] Secondly, since Jarry was primarily a writer rather than a musician, one can cite him as influence without being accused of copying his melodies or chord changes.

Thirdly, referencing Jarry and pataphysics allows popular musicians to present themselves as au fait with "high" culture while simultaneously engaged in producing a "low" cultural form such as popular music, thereby signaling a Jarryesque disregard for cultural hierarchies. Writing and popular music, after all, have different cultural values and power, and there are "rancid prejudices" around their relative cultural value.[10] For some, pataphysics is simply a byword for experimentation and leftfield work.[11] Andrew Jones's book *Plunderphonics, 'Pataphysics and Pop Mechanics*, for instance, is "remarkably silent on one word in the title: 'pataphysics."[12] Farmers Manual, although describing themselves as pataphysical, are not really able to justify such a categorization,[13] and the same might be said of numerous other artists who describe themselves in the same way. In fact, Jarry's influence on popular music is in some respects more evident in those who do not explicitly claim him as an influence; since that influence is often indirect, these artists may not even be aware that they are affected by it. They are, in other words, pataphysicians sans apostrophe.

Pataphysicians sans Apostrophe: Jarry's Indirect Influence on Popular Music

Given that Dadaism, surrealism, Fluxus, Situationism, futurism, and the Theater of the Absurd all owe a debt to pataphysics,[14] Jarry's indirect influence on popular music is profound as well as diffuse. We might regard American indie band the Magnetic Fields, named after the proto-surrealist text by André Breton and Philippe Soupault,[15] as indirectly in Jarry's debt. Musicians inspired by Dada, meanwhile, include the band Cabaret Voltaire, who took their name from the Zurich nightclub synonymous with the movement;[16] Masami Akita, whose stage name, Merzbow, derives from Kurt Schwitters;[17] and Talking Heads, whose track "I Zimbra" is made up of nonsense syllables originally written and performed as sound poetry by Hugo Ball.[18] Since Fluxus artists took inspiration from Dada,[19] Jarry also indirectly influenced Yoko Ono and, through John Cale, the Velvet Underground.[20] Since the term "art brut" was actually coined by Jean Dubuffet,[21] a member of the *Collège de 'Pataphysique*, we can trace back to Jarry not only the band of that name, fronted by Eddie Argos, but the whole notion of outsider art.[22] Jarry influenced the Situationists,[23] seen as having influenced various strands of popular music, from punk[24] and post-punk[25] to acid house duo the KLF[26] and those artists considered psychogeographic.[27] Jarry also influenced Italian futurists such as F. T. Marinetti,[28] something that fed into popular music most obviously through the label ZTT, which took its name from Marinetti's sound-poem *Zang Tumb Tuum*.[29] The list goes on—for so long, in fact, that it can seem as though Jarry had an indirect influence on almost all subsequent music, as well as on visual art and literature. As John Cage suggests, "everyone was influenced by Jarry."[30]

Even if Jarry did influence "everyone," his influence is often indirect. Many of those in his debt do not declare it; not all will even be conscious of it. In an attempt to show more concrete examples of Jarry's influence, I now go on to examine the influence of pataphysics on specific popular musicians. Some, such as Robert Wyatt (both as a solo artist and with his bands Soft Machine and Matching Mole) and Peter Blegvad (in particular on the 1977 album *Kew. Rhone.*, a collaboration with John Greaves), are self-declared Jarry devotees: 'pataphysicians avec apostrophe. Blegvad acknowledges Jarry's influence on his work;[31] indeed, he went on to become president of the London Institute of 'Pataphysics.[32] Wyatt has been a Jarry fan since Soft Machine performed a live soundtrack to Jarry's *Ubu Enchaîné* in 1967, after which they declared themselves the "official orchestra of the College of 'Pataphysics."[33] Wyatt soon took to wearing the *gidouille* logo on his hat and bass drum, and a copy of Jarry's collected works still sits on his bookshelf today.

Jarry's influence is not only evident, however, on such self-declared fans. I also examine Jarry's influence on popular music's pataphysicians sans apostrophe, including Frank Zappa, the Residents, and Don Van Vliet, better known as Captain Beefheart. Nigey Lennon, closely associated with Zappa for a period in the 1970s, was influenced by Jarry, and Hugill states that most of Zappa's output may be viewed as pataphysical, albeit not explicitly labeled as such. Both the Residents and Captain Beefheart, Hugill continues, were "clearly aware of 'pataphysics and worked it into their output," although "in a freewheeling sort of way that was inspired more by its spirit of nonconformity than by the letter of the written words."[34] After Barthes,[35] it may not matter whether Zappa, Beefheart, or the Residents saw themselves as influenced by pataphysics: the corollary of the death of the author is the birth of the reader (or listener). If readers and listeners are free to find authority where they choose, regardless of authorial intention, then these artists can be considered as pataphysical as Pere Ubu. This pataphysical aspect takes three main forms: words, music, and performance.

Pataphysical Popular Music: Jarry's Influence on Words

The first area in which we can discern Jarry's influence on popular music is words. Specifically, we can detect a pataphysical influence on popular musicians who engage in self-reflexivity, embrace scatology, voluntarily submit to linguistic constraints, and use words as game objects.

This Is the First Verse: Self-Reflexivity and What Is Being Sung

On the track "Gharbzadegi," from his *Old Rottenhat* album, Wyatt sings a line about words taking the place of meaning over and over until the line itself begins to lose semantic sense.[36] Elliott describes self-reflexivity as a Wyatt specialty,[37] and Paul Hegarty agrees that Wyatt is forever returning to the question of what is being sung.[38] Likewise, "Moon in June" from Soft Machine's 1970 album *Third* is a "self-reflexive deconstruction of the song," in that the lyrics refer to the song's own structure. The version of "Moon in June" recorded for the BBC's *Top Gear* program was even more self-reflexive: Wyatt adapted the lyrics to refer, for instance, to the tea machine down the corridor. "O Caroline" from Matching Mole's self-titled debut album is also self-reflexive, acknowledging in its lyrics that the listener might dismiss the song as overly sentimental. The epitome of self-reflexivity in Wyatt's oeuvre might be "Signed Curtain," also from *Matching Mole*: almost every line refers to the song's structure (first verse, chorus, bridge, key change).[39] In these songs, Wyatt is continuing Jarry's self-reflexive approach to language.[40]

Fast 'n' Bulbous: Scatology and the Joyously Perverse

Many pataphysical lyrics are joyously perverse as well as self-reflexive. The more scatological can be traced back to the French word *potache*, referring to adolescent schoolboy humor. As Brotchie notes, "Jarry played the [adolescent schoolboy] role with particular verve and conviction, and was loath to renounce it, even in adulthood."[41] A "delightfully vulgar wit" is identified by Jones as one reason we might consider the French group Etron Fou Leloublan pataphysical, pointing out that even their name is a pun that translates as something like "mad shit the white wolf."[42] The Coil album that features the track "Ubu Noir" is actually called *Scatology*; subject matter for Coil, meanwhile, included "the dubious pleasures of being lashed to a toilet bowl."[43] There is also a *potache* element in Captain Beefheart's *Trout Mask Replica*: Hegarty describes the album's humor as "swampy, genital, anal."[44] One phrase from the album, "fast 'n' bulbous," derives from a lubricant jelly,[45] while the track "Hair Pie" takes its name from a slang term for cunnilingus.[46]

The best exemplar of *potache* popular music, however, may be the man who worked as producer on *Trout Mask Replica*: Frank Zappa. Zappa's own work extended humor to its limits with jokes that are extravagantly physical and relentlessly scatological.[47] Zappa pushed the borders of taste with "songs about crabs, VD, S&M, anal sex and the like."[48] The track "Jazz Discharge Party Hats," from *The Man From Utopia*, is about wearing underwear on one's head; "Penis Dimension" from *200 Motels*, meanwhile, calls for chorus members to brandish illuminated sex toys.[49] "Goblin Girl" from *You Are What You Is* combines *potache* with a pataphysical love of homophony, punning on "goblin" and "gobbling" (a slang term for fellatio).[50] Zappa, it has been pointed out, took as much delight in the body and its products as any infant.[51]

The adolescent schoolboy influence on popular music extends to titles as well as lyrics, which in pataphysical music often aim, successfully or not, for humor. We might point to the "scatological 'crazy' titles" favored by bands associated with the "Canterbury sound," including Egg, Hatfield and the North, National Health, and Caravan.[52] Track titles as "Big Jobs (Poo Poo Extract)," "Big Jobs No. 2 (by Poo and the Wee Wees)," and "Lobster Cleavage Probe," from Hatfield and the North's self-titled album of 1974, all suggest a *potache* influence. Caravan, meanwhile, named their 1975 album *Cunning Stunts*. Hegarty attributes the silliness of the titles to the influence of surrealism,[53] but the source could in fact be surrealism's precursor: 'pataphysics.

Puns and Palindromes: The Voluntary Submission to Linguistic Constraints

Popular musicians influenced by pataphysics may also voluntarily submit to linguistic constraints. It is worth remembering that Oulipo, a literary movement known for its use of the palindrome, the acrostic, the lipogram, the rhopalic, and the homophonic translation,[54] was an offshoot of the *Collège de 'Pataphysique*.[55]

A number of popular musicians have employed palindromes, among them They Might Be Giants[56] and Neil Halstead,[57] while Rush[58] and Brian Eno[59] have made use of anagrams. The best example of an avowedly Oulipian popular music lyricist, however, may be Blegvad. He acknowledges the debt. "Did voluntary submission to the use of constraints (anagrams and palindromes) free me to tap into 'deep layers' of emotion?" Blegvad asks in his book about *Kew. Rhone.* "Affirmative."[60] *Kew. Rhone.* is itself an anagram (of "knowhere"), and the title track contains what may be the longest grammatically correct palindrome in popular music. "Footnote," from *Kew. Rhone.*, features various anagrams; the footnote itself, suggests Blegvad, can be considered to represent "the unconscious of the text."[61]

Ludic Lyrics: Words as Game Objects

Puns and anagrams are not only examples of the submission to voluntary constraints. They also reflect a ludic approach to language[62] and a view of words as "game objects"[63] that is common to musicians influenced by pataphysics. *Kew. Rhone.*

shares Jarry's pleasure in the ambiguity of words.[64] As Blegvad states, one theme of the album is "names and their slippery relationship to identity." Lisa Herman, who sang on *Kew. Rhone.*, writes of Blegvad stripping sentences to words, stripping words of their meanings, and ultimately facing down the alphabet. Blegvad himself points out that the trio in the song "Pipeline" are on a quest for ambiguity, and cites Sigmund Freud to the effect that words are "predestined to ambiguity."[65] The album, Blegvad elaborates, "invites interpretation even as it resists it":

> When considering the meanings of *Kew. Rhone.*, we can only guess, we can't know—which will put some people off. People who want definitive answers are unlikely to get whatever there is to be got from the *Kew. Rhone.* experience. Personally, I feel more at home with doubt than I do with certainty: what Keats called "Negative Capability," the ability to do without facts and reason. . . . Like the two gentlemen and the lady in "Pipeline" who are guessing wholes the excavated pipe might be part of. There's no telling how close they get to being "right"; they have to make their peace with not-knowing.[66]

Blegvad describes the track "Footnote" from *Kew. Rhone.* as an attempt to interrogate language, with the aim of revealing hidden meanings. Puns, or homophones, are another example of these "hidden meanings." In pataphysical terms, puns exemplify the "syzygy" of words: the humor that arises from discovery of the contradictory and recognition of unexpected conjunctions and alignments. The track "Nine Mineral Emblems" opens with a pun on the word "mine."[67] Zappa (*Sheik Yerbouti*, *Zoot Allures*) and the Residents (*The King & Eye*, *The Third Reich 'n' Roll*) also used puns in their album titles. Beefheart likewise used puns in his lyrics: the words to "Ella Guru" from *Trout Mask Replica*, to take only one example, play on the homophony of "hi" and "high," "blue" and "blew."[68]

Wyatt shares this interest, as is evident in the titles of albums (*The End of an Ear*; *Ruth Is Stranger Than Richard*; *Dondestan*) and specific tracks ("Pastafari" from *Comicopera*; "Vandalusia" and "Mass Medium" from *Old Rottenhat*; "Shrinkrap" and "CP Jeebies" from *Dondestan*). Even the name of Wyatt's post–Soft Machine band, Matching Mole, was a homophonic translation: Soft Machine was relatively successful in France, and the French for "soft machine" is *machine molle*. Wyatt also explored the reversibility and symmetry of language in the Soft Machine tracks "A Concise British Alphabet—Part 1" and "A Concise British Alphabet—Part 2" from the album *Volume Two*. "Part 1" consists of Wyatt singing the alphabet in its usual order; "Part 2" finds him repeating it in reverse. In doing so, says Elliott, Wyatt is following Jarry in "estranging, rearranging and 'virtualising' the lineament of the most basic of linguistic sense-making tools, the alphabet."[69] As Mike Barnes suggests, "Pataphyscially speaking, it meant as much, or as little, either way around."[70]

Pataphysical Popular Music: Jarry's Influence on Music

As I have argued above, pataphysical popular musicians are interested in the musicality of language: in the sound, as well as the sense, of words. In this, they are following in Jarry's footsteps.[71] Pataphysical musicians are interested in the "morphology of words."[72] The influence of pataphysics on popular music, then, extends beyond words to the music itself. Specifically, we can detect a pataphysical influence on popular musicians who embrace the musicality of language; submit to voluntary musical constraints; combine the serious and the silly; engage in bizarre and often and radically transformative cover versions and samples; play with pitch and tonality; and deploy unusual time signatures.

Muddy Mouth: The Musicality of Language

Captain Beefheart took a delight in breaking down language into vowels and consonants, using language as a vast and amusing game.[73] In place of easily comprehensible lyrics, David Thomas of Pere Ubu often favored a kind of abstract vocalese.[74] Zappa was fascinated by "the possibilities of the *nonword* or the *mouth noise*."[75] Wyatt sometimes deploys an unusual voice-as-instrument technique he calls "muddy mouth."[76]

There is a link here to jazz, a noted stronghold of pataphysical practice[77] and an influence on both Zappa and Wyatt. Wyatt's muddy mouth technique, for instance, was inspired by both vocalese and the use of mutes by jazz horn players. As Richard Elliott points out. "Jazz has an interesting relationship with words in that it was a style initially associated with instrumental playing. As a form of musicking, a way of processing musical language, it has placed emphasis on the instrumentalisation of the voice, most notable in the phenomenon of scat, but also present in the inflections and vocal experiments of most of the great jazz singers." Elliott notes that Wyatt, influenced by jazz, "escapes the prison house of language" on some recent recordings, opting to whistle or hum jazz standards on *For The Ghosts Within*, his 2010 collaboration with Ros Stephen and Gilad Atzmon.[78]

Wyatt has spoken about his interest in how words *feel* in his mouth, one reason for his interest in singing in languages such as Spanish and Italian: "Latin languages are very easy to sing, because they rhyme very easily. . . . So it was another instrument I had at my disposal. Whereas, say, Brian Eno looks for new sounds in a new synthesizer, or a new electronic technique, I just look for new things I can do with my mouth, with my body, with my hands."[79]

Uncontrolled Variables: Submission to Voluntary Musical Constraints

Above, I examine the tendency of popular musicians influenced by pataphysics to voluntarily submit to linguistic constraints. They also often submit to *musical* constraints. Consider, for instance, Wyatt's decision to reverse the tape halfway through his track "Little Red Riding Hood Hit the Road" from the 1974 album *Rock Bottom*, so that most of the instruments are played backward throughout the second half of the song. "Sight of the Wind," from *Dondestan*, again featured some parts in reverse: something akin to a musical palindrome in the tradition of Luc Étienne.[80]

We might think of reversing tape as a structural constraint. Pataphysical musicians also embrace technical restraints, sometimes in the tradition of Oulipo. There is an acknowledged Oulipian influence, for instance, on the composer Gavin Bryars[81]—also a Regent of the *Collège de 'Pataphysique*. The influence of Oulipo and pataphysics is evident in the Portsmouth Sinfonia, in whose formation Bryars played a crucial role. The concept behind the orchestra was to bring together people with little or no experience on the instruments they were playing. They were dubbed the world's worst orchestra—so bad it was comic—yet the Portsmouth Sinfonia was also thoroughly serious. Attendance at rehearsals was mandatory: "It needed a lot of hard work to be quite that bad."[82]

The Sinfonia was pataphysical in that the lack of technical ability of the players resulted in what Howard Skempton calls "uncontrolled variables," which can be understood as swerves or deviations akin to the pataphysical concept of clinamen.[83] Crucially, the submission to constraints was in many cases voluntary. Though some members of the orchestra were beginners, others were reasonably experienced musicians—yet they chose to perform on instruments on which they were not technically proficient.[84]

Anything, Anytime, for No Reason at All: Combining the Serious and the Silly

Hegarty states that the "humorousness of failure" was key to the appeal of the Portsmouth Sinfonia,[85] and Robert Barry agrees that Bryars's "pataphysical sense of irony" separates him from composers like Cornelius Cardew and Steve Reich.[86] This sense of combining the serious and the silly is highly pataphysical, related to the use of humor as a mask for boldness as well as to the pataphysical notion of equivalence. Lisa Herman, for instance, describes *Kew. Rhone.* as "playfully cerebral,"[87] and Colin Sackett makes a similar point about various related artists: the music was serious, but "compared to serious classical music its seriousness was played lightly."[88] Captain Beefheart's *Trout Mask Replica*, similarly, may be challenging, "like trying to befriend a porcupine," but also boasts "laughing-gas silliness aplenty."[89]

For all its porcupine-like qualities, *Trout Mask Replica* is rooted in the blues, while Portsmouth Sinfonia restricted its repertoire to classical music that was widely known, for instance, as TV themes. Pataphysics is uninterested in the general or generic or in distinctions between "high" and "low" culture. Jarry himself borrowed from Shakespeare as well as the more slapstick humor of Guignol puppetry.[90] Wyatt represents a similar breadth in his choice of covers, performing music made famous by the Monkees as well as by Thelonious Monk. Captain Beefheart's "Moonlight on Vermont" quotes Reich alongside the gospel hymn "Old Time Religion" and the

1940s pop song "Moonlight in Vermont."[91] Captain Beefheart's "Sugar 'n' Spikes," meanwhile, combines Delta blues with a melody lifted from the Miles Davis / Gil Evans version of Rodrigo's "Concierto De Aranjuez."[92] Frank Zappa went even further in transgressing the boundaries between "high" and "low" culture, drawing on anything from doo-wop to musique concrète,[93] from Varèse and Stravinsky to monsters and B-movies,[94] in an approach he encapsulated as "anything, anytime, for no reason at all."[95] Zappa's track "Brown Shoes Don't Make It" from *Absolutely Free*, which embraces a different style in each of its twenty-two sections, is an "exemplar *sans pareil*" of this homogeneity.[96]

As part of his interest in "low" culture, Zappa made reference to radio and TV jingles[97] and even recorded tracks like "Remington Electric Razor." Similarly, the Residents included pastiches of advertising jingles on their *Commercial Album* of 1980. Chris Cutler suggests that the group's work is so deeply ironic and eclectic as to defy all genre coding: "The Residents took pop, ironised it, processed it and tangled it in elements of other genres."[98] Cutler cites Zappa as the obvious predecessor, but this eclecticism, blending of "high" and "low" art, in fact goes right back to pataphysics.

Musical Quotations: Clinamen-Like Cover Versions and Samples

The influence of pataphysics on popular music is also evident in unpredictable and radically transformative cover versions and samples, many of which embody the concept of clinamen. We might think, for instance, of the bizarre cover versions recorded by the Residents—simultaneously tributes to and vicious parodies of pop.[99] Their album *The Third Reich 'n' Roll* is a darkly comic satire of post-Beatles pop as totalitarianism;[100] *The King & Eye*, meanwhile, features reworkings of songs previously sung by Elvis Presley. This is a pataphysical trait, also evident in Coil's version of "Tainted Love" from *Scatology* (reinvented as the "accusatory lament of someone infected with AIDS")[101] or Wyatt's cover of "I'm a Believer," featuring avant-garde musicians such as Fred Frith. Zappa's work, too, is full of musical quotations: "destructive parody" is fundamental to his work.[102] One example of the way in which Zappa's music incorporates "musical puns, quotations and slapstick" is "The Adventures of Greggery Peccary" (the title itself a pataphysical pun), on which a line about aging hipsters, for instance, is accompanied by a musical quote from Herbie Hancock's "Chameleon."[103]

Sampling tunes, in whole or in part, can be just as pataphsyical as covering or parodying them. Part of what makes this pataphysical is the sheer diversity of sampled material, spanning "high" and "low" culture: anything, anytime, for no reason at all. The approach to sampling that is most obviously identifiable as pataphysical is "plunderphonics," pioneered by composer John Oswald. A plunderphone is an unofficial but recognizable musical quote;[104] plunderphonics entails plundering well-known pop and rock songs and manipulating and/or drastically rearranging them.[105] Artists reappropriated by Oswald range from Michael Jackson to Count Basie, Beethoven to Metallica.[106] Plunderphonics was explicitly linked to pataphysics by Jones in the title of his book on *musique actuelle*, although Oswald was already, indirectly, part of the pataphysical tradition in that he was inspired by Burroughs[107]—who was inspired, in turn, by Jarry.[108]

While they might not have used the term itself, the Residents carried out a kind of plunderphonics on "The Beatles Play the Residents and the Residents Play the Beatles," on which fragments of Beatles tracks are reassembled to make a new piece. As Cutler states, the record raised copyright questions similar to those raised by Oswald.[109] In the same vein, Zappa's "plundered" his own work, through a process he called "xenochrony": extracting a musical part such as a guitar solo and inserting it into a different song, as featured on *Lumpy Gravy*, *Sheik Yerbouti* and, in particular, *Joe's Garage*.[110] Although mainly used to import guitar solos from live performances into studio projects, xenochrony could also be used, as on the track "Rubber Shirt" from *Sheik Yerbouti*, to combine an 11/4 bassline from a 1974 performance in Gothenburg with a 4/4 drum part recorded in a studio two years later.[111]

Harmonic Ambiguity and Horrible Beauty: Playing with Pitch and Tonality

Pataphysical popular musicians play with pitch and tonality as well as with words. Some move beyond a traditional Western understanding of pitch, focusing instead on rhythm and timbre—something explored by Pere Ubu, for instance, through the EMP 200 synth, equipped with a touch-tone dial rather than keyboard.[112] Beefheart removed his songs "from the security of harmony,"[113] while his Magic Band dedicated themselves to "wrenching tonality out of the rock tradition," jumping into an "atonal chasm."[114] We could draw a link between Jarry's emphasis on linguistic ambiguity and the harmonic ambiguity evident in Pere Ubu and Captain Beefheart.

Linked to a move away from tonality, and fundamental to pataphysics, is the notion of "horrible beauty," a phrase Thomas agrees aptly describes Pere Ubu's sound.[115] Jarry originally wrote about "the beauty of the horrible" in a letter to Marinetti, although Shattuck suggests it applies at least as much to Jarry himself. Shattuck also finds a musical resonance: "The refusal to drop a contradiction of logic or a raw dissonance in music is 'horrible' to the ordinary sensibility; in just such circumstances Jarry found inspiration."[116] Industrial music, clearly indebted to futurism, would be one example of "horrible beauty" in popular music.

Fives and Sevens: Unusual Time Signatures

Jarry's influence on music is also evident is on conceptions of time. Such conceptions are central to his work, his treatise on how to build a time machine being only the most obvious example.[117] Time is also fundamental to music, for instance in terms of time signatures. Unusual time signatures are evident in the music of Zappa[118] and the bands associated with the Canterbury sound.[119] As Cutler states, "Soft Machine—especially once Hugh [Hopper] had joined—was one of the first bands to really explore deeply, and more or less exclusively, the use of additive rhythm. 5/8, 7/8, 13/8 and so on."[120] Self-reflexive as ever, Soft Machine even referred to this trait on *Volume Two*, on which Wyatt mutters a line about fives and sevens as the 7/4 ending of "Pataphysical Introduction—Part 2" segues into the 5/4 "Out of Tunes."[121]

Unusual time signatures are also a feature of Beefheart's *Trout Mask Replica*. As Magic Band guitarist Bill Harkleroad, also known as Zoot Horn Rollo, recalled, "We would play in various time signatures, often at the same time. For instance, one part might be in 3/4 time while another was in 4/4 time. Only when they touched down together after twelve beats would we move on to the next section of the piece."[122]

Pataphysical Popular Music: Jarry's Influence on Performance

I have suggested that Jarry has had a profound influence on popular music—both on words and on the music itself. The third area in which we can discern Jarry's influence on popular music is on performance. Specifically, we can detect his influence on popular musicians who explore unusually long or short durations, theatrical production ideas such as the use of masks, and anti-naturalism.

The Long and the Short of It: Playing with Duration

Pataphysical musicians play with unusually long and short durations as well as with unusual time signatures. Soft Machine tunes such as "We Did It Again" could last up an hour in live performance.[123] Each piece on the Residents' *Commercial Album*, on the other hand, lasts just one minute.[124] The two appropriately titled *Miniatures* albums curated by Morgan Fisher (one of which features Wyatt) also feature extremely short pieces. Beefheart and Zappa, likewise, play with the very concept of linear time on their records.[125] Beefheart's long musical excursions can be understood as attempts to shatter time, to make it irrelevant as a point of definition or reference, and rather to explore it as an infinite playground with no imposed boundaries.[126] Likewise, Zappa's music at times ignores conventional notions of linear time to encourage the listener to engage with the music "vertically."[127] Zappa even went so far as to describe time as "a spherical constraint. Everything is happening all the time, and the only reason why we think of time linearly is because we are conditioned to do it."[128] The process of xenochrony, as evident on "Rubber Shirt," represents an unusual approach not only to time signatures but also to chronology by combining a segment from 1974 with another recorded in 1976 in a completely different context.

Bryars's "The Sinking of the Titanic" represents a particularly extreme example of pataphysical musicians playing with duration. Bryars's explicitly pataphysical concept for the piece was that the band play for eternity.[129] He initially "composed" a single page of typed A4 paper that suggested various ways in which one *might* go about creating a piece of music about the sinking of the *Titanic*.[130] As far as Bryars was concerned, the text *was* the work: in the true Oulipo sense, it was a piece of "potential music."

Theatrical Production Ideas: The Audience Itself Provides the Theatrical Event

Brotchie[131] and Fell[132] both state that Jarry's *Ubu Roi* was never intended to reach its conclusion on its infamous first night. Jarry had instructed his drinking companions to start a disturbance during the show; they duly threw missiles and even engaged in physical fights. The audience itself was to provide the theatrical event.[133] *Ubu Roi* was brought to a halt by altercations among audience members, which saw seats flying through the air.[134] The fact that Jarry, or those following his instructions, may have been at least in part responsible for the pandemonium suggests not only that he wanted the audience to be an active part of the performance, but also that he understood the publicity value of controversy. The scandal made Jarry's reputation.[135]

In a sense, Jarry is a precursor to a whole line of shock rock (Marilyn Manson, Alice Cooper, GG Allin) as well as such masters of the publicity stunt as the KLF[136] and the Residents.[137] Indeed, the history of popular music, from rock 'n' roll to gangsta rap, is one of moral panics in response to perceived controversies and scandals. Certainly, there is something profoundly punk about inviting one's audience to participate in the performance—and in using a riot as the vehicle. For a specific example of Jarry's influence on performance, we can turn to Thomas of Pere Ubu. Thomas developed alienation effects for Pere Ubu performances, which were sometimes also pataphysically self-reflexive: "Maybe I should get into some sort of audience rapport here" was typical stage banter.[138] There is a direct line back to Jarry. As Thomas states, "The thing that impressed me over the time of immersing myself in Jarry in high school and the point at which I formed Pere Ubu, was Jarry's theatrical production ideas. It seemed to me that his method called for the engaging of the audience's imaginations in the creative process, with his use of placards, pataphysical notions, and anti-naturalism."[139]

Anti-Naturalism: Theatre and Artifice, Music, and Masks

The anti-naturalism to which Thomas refers was pushed further by the Residents, who placed a considerable emphasis on playing with identity: they mutilated a Beatles cover image, for instance, for the cover of *Meet the Residents*. When the

Residents released their *Commercial Album* of 1980, with its pastiches of advertising jingles, they went so far as to buy advertising slots on a local radio station during which these tracks could be played. As Cutler observes, the group was as interested in mass marketing and advertising as it was in pop music.[140]

The Residents are synonymous with their giant eyeball masks: the group members made a fetish of not revealing their identities.[141] The cover art for Beefheart's most pataphysical album, *Trout Mask Replica*, depicts Beefheart holding a trout's head over his face, effectively using the fish's visage as a mask.[142] In Jarry's own career, according to Shattuck, masks were one of two guiding principles—the other being pataphysics.[143] The Residents' theatricality is reminiscent of Jarry: as Cutler says, the work relied on characters, closer by far to acting than to singing; "theatre and artifice" were fundamental. The Residents' work was also self-reflexive: Cutler talks of "their high consciousness of irony, their constant reference to their own situation within pop culture." The band's creation of a fictive business empire around itself is perhaps the most obvious example of this phenomenon: the group stayed completely anonymous, mediating all dealings with the outside world via the "Cryptic Corporation." The double irony, as Cutler points out, was that all the functions incorporated in this illusory network were real.[144]

Conclusion

I have argued in this chapter that Jarry's influence is not always discernible in the music of those self-declared 'pataphsyicians who claim him. "Maxwell's Silver Hammer," for instance, it not a particularly pataphsyical composition or recording. (Neither is it a critical high point: Ian Macdonald calls the track a "ghastly miscalculation" by McCartney, "by far his worst lapse of taste under the auspices of The Beatles.")[145] I have also argued that, at the same time, Jarry's direct and indirect impact on popular music is much more significant than is usually acknowledged. Jarry's influence is discernible on musicians who have not made any public acknowledgment of that influence; indeed, they may not even be aware of it. The work of these artists is diverse and divergent, yet many share core characteristics in terms of words, music, and performance.

One striking feature of musicians referenced in this chapter is the extent to which their careers intertwine. Wyatt has collaborated with Eno on several occasions and, on 1978s *Voices and Instruments*, released two tracks on Eno's Obscure label. Obscure also released records by Bryars, who played a key role in the formation of the Portsmouth Sinfonia. The producer of the first two Portsmouth Sinfonia albums? Brian Eno. Wyatt worked with John Greaves in Henry Cow; he would later sing material from *Kew. Rhone.* on Greaves's *Songs* album. Wyatt also collaborated with Blegvad's band Slapp Happy on a *Top Gear* radio session in 1974, and Slapp Happy also fused for a period with Henry Cow. Blegvad found Wyatt to be an inspirational figure and Wyatt's band, Soft Machine, was in turn inspired by Zappa.[146] Zappa also inspired Pere Ubu (as well as producing Beefheart's *Trout Mask Replica*).[147] The first review of Pere Ubu to appear in England was written by Cutler of Henry Cow,[148] who went on to play with Pere Ubu's Thomas. Pere Ubu was inspired by Beefheart, as were the Residents[149]—who performed at the Meltdown festival in 2001. Another performer at Meltdown was Chris Cutler, whose label, ReR Megacorps, has also released several of the artists mentioned above. The curator of that festival, to take us full circle, was Robert Wyatt. Also striking is the fact that pataphysicians sans apostrophe, such as Captain Beefheart, Frank Zappa, and the Residents, appear no less enmeshed than those who explicitly claim a pataphysical influence on their work.

Notes

1. Andrew Hugill, "Imaginary Music Solutions: A Survey," keynote talk, *Technologies Imaginaires: L'approche pataphysique de la musique*, conference at Université de Paris-IV Sorbonne, March 30, 2005, http://andrewhugill.com/pataphysics/Techimagin.
2. Andrew Hugill, *'Pataphysics: A Useless Guide* (Cambridge, MA: MIT Press, 2012), 2, 76.
3. Ibid., 8.
4. Roger Shattuck, "Superliminal Note," in "What Is Pataphysics?," ed. Roger Shattuck and Simon Watson Taylor, special issue, *Evergreen Review* 4, no. 13 (May–June 1960): 29.
5. Hugill, *'Pataphysics*, 27, 53.
6. Hugill, *'Pataphysics*, 76.
7. Hugill, *'Pataphysics*, 27, 53, xvi.
8. Roger Shattuck, *The Banquet Years: The Origins of the Avant-Garde in France, 1885 to World War I* (New York: Vintage Books, 1968), 187.
9. Alastair Brotchie, *Alfred Jarry: A Pataphysical Life* (Cambridge, MA: MIT Press, 2011), 308.
10. Rachel Carroll and Adam Hansen, "Writing and Popular Music: Litpop in/and/as the Word," in *Litpop: Writing and Popular Music*, ed. Rachel Carroll and Adam Hansen (Farnham, UK: Ashgate, 2014), 15.
11. Hugill, *'Pataphysics*, 27.
12. Hugill, "Imaginary Music Solutions."
13. Hugill, *'Pataphysics*, 27.
14. Ibid., 132, 137, xv; Shattuck, *Banquet Years*, 223–24.
15. David Hopkins, *Dada and Surrealism: A Very Short Introduction* (Oxford, UK: Oxford University Press, 2004), 67.
16. Simon Reynolds, *Rip It Up and Start Again: Post-Punk, 1978–1984* (London: Faber and Faber, 2005), 156.
17. Paul Hegarty, *Noise/Music: A History* (New York: Continuum, 2008), 156.
18. Reynolds, *Rip It Up*, 136; Hopkins, *Dada and Surrealism*, 31.
19. Hegarty, *Noise/Music*, 27.
20. Simon Reynolds, *Totally Wired: Post-Punk Interviews and Overviews* (London: Faber and Faber, 2009), 368.
21. Hugill, *'Pataphysics*, 95.
22. David McNamee, "Should We Go Outside?," *Plan B*, no. 15 (October 2006): https://archive.org/stream/planb-magazine-15/PlanB_15#page/n39/mode/2up; Irwin Chusid, *Songs in the Key of Z: The Curious Universe of Outsider Music* (Atlanta: A Cappella Books, 2000); Hegarty, *Noise/Music*, 30.
23. Hugill, *'Pataphysics*, 78–80.
24. Greil Marcus, *Lipstick Traces: A Secret History of the Twentieth Century* (London: Faber and Faber, 2001), 16–17; Hegarty, *Noise/Music*, 90.
25. Reynolds, *Rip It Up*, 96.
26. John Higgs, *The KLF: Chaos, Magic and the Band Who Burned a Million Pounds* (London: Phoenix, 2012), 15–16.

27. Jude Rogers, "A Sonic Postcard from the Past," *The Guardian*, June 6, 2008, https://www.theguardian.com/music/2008/jun/06/filmandmusic1.filmandmusic77.

28. See Jill Fell, *Alfred Jarry* (London: Reaktion Books, 2010), 95; Shattuck, *Banquet Years*, 240; David Toop, *Ocean of Sound: Aether Talk, Ambient Sound and Imaginary Worlds* (London: Serpent's Tail, 1995), 74; Hugill, *'Pataphysics*, 217; Christian Bök, *'Pataphysics: The Poetry of an Imaginary Science* (Evanston, IL: Northwestern University Press, 2002), 4, 47; and Brotchie, *Alfred Jarry*, vii–viii.

29. Steve Jelbert, "We Mean It, Maaan! The Lost Art of the Pop Manifesto," *The Guardian*, April 29, 2010, http://www.theguardian.com/music/2010/apr/29/pop-manifestos-manics-malcolm-mcclaren.

30. Hugill, *'Pataphysics*, 52.

31. Peter Blegvad, email correspondence with the author, January 17, 2015.

32. Hugill, *'Pataphysics*, 47.

33. Soft Machine, "Pataphysical Introduction—Part 1" and "Pataphysical Introduction—Part 2," *Volume Two* (Polydor/Universal, 2009), compact disc.

34. Hugill, *'Pataphysics*, 54, 53.

35. Roland Barthes, "The Death of the Author" (1967), in *Image Music Text*, trans. Stephen Heath (London: Fontana Press, 1977), 142–49.

36. Robert Wyatt, "Gharbzadegi," *Old Rottenhat* (Domino, 2008), compact disc.

37. Richard Elliott, "You Can't Just Say 'Words': Literature and Nonsense in the Work of Robert Wyatt," in *Litpop: Writing and Popular Music*, ed. Rachel Carroll and Adam Hansen (Farnham, UK: Ashgate, 2014), 57.

38. Hegarty, *Noise/Music*, 84.

39. Elliott, "You Can't Just Say 'Words,'" 57–58.

40. Jeanette R Malkin, *Verbal Violence in Contemporary Drama: From Handke to Shepard* (Cambridge, UK: Cambridge University Press, 1992), 164.

41. Brotchie, *Alfred Jarry*, 10.

42. Andrew Jones, *Plunderphonics, 'Pataphysics and Pop Mechanics: An Introduction to* Musique Actuelle (London: SAF Publishing, 1995), 43.

43. Reynolds, *Rip It Up*, 481–82.

44. Hegarty, *Noise/Music*, 85.

45. Kevin Courrier, *Trout Mask Replica* (New York: Bloomsbury, 2007), 107.

46. Mike Barnes, *Captain Beefheart: The Biography* (London: Omnibus, 2000), 101.

47. Hegarty, *Noise/Music*, 84.

48. Barry Miles, *Frank Zappa* (London: Atlantic Books, 2004), 276.

49. Mike Boehm, "Frank Zappa's '200 Motels' Checking In at Disney Hall," *Los Angeles Times*, October 19, 2013, http://articles.latimes.com/2013/oct/19/entertainment/la-et-cm-ca-200-motels-20131020.

50. Richard J. Hand, "Zappa and Horror: Screamin' at the Monster," in *Frank Zappa and the And*, ed. Paul Carr (Farnham: Ashgate, 2013), 23.

51. Gamma, "Poodles: A Zappological Reading of *Ulysses*," in *Academy Zappa: Proceedings of the First International Conference of Esemplastic Zappology*, ed. Ben Watson and Esther Leslie (London: SAF Publishing, 2005), 205.

52. Hegarty, *Noise/Music*, 84.

53. Ibid., 83.

54. Ibid., 70; Hugill, *'Pataphysics*, 108.

55. Bök, *'Pataphysics*, 4.

56. They Might Be Giants, "I Palindrome I," *Apollo 18* (Rhino/Elektra, 2010), compact disc.

57. Neil Halstead, "Palindrome Hunches," *Palindrome Hunches* (Sonic Cathedral, 2012), compact disc.

58. Rush, "Anagram (for Mongo)," *Presto* (Atlantic, 1999), compact disc.

59. Reynolds, *Rip It Up*, 133.

60. Peter Blegvad, *Kew. Rhone.* (Axminster, UK: Uniform Books, 2014), 44.

61. Marcus O'Dair, *Different Every Time: The Authorised Biography of Robert Wyatt* (London: Serpent's Tail, 2014), 312, 89.

62. Fell, *Alfred Jarry*, 101.

63. Malkin, *Verbal Violence in Contemporary Drama*, 164.

64. Fell, *Alfred Jarry*, 36.

65. Ibid., 28, 123, 55.

66. Peter Blegvad, email correspondence with the author, January 17, 2015.

67. Blegvad, *Kew. Rhone.*, 88, 97–98.

68. Barnes, *Captain Beefheart*, 92.

69. Elliott, "You Can't Just Say 'Words,'" 51.

70. Mike Barnes, "That Ubu That You Do," *The Guardian*, April 25, 2008, http://www

.theguardian.com/music/2008/apr/25/popandrock1.

71. Shattuck, "Superliminal Note," 27.

72. Jones, *Plunderphonics*, 174–75.

73. Courrier, *Trout Mask Replica*, 114.

74. Reynolds, *Rip It Up*, 33.

75. Michel Delville, "Zappa and the Avant-Garde: Artifice/Absorption/Expression," in Carr, *Frank Zappa and the And*, 191.

76. O'Dair, *Different Every Time*, 227.

77. Hugill, *'Pataphysics*, 53.

78. Elliott, "You Can't Just Say 'Words,'" 60–61.

79. O'Dair, *Different Every Time*, 254.

80. See O'Dair, *Different Every Time*, 206, 306; and Andrew Hugill, liner notes for *'Pataphysics*, various artists (Sonic Arts Network, 2005), compact disc, 13.

81. Robert Barry, "The Exploits and Opinions of Gavin Bryars, 'Pataphysician," *The Quietus*, April 12, 2012, http://thequietus.com/articles/08491-gavin-bryars-interview.

82. Tom Saint, "The World's Worst Orchestra," *Telegraph*, April 25, 2004, http://www.telegraph.co.uk/culture/music/classicalmusic/3617672/The-worlds-worst-orchestra.html.

83. Michael Nyman, *Experimental Music: Cage and Beyond* (Cambridge, UK: Cambridge University Press, 1999), 160.

84. Hegarty, *Noise/Music*, 93.

85. Ibid., 93.

86. Barry, "Exploits and Opinions of Gavin Bryars"

87. Blegvad, *Kew. Rhone.*, 123.

88. Ibid., 129.

89. Courrier, *Trout Mask Replica*, 17.

90. Hugill, *'Pataphysics*, 80, 211, 207.

91. Barnes, *Captain Beefheart*, 91.

92. Ibid., 92.

93. Paul Carr, "Introduction," in Carr, *Frank Zappa and the And*, 1.

94. Hand, "Zappa and Horror," 32.

95. Carr, "Introduction," 1.

96. Martin Knakkergård, "Zappa and Modernism: An Extended Study of 'Brown Shoes Don't Make It,'" in Carr, *Frank Zappa and the And*, 172.

97. Miles, *Frank Zappa*, 276.

98. Ibid., 76.

99. Ibid., 84.

100. Reynolds, *Rip It Up*, 249.

101. Ibid., 481.

102. Carr, "Introduction," 11.

103. Nick Awde, "Zappa and Satire: From Conceptual Absurdism to the Perversity of Politics," in Carr, *Frank Zappa and the And*, 97.

104. Jones, *Plunderphonics*, 132.

105. Hegarty, *Noise/Music*, 187.

106. Jones, *Plunderphonics*, 136.

107. Ibid., 134.

108. Michael Moorcock, "*Alfred Jarry: A Pataphysical Life* by Alastair Brotchie—Review," *The Guardian*, January 4, 2012, https://www.theguardian.com/books/2012/jan/04/alfred-jarry-pataphysical-life-review.

109. Chris Cutler, *File Under Popular: Theoretical and Critical Writings on Music* (New York: Autonomedia, 1993), 85.

110. Carr, "Introduction," 9.

111. Paul Carr, "Zappa and Technology: His Incorporation of Time, Space and Place When Performing, Composing and Arranging Music," in Carr, *Frank Zappa and the And*, 140.

112. Reynolds, *Rip It Up*, 33.

113. Courrier, *Trout Mask Replica*, 16.

114. Barnes, *Captain Beefheart*, 76.

115. Barnes, "That Ubu That You Do."

116. Shattuck, *Banquet Years*, 240.

117. Brotchie, *Alfred Jarry*, 31.

118. Miles, *Frank Zappa*, 25.

119. Hegarty, *Noise/Music*, 82.

120. O'Dair, *Different Every Time*, 117.

121. Ibid., 107.

122. Courrier, *Trout Mask Replica*, 39.

123. O'Dair, *Different Every Time*, 74.

124. Reynolds, *Rip It Up*, 251.

125. Courrier, *Trout Mask Replica*, 108.

126. Ibid., 56.

127. Carr, "Introduction," 10.

128. Kevin Seal, "Zappa and Religion: Music Is the Best," in Carr, *Frank Zappa and the And*, 63.

129. Hugill, *'Pataphysics*, 52.

130. Barry, "Exploits and Opinions of Gavin Bryars."

131. Brotchie, *Alfred Jarry*, 160.

132. Fell, *Alfred Jarry*, 93.

133. Ibid.

134. Brotchie, *Alfred Jarry*, 162–64.

135. Shattuck, *Banquet Years*, 155.

136. Higgs, *KLF*, 107.

137. Reynolds, *Rip It Up*, 250.

138. Ibid. 34.

139. Barnes, "That Ubu That You Do."

140. Cutler, *File Under Popular*, 79, 77.
141. Ibid., 78.
142. Courrier, *Trout Mask Replica*, 101.
143. Shattuck, *Banquet Years*, 250.
144. Cutler, *File Under Popular*, 81, 76, 82 80.
145. Ian MacDonald, *Revolution in the Head: The Beatles' Records and the Sixties*, rev. ed. (London: Vintage Books, 2008), 357.
146. O'Dair, *Different Every Time*, 223, 108.
147. Reynolds, *Rip It Up*, 34.
148. Jones, *Plunderphonics*, 15.
149. Reynolds, *Rip It Up*, 34, 248.

Chapter 9

Art and the Pataphysics of Exception

Or, How a Sieve Becomes a Time Machine

Ted Hiebert

The Sieve

What is a pataphysical gesture if not that which falls through reality to encounter itself on the other side of exception? It's no longer impossible because it has strangely happened; and yet it remains exceptional and so is not quite possible either. And yet it is here. We see it. Even if we don't quite believe what we see.

In *Exploits and Opinions of Dr. Faustroll, Pataphysician*, Dr. Faustroll sets sail around Paris on a sieve—a purposefully porous surface that acts as both a container and strainer; an object made as much from negative space as by the wires that give it shape. Jarry describes the vessel as follows:

> This bed, twelve meters long, is not a bed but a boat, shaped like an elongated sieve. The meshes are wide enough to allow the passage of a large pin; and the whole sieve has been dipped in melted paraffin, then shaken so that this substance (which is never really touched by water), while covering the web, leaves the holes empty—the number of which amounts to about fifteen million four hundred thousand.[1]

Because it is a perforated utensil, the real challenge of setting sail in a sieve is that of keeping the water from seeping in; it requires a constant attention to the act of bailing out the boat in order to maintain a precarious balance at the intersection of imminent submersion and pataphysical buoyancy. This is not simply to "suspend disbelief" as Samuel Taylor Coleridge prescribed for readers about to embark on vicarious poetic journeys.[2] To set sail in a sieve is to make suspension one's immediate priority, not simply a mechanism of belief or of willingness, but a material condition of imaginative engagement. The sieve is a vessel that requires the constant attention of participants—what Peter Sloterdijk calls a form of "critical proximity" required for embodied philosophical engagement.[3] Pataphysics, in this way, might be thought of as an insistence on suspension as the exceptional condition of engagement—as an act requiring concerted and sustained attention.

But it is worth spending some time imagining the details of this vessel—the bed that is a boat that is a sieve—since the entire journey of Dr. Faustroll, and in a sense the consequent buoyancy of pataphysics, is implicated in the question of how such a vessel stays afloat. It is a paradoxical question, for the goal cannot be to simply plug the holes—a utilitarian solution that might well increase the floatation capacity of the vessel but with the unfortunate side effect that the sieve then becomes merely a boat and the constant attention of the participant is no longer required. One must maintain the holes in the sieve, perhaps even the holes in the believability of the story; the aspirations of pataphysical proposition must always remain overextended. It is an argument that only makes partial sense, premised as it is on the flotation capacity of a porous vessel.

Yet for Jarry even porous vessels can retain buoyancy, in part through the labor of those who bail out the interior and in part through the surface tension created between the holes in the sieve and the molecular membrane of the water underneath it. One might even propose that any surface that is perforated with holes—or questions—might be thought of as a sieve, and open up the metaphor of the sieve as a vehicle for the artistic imaginary. Many thinkers of the past have proposed variations on this theme, from Aristotle's "plausible impossibility"[4] to Immanuel Kant's gaze of "disinterested interest"[5] to Marcel Duchamp's "art coefficient,"[6] but Jarry goes beyond this to suggest an ideology of aesthetic engagement that is *technologically facilitated.* That is the promise of the sieve: nothing short of a machine designed to facilitate aesthetic engagement, a machine in the form of an imagined vessel, indeed an imagined solution to the problem of there not being a functional vessel. In fact, the sieve is not even just a vessel machine in this case, but a time machine as well, reinforcing the duration of aesthetic experience and, in so doing, making exceptional the moment of viewer interaction.

What follows are three suggestions for ways to approach the pataphysical question, each of which treats Jarry's life and thought as catalysts for thinking about works of contemporary art. These suggestions explore the ways that Jarry's science of imaginary solutions travel alongside the evolution of creative thought, manifesting in the future that is now, following a vision of speculation that "consists of a 'what if' . . . , that treats this unreal navigation in the most rigorous possible way."[7]

Each of these suggestions might also be seen as a speculative suspension of creative thinking, exceptions that are sieves that are also time machines that amplify the duration of aesthetic engagement: by taking the imagination literally; by thinking of pataphysics as a friendship; and by examining how a pataphysical imagination can dissolve the boundaries between the speculative and the real.

Taking the Imagination Literally

A first suggestion for approaching pataphysics might be seen as the simple act of taking the imagination seriously (and by seriously one might imply literally), engaging with acts of imagination precisely with a scientific candor that insists on taking for granted the story that presents itself, replete with details that seem insignificant but can (and perhaps must) be accounted for, even if the act of counting undermines the story from which we began.

The Time Machine

Jarry's conception of his time machine was anchored in the idea of finding a mechanism to isolate a body from duration—to slow one down relative to the temporal succession of the world around us and thus open perception to the infinite flow of space instead. For this reason, Jarry also called his time machine a "machine of absolute rest" since it was premised on the idea of making its pilot transparent to the succession of events:

> By gyrostatic action, the Machine is transparent to successive intervals of time. It does not endure or "continue to be," but rather conserves its contents outside of Time, sheltered from all phenomena.[8]

From this moment of "absolute rest," the machine would accelerate gyroscopically. Under normal conditions the machine simply isolates the voyager from time by providing a gyroscopic "counter-momentum" to the usual progression of moments. When the machine speeds up, it first moves into the future, then begins to exceed the momentum required to witness the future and actually starts to travel backward—past the moment where one entered the machine (which Jarry termed the "imaginary present") and into the past itself.

From a certain perspective, the details of the machine do not really matter. Instead, what is most important about Jarry's essay is the way it functioned as a social catalyst, piquing the curiosity of artists and scientists who—even if unconvinced, annoyed, or angry—took the time to engage with his ideas.

To make this claim is to recast Jarry's time machine for its social effects, sustained by harnessing the time others take to engage. This reinforces what many critics insist is the necessary condition of artistic interpretation—namely, the viewer's investment required to sustain the operation of the machines of speculation.[9] And while Jarry's theory might have holes, in this case the holes create a sieve that reinforces the lived attention required in order to sustain its speculations. For a time machine without a pilot is not a machine—it's just time. The pilot adds the necessary ingredient of social engagement to the equation, required in order to keep the machine afloat. It's as if Jarry in some way anticipated what Marina Abramović would popularize a hundred years later: projecting himself into the future propelled by those who continue to take the time to engage.

The Artist Is Present

In a widely celebrated 2010 performance, Marina Abramović sat at a table at the Museum of Modern Art in New York and spent more than seven hundred hours staring at people who waited in line to sit down across from her.[10] The performance, *The Artist Is Present*, was an extension of a lifestyle philosophy the artist has created (known as the Abramović Method), a compelling process of elongating activity to emphasize the durational moment of time itself. In some ways it's the opposite tactic of Jarry, not isolating the body from duration, but making it hyper-aware, so a new sense of duration is created. The strategy is simple and purposely time-consuming, outlined with basic exercises such as drinking a glass of water slowly, so slowly that it might take fifteen minutes or more, or taking the time to count, one by one, every grain in a bag of rice, an exercise that could take as long as twenty hours and creates an absolutely new sense of duration for the person actively engaged.[11] It is as radical as it is simple: attuning to one's place and activities and, in so doing, entering into a fundamentally different relationship with time.

This is not a *dérive* of the wandering twentieth century but a concerted counter-attention that responds to the politics of digital speed by creating, out of one's own body, a machine of absolute rest, focused as it is on the enduring present rather than on the efficiencies of on-demand productivity. This is to make out of one's own body what Jean Baudrillard calls a "useless function," an imaginary solution to the problems that arise from a culture of hyperactivity, a resistance tactic that can be effective because it precisely refuses to participate in an economy of streamlined efficiency, preferring the playful to the useful; the ridiculous to the operational; the imaginary to the real (even if, from some perspectives, it makes no sense to do so).[12] Instead, for Baudrillard, when the social and political world increasingly prioritizes "intelligent" solutions, the only effective resistance strategy is to embrace that which is literally counter-intelligent:

> When the hypothesis of intelligence ceases to be *sovereign* and becomes *dominant*, then it is the hypothesis of stupidity that becomes sovereign. A stupidity that might be said to be a sort of higher intelligence, on the verge of a radical thought—that is to say, beyond truth.[13]

It is in this notion of radical unproductivity that the pataphysical importance of the Abramović Method begins to truly congeal, counter-tactics to the operationalized speed of a culture of productivity—taking time and, in so doing, reclaiming time—redistributing attention in ways counter to the currency of operational culture.

In the case of *The Artist Is Present*, Abramović herself sat at the table, waiting for people to sit down and meet her stare. And people quickly lined up for their turns, spilling out of the museum and around the block, curiously making time not just to sit down and look at the artist, but to wait in line for their turns. Indeed, while the title of the piece focuses on the presence of the artist, the real effect of the work itself is that the viewers become hyperaware of their own presence, intensified under the gaze of the artist but, perhaps more importantly, building anticipation along the way as they wait alongside many others. With this in mind, one might recast *The Artist Is Present* for an even more radical redistribution of time: not the ambitious durational performance of the artist herself; nor even the intensity of the moment when a viewer sits down to look at Abramović; but the seemingly tangential experience of waiting in line for one's turn. The point of the performance is its exception, that which is precisely not seen but nonetheless transpired in anticipation of the encounter, the long lines of people patiently waiting, taking time before they even take their turns in the presence of the artist. People will wait for their moment in time.

Drawing Your Attention

Ironically, what is truly radical in a culture of digital speed and high-performance efficiency is to take literally the premise for Jarry's time machine as a machine of absolute rest and to begin to visualize ways to put rest into motion, suspending time to bring attention to the space of the moment. Why not make waiting itself the project? Such is the innovation of Seattle-based artist Andrew Buckles's performance work: waiting at a bus stop, waiting tables in a restaurant, asking other people what they are waiting for in life. It is not a spectacle. In fact, it is perhaps the opposite of a spectacle: cut out the spectacle altogether and just focus on the waiting. The project *Why Wait?* is ephemeral, relational, social, and involves nothing more than treating every moment of the day as one that leads to the next: a catalyst for prolonged and purposeful engagement.

In one iteration of the project, Buckles sits waiting for a bus with a notepad and a pen, drawing his surroundings, refusing to let moments of transience disappear into the boredom of directional time (fig. 9.1). The bus stop is not (or not only) a place between work and home, but a site of creative possibility, activated as much philosophically as it is artistically, by the act of waiting on purpose. In doing so, Buckles also becomes a social catalyst for others, literally drawing their attention at the same time as he's drawing the scene around him, drawing others into

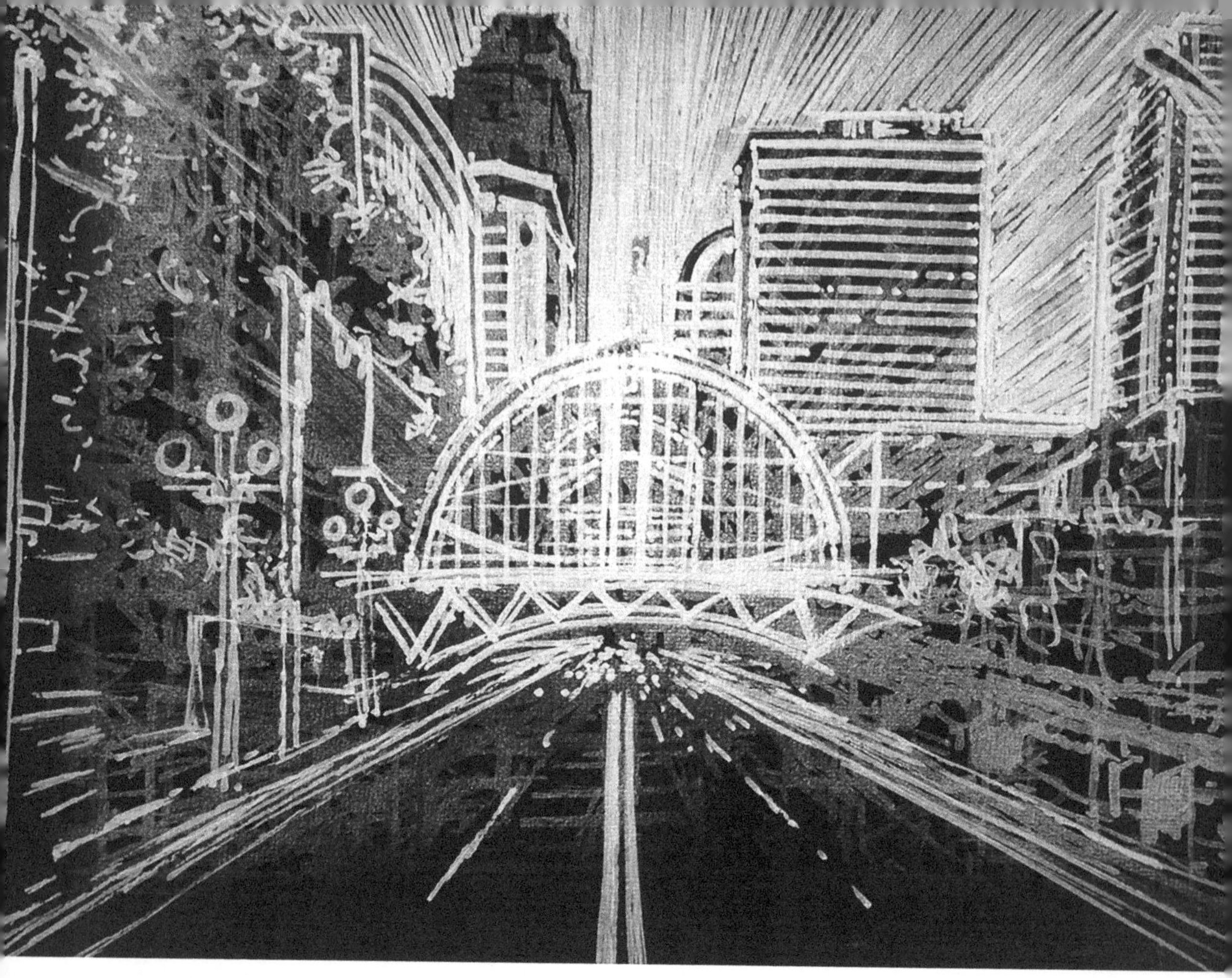

9.1. Andrew Buckles, from the *Why Wait?* series, 2013. Acrylic on canvas, 11 × 14 inches. Image courtesy of the artist.

the conversation about what they are waiting for. This takes the act of waiting literally, for its complex speculative possibilities, but also something more important: to "take the imagination literally" as Buckles insists, as a real solution to the challenge of creative engagement.[14]

The suggestion seems simple but has sophisticated possibilities, some of which have potential for disruption. In some ways it is almost like suggesting that the imagination is the accident of the real, following Paul Virilio's logic by which every invention of a technology or method heralds the invention of a new accident:

> When you invent the ship, you also invent the shipwreck; when you invent the plane, you invent the plane crash; and when you invent electricity, you invent electrocution. . . . Every technology carries its own negativity, which is invented at the same time as technical progress.[15]

With the invention of accelerated living comes the accident of waiting, just as with the invention of the real comes the accident of the imaginary solution, that counter-intelligent solution that undermines the world of the everyday by injecting a form of suspended contemplation, time machines that slow us down to the state of absolute rest, from which new imaginative possibilities begin to emerge. For Buckles, the question of "why wait?" is not rhetorical; it is philosophical, requiring an answer that is also a proposition that is also inevitably an imaginary solution to the question of what one is already doing anyway. And to see waiting in this way is compelling precisely because it avoids the spectacle of duration altogether in favor of simply engaging in life as it is already lived.

In the end, the time machines created by Abramović and Buckles are exceptional not because they take us to the future or the past but because they bring us back into the present, accentuating the fact that it takes work to keep a moment in play. The future is here, and we are living it already in our minds and imaginations. These artworks are important because they reveal the pataphysical undercurrent of social misunderstanding. We need a machine to get us back to the everyday moment. In a strange twist, taking the imagination literally actually moves us through time: beginning in the future where our minds are already focused, to the past that began with Jarry's time machine, and then back to the present where our engagement holds steady the pataphysics of speculation.

More Like a Friendship

A second suggestion for approaching pataphysics might be seen as the act of treating the imaginary as if it were more like a friend than a phenomenon, developing a relationship with the imagination in ways that personalize, and perhaps even personify, the stories we engage, making literal the interpersonal dynamics by which both anecdotes and friendships are sustained beyond the situations from which they arise.

The Toothpick

Legend has it that, while sick in the hospital at the very end of his life, Jarry's final words were a whispered request for a toothpick. Nobody present had one, and so in true collegial spirit one of his friends went out to get some, returning shortly with a package of toothpicks, which he offered to Jarry. As the story goes, upon taking one, "an expression of joy crossed his face" and a moment later he was dead[16]—the Cheshire image of a lingering smile might be imagined as Jarry's last performance for the world around him.

One might even think of this philosophically, as an extension of Michel Onfray's argument that the foods we ingest actually influence how we think. For Onfray, there is nothing innocent about dietary choices, insisting instead that the choice of food is "an existential choice through which one accedes to self-constitution."[17] And seen in this way one might look to the dietary habits of Jarry as well, to foreshadow the story of the toothpick. For it has been said that Jarry's eating habits were perhaps as eccentric as his ideas, that when dining out he ordered and ate his meals backward, beginning with dessert and ending with soup. When eating at home his meals often consisted of fish he caught himself from the Seine, or chickens he caught from his neighbor's yard with a fishing rod.[18] But Jarry's best-known dietary fondness was for absinthe, which he consumed liberally—sometimes even (when finances were tight) mixing it with ink:

> Once, when he was dying of thirst and there wasn't enough absinthe for a good gulp, Jarry got to experimenting around in his own inimitable fashion and came up with . . . a glassful of absinthe, vinegar, and ink.[19]

Absinthe is thoroughly mythologized for its psychotropic effects, so it is easy to claim that it had an influence on Jarry's way of thinking. The act of adding ink to absinthe links the drink itself to Jarry's written words,[20] anticipating Antonin Artaud's notion of "thought as incantation" by turning willful ingestion into an anticipatory manifestation of thought.[21] For, according to Onfray, the choices of what we consume must ultimately be seen as "a stratagem for the construction of the self as a coherent work of art," a reversal of how we generally think about food, no longer simply a required energy source to sustain the human body and mind but itself implicated in the intellectual destiny of the minds it feeds.

Untitled 1992 (Free)

To take literally the idea that what we eat influences the way we think would be to reevaluate some of the social and artistic rituals surrounding food consumption and relational proposition. In 1992 Rirkrit Tiravanija converted 303 Gallery in New York into a kitchen, serving Thai food to those in attendance and revolutionizing the connection between social space and artistic production in the process. Indeed, the work—*Untitled 1992 (Free)*—was a provocative intervention because it bypassed expectations for artistic objects and instead presented something simpler, a meal and a gathering, as a gesture of creative hospitality.

Tiravanija, prominently featured in Nicolas Bourriaud's 1998 book *Relational Aesthetics*, has established a celebrated artistic career by doing many other similar works, bringing people together for an evening, for a conversation, over a meal—often green curry, tom kha soup, or pad thai. What caught Bourriaud's attention so forcefully about Tiravanija's work is the way that it prioritizes social interaction as its medium; "lots of people" is often among the list of artists materials on his gallery labels.[22] In a sense, however, Bourriaud's point wasn't about a really new practice, but a recasting of Joseph Beuys's notion of "social sculpture" from the 1960s: the idea that collective engagement creates shared social futures (hence, for Beuys, "everyone is an artist").[23] What is new with Tiravanija is the spotlight on food as the catalyst for shared experience—the medium or even the machine, so to speak, through which the social spaces are formed.

To supplement Bourriaud's reading of Tiravanija's work through the lens of Onfray, then, would be to make another suggestion: that it's about creating unified social conscience, not through conversation or shared community but by recasting the people involved as choreographed ideologues, digestively unified into similar ways of thinking. Food is scripting the thoughts of the participants, taking literally the claim that we are what we eat and coming to the conclusion that a work of this sort can be powerful, not because of the social spaces it creates, but because of the ways it aligns participants' bodies at a precognitive, digestive level. If the food is the script, Tiravanija's work turns each of us into an actor in the drama of the meal itself. Making literal Jarry's act of drinking delirious ink, Tiravanija's work scripts the shared ideological experience of those brought together through food. It's not that strange; however, it is different from the way we normally think about social space—and about food. This performance is not just designed for the mind, nor even for creative interpretation, but for digestive response: an artwork directed toward the very physiology of human experience itself. This amplifies Bourriaud's ideas: not just creating social space but literally turning each of us into a host for the artwork, animating bellies that synchronize bodies that unify minds. That each of us still remains ourselves is the great illusion that is also the hole in the interpretation, an artwork in the form of a sieve where each of us is a hole in an otherwise unified social moment.

It is one thing to assert that pad thai unifies us digestively (and thus ideologically), and quite another to ask what pad thai makes us think, the digestive unconscious hard at work building its social future. All this is speculative until the point where food, or stomachs, become something more than metaphors for social observations. The risk is that, at a certain point, the idea that what we eat influences how we think becomes more of a rhetorical gesture than one with lived implications, unless the proposition can be made more literal. If it could be made more literal, it would become more scientific and more imaginative at the same time, more solution-oriented while also more speculative—that is, more pataphysical.

When the Canadian artist Doug Jarvis wanted to find out what his stomach was actually thinking, he attached a brainwave sensor to his belly to register and record its musings. It's not quite as strange as it sounds: Jarvis had read Michael Gershon's 1999 book *The Second Brain*, in which the author outlines research showing that there are neurons in the stomach, forming a second neural network in the human body.[24] Taking this research literally, Jarvis initiated a series of performances, collectively titled *Minding the Belly Brain*, in which he stimulated his stomach in different ways, ingesting different types of food and drink, sometimes while exercising vigorously or subjecting himself to media stimuli that might make one's stomach feel weak (fig. 9.2).[25]

In one iteration of the project, Jarvis watched disaster videos on YouTube, comparing his physiological responses to seeing the 2011 tsunami that hit Japan, horror movies, and animated caricatures, curated purposefully to make him queasy. In this series of actions, the stomach became the audience for the work, and the work became a conversation between Jarvis's two different brains. The result was "more like a friendship" than an experiment, in the artist's words; a purposefully extended proposition brought from the imagination into the world of material (and digestive) reality.[26] The language used to frame the project is important, because it suggests a social interaction between the belly and the mind, not reducible to either but interdependent in ways that promise conversational and creative possibilities.

One might even go as far as to think of this project as taking a trip with one's own body aboard a vessel made from scientific literature. And what's particularly interesting here is that such an approach might be made of any type of literature, since at its core this kind of approach involves making an interpretive error, purposefully overextending the claims of the research to build out an alternative form of presence, if not another form of reality. Insofar as it involves overextending the terms of the literature itself, it is a reality filled with holes, but built on a gesture of interaction and cocreation that is not bound to conventional social codes. This might even be seen as a tenuous—but possible—application of William Rawlins's "dialectic of friendship," which outlines a series of contextual and interactional dialectics such that "appropriate behavior is determined within the friendship and is upheld principally by each individual's affection for and/or loyalty and commitment to the other,"[27] and not in any real way by established norms and codes of more formalized relationships. For Rawlins, friendship is based on a series of "contradictory requirements," some of which involve

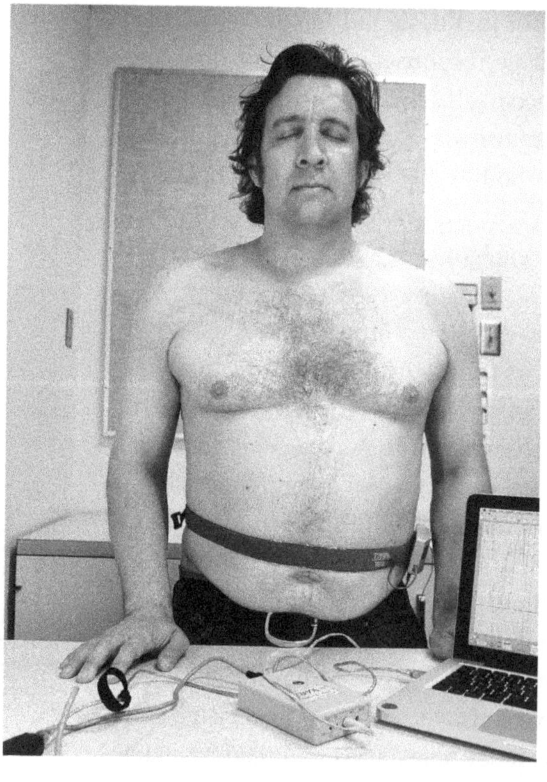

9.2. Doug Jarvis, *Minding the Belly Brain*, EEG performance, 2011. Image courtesy of the artist.

upholding untruths strategically, even lying at times in order to preserve the trust, the feelings, and the good intentions at the core of the relationship.[28] And while Rawlins's text stops short of discussing imaginary friendships, one might suggest that many of these same principles would hold true in a pataphysical context: what matters is not whether a friend is real or imagined, but whether one can sustain the reality of the relationship without compromising the social intentions on which it is based.

The idea of thinking about the imaginary as if it were a friend is not that radical. It is to purposefully develop an imaginary friendship that takes exception to the idea that the world around us is reducible to the real, instead insisting on our inalienable right to imagine.

More Like a Friendship

Seen as time machines, the works of Tiravanija and Jarvis are exceptional not because they transport us out of the present and into some other timeline of engagement, but because they reveal that other timelines are already present—time progresses differently depending on the perspective one adopts. To gain access to the social spaces of community engagement, the biological spaces of digestive process, or the contradictory spaces of imaginary friendships is, in each case, to transport oneself into a different form of interaction. These are works that speak powerfully to the imagination because they are made out of desire, imagination, and a belief in the human capacity for relationships. They constitute artistic propositions less as creative interventions and more as friendships, thus acknowledging the shared social spaces that become catalysts for the pataphysical imagination.

Into Which Things Dissolve

A third suggestion for approaching pataphysics might be seen as the act of integrating the imagination into the medium of life, recasting imaginary solutions not as answers to riddles but as performative substrates, pools of liquid into which one jumps, or on which one sets sail, as if to suggest that pataphysics may be less a way of thinking than an environmental trajectory that sets in motion our stories well in advance of the moments we encounter them for ourselves.

The "Ha Ha"

Much has been made of the eccentricities of Jarry's writing and ideas, though one cannot underestimate the importance of always insisting on an essential linkage between the concept of pataphysics and its practice. The destiny of pataphysics is to be a mode of engagement. Deeply performative in its implications, what pataphysics does so well is highlight the lived and experiential absurdities of imaginary practice. This "science" is not so much about providing solutions as it is about injecting the imaginary—in real ways—into the everyday world that the artist inhabits.

It is not an exaggeration to say that this perspective, by which pataphysics is best understood as a performative philosophy, finds correlations in Jarry's own life, and there is perhaps no better example than the way he adopted performance as a central and integrated component of speech itself. Well known for his affectations, Jarry's way of speaking involved "hammering out each syllable, inventing bizarre words, strangely deforming others"[29] and was marked "by the habitual use of the phrase 'celui qui,' meaning 'he/she who' or 'that which'":[30]

> Alfred Jarry had a very particular way of speaking that was disconcerting to those who heard it for the first time. He said "we," when referring to himself and substituted verbs for nouns, in imitation of ancient Greek. Example: "celui qui souffle" (that which blows) for the wind, and "celui qui se traîne" (that which crawls along) for a train, even it if was an express![31]

Jarry's practice of verb-based speech is of the utmost importance for its emphasis on the function and performance of things, rather than their static or objectified states; and what seems a mere quirk of character is in fact the materialization of Jarry's philosophy of life. By extension, one might insist on an equally performative definition of pataphysics: perhaps thought of as "that which imagines" or simply as "that which laughs." To suggest this latter is to tie the verb-based ways of thinking about pataphysics back to *Faustroll*, wherein the laugh of Bosse-de-Nage, the dog-faced baboon, is perhaps the paradigmatic pataphysical response to the challenge of the real. The "ha ha" by which Bosse-de-Nage periodically punctuates the conversation is a social toothpick that preserves the porous nature of relationships by injecting opposing perspectives when needed, which is to say at every moment.

The reversibility of "that which laughs" means that it must laugh at itself, too: a joke that never quite ends and always continues into its next iteration, a spiraling logic necessary to keep in motion this most performative way of thinking. That a tension arises between the realities we take for granted and the new possibilities that emerge is purposeful—the suspended engagement that always demands a return to the sieve for its ability to insist on constant attention and care. The sieve is not just a joke; it is a broken vessel requiring consistent timing in order to sustain the communities its journeys make possible.

Take Care of Yourself

There is an art to laughing at oneself during moments of duress, and an equal art to creatively reinventing the world to accommodate one's act of the imaginary. One might go as far as to call it an act of building a shared imaginary space—the constitution of a world in which others can similarly imagine together. Sophie Calle created such a space (and made headlines) at the 52nd Venice Biennale in 2007, forming a creative community around interpretations of an electronic breakup letter she had received. The project, *Take Care of Yourself*, included works by 107 women, who were each asked to interpret the breakup letter in their own way, according to the parameters of their professions: from anthropology to criminology, opera to psychiatry to athletics, yielding works that included songs and dance, scientific analysis, crossword puzzles, origami, a shooting target, a parrot, and a forensic study.[32]

Calle's work is often acclaimed for the ways she humorously troubles clear boundaries between privacy, public living, and the imaginative reinvention of the lives of those around her. This project also does something else, however, bringing together communities united by imaginative responses to a real-life event. In defiance of many internet theorists who insist on the ways electronic culture increasingly isolates human sentimentality and interaction, this work precisely does the opposite, using an email as a catalyst for real-world interaction. In a way, Calle's work refutes Sherry Turkle's argument that electronic living threatens to leave us "alone together,"[33] by providing a platform that brings together perspectives that would otherwise be isolated—united through the extended contemplation of electronical correspondence.

Unified by art, and making artworks out of what were previously discrete professional activities—psychoanalysis as art; grammatical analysis as art; Braille as art; parrots as art—*Take Care of Yourself*, is at once about laughing at Calle's situation and about taking care of others. The project provides a platform for voices of interpretation that transform Calle's breakup forever; it is no longer just a breakup, but a catalyst for collective creative action, and indeed laughter. This is not just an imaginary solution but the creation of a culture of care, a bringing-together of imagined responses and contributions that collectively animate and interrogate the electronic breakup, reattaching it to the cultural world in the process.

In a sense, using the electronic breakup letter as a catalyst of this sort is also to push it out to sea, to turn it into a vessel on which others can sail, too. In this act of curatorial self-extension, Calle begins to reverse the direction of digital ideology, no longer a system of communicative data, but one that facilitates the seductive celebration of cultural catharsis. It could even be made to seem like the next evolution of the readymade—not simply objects waiting to be repossessed, but activities, too, making artworks where there were none before, and literally growing a culture of artists. Less a project than a collective setting-sail on the back of the breakup letter itself, with Calle having the last laugh—a laugh that is also the theme song for the voyage.

Observation Diary of a Hydroponic Nose Hair

Imaginative encounters can be compounded by taking literally their terms of engagement. Such a strategy embraces different kinds of cultures and different forms of solutions, like those alchemical solutions that the Japanese artist Tetsushi Higashino

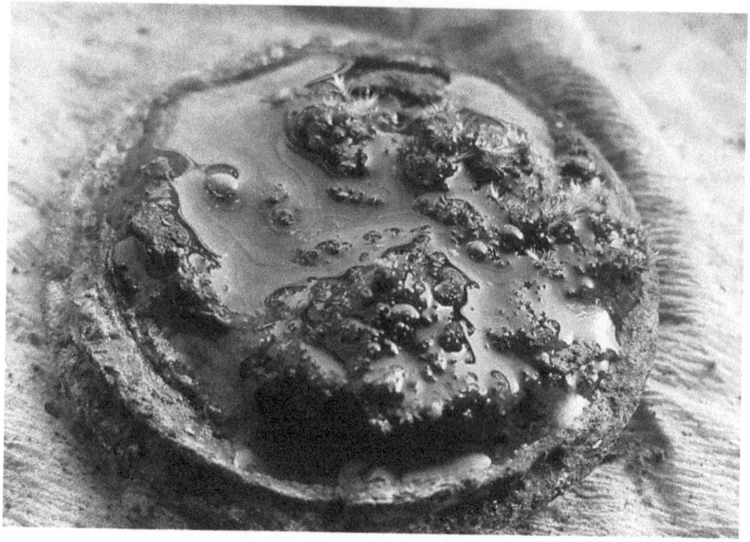

9.3. Tetsushi Higashino, *Observation Diary of a Hydroponic Nose Hair, Day 3939, May 28, 2020*. Nose hair, petri dish, 4 × 4 × 2 inches. Image courtesy of the artist.

uses to culture an artwork he has been growing. The work, *Observation Diary of a Hydroponic Nose Hair*, consists of a nose hair that the artist planted in a petri dish (fig. 9.3). Since August 2009 he has been waiting to see if it will grow, nourishing it with various solutions: hair-growth formulae, plant nutrients, even energy drinks like Red Bull. The nose hair resists but Higashino keeps trying, in a dedicated comedy of persistence, until whatever he has been doing has the exceptional consequence of making the petri dish grow instead. The artist continues to nourish this unexpected cultural growth, carefully documenting the nose hair and the petri dish each day. And now, for more than ten years, this petri dish has been growing its own jungle of molds that fester and stagnate and expand, the explosive pataphysical potential of the project revealed in exactly the unintended consequences of an artistic proposition.[34]

In many ways it is the perfect solution, a nonsolution, an answer that resolves the question before it is even constituted as a question. It is also a solution of a different sort: a mixture rather than a combination, or a dissolution rather than a solution proper. One might adopt Jarry's vernacular and call it "that into which things dissolve," highlighting the various nutrients that are absorbed by the nose hair and the dish. Or one might equally adopt the opposite tack and name it "that out of which new things grow," despite the fact that the growth is an accidental byproduct of a ludicrous experiment. In a curious twist, what is so compelling about this project is the way it extends the vernacular of care from a gesture of shared imagination to one that is transformed into a properly ecological manifestation. It is almost as if the nose hair developed a mind of its own, or decided it was going to contribute to the culture around it rather than focusing only on its own well-being. One might even go as far as to attribute a properly nonphilosophical imperative to this project, building an analogy between François Laruelle's "non-philosophy project" and Jarry's 'pataphysics. For Laruelle, "the question 'what is non-philosophy?' must be replaced by the question about what it can and cannot do," which is also to say that "non-philosophy is performative and exhausts itself as an immanent practice rather than as a program."[35] Indeed, the destiny of nonphilosophy is precisely to disappear to itself, to simulate philosophy until the point where—without even intending it—philosophy becomes not something one thinks but simply something one does. To make an analogy of this sort is to claim that, like Jarry's affected speech, pataphysics is a verb-based ideology, focused on performance and suspension to ultimately become (like nonphilosophy) "performed without an act of performance."[36] Higashino's nose hair functions in exactly this way, the imagination exhausting itself by finding a new kind of solution in which to grow.

From the care involved in the cultivation of an imaginary community to the imagination that grows a culture of its own, a theory of nonimagination is born: a performance that makes real what would otherwise only be imagined, suspending the imaginary in a mixture, a solution or concoction called reality.

Into Which Things Dissolve

To call these works time machines is to understand that both Calle and Higashino have premised their work on the creation of a future context—a solution in the biological sense of the term such that the "science of imaginary solutions" begins to look more like alchemy than idle speculation, creating concoctions within which life and the imaginary fuse and grow. Perhaps the destiny of pataphysics is to become "that into which things dissolve," exactly realizing the project of the speculative imagination by exhausting the imagination. This is a time machine that sets in motion future cultures and future imaginations, building on the non-imagination of a realized pataphysics, tempered only by the lingering laughter of the artists from which they were initiated.

Conclusion: How a Time Machine Becomes a Sieve

The artwork of Steven Rayner provides the perfect image with which to conclude an essay such as this—a collection of "sieves" in the shape of artworks. These works—shovels and tables and plastic skulls and garbage bins—have been ravaged by a hand drill and an artistic imagination, punctuated and perforated until all that remains is the connective tissue between hundreds of tiny holes. Interestingly, they are not conceived as objects at all, but as "air sculptures," opening up the objects to allow the air around them to take new shapes (fig. 9.4).[37]

Like Rayner's work, this essay is built to be full of holes, filled with porous moments that allegorically come together to render an oblique and ephemeral idea:

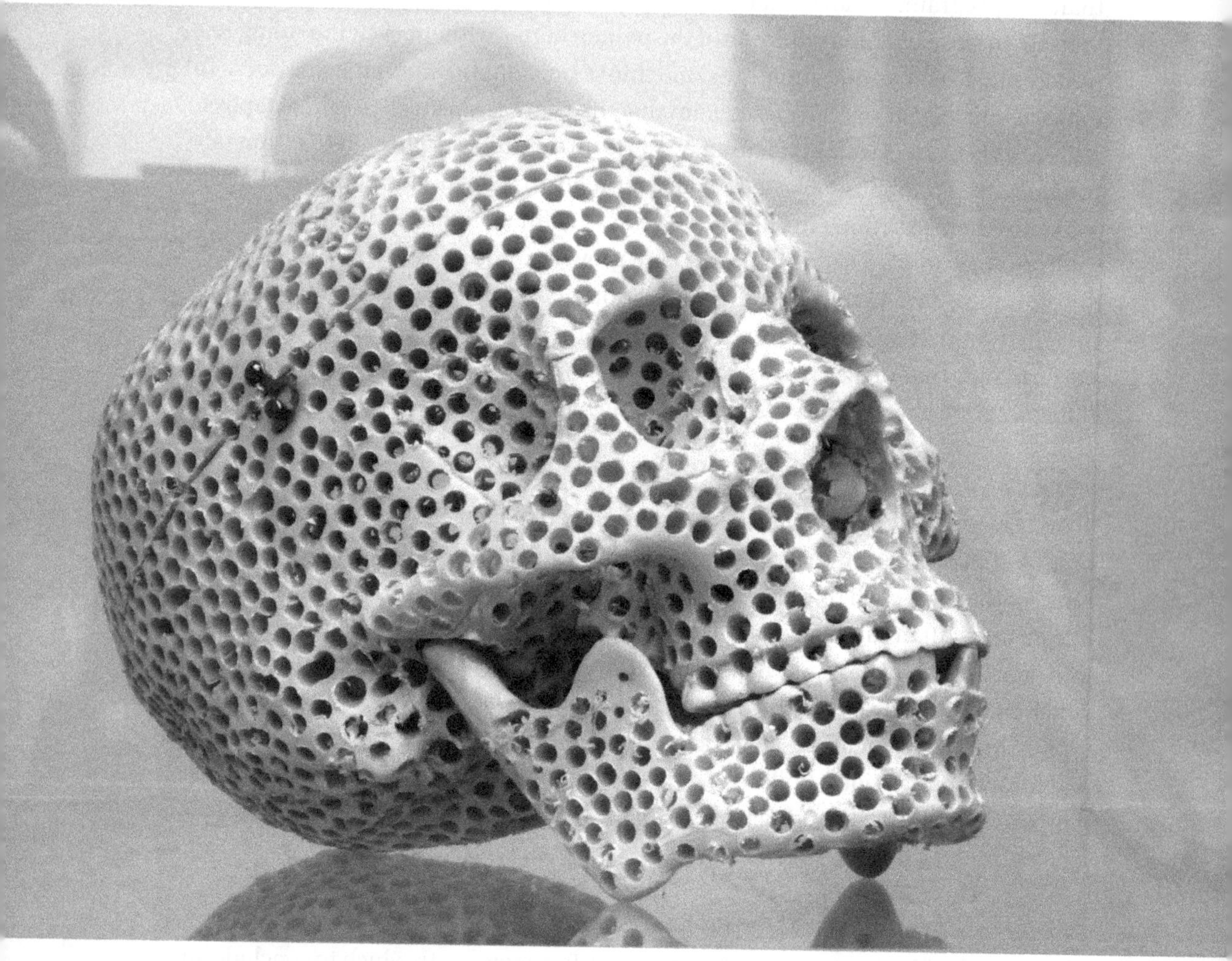

9.4. Steve Rayner, *Something*, air sculpture, 2012. Plastic skull, air, 8 × 8 × 8 inches. Image courtesy of the artist.

that the exceptions provided by pataphysics are in no way exceptional. That is the only possible conclusion, since, as that which surpasses metaphysics, pataphysics is only viable from within. As such, it is a vehicle, a machine, a relationship, an environment, a solution. Insofar as it affects modes of movement through life, it is a time machine, too. This is not to state the obvious, but to make obvious what cannot quite ever be stated—to contour the holes that allow the sieve to float and prevent it from otherwise becoming just a boat. In this, perhaps Rayner's work gives another suggestion, that the task of art (and perhaps of pataphysics, too) is not simply to make, but also to unmake: to allow life itself to be penetrated by the imaginary, even if that means a constant state of mediation, of presence, and indeed of exception to the rule. To poke holes in this way is to make a sieve out of time, to rupture the contour of temporal thinking, offsetting the way time is supposed to work by adding an imaginary counterpart. To drill holes in reality is to provide new shapes for the imagination to take: artworks that are not artworks but sieves shaped like artworks, time machines that allow us to travel through reality on the back of an imaginary friend.

Notes

1. Alfred Jarry, *Exploits and Opinions of Dr. Faustroll, Pataphysician (A Neo-Scientific Novel)* (1911), trans. Simon Watson Taylor (Boston: Exact Change, 1996), 14.

2. Samuel Taylor Coleridge, *Biographia Literaria* (1817), ed. John Shawcross (Oxford, UK: Clarendon Press, 1907), chapter 14.

3. Peter Sloterdijk, *Critique of Cynical Reason* (1983), trans. Michael Eldred (Minneapolis: University of Minnesota Press, 1987), xxxiii.

4. Aristotle, *Poetics*, trans. Malcolm Heath (London: Penguin Classics, 1997), xxv.

5. Immanuel Kant, *Critique of Judgment* (1790), trans. Werner S. Pluhar (Indianapolis: Hackett, 1987), 173–74.

6. Marcel Duchamp, "The Creative Act" (1957), in *Marcel Duchamp*, by Robert Lebel (New York: Paragraphic, 1959), 77–78.

7. Andrew Hugill, *'Pataphysics: A Useless Guide* (Cambridge, MA: MIT Press, 2012), 219.

8. Alfred Jarry, "How to Construct a Time Machine" (1899), in *Selected Works of Alfred Jarry*, trans. Roger Shattuck (London: Patakosmos Press Open Access, 2013), 12.

9. Consider Roland Barthes's eloquent anchoring of the photograph using the self as foundational mediator of the image (*Camera Lucida*, trans. Richard Howard, New York, Hill and Wang, 1981, 8–9) or—equally—his assertion in "The Death of the Author" that the reader is the site upon which meaning is made (*Image, Music, Text*, trans. Stephen Health, London: Fontana, 1977, 148). Nicolas Bourriaud's puts it still more bluntly, insisting that a viewer who finds no meaning in an artwork is not trying hard enough, effectively shifting the interpretive operation to the viewer themselves (*Relational Aesthetics*, Paris: Les presses du reel, 2002, 80).

10. See the Marina Abramović Institute, http://www.mai-hudson.org/about-mai.

11. Marina Abramović, "Have You Got What It Takes to Follow the Abramović Method?," *The Guardian*, May 12, 2014, http://www.theguardian.com/artanddesign/video/2014/may/12/marina-abramovic-method-video.

12. Jean Baudrillard, *Impossible Exchange* (1999), trans. Chris Turner (London: Verso, 2001), 40.

13. Jean Baudrillard, *The Intelligence of Evil or the Lucidity Pact* (2004), trans. Chris Turner (New York: Berg, 2005), 179.

14. Andrew Buckles, interview with the author, January 2014. See also Stacey Soli, "Thirty Art Works This Month? I'll Start Them Tomorrow," Crosscut, October 2, 2012, http://crosscut.com/2012/10/stacey-solie-30-day-art-challenge.

15. Paul Virilio, *Politics of the Very Worst: An Interview by Philippe Petit* (1996), trans. Michael Cavaliere (New York: Semiotext(e), 1999), 89.

16. Jill Fell, *Alfred Jarry* (London: Reaktion Books, 2010), 194.

17. Michel Onfray, "Introduction: The Banquet of Omnivores," in *Appetites for Thought: Philosophers and Food* (1989), trans. Donald Barry and Stephen Muecke (London: Reaktion Books, 2015), 13.

18. Nigey Lennon, *Alfred Jarry: The Man with the Axe* (San Francisco: Last Gasp Books, 1990), 59–60.

19. Ibid., 60.

20. The role of the vinegar here might be as simple as that of a household preservative, or as complex as a symbolic reference to the vinegar that Jesus was given to drink on the cross.

21. See Antonin Artaud, *The Theatre and Its Double* (1938), trans. Victor Corti (London: Calder, 1970), 35–71.

22. Bourriaud, *Relational Aesthetics*, 25.

23. See Laurie Rojas, "Beuys' Concept of Social Sculpture and Relational Art Practices Today," *Chicago Art Magazine*, November 29, 2010.

24. Michael Gershon, *The Second Brain: A Groundbreaking New Study of Nervous Disorders in the Stomach and Intestine* (New York: Harper Perennial, 1999).

25. For more on Doug Jarvis's *Minding the Belly Brain*, see http://www.dougjarvis.ca/belly-brain.html.

26. Doug Jarvis, interview with the author, July 2012.

27. William Rawlins, *Friendship Matters: Communication, Dialectics, and the Life Course* (New York: Aldine de Gruyter, 1992), 9.

28. Ibid., 22.

29. André Gide, quoted in Fell, *Alfred Jarry*, 7.

30. Alastair Brotchie, *Alfred Jarry: A Pataphysical Life* (Cambridge, MA: MIT Press, 2011), 181.

31. Rachilde, quoted in ibid., 181.

32. Louise Neri, "Sophie Calle," *Interview Magazine*, March 7, 2009, http://www.interviewmagazine.com/art/sophie-calle.

33. Sherry Turkle, *Alone Together: Why We Expect More from Technology and Less from Each Other* (New York: Basic Books, 2012).

34. For more on Tetsushi Higashino's *Hydroponic Nose Hair*, see http://hnh.workth.net.

35. François Laruelle, *The Non-Philosophy Project: Essays by François Laruelle*, ed. Gabriel Alkon and Boris Gunjevic (New York: Telos Press, 2012), 207.

36. Ibid., 219.

37. Steven Rayner, "Air Sculptures," https://www.stevenrayner.net/new-index-1.

PART 3

“Written in the Curves of the Limbs”

PATAPHYSICAL CRITICISM

Chapter 10

Reading, Writing, and Rhythmatic

Jerome McGann

I think the way a girl takes off her dress.
—George Bataille, *Méthode de méditation*

This is a story of how I began to learn to read. I actually learned to write before I learned to read, and that is why I became such a poor reader. Publishing what I wrote only made matters worse. My problems began very early because all my teachers insisted I was an excellent reader—the best in the class, they often said. I believed them. And when I began writing essays and books about what I was reading, and getting my work published, I was quite certain I was a top-notch reader. Everybody said so.

Everybody except my children. My children have always told me my writing is unreadable. Although they never called it "nonsense," it certainly made no sense to them—in the sense that it wasn't worth the trouble to try deciphering. When it came to nonsense that made sense, they voted for Edward Lear and Dr. Seuss. And while we all shared a lovelong life for "The Jumblies" and *Green Eggs and Ham*, many years would pass before I began to understand why homo ludens was more productive than homo economicus. When I did begin, nonsense proved a good place to begin learning to read, being where I had been working all along without realizing it. This essay is an account of some of the research work that followed. Listening for the songs of the open road, I began to read and hear and see the lay of the land.

Because it was (I discovered) all a "Land of Cockayne," I began by drawing maps of misreading: misreadings of myself, first of all, then of Felicia Hemans, Joyce Kilmer, Walter Scott, Henry James, Haruki Murakami—many others.[1] A significant breakthrough came when these experiments turned up scores of deformance, thus exposing both the n-dimensional and transmedial nature of the data.[2] But what proved decisive, for me personally, came as a late, perhaps desperate act of filial generosity. One of my children read one of my books simply to demonstrate that it could be done. This turned out to be what Laura Riding once called, and delivered as, a "Last Lesson in Geography."[3] I arrived where I started and, as the poet said, I knew the place for the first time.

From Raymond Queneau to Edward Lear

I now judge that my travels actually began with my fascination for the morphogenetic Nonsense of William Blake, with G. Spencer Brown's metamathematical *Laws of Form*, and with the Blessed Ramon Llull's combinatoric masterpiece the *Ars Magna*. I moved to Alfred Jarry's *Exploits and Opinions of Doctor Faustroll, Pataphysician*, spent some rigorous months exploring Randall McLeod's close empirical studies of Obliterature, and then settled down to experiment with exercises drawn from the work of Llull's twentieth-century namesake, Raymond Queneau.[4] Because I was working at such an academic deficit, I found Queneau's elementary *Foundations of Literature* a helpful students' guide.

Foundations of Literature is an axiomatic treatise on poetical forms. Its immediate relation is to David Hilbert's equally seminal mathematical treatise of 1899, *The Fundamentals of Geometry*. But its *foundations* were laid in the early fourteenth century by Ramon Llull in his *Ars Magna*. For my purposes, the key passage in Queneau comes as Theorem 3 and its natural consequent, Theorem 7, both of which he derives from the third of the second group of his foundational axioms, the "Axioms of Order."

According to Theorem 3, "Where two words are present, the sentence in which they appear includes at least one word between these two words." Consequently, Theorem 7: "Between two words of a sentence there exists an infinity of other words." Anticipating the "surprise" that these two theorems can occasion, Queneau adds the following comment: "To overcome his astonishment and understand these theorems [the reader] need only admit the existence of what we shall call . . . 'imaginary words' and 'infinitesimal words.' Every sentence contains an infinity of words; only an extremely limited number of them is perceptible; the rest are infinitesimal or imaginary."

Of course one cannot *see* those imaginary words—or, at least, *I* could not see them. (In fact, as I was later to learn, such imaginary words are quite accessible to certain eyes trained to an acuity of vision of which I was not capable.) But because the sounds they code can be heard (made) and their rhythms felt (performed), the "imaginary" words can be reconstructed. So an ideal light dawns from the shadows that light made possible, flooding the world of the infinitesimal words.

"The Courtship of the Yonghy-Bonghy-Bò" is one of many experiments Edward Lear ran to prove the existence of that world. Powerful as those demonstrations were, they never forced conviction because they had not been replicated. In 2003 when the ARP Laboratory (Applied Research in Patacriticism) was established, replicating Lear's work and the work of other pataphysical investigators was one of my top priorities.[5] After ten years I was able to report on the first successful replication of Lear's work: *The Invention Tree*, with illustrations by Susan Bee (published by Chax Press in 2012). The experiment proved that the prosodic body of Lear's poem hid an invisible double, and in revealing that double I was able to show how an indefinite number of mirror texts could be, with the application of a rigorous method, extruded from the source document. I had actually derived a new theorem for Queneau's *Foundations of Literature*: "For a given set of real words (S), any number of equivalent sets (E) may be extruded by reordering the set numerically (fN), thus yielding a real equivalent set (SE)." fN is the Nonfunction or Nonsense function that reveals the n-dimensional worlds of any given word set.

To prove the theorem I ran fN on "The Courtship of the Yonghy-Bonghy-Bò" and discovered the following:

The Ballade of the Vast Invention Tree
1.
In a Land Transoceanic
Past the vast Immensett Sea,
By the river Twaddlequiver
Rose the great Invention Tree,
Guarded in a garden closely
By Lord Luminosity.
In serapes and sarongs,
There the Bos and Nims and Quongs
Grow up pictures, poems, and songs,
In the Land Transoceanic
Past the vast Immensett Sea.

2.
Ages ancient and anterior
Hid in beatific bowers,
Stirred a Vision Bird to tell of
Flagrant hands with dreamy powers

Flicking flakes of fragrant showers
Hours and hours on vagrant flowers.
"'T is our Being Beatific
(Sang the Bird in tones terrific)
Our amazing beatific
Lady Luminosity
Lady Luminosity."

3.
But on Isolation Island
Ruled the demons Don't and Never,
Among rocks and scrubby sages
Skinny characters and clever
Fixing number, weight, and measure,
To translate and name that treasure
With their strict insistency,
That creation of the Lady,
The Impossabilla Tree
Skinny demons Don't and Never
Dried-up demons Don't and Never!

4.
Lady blively, magic, sainted,
Scans her land majestically
"Would that once upon our Wood Land
Grew a great Invention Tree!"
Trochees straight turn anapaestics
Wood Lands dream of hypermetrics,
(Don't and Never turn dyspeptics—
"Rhymes and lines are running free!")
"Homonymphs and Synonymphies
Call the Dimplies and the Simplies
And the Smarties and the Pimplies
Para no masiacly
Para no messiacly."

5.
Then the little letters lightly
Litter light along those lawns,
While the long are lighting out for
Limpid glimpses of that dawning

Where the Funny Nims, reborn,
Watch the Silly Belles of morning,
Lyric ladies, ludic, lisping,
Unheard melodies are listing—
All the nymphs are unresisting
Where the long and little letters
Lightly lisp along the lawn.

6.
"What? a Would Land in a Wood Land,
And some Village—Though or Maybe?
Simply squishy, suppositious."
All things special and propitious,
Weather wishous or delicious
They pronounced both mad and vicious.
"Bonny burdies and absurdies
Spinning tunes on hurdy-gurdies
We transform to dirty wordies"—
Bonny burdies and absurdies,
Happy tunes on hurdy-gurdies.

7.
So 'mid rocks and scrubby sages
Shrinking from those winds of whims,
These crazed demons take to shouting
"Silly Belles and Phoney Nims
Do not multiply yours sims,
Here are Information Hymns!
Border ballads of disorder,
Siren songs on Pan's recorder—
Bad words—Silence!—come to order!
Here are Information Hymns,
Hear our Information Hymns."

8.
Demon dumbsters Don't and Never
Dance a puppet pantomime
Faster masters of disasters
Raining ruin out of time
Growing rich in runic crime
Through this coo-coo clock of rhyme.

All the simplies and the dimplies,
All the smarties and the pimplies,
Look and giggle at your disease
Demon dumbsters caught for ever
In this coo-coo clock of rhyme.

9.
And the Funny Nims inflected,
(Clearly here the spell they're under)
List the Lady's ludic lisping,
While the Lord of mimic thunder
Shook the Silly Belles asunder,
Turning all that world to wonder
At a Lady sailing hither
Shedding starlight like that river,
Called the noble Twaddlequiver—
Lady Luminosity!
Lady Luminosity!

10
Past the Land Transoceanic,
Past the vast Immensett—See!
Demons turn to Demon Lovers
At the great Invention Tree,
Singing "Beatific Lady,
We have come here to be free."
Then the Bos and Nims and Quongs
Show how synonymphy songs
Sung to homophonic gongs
Can set time to run for ever
In this coo-coo clock of rhyme.

Although this was my first successful ARP Lab effort to replicate Lear's work, it was soon followed by a series of other rewarding breakthroughs: most importantly, perhaps, "The Klupzies," "The Wordor of Nott," "The Howl of the Copycat," and "The Nothing that Nobody Knows."[6]

It also spurred a return to interesting experiments by other pataphysicians, many not known (even to themselves) to have been involved with such work. These have included transactions with Robert Frost's "Stopping by Woods on a Snowy Evening" ("Shopping for Woulds with the Disbelieving"), Frank O'Hara's "Why I

Am Not a Painter" ("Why I Am Not a Poet"), and Henry Wadsworth Longfellow's "The Children's Hour" ("A Chilled Rum Sour"). One of the most important was the replication of an (in)famous early twentieth-century experiment, Joyce Kilmer's "Trees." Long believed an experimental failure, the appearance of the replicant "gods" showed how mistaken that view of Kilmer's work had been:

gods

I think that I should like to see
A god that's got a history.

A god who often feels hard pressed,
And pleased to come up second best.

A god made out of curds and whey
Or potter's clay from Claude Monet.

(Who might be best to disobey
Or—just a little—lead astray)

A god whose Book of Common Prayer
Recounts a tale of wear and tear,

Who lives in an intense inane,
And falls in love with Mary Jane.

Oh Holy See! Oh D.O.D.—
May gods be made from ring-bo-ree.

In this case, the laboratory result proved important because it corroborated an early theoretical argument that pataphysical conditions could be exposed through inter- and crossmedial interventions.[7] Susan Bee's graphetical transforms of the initial experiment on "The Courtship of the Yonghy-Bonghy-Bò" were particularly fruitful. They also exposed a small but important technical flaw in the experiment's initial line of code.[8]

Swinburnian Rhythmatics

The ARP Lab experiments raised an interesting question about whether similar research might have been carried out earlier. Focusing our attention on the period of Lear's work, we soon found two such experiments, both by Algernon Charles Swinburne. Our historical research continues and we are confident that other early research work will be discovered. But the Swinburne case is important because his research was grounded in premises that were far more traditional than Jarry's or Queneau's.

Swinburne's most elaborate experiment was his second (published in 1882 in the volume *Tristram of Lyonesse and Other Poems*). It was a clear effort to replicate his earlier work, which he undertook sometime in the early or mid-1860s and published in 1866, in the volume *Poems and Ballads*. According to his laboratory notes (which survive at the University of Texas Humanities Research Center), he worked up the experiment as part of a larger project he first called "Philocris," but subsequently changed to the name by which it has always been known, "Anactoria."

"Anactoria" is a demonstration of what Swinburne described as his "own scheme of movement and modulation . . . which I consider original in structure and combination."[9] The poem's combinatorics are most dramatically realized in a pair of mirror texts (lines 35–46 and 47–58), where prosodic rather than linguistic structure governs the poetic transformations—a clear instance of the operation of *fN*. The terminal rhyme words locate a scheme where verbal units—words, word phrases, and even sentential units—are handled primarily as prosodic rather than semantic elements, with grammar emerging as a musical rather than a logical structure. The twenty-four lines play astonishing transformations on words like "all," "fire," "flower," "eyes," and "blue," and these in turn play out further transformations in phrasal units both large and small:

> Fierce at the heart with fire that half comes through,
> But all the flowerlike white stained round with blue; (41–42)
>
> Coloured like night at heart, but cloven through
> Like night with flame, dyed round like night with blue, (53–54)
>
> Thine amorous girdle, full of thee and fair,
> And leavings of the lilies in thine hair. (45–46)
>
> Thy girdle empty of thee and now not fair,
> And ruinous lilies in thy languid hair. (57–58)

This is poetry aspiring to the condition of music. Paradoxically, because the aspiration appears through such deliberated artifice, the poetic motifs become what Franz Liszt called "personifications of ideas."[10] At the most general level, the verse embodies ("personifies") the idea of poetry as a self-aware and purposive intellectual practice. Furthermore, as "personified" the ideas resist being translated into abstract terms (nominalizations). Although translations and transformations emerge and mutate through the verse of "Anactoria," the linguistic forms (words, phrases, syntaxes) come before us so purified of abstract (cognitive) reference that even the poem's semantic features—the idea of being sickened with love, for instance—get subordinated to the logic of musical and sensuous transformation. So the *idea* of love is here musically translated into multiple possibilities of meaning: it lifts and abashes, it is insatiable, it is wearied out, it is sweet, it is bitter. In short, the forms it can assume are numberless:

> Ah sweet, and sweet again, and seven times sweet,
> The paces and the pauses of thy feet. ("Anactoria," 118–19)

So far as poetry is concerned, the forms are limited only by the expressive capacities—the musical transformations—latent in the dataset. Lines 35–58 are much more than a tour de force demonstration of Swinburne's virtuosity as a research scholar. *Ex*posing the general dynamic order of the poem tout court, the passage is also *pro*posing a general theory of poetic action. Lines 57–58 are more than an extrusion of lines 47–48, more than a set of that couplet's hitherto unobserved infinitesimals. They prove that further extrusions are not only possible, they are inevitable:

> Ah sweeter than all sleep or summer air
> The fallen fillets fragrant from thy hair. (119–20)

And out of that form will come further forms and transforms, as "note is struck from note" (137)—

> With thwartings of strange signs, and wind-blown hair
> Of comets, desolating the dim air (161–62)

—including forms that reach beyond themselves—in prosodic terms, forms that escape their normative couplet structure—to expose another kind of generative rhythm,

> Nor any memory of thee anywhere:
> For never muse has bound about thine hair
> The high Pierian flower whose graft outgrows
> All summer kinship of the summer rose
> And colour of deciduous days, nor shed
> Reflex and flush of heaven about thine head,
> Nor reddened brows made pale by floral grief
> With splendid shadow from that lordlier leaf. (193–200)

The first couplet in this passage both rhymes with its precursors (45–46, 57–58, 119–20, 161–62) and then breaks their prosodic pattern with its extreme end-stop.

Paradoxically, from the platform of that cloven couplet flows a heavily enjambed movement that enacts the fractal inertia that is the law of the poem.

The soft strange ways of such verse seem endless, like the endless ways of love:

> And all the broken kisses salt as brine
> That shuddering lips make moist with waterish wine, (37–38)
>
> Yea, thou shalt be forgotten like spilt wine,
> Except these kisses of my lips on thine (201–2)

Motivic though they are, the end rhymes need not key the poetic transformations. When words and phrases recur—for instance, "reluctation," (33) and "reluctance" (164)—the altered contexts supply them with verbal associations and relationships that can be exploited. "Shuddering" (34, 38) gets defined as a motivic word explicitly associated with the "intense device" (28) of Swinburne's versification:

> Relapse and reluctation of the breath,
> Dumb tunes, and shuddering semitones of death (33–34)
>
> But in the light and laughter, in the moan
> And music, and in grasp of lip and hand
> And shudder of water that makes felt on land
> The immeasurable tremor of all the sea,
> Memories shall mix, and metaphors of me.
> Like me shall be the shuddering calm of night. (210–15)

Thus one can say that the unfolding network of *motivic* modulations in "Anactoria" is less important for the empirical results of Swinburne's experiment—the poem's set of identifiable forms and transforms—than for its proof of a general transformational rule: the fractal algorhythm that the data itself instantiate. It is worth a passing note that Swinburne's decision to use the couplet form to execute his experiment seems uncannily shrewd: the form itself signals the presence of the work's fractal geometry.

I shall leave to others an account of the more elaborate experiment Swinburne carried out with "Tristram of Lyonesse." Suffice it to say that he generated a set of mirror texts, each of forty-four lines, that would serve as the work's fractal matrix. He set one at the beginning of the work ("The Prelude, Tristram and Iseult," lines 1–44) and the other at the beginning of the ending ("The Sailing of the Swan," lines 1–44). Because the entire work extends to 4,481 lines ("Anactoria" has a mere 304 lines), the code structure of that enormous dataset is more complex. The language the code is written in, however, is exactly the same.

From Grammatics to Graphetics: Comte de Lautréamont, *Les Chants de Maldoror*, Chant 6

The heavily thematized poetics of twentieth-century academic research and practice forgot to remember how many ways Swinburne demonstrated his work's large theoretical claims. Rhyming Faustine's name forty-one times in the forty-one quatrains of her poem was a move of truly Faustian poetic pretension. His procedural approach is clearest in his translations, his pastiche writings, and his poetic parodies, at least one of which—"Poeta Loquitur"—is nonsense of the highest order, like "Dolores." But despite some of Wallace Stevens's best early work, despite the high cultural celebrity of Gertrude Stein and *Finnegans Wake*, the profession of English and American modernism did not hold this line of poetics in great regard.

The European view—an avant-garde view—was quite different, and was accessible even in certain English and American quarters. A work like *The Importance of Being Earnest* (1895) made serious nonsense of high seriousness and the English idea of a great tradition. The view captured the immense significance of Edgar Allan Poe and, even more remarkably, of Lautréamont's comic masterpiece *Les Chants de Maldoror*.[11] In contrast to the splendidly sentimental nonsense of Lewis Carroll and Edward Lear, drawn out of the archive of nineteenth-century children's literature, Lautréamont turned to nonsensify the high Romantic satanism that stretched from Johann Wolfgang Goethe through Lord Byron, Charles Robert Maturin, Poe, Adam Mickiewicz, and Victor Hugo, and reached its apogee in Charles Baudelaire and Richard Wagner.

Lautréamont demonstrated his poetics most clearly in the sixth chant of *Maldoror* where the texts of Romantic genius get their hypocritical hearts laid bare. "Personal poetry has had its day of relative jugglery and contingent contortions," Lautréamont declares. What is necessary now is a return to "the indestructible thread of impersonal poetry" (317/ 271; *le fil indestructible de la poésie impersonelle*). His approach inherits the method Poe laid out most clearly in "The Philosophy of Composition." But while both pledge a cold allegiance to conscious artifice, Lautréamont makes an advance on Poe by collapsing the traditional distinction between method and practice, or what he calls the "theorem" and its "application" (289–90/335).[12] More than fifty years before Gertrude Stein presented her view of *Composition as Explanation* (1925–26), chant 6 of *Maldoror* gave the theory a practical demonstration.

The chant is divided into two parts: a prose poem in two strophes (called a "hybrid preface") is followed by "a little novel in thirty pages" arranged as eight brief chapters. The hybrid preface has two principal functions. The first is to underscore the artifactuality of the entire work. It is full of surprises that are doubly disorienting because the writing foregrounds the Maldororian war with conventionally ordered arrangements and expectations. The hybrid preface also reveals that the first five chants were not exactly the series of bizarre, discontinuous reports of the exploits of Maldoror that they seemed to be. Chants 1–5 were actually "the frontispiece of my work, the foundation of the construction, the preliminary explanation of my future poetry" (222/256; *le frontispice de mon ouvrage, le fondemont de la construction, l'explication préalable de ma poètique future*). In appearance a set of strange fictions, they were actually an analytic "explanation" of *Maldoror*'s aesthetics.

Indeed, the term "préalable" shows that the "explanation" is a required precondition of "ma poètique future." The textual condition is thus proto-Steinian in a double sense: the explanation of "ma poètique future" precedes its narrative unfolding and composes itself in a tale-telling mode. The wordplay in the phrase "ma poètique future" announces a new kind of poetical work: writings that do not forecast unimaginable futurities but execute them before any report of their occurrence. Crucially, these are not memorial realities offering themselves to philosophic meditation or reflexive imagining. The algorhythm for accomplishing their future realization is already clear and present. *Pre*meditated realities, they are truths only discoverable through a project of textual research like the one carried out in chant 6 of *Maldoror*.

Lautréamont's initial demonstration of his "poetique future" comes as the final sentence of the hybrid preface:

> How could the Carrousel Bridge maintain the constancy of its neutrality when it heard heart-rending screams apparently uttered by the sack! (225/261; *Comment le pont du Carrousel put-il garder la constance de sa neutralité, lorsqu'il entendit les cris déchirants que semblait poussser le sac!*)

The sentence disorients because, read in context, it seems to have no context. It reads as if it were some out-of-place fragment of narrative that has dropped by chance into *Maldoror*. Only when we enter chapter 8 of chant 6, *Maldoror*'s final section, will we finally be reading a narrative where that sentence makes narrative sense—more precisely, where that sentence has been made to make sense.

Chant 6 is organized around a series of six such sentences, of which the following are the next four:

> Do you know that when I think of the iron ring concealed beneath the stone by the hand of a maniac, an irrepressible shudder passes over my scalp? (229/266; *Savez-vous que, lorsque je songe à l'anneau de fer caché sous la pierre par la main d'un maniaque, un invincible frisson me passé par les cheveux?*)

> Go now to where the swan-lake is. And I shall tell you later why one swan there among them is completely black, with a body bearing an anvil surmounted by the putrefying carcase of a crab, and rightly inspiring mistrust

in the rest of its acquatic comrades. (232/271; *Dirigez-vous du côté où se trouve le lac des cygnes; et, je vous dirai plus tard pourquoi il s'en trouve un de complètement noir parmi la troupe, et dont le corps, supportant une enclume, surmontée du cadavre en putréfaction d'un crabe tourteau, inspire à bon droit de la méfiance à ses autre aquatiques camarades.*)

> The fish's tail will fly only three days, it is true; but alas! The beam will be burned just the same; and a cylindro-conical bullet will pierce the rhinoceros's skin, despite the daughter of the snow and the beggar! It is that the crowned fool has uttered the truth concerning the fidelity of the fourteen daggers. (237/278; *La queue de poisson ne volera que pendant trois jour, c'est vrai; mais, helas! La poutre n'en sera pas moins brûlée; et une balle cylindro-conique percera la peau du rhinocéros, malgré la fille de neige et le mendiant! C'est que le fou couronné aura dit la vérité sur la fidélité des quatorze poignards.*)

> The prophecy of the cockerel will be realized when he glimpsed the future at the bottom of the candlestick. May it please heaven that the crab will rejoin the caravan of pilgrims and apprise them in a few words of the narrative of the ragpicker of Clignancourt! (239/280; *Ainsi, sera réaliséé la prophétie du coq, quand il entrevit l'avenir au fond du candélabre. Plût au ciel que le crabe tourteau rejoigne à temps la caravane des pèlerins, et leur apprenne en quelques mots la narration du chiffonnier de Clignancourt!*)

Each of those passages has been composed in and as a "poetique future" in a literal sense: they make true declarations that are only subsequently proven true in the fairy tale being composed as chant 6. When first read, they operate the same disorienting method as the first one in the hybrid preface.

While each of those algorhythmic passages would repay the closest kind of reading, I shall limit myself to a closer study of the first. Notice the sentences that immediately precede it.

> First of all, I shall blow my nose, because I need to. And then potently assisted by my hand, I shall again take up the pen-holder that my fingers had let fall. (225/261; *Je vais d'abord me moucher, parce que j'en ais besoin; et ensuite, puissamment aidé par ma main, je reprendrai le porte-plume que mes doigts avaient laissé tomber.*)

In normal narrative, these sentences would set up the cause and effect logic of the next, just as these two sentences are joined in a narrative logic, the first preparing us to understand the second. But in this case that logical relation seems missing.

But if we alter our perspective slightly we discover a different logic. Suppose the narrative context for the Carrousel Bridge sentence is not in a story out of Paris but in the story of the making of a story out of Paris. Now we see the context and grasp why the narrator had let his pen fall, and why the narrative was briefly interrupted, and why that interruption was both a sign and an invitation for a way of reading. Now in fact we perhaps begin to become part of *that* story, as we were warningly invited to do at the beginning of chant 1. Now we may start to undertake the difficulty of paying close attention. There is a rigorous procedural rhythmatic organizing this work. Lautréamont's *poetique future* is algorhythmatic.

Notice, too, that the exclamation point at the end of this algorhythm doubles its significance. It is both a question about a possible future (a factual question) and an exclamation of surprise about an accomplished event (an affective response): "*how* could x have happened"; and "how *could* y have let x come about." The narrative brilliance of the sentence involves its demonstration of how to command the unimaginable (how to imagine what you don't know).[13] You do this by treating your scripts as executable code.

Maldoror's final demonstration of this *poetique future* comes as the work's last sentence:

> It is nonetheless true that the draperies in the shape of a crescent moon no longer derive the expression of their definitive symmetry from the quaternary number: go there and see for yourself if you do not wish to believe me. (255/303; *Il n'en est pas moin vrai que les draperies en forme de croissant de lune n'y recoivent plus l'expression de leur symétrie definitive dans le nombre quaternaire: allez-y voir vous-même, si vous ne voulez pas me croire.*)

In this case, not only does the sentence lack a prevenient narrative context, it appears to have no textual future where it might be made to come true. But when Lautréamont tells his reader to "go there and see for yourself," he uses his readers to prove the truth of his algorhythmatic poetics. Could *you* write a tale that proved the truth of those draperies? Surely you could. Could you write ten tales, a hundred . . . perhaps a thousand and one?

Although we are accustomed to reading books typographically, that represents only one of the dimensions organizing their "Textual Condition." Every textual event is n-dimensional.[14] At the same time, the law of the Textual Condition operates through a defined set of dimensions that can be called to act in an indefinite number of unique dynamic arrangements.[15] Not only is every edition of *Maldoror* a unique arrangement of the work's possibilities, but every copy of every edition is itself a unique arrangement. Each edition of *Maldoror* is a particular abstract conception (or reflection) of how the work's dimensions might be organized.

In the case just considered, Lautréamont achieved a notable literary result by a simple manipulation at the level of *Maldoror*'s rhetorical dimension. He collapsed the distinction between an expository and a narrative encoding, making free substitutions throughout the book. We register that move throughout the first five chants in our uncertainty about the identity of the work's hero. Who addresses the reader: Is it a person named Lautréamont (or Ducasse)? Is it Maldoror? That duplicity gets continually reinforced because the book's rhetoric switches arbitrarily from first to third person, from tale-telling to abstract reflection.

In this elementary respect, *Maldoror* is a practical lesson in certain reading and writing affordances of a textspace. Lautréamont makes other manipulations of his textspace that also serve his purpose to dis- and reorient the practice of reading. Except when dialogue is being represented, *Maldoror* is laid out in great blocks of unparagraphed writing, each a single poetic stanza (strophe).[16] This manipulation of the work's bibliographical dimension further collapses the distinctions that traditional narrative and exposition commonly mark and exploit. By graphically (typographically) marking the absence of those distinctions, *Maldoror* creates an echo chamber and network of relations that will seem intolerable if we try to read it in traditional terms.

Still, *Maldoror*'s unusual textspace carries the significant message that texts are also spatial events and that textual space can be made significant as space, that text has a graphical dimension. Maps, illustrations, and illuminations are the most dramatic devices for exploiting a text's graphical dimensionality: Blake's engraved works, children's books like Carroll's and Lear's, Charles Rickett's design for Wilde's *The Sphinx*, Tom Phillips's *A Humument*. Wilde solicited Aubrey Beardsley's illustrations for *Salome*, but when he saw them he was seriously unpleased. They brought to Wilde's play a shockingly clear interpretation that Wilde had wanted to leave in the suggestive interstices of his work's purely linguistic dimension.[17]

No one who writes or publishes can be quite sure what they have done, what their work might mean. Not until Blake reconceived and rewrote *Paradise Lost* did we know (did *I* know!), or could Milton himself have guessed, that Satan might be considered the work's true hero. Blake took it as his obligation to reread what he ironically called the "sacred codes" of religion, history, philosophy, and science in order to expose "the infinite which was hid" away in them.[18] While many late twentieth-century academics interpreted Blake's move "against the grain" of tradition as a deconstructive move, it was far more ambitious. Cleansing the doors of perception was for him "the necessary precondition for the revelation of an infinite world" (*l'explication préalable de ma poètique future*), the "delight" of a "Prolific" power of which he was such an extraordinary example.

The Return of the White Knight

Academics like me have internalized a Romantic view of memory and culture. It is the licensed way to glorify individual talent by reglorifying the declared masterpieces of tradition. Nonsense descends on this historical situation to argue that what seems trivial and inconsequent—paradigmatically, children's literature—might be subjected to a formal glorification. Lewis Carroll's treatment of the White Knight in *Through the Looking-Glass* (1871) gives a perfect demonstration of the method. A traditional heroic figure is ludicrously diminished as a gift to a young girl. In that sentimental transformation, no Western Hero need ever again be taken seriously. The Hero is stripped of his traditional function and delivered to a world of small things. This is the Hero Stripped Bare of His Girlfriends, Even.

But the Masters of Culture resist that move against Tradition's power and significance. Their defense against Lewis Carroll has been to make a place for him in the Pantheon. But we do better, I think, to read his work in the same spirit that he wrote it. His work is the mirror image of the person to whom it was addressed, Alice Liddell, a girl of no importance—or, rather, a girl of importance only for a fleeting moment of time, in a tiny place, among a small circle of family and friends.

A *popular* girl, as Edgar Allan Poe was a popular poet, a poet Emerson called "the Jingle Man," meaning to separate him from the great world of Representative Men and their poetic representatives. I wrote a book once-upon-a-time (ca. 2013 CE) to argue, against High Emersonian Culture, that Poe was a figure of great cultural consequence. The traces of that argument can be traced in this essay, for once having enlisted in the armies of Culture, one does not easily—or perhaps ever—escape their seductive power. To a popular imagination, perhaps a Common Reader, perhaps simply my children, such books appear unreadable. But they can be attacked by the White Knight; they might be read by Humpty Dumpty.

All sacred codes, however trivial or pedantic, await the visitation of an unimaginable redeemer, a Demon Lover. Nor can we be sure who that alien angel will be, or when he will come, or what she will reveal. His name is Legion. If someone can see heaven in a wildflower, or hear the lamentation of Beulah over Ololon in the trills of a nightingale or a skylark, someone might transmediate my book *The Poet Edgar Allan Poe: Alien Angel* in order to show and tell something like color plate 15.[19] The representation is so drastic at so many levels and in so many directions that commentary's only safe resort seems to be pointing: to the selection of colors and their explosive arrangement, in particular the tiny flecks of gold that look like cosmic dust scattered from some Big Bang of the primal textual event, the (uncollected) letter from Poe to Professor Jerome; to the demonic figures spilling from the death's head, their spears either driving back or drawing out a brainhoard of raging, incoherent letters and pixilating sigla; to the flight of bats each bearing forward from some remote darkness a single unique letter; to the cryptic message plucked from what was once an orderly academic text, but that now, having submitted to this violation—who did it?—has become the image of a random set of data or an archaic memory bank here being shocked into life, like Frankenstein's monster: "The recognizable event plunges Like fire into ambiguous unexpected wonder The ancient sentimental shadows."

Thus is *The Poet Edgar Allan Poe: Alien Angel* raised from the dead in one hundred separate resurrections. The leaves of the book's openings are each spread out to a pair of winged pages that then fly free, even as they declare the imprisonment that has driven them to take flight (color plate 16). Is Poe looking out at us or are we looking in at him? Why does he smile so warmly, has he learned a new, more perverse, and more sentimental irony from that saintly child who holds out her scrawled red Halloween request? Who is she? And who would dare to take a candy from that dish? It is clearly poisoned. But when was it poisoned, and by whom? A learned book is being transformed into a box of Chinese fortune cookies, each with some unnerving message: "The popular life throws man to self-betrayals the extreme world is far worse." Having been torn from its murdered context, what does that disorderly sentence—is it a sentence?—*mean*? I now know that it is impossible to know what it means, though I also now know that it is far from impossible to show and tell.

Popular or extreme (popular with whom? in what sense extreme?), *The Poet Edgar Allan Poe: Alien Angel* has here been invited to join the transhuman world of Nonsense Visible. But other views of the book are very different (color plate 17). *There* is a reading of Poe that oft was thought but ne'er so well expressed. Parodically disguised as Groucho Marx parodically disguised as Sherlock Holmes, Poe strides against a blast of windy words, sweeping away all beyond their coldest truest core: "thus unfolds willful loneliness at first cherishing confrontation. But two kinds both alienated and affectless forcing us to cold subjects." It is the eternal Jingle Man caught in the twinkle of a coldly comic Private Eye. It is Auguste Dupin showing and telling something about how to read (in the twinkle of an eye): look both ways when you cross a word (color plate 18).

These are four glimpses of one Poe, a random Maldororian quaternary plucked from a *Wunderkammer* of a hundred. A White Knight is driving through a great Western desert, taking his stop-motion pictures. And then suddenly

In the desert a fountain is springing[20]

and I am thinking someone somewhere must be seeing Hokusai's *One Hundred Views of Mount Fuji*. And someone else somewhere is reading about "nothing that is not there and the nothing that is" (fig. 10.1). I am reading pages 158 and 159, and seeing them for the first time. Here is the Meaning of Meaning: that textspace may be so shattered and swept clean it can be fruitfully explored at will. These fragments do not insist on the order of their going. Set before this whited-out sky, I stare at

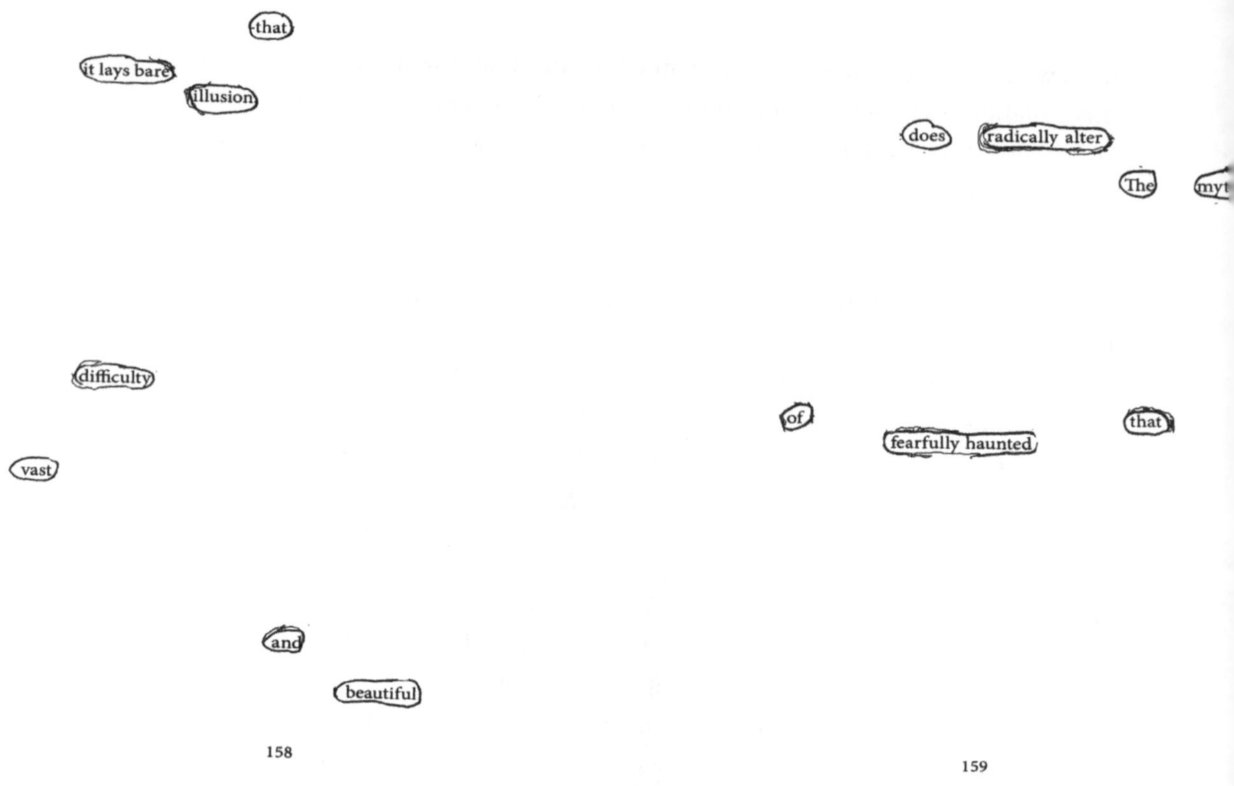

10.1. Geoffrey McGann, "The Meaning of Meaning," from *ALIEN*, 2015. Privately published by the artist in Los Angeles. Published with the permission of the artist.

starwords that have lost touch with the constellations that might explain them. But for consolation I am left with the blank space of Queneau's "infinity of words," where an "infinitesimal" remnant will always bereft to be seen.

Notes

1. Jerome McGann, "Marxism, Romanticism, and Postmodernism: An American Case History," *South Atlantic Quarterly* 88 (Summer 1989): 605–32; Felicia Hemans, "Literary History, Romanticism, and Felicia Hemans," *Modern Language Quarterly* 54, no. 2 (June 1993): 215–36; Joyce Kilmer: "The Alice Fallacy; or, Only God Can Make a Tree: A Dialogue of Pleasure and Instruction," *Chain* 3, no. 2 (Fall 1996): 108–34; Walter Scott, Henry James, Haruki Murakami—many others: I refer to the series of IVANHOE games that I played with everyone involved in the ARP Lab. See *Text Technology* 12, no. 2 (2003); and Jerome McGann, "Like Leaving the Nile: IVANHOE, a User's Manual," *Literature Compass* 2 (2005): 1–27.

2. Jerome McGann and Lisa Samuels, "Deformance and Interpretation," *New Literary History* 30, no. 1 (Winter 1999): 25–56.

3. Laura Riding, *Progress of Stories* (1982; repr., New York: Persea Books, 1994), 236.

4. William Blake Archive, http://www.blakearchive.org; G. Spencer Brown, *Laws of Form* (London: Allen and Unwin, 1969); Ramon Llull, *Ars Magna* (1305), in *Selected Works of Ramon Llull*, trans. Anthony Bonner, 2 vols. (Princeton, NJ: Princeton

University Press, 1985); Alfred Jarry, *Exploits and Opinions of Doctor Faustroll, 'Pataphysician (A Neo-Scientific Novel)* (1911), trans. Simon Watson Taylor (Boston: Exact Change, 1996); Raymond Queneau, *The Foundations of Literature (After David Hilbert)* (1976), in *Oulipo Laboratory*, trans. Harry Mathews and Iain White (London: Atlas Press, 1995). Although Randall McLeod's work on Obliterature has been a lifelong endeavor, the key essay is "Obliterature: Reading a Censored Text of Donne's 'To His Mistress Going to Bed,'" *English Manuscript Studies, 1100–1700* 12 (2005): 83–138; see also "THE UNEDITOR: Randall McLeod in Conversation with Mark Owens, July 2008," *Dot Dot Dot* 18 (August 24, 2009): 40–57.

5. The ARP Lab, founded in 2002 at University of Virginia, is no longer operating. The Wiki notice of its work is unhelpful. While the work at the Lab was highly collaborative, other researchers—Johanna Drucker, Andrea Laue, and Bethany Nowviskie in particular—had different priorities: for example, temporal modeling, graphesis, and ludic algorithms.

6. The results of two of those experiments were published in the *Antioch Review* 71, no. 3 (Summer 2013).

7. Of particular importance is the experimental work of Johanna Drucker; see especially *Graphesis: Visual Forms of Knowledge Production* (Cambridge, MA: Harvard University Press, 2014).

8. "Inter- and crossmedial interventions" refer to certain patacritical transpositions that can be enlisted to support the pataphysical hypotheses. That such support might be important was first argued in an essay that antedates ARP by seven years: Jerome McCann, "The Alice Fallacy; or, Only God Can Make a Tree: A Dialogue of Pleasure and Instruction," *Chain* 3, no. 2 (Fall 1996): 108–34. Because the essay's proposals were thoroughly ideatic, they anticipated and even called for the field tests (dramatic performances) that were carried out shortly afterward at SUNY Buffalo, University of Virginia, and University of North Carolina. The results were promising but inconclusive. Susan Bee's remediations (2011–12), however, were a brilliant success—so much so that they exposed a flaw in a line of the initial code that could have vitiated much of the lab's later work with Lear. After 2012 "The Invention Tree" was recoded as "The Ballade of the Vast Invention Tree," which is the script given here.

9. Algernon Charles Swinburne, *The Swinburne Letters*, ed. Cecil Y. Lang, 6 vols. (New Haven, CT: Yale University Press, 1959–62), 2:73–74.

10. Jerome McGann, "Wagner, Baudelaire, Swinburne: Poetry in the Condition of Music," *Victorian Poetry* 47 (Winter 2009): 625.

11. Lautréamont, *Œuvres complètes*, ed. Jean-Luc Steinmetz (Paris: Gallimard, 2009); for an English translation, see Lautréamont, *Maldoror (Les Chants de Maldoror), Together with a Translation of Lautréamont's Poésies*, trans. Guy Wernham (New York: New Directions, 1943, 1965). Wernham's translation has been justly criticized as sometimes less than literally accurate, but in imaginative equivalence it seems to me easily the best English translation available. In citing *Maldoror* I give two page numbers: first Steinmetz, then Wernham. Lautréamont was the nom de plume of Isadore Ducasse.

12. Poe published "The Philosophy of Composition" as an ex post facto commentary on "The Raven." In so doing, he seemed to leave intact the distinction between "composition" and "explanation." But as Stéphane Mallarmé was the first to understand, the essay was primarily a work of imaginative fiction, just as the poem was primarily a demonstration of prosodic method. In that view, which of those two works is "composition" and which is "explanation" is left undecided. (Reading "The Philosophy of Composition" as a fiction, a short story, is a decidedly useful interpretive move.) The strength of the conventional view that separates the provinces of prose and poetry, particularly as that view was reinforced by Romantic aesthetic theory, has made Poe's innovation difficult to appreciate.

13. "Imagining what you don't know" was Lisa Samuel's reformulation of Percy Bysshe Shelley's famous call (in his *Defense of Poetry*) to "imagine what we know." See Jerome McGann and Lisa Samuels, "Deformance and Interpretation," *New Literary History* 30, no. 1 (1999): 25–56.

14. Jerome McGann, "Texts in N-Dimensions and Interpretation in a New Key," *Text Technology* 12, no. 2 (2003): 1–18.

15. Jerome McGann, "Marking Texts in Many Dimensions," in *A Companion to Digital Humanities*, ed. Susan Schreibman, Ray Siemens, and John Unsworth (Oxford, UK: Blackwell, 2004), 198–217. In my initial ARP Lab reflection on textual dimensionalities, I theorized textuality in terms of six dimensions. No one at the time regarded these six dimensions as more than hypothetical, which gave rise at the time to interesting critical discussions. My current view is that those original six dimensions represented my reading of the world history of documentary representations. I now think it would be useful if a preliminary "Dublin Core" of dimensions were hypothetically established and widely tested for results. Explanatory models would emerge whose limits and affordances could then be rethought and redesigned.

16. Not all editions respect this bibliographical design installed by Ducasse in the first editions (1868–69). Wernham introduces numerous breaks in the prose poetry, presumably in the interest of supplying the texts with greater cognitive clarity.

17. For a closer discussion of Ricketts's *Salome*, see Jerome McGann, "Literature by Design Since 1790," *Victorian Poetry* 48, no. 1 (2010): 24–32.

18. In this and the following sentences I am quoting from Blake's *The Marriage of Heaven and Hell*, plates 4, 13, 16.

19. Plates 15–18 as well as figure 10.1 are drawn from Geoffrey McGann 's *ALIEN* (Los Angeles: privately printed, 2015), a parodic transmediation of my study of Poe.

20. Byron, "Stanzas to [Augusta]," 45.

Chapter 11

The Patacritical Demon, Two Decades Later

Johanna Drucker

The concept of the "patacritical demon" emerged in the context of the Speculative Computing Lab (SpecLab) at the University of Virginia in the early 2000s.[1] The loosely formed and barely institutional SpecLab was a forum for conversation and exploration of possibilities that aimed to push the boundaries of the then-nascent digital humanities. My colleague and cofounder, Jerome McGann, and I shared an enthusiasm for the experimental tradition in literary and aesthetic work. That included a conviction that various precedents might be drawn on to inform projects against the grain, so to speak, of the algorithmically correct direction that was already becoming dominant in the emerging field of digital humanities. The critical legacy of deconstruction, with its tenets of historical and cultural relativism, emphases on reading practices, and impulses to produce knowledge in accord with post-Cartesian models, was difficult to incorporate into the planning sessions of digital humanities projects. The exigencies of computational logic made any interpretative approach to production difficult, if not impossible, at the level of infrastructure or procedure. As we duly learned our lessons of code, of markup languages and nested hierarchies, decision trees and regular expressions, recursion and parsing, we watched many closely held beliefs about humanistic methods evaporate. The machines, it seemed, could *produce* an infinite amount of nonsense through the use of logical statements, but could not *process* any illogical, ambiguous, contradictory, or conflicting statements. Computers, in other words, are good for what computers are good for: automation of explicitly articulated tasks and functions. Hardly news, but rather a cold bucket of water thrown on those for whom natural (not formal) languages are the touchstone of experience and for whom interpretative (not objective) modes of knowledge are the core of our professional work and personal beliefs. For us, the goal of digital work was *not* to approach the condition of science—quite the contrary, it was to promote humanistic methods.

Our effort to push a wedge into the rapidly closing window of that possibility was meant to keep at least part of the digital humanities field from a complete capitulation to the rules of those formal languages and to imagine, at least speculatively, that humanistic, poetic, aesthetically adventurous methods might find a place in the foundations of our work. In other words, aesthetic artifacts were not merely to be objects of study, the material under examination in new digital frameworks, but were to serve as methodological models for creating platforms and procedures in these technologies. So we gleaned principles from Lucretius, inflected by Alfred Jarry, with a conviction that pataphysics could be brought to bear on the formulation of an experimental operation. That operation would be the patacritical demon—a platform for exposing the non-self-identical character of texts through a hermeneutic link between production and reception. The demon would expose anomalies within all systems, show the exceptional as a fundamental condition of phenomena, and play with the generative and provocative potential of representations—surrogates, derivatives, those always constructed expressions of what supposedly *is*. From such theoretical abstractions, grounded in the constructivist traditions of epistemology, our demon would be able to do something—but what exactly?

To put this into some kind of reasonable context, to offer something sufficiently concrete to communicate at least an outline of the specter that haunted our imaginations, I have to sketch a few more reference points. McGann and I, along with a handful of variously willing and skeptical colleagues and graduate students, had created two experimental projects in which interpretation was a central feature. One was Temporal Modelling, which attempted to model nonlinear temporal relations using nonstandard metrics, "rubber timelines," and other graphical devices that would in turn generate structured data. The other was the Ivanhoe Game, an environment for multiplayer rewriting of literary texts. Both platforms supported imaginative activity, but trying to coax a computer into interpretative acts was another matter. One day we used a scanner and an OCR (optical character recognition) program to conduct a series of experiments. A text, placed on the scanner, was sent through a sequence of processing attempts. Nothing was changed between one scan and the next. The text sample stayed in the same place, the settings on the scanner were kept constant, and the instructions to the OCR program were identical—but the results were slightly altered. This moment (so trivial but so revelatory) enacted the principle that reception *is* production, even in a fully automated environment. Agree or disagree as you like (I am inclined to a fairly modest appraisal of the interpretative capabilities of the scanner software), the experiment allowed variation in each reading/scanning to register as significant.

Now, keep in mind that the driving impulse of SpecLab was play; the overriding rubric under which its activities were undertaken was another one of my neologisms, "de-lightenment," and the invention of the patacritical demon was designed to instantiate the ever-unachievable goal of exposing interpretation as a complex act of textual production. Our attachment to anomalies ruled over systematic reason, as per Jarry's insistence on exceptions. This investigation of exceptions drew (loosely) on the statistical origins of Jarry's 'pataphysics—its attention to probabilistic rather than mechanistic rules. But whereas the "science" of statistics had been put at the service of administrative and actuarial implementations (the original term derived from collecting data about nation states as "political arithmetic"), we saw 'pataphysics (in the original formulation) outstrip the bounds of probabilistic discipline into poetic play. While it would be a mistake to conflate statistics (data production) and probability (estimates of likelihood/outcomes), they each had a role to play in our conception of Jarry's work.

By coining the term pata*criticism*, I shifted Jarry's original study of phenomena into an applied method of engagement with aesthetic objects on terms appropriate to their specificity (aligned with Jarry's concern with "the particular" by contrast to generalizable tenets of natural science). The desire to provide a foundation for critical action undertaken with pataphysical influence drove the design of this project (fig. 11.1). The failure of the project remains one of its points of success—it could not succeed. But more on that below.

11.1. Johanna Drucker, design for business cards for Applied Research in Patacriticism, 2003. © Johanna Drucker.

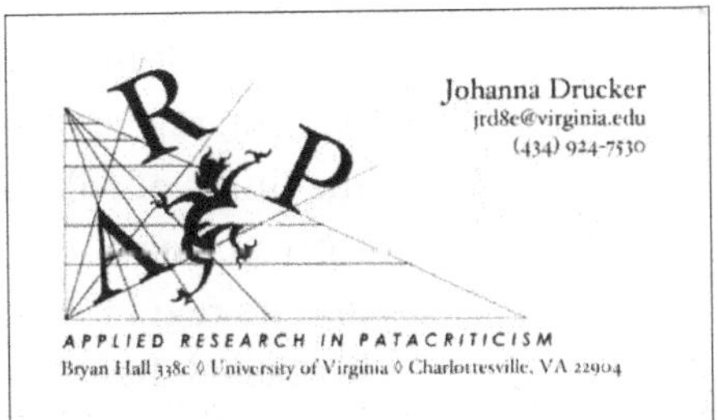

This patacritical work was undertaken between 2001 and 2003 at the University of Virginia, where digital humanities activity was exemplary and cutting-edge. But its techniques (necessarily, from a strictly practical perspective) were far from poetic methods, however, and even antithetical to them. The idea of an "aesthetic provocation" was not easily reconciled with parsing a document or running a program. Inventing the demon, even as a concept, was a way to signal the need to keep the spirit of the imaginative avant-garde (and some of its important predecessors) alive within the creation of digital projects. For me, Jarry, the French symbolists Arthur Rimbaud and Paul Verlaine, the Dada and surrealist poets, the radically inventive Comte de Lautréamont, and the visionary Antonin Artaud, among others, were figures of substantive idiosyncratic thought. Jarry's 'pataphysics had been given a renewed currency through the interest of a cluster of visual and conceptual poets in the 1970s and 1980s—Steve McCaffery and bpNichol (who invented the "Pataphysical Hardware Company), with their coinage of Canadian "Pataphysics—and the brilliant next generation they inspired, specifically, Christian Bök and Darren Wershler. So the reach toward Jarry was hardly unusual among literary practitioners. Our focus on Jarry was also motivated by the fact that pataphysics was, in McGann's opinion, a response to the dominant models of late nineteenth-century statistics. In traditional quantitative analysis, anomalies were characterized as outliers. They were not seen as indicators of significance, and certainly not as indicators of the greatest significance. Early statisticians, in fact, were highly unlikely to see anomalies as points of light shining from within the abyss of the as-yet-unknown, signaling directions for exploration ahead. But Jarry did see them this way, and McGann and I were sympathetic to that sensibility.

An excerpt from a piece I wrote at the time (around 2003), makes our interpretation of pataphysics clear:

> Rather than generalize from observation of empirical phenomena towards a set of rules that appear to hold true in accounting for the physical world, pataphysical attention to exceptions emphasizes the particular. Anomalies are not merely statistical outliers, but independent instances, real, actual demonstrations of the mutability of all energy in its existence as matter. While such principles are easily grasped and intuitively sensible, the nasty traditions of western science, with their reductive empirico-positivist bent, repress nothing so much as the capacity of imagination to escape the limits of rule-bound deductive logic. Nothing constrains our capacity to perceive so much as the expectation imposed by the order of reason and its regulated methods of description. Anything that doesn't fit gets bracketed. But the unfit and the particular are the stuff of the pataphysical world. And patacriticism is the interpretive method developed to apprehend the infinitely varied and highly specific character of each instance of the mutable condition of existence.[2]

I set out to visualize the process of patacriticism in drawings of interpretation as a generative method. In these diagrammatic demonstrations, the "event space" of reading (interpretation) is not presented as an act of positivist or empirical perception, but as a subjective intervention in a discourse field of potentialities. I was making use of techniques I had developed decades earlier in making drawings of events. I thought of these as "trace" drawings, records of processes and occurrences. Revisiting these approaches in the context of the patacritical demon, I combined these graphic methods with schematic diagrams of reading practices in order to create images of textual production as provocation. These were meant to be speculative rather than fanciful, to embody a possibility, not a fantasy. I called these "poetentialities," the poetic visualization of potential texts. The sketches were based on a post-poststructuralist paradigm in which a third term was introduced to create a trialectic that extended the dialectic into the realm of infinite play. The demon was envisioned as a program or application that would expose interpretation—show that an act of reading makes a work, in each instance, as a *particularity*, in the spirit of Jarry's "science of the particular" in which "each thing and each event" is "the singularity that makes it an exception."[3] We didn't actually *make* the demon; rather, we simply constantly invoked it, kept the idea alive, gestured toward it with sketches and conversation—in other words, the demon itself remained an "imaginary solution."

Ultimately, the creation of the concept was a commitment to keeping aesthetic, imaginative, interpretative methods foremost in an environment (work in digital humanities) that largely precluded them from consideration on practical grounds. In other notes I wrote at the time, I said, "The goal of patacritical computing is to keep digital humanities from falling into mere 'instrumental' operations (either administered information management or engineering/statistical calculations)." This, to return to the thread left hanging above that referenced the necessity of failure, was why the project could not succeed. Any final version of the demon that might actually implement its principles according to systematic and repeatable protocols would, by definition, be in violation of those principles. The idea of creating a program or platform for the demon that *worked* would only be undertaken by someone who "*like totally*, did not *get* the demon." That is, of course, not a scholarly citation. Nor was the demon a scholarly tool or instrument. It was an intervention, a provocation.

The pataphysical, to paraphrase my earlier remarks, recognizes the exceptional as the condition of being. Deviation is a principle to demonstrate that systematic consistency is merely a conceit, the effect of letting generalities impose themselves on the particularity of being. We felt then, and I still feel now, that invoking pataphysics was a way to think about computing outside of the problem-solving, engineering sensibility and to create open-ended, generative capabilities for humanistic, imaginative, interpretative work. As part of a larger agenda to inform the digital with humanistic methods, poetic and aesthetic techniques, the idea of the demon remains useful—perhaps most valuable as an unachievable goal, one meant to inspire experimentation rather than provide solutions.

So, two decades later, what assessment would I make of this project? What implications does it still have for how we are thinking about pataphysics within poetic and/or critical practice? And how does it, in hindsight, relate to the development of digital humanities?

Almost from its inception, the *digital* humanities was implemented as *computational* humanities. This means it depended on processes that made use of discrete and explicit instructions. These would then be carried out on files that had been parameterized (or tokenized, broken into computable units) in formal, explicit terms. Though these formal processes were themselves interpretative (any algorithm is a human-authored text and parameterization is performed according to protocols that bear the imprint of the decisions that shape their operations), they are operationally mechanistic. Once these scripts were written, they worked automatically, excluding the interpretative methods that are central to the humanities—and certainly excluding anomalous exceptions to rules. Simply by being executed in computational environments, the digital humanities made concessions from the outset that largely abandoned traditional humanistic values.

In contrast to this, we had envisioned the demon in a ludic spirit. Invoking the pseudoscientific foundations of Jarry's thought, in particular his interest in anomalies, the patacritical method was committed to play. Play takes on a resonant meaning here, not as something trivial or insignificant, but as a fundamental feature of epistemology and interpretation. Play is the space of intellectual mobility and flexibility, that which keeps any object of intellectual inquiry (text, image, performance, artifact) from simply being understood in a one-dimensional construction of its identity. Even more important, play is the activity that keeps an object from being identical to itself, from being an object whose ontological status is the same as its epistemological one. Play is the hermeneutical space in which the apprehension of an object constructs what it appears to be—an interpretation.

But digital humanities, as noted, developed with very different constraints. Roberto Busa's famous first engagement with computational method shows how certain original formulations of the intersection of humanities and computing set the pattern for subsequent work. Busa's digitized version of his fifty-six-volume concordance, an index to the work of Thomas Aquinas, is considered by many to be the founding project in digital humanities. Commonly referred to by a short version of its title as the *Index Thomisticus*, this was a project with a long history. Busa's 1942 dissertation had been titled "The Thomistic Terminology of Interiority."[4] Busa's focus on terminology made it particularly suitable for early digital humanities work, and in fact, *linguistic computing* was the phrase under which this early activity was identified. Texts could be processed unambiguously at the level of basic encoding, because of their structure as discrete characters and spaces. But text processing is not the same as interpretation or reading. The questions inherent in Busa's work (though not formulated by him) about the distinction between the ontological identity of a word and its epistemological resonance within a probabilistic space of interpretation remain at the heart of the impasse faced by digital humanities. The demon was designed to force that space into view as a disturbance in the hermeneutic field.

Busa's original research (first for his dissertation and then for the *Index*) was executed using the then-standard method of writing information on index cards by hand.[5] A concordance is a word list, a way of creating a cross-reference to terms within a corpus. But the question of how and when a word is the same as another is not trivial ("the *mother* sheltered her children as the *mother* of all storms approached"). Aside from the unwieldiness of the sheer scale of the project (he apparently tracked about nine million instances), its subject matter and its analytic methods posed significant challenges with or without computational assistance. In addition to the concept of interiority in Aquinas, Busa focused terms related to the metaphysics of *presence*. By definition, these are elusive concepts, difficult to pin to specific words: Where does exteriority leave off and interiority begin in processes of prayer, reflection, or faith? And how can *presence*, indicated by a word that signifies by referencing an *absent* meaning, appear within a text? The interpretative dimensions of determining how words signify, crucial to humanities work, are immediately apparent as conundrums rather than ideas that can be specified mechanistically. In addition, the complexities of language required that all variants and related versions of the terminology be able to be cross-referenced (e.g., cognitive, cognition, incognito).

The manual work of identifying these terms and their place in Aquinas's texts was already done by 1949, when Busa met Thomas Watson, head of IBM, and they decided to undertake a digital version of the *Index*.[6] The initial digital version of this project took twenty-five years (!) to complete (remember, this was not online, just automated). The design puts the contradictions between methods and concepts into focus—between the explicitness enacted by the computational environment and the elusive resonance of the terminology of a metaphysics of presence. If ever a project is plagued by the demon, it is this one, doing its absolute best to eliminate play and guarantee certainty in relation to terms that do not lend themselves to disambiguation.

A look at the still-working site shows how the search protocols are designed (to find X, do Y). Search terms are defined from specific to more broadly inclusive: the "desired word form," a "lemma entry," or a "word form" that will select "all of the forms belonging to the same lemma." Standard Boolean operations included wild-card characters and so on. But such a search cannot bring forth a word linked by interpretation or implicit association. One might find a "mysterious presence" by searching the term *praesentia* but not a "suffused sensation of connection" or other descriptions. The very specificity that undergirds automated search negates the possibility of finding concepts expressed in vague, allusive, paraphrased, or metaphoric terms. Furthermore, the possibility of ambiguous expressions, or multivalent ones, cannot be accommodated in the formal procedures of automated search. This remains true; even if more recently developed text analysis and data mining tools can analyze statistical features of texts to extract inferences, making use of probabilistic methods, they still process the literal character string mechanistically. As Dino Buzzetti has pointed out, computational operations work on the plane of discourse while pretending to work on the plane of reference.[7] He was specifically referring to markup languages and the insertion of interpretative tags into the character string of the file. This conflation is highly problematic, as the plane of reference (the "told") is a construct, while the plane of discourse ("the telling") is palpably present. The irony of Busa's engagement with presence becomes clearer as the absent referent is so wonderfully suited to the questions the process engages.

Much more could be said about Busa's work and its peculiar aptness as a founding instance of digital humanities. However, I want to consider the way this project is emblematic of the ways digital humanities developed into the present—and the work the demon might still do. The original aspirations of digital humanities varied according to project, but were generally and collectively utopic and visionary. Computational linguistics took up issues of stylometrics that were used for authorship attribution, for instance, in an era when such discussion was still a burning issue. Another early endeavor focused on machine translation. This involved elaborate investigations of syntactical structure, vocabulary and morphological equivalence across different languages. This was in turn bound up with reflections on language acquisition and cognition in humans, investigations that were linked to early artificial intelligence (AI), as well as work by Noam Chomsky and others. These began with the idea of modeling human intelligence and gradually came to terms with the recognition that knowledge was informed by an embodied life. Embodiment and the details of experience—trivial as well as more general knowledge—were required to build intelligence.

While AI discussions still continue to emerge, the ideas of silliness, playfulness, and even sly play elude its predictive formulations. John Seabrook's recent piece "The Next Word," by illustrating the extent to which a machine could learn to write for the *New Yorker*, outlines the current capabilities of automated text-generating engines.[8] The unstated but surprising takeaway from that piece (not Seabrook's own argument) is that the irrational playfulness of experimental writing from the avant-garde to innovative contemporary poetics (and with a healthy heap of Lear-and-Seuss-type nonsense along the way) might be the only compositional mode to escape predictability. Claims for the social value of nonnormative syntax may yet have a role to play in keeping open imaginative spaces of engagement with experience. The ghost of Viktor Shklovsky may yet perturb the workings of the machine.

Much more could be said about the way digital humanities emerged. Computational approaches to exploring the possibilities of networked environments, hypertextual editing, virtual aggregation of distributed materials, crowdsourced projects, and web presentation in nonlinear formats are all part of its inventory.

Methods of construction, presentation, and electronic infrastructures can be used to advance humanistic work. But they do not use or incorporate humanistic methods in their design, because hermeneutic processes of interpretative engagement are almost always precluded from the efficient operations and formal logic of computation. Like Busa's concordance, computation collapses the metaphysical and metaphorical into the literal. In the process, it precludes the possibility of play in the system. Play would incorporate whim, taste, idiosyncrasy, the shifts of mood and attitude that characterize the specificity of human processing as understanding—in which no reading is ever the same as a text or experience, but is always inventing anew (even if that newness is ennui, boredom, or disaffection with the experience). But the idiosyncratic, subjective specificity of hermeneutic experience is not structured into our tools and platforms.

The digital humanities may aspire, now, to many things: to augment human experience through integrating the cultural record into an accessible dimension of daily life; to expose cultural differences and community values within a system that sustains universal access to that material; and to support equitable participation among a wide range of demographic groups. The digital humanities may continue to try to save the humanities from institutional extinction, to revive and perpetuate the legacy of aesthetic, historical, political, and cultural materials through a participatory environment—or, alternatively, to create tools and platforms that allow interrogation of current practices in their ideological dimensions. These and many other goals inform the projects of invention and reparation that motivate digital activity and its innovations. But all concede, fundamentally, to the need for such work to be done within the terms set by the technology. Sadly, these are not playful, nor are they imaginatively engaged.[9] They do not derive from the conditions of embodied, partial, and situated knowledge in all of its nonreplicable, nonstandardizable specificity and particularity. The digital humanities depends on procedures and protocols borrowed from the natural and social sciences that do not entertain play or hermeneutic particularity.

The demon was meant to do this—but not in an instrumental way. The poetics of patacriticism, its own aspiration to made-ness, was of course to be realized in the participle form—as making. Traditions of pataphysics continue to inspire new work. The concepts have a generative capacity that still functions as an imaginative engine. Taking up the mantle of any early form always risks mere mimetic anachronism—contemporary Dadaist and surrealist works do not produce the same frissons as did their first appearances a century ago. But forms and traditions exist to be used, reused, remade anew, and pataphysics has a legitimate place in the canon of poetic practices.

Patacriticism was a novel invention, one that embraced the anomalous nature of interpretative activity as a fully perverse act, far from the normative terms of academic practice and pedagogy. It was meant as a nose-thumbing gesture, an expression of full irreverence, an embrace of the foibles and follies of imagining an act of interpretation could ever be equivalent to or exhaust its object. It was a dedicatedly nonmimetic and nonrepresentational approach to criticism and, by extension, to the intellectual work of the humanities. I know because I invented the term and designed the creature. Any attempt to build a demon that actually worked would be at odds with the pataphysical demon's conceptual underpinnings to make a performative and generative concept that could not be realized. We realized other kinds of interpretative activity in the Ivanhoe Game and in Temporal Modelling to a limited but still significant degree. But the unique character of the demon was to be its own iterative *un*realizability, a particularity that exists always just beyond instantiation in any form that might become recognizable and familiar, and thus, appear to be the same as itself.

Notes

1. The patacritical demon would not have existed without Jerome McGann as a partner in its conception, but the Wikipedia article on ARP (Applied Research in Patacriticism) mistakenly cited him as the sole founder of SpecLab. Though this error has since been rectified (Wikipedia entry accessed May 29, 2020), it still does not note that I coined the term "patacriticism," drew the logo, and designed the cards we carried. Our conversations and mutual engagement in the project brought it about, always as a joint endeavor. The same was true of the Ivanhoe Game. Temporal Modelling, however, was my project, and the first of these. Bethany Nowviskie, who we were fortunate to have as our graduate student at the time, played a major role in implementation of both of those projects, which were meant to actually function—unlike the fully perverse demon.

2. Taken from unpublished notes; for drawings and another discussion, see Johanna Drucker, "The Patacritical Demon," in *SpecLab: Digital Aesthetics and Projects in Speculative Computing* (Chicago: University of Chicago Press, 2009), 119–26.

3. Roger Shattuck, "Superliminal Note," in "What Is Pataphysics?," ed. Roger Shattuck and Simon Watson Taylor, special issue, *Evergreen Review* 4, no. 13 (May–June 1960): 28.

4. Nico Sprokel, "The 'Index Thomisticus,'" *Gregorium* 59, no. 4 (1978): 739–50. This is an excellent description of the project in full detail including each step of the process.

5. Daniel Esparza, "The Jesuit Who Invented Hypertext," *Aleteia,* September 16, 2016, https://aleteia.org/2016/09/16/the-jesuit-who-invented-hypertext.

6. The working version of the *Index* provides a useful introduction to the dimensions of the project: https://www.corpusthomisticum.org/it/index.age.

7. Dino Buzzetti, "Digital Text Representation: Expression and Content," in *Contexts: Proceedings of Alternative Natural Philosophy Association (ANPA), 31st International Meeting,* ed. A. D. Ford (Cambridge, UK: Wesley House, 2010), 124–45.

8. John Seabrook, "The Next Word: Where Will Predictive Text Take Us?," *New Yorker*, October 14, 2019, https://www.newyorker.com/magazine/2019/10/14/can-a-machine-learn-to-write-for-the-new-yorker.

9. The work of Andrew Hugill and Jim Hendler, described in their chapter in this volume, is a welcome counterexample.

Chapter 12

Reflections on Applied Research in Patacriticism

Prism and Reading's Shape

Brandon Walsh

In his introduction to *Dr. Faustroll, Pataphysician*, Roger Shattuck suggests that Alfred Jarry deliberately plants the "recalcitrant reader's response"[1] to his absurd text in the mouth of Bosse-de-Nage, Dr. Faustroll's baboon companion: "Bosse-de-Nage, inordinately interested, forgot himself so far as to think visibly: 'Ha ha!'"[2] The analysis makes good sense: Bosse-de-Nage acts as the most representative reader of the textual world around him, even if his response is only ever represented to the holder of the novel as twin laughing syllables. Bosse-de-Nage's laughter visibly shakes him, to be sure, but his thought becomes visible in a second sense, as ink on the read page. The moment is not one of passive reception but rather one of active participation in the textual universe. The baboon's laughter takes shape as a running reader's commentary on the text, printed as part of the novel proper. Bosse-de-Nage becomes a figure for writers, those visible thinkers who negotiate such transformations from thought to ink on a regular basis. Interpretation fuses with text, each structuring one another in a single laughing moment from the same character. To explore just this complex point of intersection, over a century later the Praxis Program team[3] at the University of Virginia's Scholars' Lab developed Prism,[4] a browser-based application that crowdsources textual interpretation to discover trends in collaborative reading. Users mark texts with traces of their own analyses, and Prism visualizes the ways in which such interpretations reshape text and reader alike.

Jarry suggests that a text and its reception can structure one another, and the digital environment offers new and powerful ways to rethink how we have always read. As Johanna Drucker and Bethany Nowviskie suggest of the uses of pataphysics and speculative computing for digital humanities, "interpretation of subjective activity can be formalized *concurrent with* its production," and we can conceive of user interfaces and tools that incorporate "subjective perspectives into *the process* of digital humanities."[5] Prism aims to be one such tool, dynamically visualizing the subjective interpretation of complex documents by groups of readers. The application asks users to configure their reading of a short text along a series of axes, or facets. After a user reads and marks a text according to these categories, Prism records the user's interpretation and aggregates it along with all other users' readings of the text, producing visualizations that offer glimpses of trends in the subjective reading of the document. Users asked to mark words and phrases in *A Portrait of the Artist as a Young Man* according to the categories of modernism and realism, for example, can see how their understanding of literary aesthetics maps onto the larger group's analysis. *Portrait*, which might have seemed static and fixed, becomes a loose spectrum of individual and shared interpretations playing across the page, a rainbow-colored visualization of where modernism ends and realism begins. The text alters before the eyes of the user, morphing and changing shape according to these meanings as text, size, and color come to reflect the collective interpretation of the group.

Prism emerged from a long tradition of speculative thought by Drucker, Jerome McGann, Nowviskie, and other pioneers at the University of Virginia's SpecLab. In their digital experiments, SpecLab participants imagined the intervention of pataphysics as a means by which they could preserve the infinite subjective possibilities of interpretation in a digital world whose markup schemas and hierarchical classifications were ill suited for complex humanities documents.

Interpretation feeds into visualization, which then retroactively changes the understanding of the text. In this spirit, the reading interface produced by Prism is a playful bit of quantitative sleight of hand: the interpretations carefully and dutifully supplied in the first segment of the exercise are suddenly quantified, aggregated, and displayed. Humanistic inquiry meets exactly the sort of computational approach that is often held up publicly as the disastrous future digital humanities will bring to literary study. But, of course, such data is never meant as an end in itself: Prism's visualizations lean toward aesthetic provocations and humanistic conversation precisely because they masquerade as quantitative "imaginary solutions" to interpretive questions: one might ask and be answered, "Is [James] Joyce being modernist or realist when he uses the word 'toocoo' in this passage? Well, according to Prism (at the time this essay was written), it is exactly 88.5 percent modernist. Problem solved." The absurdity of such mathematical statements produced by Prism generates the need for further inquiry, exploding the interpretive dimensions of the text under discussion rather than narrowing them to a fixed point. To return to our central optical metaphor, Prism refracts interpretation in new and unexpected directions, and it does so by way of computation. Prism's three fixed interpretive categories (themselves adjustable at the outset of a Prism "game") allow for changeable paths into a text, reconfiguring our understanding of what it means to read it in the first place. In the process, the tool exposes the deeply humanistic origins of quantitative approaches to literary interpretation.

At the same time, reading through Prism exposes the mechanistic nature of literary interpretation. The application smashes interpretation against the engine of the machine: a decision by the user to interpret a particular word of *Portrait* as realism becomes a number added to a particular database field. Interpretation becomes quantified, or rather it reveals itself to have been quantifiable all along. As Stephen Ramsay argues, "The apparently objective realms of mathematics and computing can be made to fit with the insistently subjective processes of interpretation precisely because computational processes, when motivated by interpretive questions, are already fully aligned with the imperatives of humanistic inquiry."[6] Scansion, close reading, structuralist theory: all of these are forms of reading that rely, in some sense, on counting and the recognition of patterns. Prism dramatizes a pattern-based approach to literary study after the fact, but moreover clarifies how every aspect of computation requires interpretative decisions on the part of its implementers. In the case of our tool, for example, the decision to use a constrained vocabulary reflects a poststructuralist assumption that the close scrutiny and juxtaposition of binaries or trinaries will cause them to break down. By standing in both humanistic and computational worlds, Prism exposes how one cannot exist without the other. By reconnecting the two, we can revitalize our sense of the possibilities contained by a text and how our reading shapes it.

Beyond serving as the focal point for writing and reception, Bosse-de-Nage's laughter also captures the playful spirit that Prism hopes to recover for reading and interpretation. Prism was under active development by two cohorts of Scholars' Lab graduate fellows, from fall 2011 to spring 2013. During that time, the interface was radically redesigned in favor of a playful, tactile experience: color schemes were brightened, supplemental content minimized, and the general tone of the project modified to conceive of the activity in gamelike terms. We hoped to recover the sense of possibility that a childlike sense of play brings with it, when an exploratory freedom to fail offers the richest ground for exploration.[7] If 'pataphysics is a science of exceptions, we offered Prism as an attempt to render such exceptions visible. By making tactile and visual the normally invisible processes of reading and interpretation, Prism allows users to experience these activities anew. The attempt to return to an earlier scene of reading was, in many ways, more successful than anticipated: Prism has seen strong use in primary and secondary school classrooms, among communities of teachers more interested in how we *teach* reading than in how we conceive of it. Pataphysics offers a model for subverting and, ultimately, rethinking institutionalized approaches to reading, digitally or otherwise. By infusing reading with a sense of pataphysical play, we counter what has been described as the hermeneutics of suspicion[8] with the baboon's laughter: an equally valid response that unfolds new avenues of textual study rather than closes them off.

Analysis at the level in which Prism trades may seem like small stakes, but pataphysics suggests that such trivial matters, such games, are always serious business: "Thus pataphysics is impossible. Must one kill oneself to prove it? Indeed, since it is not serious. But it is exactly this which is its seriousness."[9] Prism is all the more serious for its apparent triviality. Interpretation always involves a personal sacrifice to another text, person, or group. Something is always given away, something transformed. After all, Bosse-de-Nage "forgot himself" when laughing his thought into existence. Interpretation is a dangerous game, but it is one that we must all play. Prism's most helpful intervention is in how it unsettles received notions of how the reading process takes shape. It just might help us remember something of ourselves as we play along.

Notes

1. Roger Shattuck, introduction to *Exploits and Opinions of Doctor Faustroll, Pataphysician (A Neo-Scientific Novel)* (1911), by Alfred Jarry, trans. Simon Watson Taylor (Boston: Exact Change, 1996), xviii.

2. Jarry, *Faustroll*, 54.

3. For a full list of contributors, see http://prism.scholarslab.org/pages/about. The project was developed by graduate student fellows in the Scholars' Lab alongside the Lab's faculty and staff.

4. Source code available at https://github.com/scholarslab/prism. Experiment with Prism at http://prism.scholarslab.org.

5. Johanna Drucker and Bethany Nowviskie, "Speculative Computing: Aesthetic Provocations in Humanities Computing," in *A Companion to Digital Humanities*, ed. Susan Schreibman, Ray Siemens, and John Unsworth (Oxford, UK: Blackwell, 2004), 433, 441.

6. Stephen Ramsay, "In Praise of Pattern," *TEXT Technology: the journal of computer text processing* 14, no. 2 (2005): 178.

7. For more on such an ethos of critical failure in the context of the Scholars' Lab, see Bethany Nowviskie, "Too Small to Fail," *Bethany Nowviskie* (blog), October 13, 2012, http://nowviskie.org/2012/too-small-to-fail.

8. The term comes from Paul Ricoeur, though Rita Felski, among others, has critiqued the practice as it pervades literary studies.

9. Jean Baudrillard, "Pataphysics," trans. Drew Burk, CTheory.net, January 4, 2007, https://journals.uvic.ca/index.php/ctheory/article/view/14496/5338.

Chapter 13

The Pataquerical Imagination

Midrashic Antinomianism and the Promise of Bent Studies

Charles Bernstein

I. [Facsimile]

A specter is haunting official verse culture—the specter of pataquericalism. All the forces have entered into a nepohumanist alliance to exorcise this specter: Associated Writing Programs and Pulitzer, *New Yorker* and *New York Review of Books*, elliptical lyricists and hybrid centrists.[1] Over the past two decades, the stranglehold of Cold War scenic-voice poems has loosened under the pressure of the literary in(ter)ventions of *L=A=N=G=U=A=G=E* and its partisans to let a soupçon of flowers bloom in official verse culture greenhouses. The forms demonized a few decades ago are now embraced as a mark of new inclusiveness, a fair and balanced approach to poetry styles, marking not the end to poetic ideology but an indefinite cessation.

It is high time that pataquericalists should openly, in the face of the whole poetry world, display their views, parade their aims, parody their tendencies, and meet this old husband's tale of the specter of Bent Studies with a whoosh & higgly hoot & a he-ho-hah.

The history of all hitherto existing poetry is the history of pataquerical struggles. Normal and perverse, highbred and vernacular, metered and unmetered, versed and averse, national and barbaric, couth and uncouth, proper and wrong, manly and unmanly, black and white, jew and goy, pigeon and sparrow, fancy and imagination, miscegenated and pure, assimilated and ideolectical, dominated and dominatrix—stood in constant opposition to one another, carried on an uninterrupted, now hidden, now open fight, a fight that each time ended either in a revolutionary reconstitution of poetry at large or in the triumph of the mediocracy. The modern necrohumane society that has sprouted from the ruins of the poetry wars has not done away with these antagonisms. It has established new hybrids, new conditions of normalcy, new forms of correctness in place of the old ones.

III. Com(op)positionality

In *Wordsworth's Philosophic Song*, Simon Jarvis counters a corrosive assumption about ideological critique.[2] In *The German Ideology*, Jarvis reminds us, Karl Marx takes to task the idealists known as Young Hegelians for their iconoclastic hubris: the assumption that by debunking false consciousness—idol smashing—they will free themselves from idols once and for all. The mistake of the Young Hegelians was to see debunking as an end in itself rather than as a part of a dialectical process of critique, to take an Emersonian rather than a Marxist swerve, a process that has no terminal point but, like a Klein bottle, doubles back on itself (or like sweaters at the old Klein's department store, is always on sale at a better price).

The legacy of romanticism haunts the contemporary imagination of poetry. Romantic ideology, in Jerome McGann's sense, underwrites the hegemonic ideology of postwar US poetics—that poetry, through its commitment to lyric sincerity (high lyric) and refined craft (highbred) can be a universal expression of human sentiment.[3] Poetry, in its highest, and often dullest, forms, is able to transcend partisan bickering and divisive position taking. It is a bulwark against the inhuman tyrannies of hypernationalism, fascism, and Pol-Pot-Stalin-Mao-Tse-Tung thought: regimes of totalitarian violence that are an affront to humanity. Except that these monstrous irruptions are entirely human and define us as much as moral sentiment or ethical conduct.

In our time, the dominant strain of official verse culture is defined by its presumption of being above the fray of special interests, bickering movements, and groups. The recent rise of elliptical and hybrid poetics is a case in point, for this is not a movement but a strategy to contain disruptive and unruly ideological and historical—which is to say *aesthetic*—challenges.[4] It is a poetics of assimilation and accommodation, and, as such, is very much in line with the traditional values of much American poetry and poetry criticism of the Cold War.

There is no escape from aesthetic ideology, despite the fervent insistence of the fair and balanced idealists in their rejection of excess, dissidence, and oppositionality—that is, aversion of the three *q*'s: queered, quixotic, querulous. The repression of aesthetic ideology under the banner of convention, accessibility, compromise, refinement, or humanist literary values has the effect of naturalizing the idealists' unacknowledged positions and group affiliations. This subliming fosters a poetry of capitulation and compromise whose telltale signs are often stylistic restraint and lyric self-regulation, which as an aesthetic position could be promising but in a humanist vacuum are merely proto-professional. This is the difference between craft and method, positivism and the dialogic, Christian universalism and Minute Particulars, homogenization and the syncretic.

To imagine that there is a neutral space, a craft of poetry, that is free of ideological domination or contamination is positivism. In poetry culture, it is the most virulent form of ideological self-deception because it cannot open up to contradiction, difference, or dialectic, that is, to *com(op)positionality*.

To transcend ideology, aesthetic partisanship, movement, groups, and positions is to be blinded by idolatry.

A poetics is valuable to the degree that it is able to engender other positions in response, both complementary and oppositional. The cyclical triumphalism of postpartisanship in postwar US poetry, insofar as it intends to end the argument rather than foment it, is the most disingenuous form of position-taking.

This triumphalism mirrors, rather than counters, the avant-gardism of formalist progress, which eradicates the prior and the other almost as fast as it eradicates itself.

Insofar as postpartisan cultural formations align themselves with the dominant forms of poetic practice, both more radical and more conventional at the same time, they will enjoy flickering moments of hegemony, having absorbed into their fold the insurgent counterhegemonic flows of the immediate past. But such postmodern turns in official verse culture can be successful only to the degree that they elide the most challenging and dynamic poetic innovations that are newly emerging or as yet unsettled (including ones that provoke bewilderment, disgust, hostility, and genre concerns). The degree to which the postmodern turn in official verse culture accommodates and contains the radical innovations of the recent past is the degree to which official verse culture is incapable of acknowledging the uncontainable inventions of the ever-actualizing, ever-shifting present.

The task of bent studies is to move beyond the "experimental" to the untried, necessary, newly forming, provisional, inventive. Innovation resists maps. I want a poetics that rejects the historical avant-garde's colonic high ground of single best solution but also rejects its dark twin, the bottom-feeding low ground of official verse culture's lobotomization of poetic invention.

Conflict is art's quiver.

The pseudoromantic idea of overcoming conflict, camps, antagonism, is the greatest provocation to partisanship. Indeed, the most aggressive position, most focused on dominance and control, is one that attempts to defeat conflict *in theory*, by fiat.

The attempt to quell the poetic other is the ultimate provocation to write more poetry and write it otherwise.

V. Varieties of Poetic Experience

The dialectical possibilities for poetry involve multiple overlapping and discrete sites of activity:

> the multilectical and multilingual
> site-specific/fieldwork
> appropriation via transcription, reframing, and resiting
> web data mining
> ec(h)opoetics—exploring a reciprocal relation between the human and nonhuman, world and earth, as well as a practice of mimicry and repetition within and across human cultures and languages
> omnidirectional, homophonic, and heterosemantic translation, transcreation, and remediation, including transposition, resetting, and restaging across media platforms
> constraint-based work
> ESL (writing in English by those from non-English regions, via web-intensified global affinity clusters)
> poetry in programmable media
> sound/performance in/as recording (deformations/rearticulations of audio archive)
> collaboration
> syntactic involution

Along with these are newly emerging in the broad area of "bent poetics":

> disability and the defamiliar and imaginary body
> identity formations as/in textual/sexual medium (queerencies)
> nude formalisms (distressed metrics)
> junk space
> ambience
> ideolect
> sprung lyric
> mixed/syncretic poetic genres
> modularities
> music/poetry
> visual-art/poetry collaborations, book art

VII. The Poetic Principle

The tomb of Edgar Poe is the birthplace of pataqueasics.

I love the irony that Poe's poetics—Poe is, after all, an emblematic American writer (to use his term from "The Poetic Principle")—remains largely unread, its aestheticism roundly rejected ("only this and nothing more"). "The Poetic Principle" (1848) is a founding document of the pataquerical line of American poetics:

> I would define, in brief, the Poetry of words as *The Rhythmical Creation of Beauty*. Its sole arbiter is Taste. With the Intellect or with the Conscience, it has only collateral relations. Unless incidentally, it has no concern whatever either with Duty or with Truth.[5]

Poe recognized early in American literary history that high-minded moral and didactic principles suffocate aesthetic creation, as a body buried alive, even in a coffin made of the finest Brazilian mahogany and lined with pages of Henry Wadsworth Longfellow, slowly and painfully loses consciousness. Worse, aversion to transient and nonproductive sensation cripples ethical judgment, as a steady diet of stale bread not only takes away the taste for fresh goods but also makes the habitué of the desiccated contemptuous of flavor.

In Poe's lampooning of poems with superstructural import that rely on ideas rather than "Taste," moreover that view taste and sensation with suspicion, he echoes William Carlos Williams's formulation seventy-five years later: "Say it! No ideas but in things."[6] Ironically, Williams would insert the relatively short multipart poem where his aphorism first appears—indeed he liked the aphorism so much he repeats it three times in that poem—into *Paterson*, his foray into the long poem form, which, to echo Poe, reads better as a series of short hits than as an epic.

Poe's deadpan insistence that the long poem does not exist rests on Zeno's paradox by way of *The Confidence Man*. The logic is impeccable: no matter how much the long poem tries to make a whole greater than its parts, the parts, the "intense" "moments" of "excitement," as he puts it in "The Poetic Principle" are "*when*"—not *where*—"the meanings are," to quote Dickinson.[7] This is a poetics of temporal *now*ledge rather than atemporal knowledge.

XI.

Poetry is a weak thing and that is its strength.

XXVI. Expression by Other Means

Craig Dworkin, in his introduction to *Against Expression: An Anthology of Conceptual Writing*, the work he edited with Kenneth Goldsmith, emphasizes the importance of framing in determining the reading of any work. Dworkin's focus on the primacy of framing brings to mind Erving Goffman's exemplary practice of "frame analysis."[8]

Goffman's counterintuitive idea is that an "event" (including an art "object") does not speak for itself but is recognizable only by its frame or context. For this reason, the discussion *about* an event can exceed the duration of the "event" itself. An event, or work of art, like a dream, may elicit multiple—incommensurable or discrepant—frames. Some frames are sticky, become *stigma*.

Frames are cued or keyed, and, for Goffman, what is out-of-frame is often (in the end) most significant: what is is defined by what it isn't. Goffman's frames are related to ideology (in Louis Althusser's sense) and also to "metaphors we live by" and categories (in George Lakoff's sense): frames are the lens, the language, through which we perceive/value. Think of how Wittgenstein proposes the fundamental nature of "seeing as" in *Philosophical Investigations*.

One of the hallmarks of *Frame Analysis* is Goffman's obsession with frauds, which he analyzes as undetected changes of frame: in a crap game, the mark keeps his eyes peeled on the handling of the dice, while out of frame are the winking eye signals of the con men.

All poetry, IMHO, is a con, but some cons are more evocative than others. And some cons help us to learn to dodge better. Goldsmith, a trickster figure par excellence, touches on this in his introduction to *Against Expression*, where he makes fun of Oprah-pitched memoir frauds.[9] He notes that such literary frauds have not taken hold in the art world, which, at present, is less invested in subjective "originality" than in market signature. Which only means that in the art world you have to look for other kinds of fraud, perpetuated by a system that is based on establishing market values as opposed to discovering aesthetic merit.

Dworkin and Goldsmith are good collaborators because, though they surely share an enthusiasm for the work collected in this anthology, their approaches to poetics have always been so very different. Dworkin's social formalist commentaries and compendia are both provocative and mesmerizing. He gives detailed readings of forms, structures, and bibliographic codes (rather than themes and subject matter), with special attention to potentially unnoticed discrepancies, elucidating the warp and woof of a series of hard-core and uncanny art practices in which the "remove of literature" (erasure of signal, voiding of medium, foregrounding of paratext) opens the floodgates of a sublimely nude poetics of blank: the noise of silence. ("Nothing but the blank": "only this and nothing more.")

Dworkin is an ingenious reader; he shows a profound engagement with extreme textual practices, writing that stresses the limits of legibility, comprehension, and perceptibility. What's profound about Dworkin's approach is its ecstatic superficiality: he refuses to jump to conclusions, putting a conventional reading or envisionment of the poem in suspension so he can observe textual anomalies and counterintuitive semantic flows. Dworkin tells you not what you already know, or can see for yourself, but what goes undetected until recognized. There is an athletic struggle in many of his hyper-close readings; one senses that his search for meaning requires singular focus and uncanny endurance.

Dworkin's essays are often about finding meaning—finding expression—in textual dynamics or traces that most of us would overlook, indeed, which the author might also have not been fully aware of (or aware of at all). Dworkin excavates meaning and expression in what Goffman calls the disattend track: the place where you are not looking. The result is that Dworkin finds a surplus of meaning in the folds of textual production; who or what is "expressing" this becomes an issue that he often, as a constraint, refuses to address.

In contrast, Goldsmith sometimes likes to say you don't need to read his work, all you need to do is get the concept. With Dworkin in mind, I take this to mean you need to reread the work, read it pataquerically, against the grain (against habitual reading habits), and look for the way it swerves from its proposed course. "By looking beyond received histories and commonplace affiliations one could more clearly see textual elements that otherwise remained obscured or implicit," Dworkin writes in the anthology's introduction. "The simple act of reframing seemed to refresh one's view of even familiar works, which appear significantly different by virtue of their new context."[10]

Dworkin responds to those who may want to take the title *Against Expression* a tad too literally, imagining that the claim is that the works in the anthology are not as expressive as those in other poetry anthologies. For the last forty years, the argument has been that a certain formulaic linguistically I-centered, conceptually sovereign-self-centered lyric is a barrier to affect and expression. Pataquerical poetry is not antilyric, antivoice, antihuman, antisubjectivity, antimeaning, antiself; it just doesn't buy that the conceptually empty genre rules for much of official verse culture allow for expressions, voicings, and our "it's complicated" selves.

To be "against expression," in the necrohumanist sense of expression, is to be for expressions in the wider field of the bent studies.

Expression by other means.

This is clear when Dworkin writes, "Our emphasis is on work that does not seek to express unique, coherent, or consistent individual psychologies and that, moreover, refuses familiar strategies of authorial control" (xliii). The delightful polemic kicks in when Dworkin insists that methods of "noninterference" and "minimal intervention" are preferred: "Frequently, we had to admit that works we admired were not quite right for this collection because they were simply too creative—they had too much authorial intervention, however masterful or stylish that intervention might be" (xliv). A whole heap of masterful intervention was necessary to create the anthology. And while the intention may be more in complex framing choices than in individual word choices, stylish intervention it nonetheless is. I recall Jackson Mac Low being pained by his work being described as derived by "chance" rather than being, in his phrase, quasi-intentional. That's where I see Dworkin's calling card as a critic: hyperclose reading, and classification, of quasi-intentional linguistic phenomena. This is not an evasion of reading or intervention but a raising of the stakes and a sometimes ecstatic commitment to the power of framing.

Dworkin writes that the poetry he anthologizes "is neither depersonalized nor unemotional. Rather, the formal conceit attempts to discover or more closely approach emotional conditions by avoiding the habits, clichés, and sentimentality of conventional expressivist rhetoric."[11]

XIII.

We are most familiar with the estranged.

XXXIII. Anaesthetics

The turn away from beauty or emotion, like the aversion of identity or expression, may be both a response to the shallowness of what is accepted as beautiful or emotional and a mark of the search for beauty or affect, a beauty or affect not already trapped and tamed. For if you say what I find beautiful is worthless, then I may say I reject beauty, but that is just a measure of my recognition of how categories of the beautiful anesthetize you from the experience of beauty. For some, it is only in renouncing the beautiful that the possibility of beauty opens. And those of you who lament this turn away from beauty or emotion, compulsively proclaiming its return, do not and perhaps cannot understand what it is to be outside the script, dead as you are to sensation, oblivious to beauties that cannot be dreamt of in your moralities.

And I mean that *you* in the most personal possible way.

XL. Disclaimer

The views in this essay do not necessarily represent the opinions of, and should not be attributed to, the University of Pennsylvania's English Department, Donald T. Regan, Ronald Reagan, Bernice Johnson Reagon, or the author. The views expressed are solely those of the essay.

XLVII. *I'm Special, Who Are You?*

It's funny. In Portuguese *esquisito* means something exquisitely different from *exquisito* in Spanish.[12]

Funny odd or funny peculiar?

Pataque(e)ricals are markers of stigmatized difference. In order for a difference to be stigmatized or scapegoated, it first needs to be noticed, much the way language is called to (or put on) notice when it is used in poetry (at least in one way of defining poetry).

The pataquericals in my lists are negatives. But negatives have a queer way of becoming positives, especially for those for whom such tactical reversals might create a space of greater freedom, as Michel de Certeau discusses in *Arts de faire* (arts of doing, or *The Practice of Everyday Life*). Reverse pataquericals are honorific rather than stigmatic terms for things that fall out or don't fit in: *innovator*, *rebel*, *extraordinary*, *exceptional*, *iconoclast*, *genius*, or the one made so exemplary in its ordinariness by Mr. Rogers, *special*, which, after all, is not without its de Certeauian or Blakean spin, if we take *special* to mean *Particular*.[13] Another kind of reverse pataqueasical is simply to take on the stigma as a badge of honor, if not with pride then with defiance (as when pataquericals become literary terms or, paradigmatically, in the case of *queer*).

Stumpling clumpsiness for one, the eloquence of the gods for 'nother.

However, a more frequent response to stigma is internalize it, which is the basis of what, in *Jewish Self-Hatred*, Sander Gilman calls a form of self-scapegoating.[14]

Then again, the American way is assimilation: if thy nose offend, fix it (I am avoiding saying "cut it off" as I don't want to descend into a crude castration fantasy).

In these investigations I am less interested in sexual difference than in aesthetic difference and, specifically, the way the sexual and sociocultural differences are articulated symbolically, or allegorically, within an aesthetic field such as a poem.

L.

The extraordinary is never more than an extension of the ordinary.

LXXIII. Anti–Bachelor Machines

As a term for poetic constructions, *bachelor machine* suggests nonproductive, nonprocreative, onanistic processes, vicious (or self-enclosing/collapsing) circles, an apparatus that is unable to get outside itself. There is a connection to *délire* (delirium, with special reference to Jean-Jacques Lecercle)—that which goes astray, deviates from the rational, errs, raves.[15] Though perhaps it would be better to call pataque(e)rics an anti–bachelor machine. The term "bachelor machine" (*machine célibataire*) comes from Duchamp's "Bride Stripped Bare by Her Bachelors, Even" (the lower part of *The Large Glass*, e.g., "Chocolate Grinder"). Michel Carrouges (in his book *Les Machines célibataires*) extended the term to incorporate the disciplinary apparatus of Franz Kafka's *The Penal Colony* and also to Raymond Roussel's *Impressions of Africa*, and some of Poe's machines as well, and, crucially, to the work of Alfred Jarry. This formulation has been adapted by Gilles Deleuze and Félix Guattari in *Anti-Oedipus* and also by Michel de Certeau in *Arts de faire*.[16]

XLVI.

Unlike sincerity, insincerity is at least pointed toward truth. That is where the sin is.

XC. Pataqueronormativities

I just want to be like everyone else like me.

The history of art, no less than the history of societies, is replete with the normalization of stigmas. From time to time, as moral and aesthetic values change, poetics and persons previously subject to negative judgment by those who evaluate poetry in terms of dutifulness and virtue are redeemed. For Young Hegelian debunkers, such redemption inaugurates a rule of renormalization (subliming), in which the aims of art remain duty and morality; but now it is a new, ethically improved morality and a radicalized, purified aesthetic duty that reigns.[17]

But aesthetics is not a tool of morality, nor is it bound to it or by it. Aesthetics is not applied ethics.

It is practically an Ironclad® law of nature that new orthodoxies replace old ones,[18] just as it is a delusion of starry-eyed romanticism to think anything else is possible.

Yet THINK WE MUST FOR A GROWING IMAGINARY.

XCIV.

THIS SECTION INTENTIONALLY LEFT BLANK.

CV. In Praise of Disfluency

> To be crippled means to be institutionalized, infantilized, unemployed, outcast, feared, marginalized, fetishized, desexualized, stared at, excluded, silenced, aborted, sterilized, stuck, discounted, teased, voiceless, disrespected, raped, isolated, undereducated, made into a metaphor or an example. To be crippled means to be referred to as retard, cute, helpless, lame, bound, stupid, drunk, idiot, a burden on society, in/valid. To be crippled means to be discounted as a commodity or regarded as mere commodity.
>
> —Jennifer Bartlett, *Autobiography/ Anti-Autobiography*[19]

The poetics of disfluency and disability is the horizon for a querical poetics of de-arrangement.[20] For the purposes of these quarlsome quarries, I am less interested in narratives of social/cultural identities or disabilities than in how such frames (and the experiences they embody) transform both the writing and reading of poems: difference making for difference, not difference expressed through sameness.

This is a theme explicitly taken up by Amanda Baggs in her video "In My Language."[21] Baggs divides the video into two parts. The first aims to present a primary experience of autistic consciousness; it resembles works of radically deranged art but is framed as expressive of Baggs's state of mind and modes of perceptual grappling and communication. The second part of the video is a pata-translation of the first part into more normative language, which has the effect of framing the first part not as unintelligible but as *otherwise intelligible.* Charges that Baggs's video is a fraud, that she is not really autistic, which Baggs documents on her website,[22] add a devilish twist to the work, since the humanist need to pity authenticated suffering metamorphoses into a virtual Tarr and Fethering by her accusers.

If Todd Browning's *Freaks* (1932) remains the signature work of pataqueasical scopophilia, our age demands its freak shows "tamed by Miltown" into memoirs whose reliability is comparable to (and often as financially advantageous as) junk bonds.[23] Browning's cinema creates a Brechtian self-consciousness on the part of the viewer via repulsion and fascination; Chaplin's Little Tramp is the converse, eliciting empathy and identification, without pity. Baudelaire's "À une mendiante rousse" remains the paradigm for the aversion of objectification. In "Pastoral," Williams's approach to the "the houses / of the very poor" is exquisitely oblique: the "weathered," haphazard scene "smeared a bluish green" occludes voyeurism.[24] In contemporary poetics, Leslie Scalapino's "Bum Series" (*Way*, 1988) revisits this dynamic voyeurism and displacement to create an ontological space for turning toward (averting aversion).[25]

Following Blake and Emerson, Baggs turns pity back onto the beholder as she holds her own ground. "In My Language" turns many of the tropes and quirks of defamiliarizing poetry on their head, returning the metaphors to their source—or rather returning the source to its metaphors and to its criteria, in Wittgenstein's sense: "An 'inner process' stands in need of outward criteria."[26] Baggs confronts a misleading binary picture of inner process and outer expression, the idea that there is a core, privately experienced, "truth" that needs to be translated into the memoir's outer expression.[27]

In a 2001 talk on stuttering and torture, Jordan Scott, charting the interrogator's relentless search for hidden truth, twists a linguistic knife into actual flesh. In his talk, Scott presented examples of interrogators interpreting outer expressions of verbal disfluency as concealing the sought-after inner truth.[28] Yet the impulse of the torturer to push against the stutter only intensifies the subject's stutter. Scott's own stuttering while he lectures collapses the stadium of explanation of academic discourse onto itself: Scott not only talks about stuttering but lacerates his discourse with verbal interruptions, except that these irruptions don't interfere with, or compromise, his talk; rather, they make it palpable.

In Scott's collection of poems, *Blert*, he sets out to create works that trip his tongue in performance.[29] To hear Scott read is to be aware of stuttering as a literary device collapsing into stuttering as animalady. Scott's work is a spiky reminder that disability is not (only) a metaphor. *Blert* plays on its difference from poems that use stuttering for sound or social or semantic effect—but not by insisting on his real disability versus another's metaphoric use of disability. Like Baggs, he compounds and propounds the difference. What would happen if his stuttering was cured? Would he lose his poetry street cred? Or would he be better off increasing his stutter, as the professional Frenchman's accent grows stronger each year he lives in the New World? Or does that just bring us back to *Freaks*?

"The Human Abstract" is echoing on the green: "Pity would be no more. / If we did not make somebody Poor."

CIX. Passing

> After trying my animal noise
> i break out with a man's cry
>
> —Larry Eigner[30]

American culture is filled with both the desire to pass and a resistance to passing: to be absorbed by the dominant culture or to remake that culture. Assimilation is motivated as much by fear as by desire.

Twentieth-century American popular entertainment, from vaudeville to popular song, is rife with examples of ethnic and racial performance, where stigmas are flaunted by their putative victims for an audience that identifies with these stigma—or are displayed to indulge the racialist fantasies of nonidentifying audiences. Or both: for the play of same and difference is always a lure. Starting in the 1910s, the Ziegfeld star Fanny Brice (born Fania Borach in 1891) performed Yiddish-accent shtick (most famously "Cohen at the Beach"), but she also used her Yiddish accent to create an outrageously incongruous comic effect to her American immigrant rendition of "I'm an Indian" ("O look at me I'm an Indian, that's something that I never was before"): *from shtetl to reservation*, Jewface as redface.[31] An obtrusive nose visually represents Jewface: Brice got plastic surgery to remove this difference in 1923.[32] By the mid-1940s she had perfected her ventriloquized foreignness, rocketing into mass culture with another of her Ziegfeld shticks, the weird but not ethnically marked pataquerical radio voice of Baby Snooks. All the while, Brice sang less-accented torch songs such as "When a Woman Loves a Man"—her middle voice, which Brice explicitly tied to universal socialist values in "The Song of the Sewing Machine" (1927):

> There is no song, there is no birds
> And God is just another word
> If you listen to the song of the sewing machine[33]

The dream of American "liberty" doesn't pass the sweatshop test ("America never was America to me," as Langston Hughes more famously put it):[34] it is class consciousness, not nose jobs, that erases difference, understood here as economic, not racial or ethnic.

Beyond the fear of ethnic or racial difference is the fear of animal difference. The fear of animalady manifests as the need to pass as human (cultivated, learned, well mannered, well dressed), which is figured, in the tale of Dr. Tarr and Professor Fether, as the need to pass as *not insane*.

Michael McClure directly confronts the phobia of *not passing* as human in "Ghost Tantra" 49, in which he not only invents a zaumist "beast language" but also performs the poem to growling tigers, exceeding his own expressionist linguistic acrobatics in the final minute (in the audio recording) of the lion's sounds that persist beyond the poem, theatricalizing a full dissolve of the human into animality.[35] It's a marvelously incantatory, almost satiric exorcism of the human. The conceit of McClure's performance is not man taming the beast. Rather the performance is a coming to literary terms with our inner beast, not as noble or even more human than we are (à la Jean Cocteau's "Où est ma bête?")[36] but as something that, like the body, marks animal being as a base level of human being. But any such literary effort necessarily courts—either by romanticizing or by stigma—jungleification, primitivism, savagery.

In Curt McDowell's *Thundercrack!* (1975), George Kuchar (who wrote the script) plays a circus truck driver who has fallen in love with the female gorilla in his charge. In the final, touching scene we see the driver in bed with someone in a very campy gorilla costume. From Baudelaire's "À une mendiante rousse" onward, artists have tried to find a way to portray society's "others" without voyeurism, pity, condescension, or romanticizing. Kuchar in bed with an actor in a gorilla suit is the perfect realization of the possibility of the pataque(e)rical as a quest for what Kuchar calls "otherworldly humanity."[37] Like many pornographic films, *Thundercrack* portrays a descent into animalistic sexual drives, brought to a head in this last scene. With its parodic bestiality, Kuchar reverses the normal direction of assimilation: he wants to pass as animal.

As if on cue, on July 30, 2009, Fox News ran a segment with Megyn Kelly that attacked the National Endowment for the Arts for supporting a movie series showing *Thundercrack!*, a film that was disgusting, according to Kelly, because it showed sex between a man and a gorilla.

Moral repugnance is the last refuge of scoundrels.

CXXXVI.

PROVIDE FEEDBACK ON THIS ESSAY

Did this essay solve your problem?
__ Yes __ No __ I don't know
Was this essay relevant?
__ Yes __ No
What can we do to improve this essay?

Notes

Excerpts from the final essay—"The Pataquerical Imagination: Midrashic Antinomianism and the Promise of Bent Studies (A Fantasy in 140 Fits)"—in Charles Bernstein, *Pitch of Poetry* (Chicago: University of Chicago Press, 2016), 293–344.

1. *Nepohumanism* (also called *necrohumanism* and *hypohumanism*) universalizes one's immediate preferences while stigmatizing as barbaric those that are not immediately intelligible.

2. Simon Jarvis, *Wordsworth's Philosophic Song* (Cambridge, UK: Cambridge University Press, 2009).

3. Jerome McGann, *Romantic Ideology* (Chicago: University of Chicago Press, 1983). See Charles Bernstein, "McGann Agonist," in *Attack of the Difficult Poems: Essays and Inventions* (Chicago: University of Chicago Press, 2011), 160–70.

4. See David St. John and Cole Swensen, eds., *American Hybrid: A Norton Anthology of New Poetry* (New York: W. W. Norton, 2009); and Stephanie Burt, review of *Smokes*, by Susan Wheeler, *Boston Review* 23, no. 3 (September 1998); "The Elliptical Poets" feature, *American Letters and Commentary*, no. 11 (2007). See also Craig Dworkin, "Hypermnesia" and Brian Reed, "Grammar Trouble," in "American Poetry After 1975," ed. Charles Bernstein, special issue, *boundary 2* 36, no. 3 (Fall 2009).

5. Edgar A. Poe, "The Poetic Principle" (1850), Edgar Allan Poe Society of Baltimore, updated March 18, 2015, https://www.eapoe.org/works/essays/poetprnb.htm. See Jerome McGann's *The Poet Edgar Allan Poe: Alien Angel* (Cambridge, MA: Harvard University Press, 2014), which restores Poe to his foundational role for American, and nineteenth-century, poetics; McGann's breathtaking scholarship makes Poe's work thrillingly present and hauntingly prescient.

6. William Carlos Williams, "Paterson" (1927), in *The Collected Poems of William Carlos Williams*, vol. 1, *1909–1939*, ed. A. Walton Litz and Christopher MacGowan (New York: New Directions, 1986), 264.

7. Emily Dickinson, *Poems*, ed. Thomas H. Johnson, 3 vols. (Cambridge, MA: Belknap Press of Harvard University Press, 1955), no. 258, 1:185.

8. Craig Dworkin and Kenneth Goldsmith, eds., *Against Expression: An Anthology of Conceptual Poetry* (Evanston, IL: Northwest University Place, 2011); Erving Goffman, *Frame Analysis: An Essay on the Organization of Experience* (Boston: Northeastern University Press, 1986).

9. Kenneth Goldsmith, "Why Conceptual Writing? Why Now?," in Dworkin and Goldsmith, *Against Expression*, xx. See my discussion of frauds in "Fraud's Phantoms," in *Attack of the Difficult Poems*, 206–26.

10. Craig Dworkin, "The Fate of Echo," in Dworkin and Goldsmith, *Against Expression*, xxiv (hereafter cited parenthetically in the text).

11. Craig Dworkin, introduction to "Skin Deep," by Walter Abish, in Dworkin and Goldsmith, *Against Expression*, 8.

12. Christina Hesketh pointed this out to me: the Portuguese means bizarre, the Spanish is close to the English equivalent.

13. "You are special / You are my friend / You're special to me. / You are the only one like you." Fred Rogers, "You Are Special" (1967), accessed September 13, 2019, https://pbskids.org/rogers/songLyricsYouAreSpecial.html. This inevitably also brings up the euphemism "special needs." We're all special and all have special needs. Pataque(e)rical euphemisms substitute positive attributes for stigmatized negative attributes: *challenged* for deficient.

14. I discuss Sander Gilman's *Jewish Self-Hatred: Anti-Semitism and the Hidden Language of the Jews* (Baltimore: Johns Hopkins University Press, 1990) in *My Way: Speeches and Poems* (Chicago: Chicago University Press, 1999), 37, 188, 216. See also Erving Goffman, *Stigma: Notes on the Management of Spoiled Identity* (New York: Simon and Schuster, 1963).

15. For more on *délire*, see Jean-Jacques Lecercle, *Philosophy Through the Looking-Glass: Language, Nonsense, Desire* (La Salle, IL: Open Court, 1985).

16. I provide a list of my own anti–bachelor machines at "What, Me Conceptual?," with special reference to "Recantorium: A Bachelor Machine After Duchamp after Kafka," modified January 14, 2020, http://writing.upenn.edu/pennsound/x/Bernstein-Tucson.html. "Recantorium" was collected in *Attack of the Difficult Poems*, 269–70. See Michel Carrouges, *Les Machines célibataires*, 2nd ed. (Paris: Éditions du Chêne, 1976). De Certeau discusses the "celibate machines" of Jarry, Roussel, Duchamp, and Kafka in *The Practice of Everyday Life* (1980), trans. Steven. F. Rendall (Berkeley: University of California Press, 1984), 150–53. Gilles Deleuze and Félix Guattari discuss "celibate machines" in *Anti-Oedipus: Capitalism and Schizophrenia* (1972), trans. Robert Hurley, Mark Seem, and Helen R. Lane (Minneapolis: University of Minnesota Press, 1983), 17–19. See also Lecercle, *Philosophy Through the Looking Glass*.

17. For a case study, see "Disfiguring Abstraction" in *Pitch of Poetry*, 48–59. The Hegelian orthodontics of the avant-garde was exemplified in a discussion at a planning meeting at the Museum of Modern Art, discussed in the essay. My suggestions that the most radical and contradictory energies of modernist art were at risk of being contained by museum abstraction were rebuffed in a telling instance of how aesthetically challenging art can been subsumed into the new normal. Avant-garde poetry and art, by definition, are susceptible to the lure of the pataqueronormative: it is, for us, as powerful as the sirens for Odysseus.

18. "The iron hand crushd the Tyrants head / And became a Tyrant in his stead," as Blake succinctly puts it in "The Grey Monk." I read the poem here: "Charles Bernstein Reads 'The Grey Monk' by William Blake," Romantic Circles, June 14, 2007, https://www.rc.umd.edu/pop-blog/charles-bernstein-reads-grey-monk-william-blake.

19. Jennifer Bartlett, *Autobiography/Anti-Autobiography* (Palmyra, NY: theenk Books, 2014), 11. See Bartlett's preface to *Beauty Is a Verb: The New Poetry of Disability* (El Paso, TX: Cinco Puntos, 2011) and the interview with her at Charles Bernstein, "Jennifer Bartlett in Conversation with Jane Joritz-Nakagawa," *Jacket 2*, August 9, 2014, https://jacket2.org/commentary/jennifer-bartlett-conversation-jane-joritz-nakagawa.

20. See Michael Davidson's groundbreaking *Concerto for Left Hand: Disability and the Defamiliar Body* (Ann Arbor: University of Michigan Press, 2008).

21. See Amanda Baggs, "In My Language," uploaded January 14, 2007, YouTube video, https://www.youtube.com/watch?v=JnylM1hI2jc, which has received over 1.6 million views (as of early 2021). See also David Wolman, "The Truth About Autism: Scientists Reconsider What They *Think* They Know," *Wired*, February 25, 2008, https://www.wired.com/2008/02/ff-autism.

22. See "Amanda Baggs Autism Controversy," updated February 29, 2020, http://abaggs.blogspot.com.

23. "The age demanded an image / Of its accelerated grimace . . . / Not, not certainly,

the obscure reveries / Of the inward gaze; / Better mendacities / Than the classics in paraphrase! . . . / A prose kinema." Ezra Pound, "Hugh Selwyn Mauberly" (1920), EPC Digital Library, updated February 20, 2020, http://writing.upenn.edu/library/Pound_Ezra_Hugh_Selwyn_Mauberly.html. "Tamed by Miltown" is from Robert Lowell's "Man and Wife" (1959), in *Selected Poems* (New York: Farrar, Straus and Giroux, 1976).

24. Williams, *Collected Poems*, 64. He ends the poem with the pataquerical imperative: "No one / will believe this / of vast import to the nation." Only *this* and nothing more. He comes back to the ontology of voyeurism in "The Young Housewife."

25. Duchamp's bachelor machine, "Étant donnés" turns the gaze back on the gaze. See also "Reznikoff's Nearness" in my volume *My Way: Speeches and Poems*, 197–228.

26. Ludwig Wittgenstein, *Philosophical Investigations*, trans. G. E. M. Anscombe (Oxford, UK: Basil Blackwell, 1953), §580.

27. Ibid., §305:

"But you surely cannot deny that, for example, in remembering, an inner process takes place."—What gives the impression that we want to deny anything? When one says "Still, an inner process does take place here"—one wants to go on: "After all, you *see* it." And it is this inner process that one means by the word "remembering."—The impression that we wanted to deny something arises from our setting our faces against the picture of the "inner process." What we deny is that the picture of the inner process gives us the correct idea of the use of the word "to remember." We say that this picture with its ramifications stands in the way of our seeing the use of the word as it is.

28. *North of Invention: A Canadian Poetry Festival*, University of Pennsylvania, January 21, 2011, http://writing.upenn.edu/pennsound/x/North-Of-Invention.php.

29. Jordan Scott, *Blert* (Toronto: Coach House Press, 2008).

30. Larry Eigner, *Selected Poems* (Tuscaloosa: University of Alabama Press, 2016), no. f9, September 1954.

31. The Library of Congress streams a 1921 recording of Brice performing "I'm an Indian" (lyrics by Blanche Merrill, music by Leo Edwards), updated October 13, 2015, http://memory.loc.gov/diglib/ihas/loc.natlib.jukebox.8288/default.html. This song is not to be confused with, but is worth comparing to, the later Irving Berlin song from *Annie Get Your Gun* (1946), "I'm an Indian Too," which has been criticized as racist. For "Mrs. Cohen at the Beach," see "Fanny Brice Collection, 1925–1935," Internet Archive, updated August 3, 2011, https://archive.org/details/FannyBriceCollection1927-1930Complete/Mrs.CohenAtTheBeachPartOneTwo1927FannyBrice-Victor21211.m4a. More discussion on this topic can be found in "Objectivist Blues: Scoring Speech in Second-Wave Modernist Poetry and Lyrics," in *Attack of the Difficult Poems*, 139–57.

32. Herbert G. Goldman, *Fanny Brice: The Original Funny Girl* (New York: Oxford University Press, 1992).

33. Lyrics by Ballard MacDonald and Billy Rose (born William Rosenberg in 1899), who had also written "Mrs. Cohen at the Beach." Full lyric and sound file available at Charles Bernstein, "The Song of the Sewing Machine," *Jacket 2*, January 6, 2014, https://jacket2.org/commentary/song-sewing-machine.

34. Langston Hughes, "Let America Be America to Me" (1936), in *The Collected Poems of Langton Hughes*, ed. Arnold Rampersad (New York: Alfred A. Knopf, 1994), 189.

35. Charles Bernstein, "Michael McClure Reads to Lions: Tantra 49 and 1974 Olson Memorial Lectures at Buffalo," *Jacket 2*, July 31, 2014, https://jacket2.org/commentary/michael-mcclure-reads-lions.

36. So says Beauty confronted with the loss of her beast in Jean Cocteau's 1946 film *La Belle et la Bête*.

37. Kuchar uses this term in one of his last films, *Lingo of the Lost* (2010).

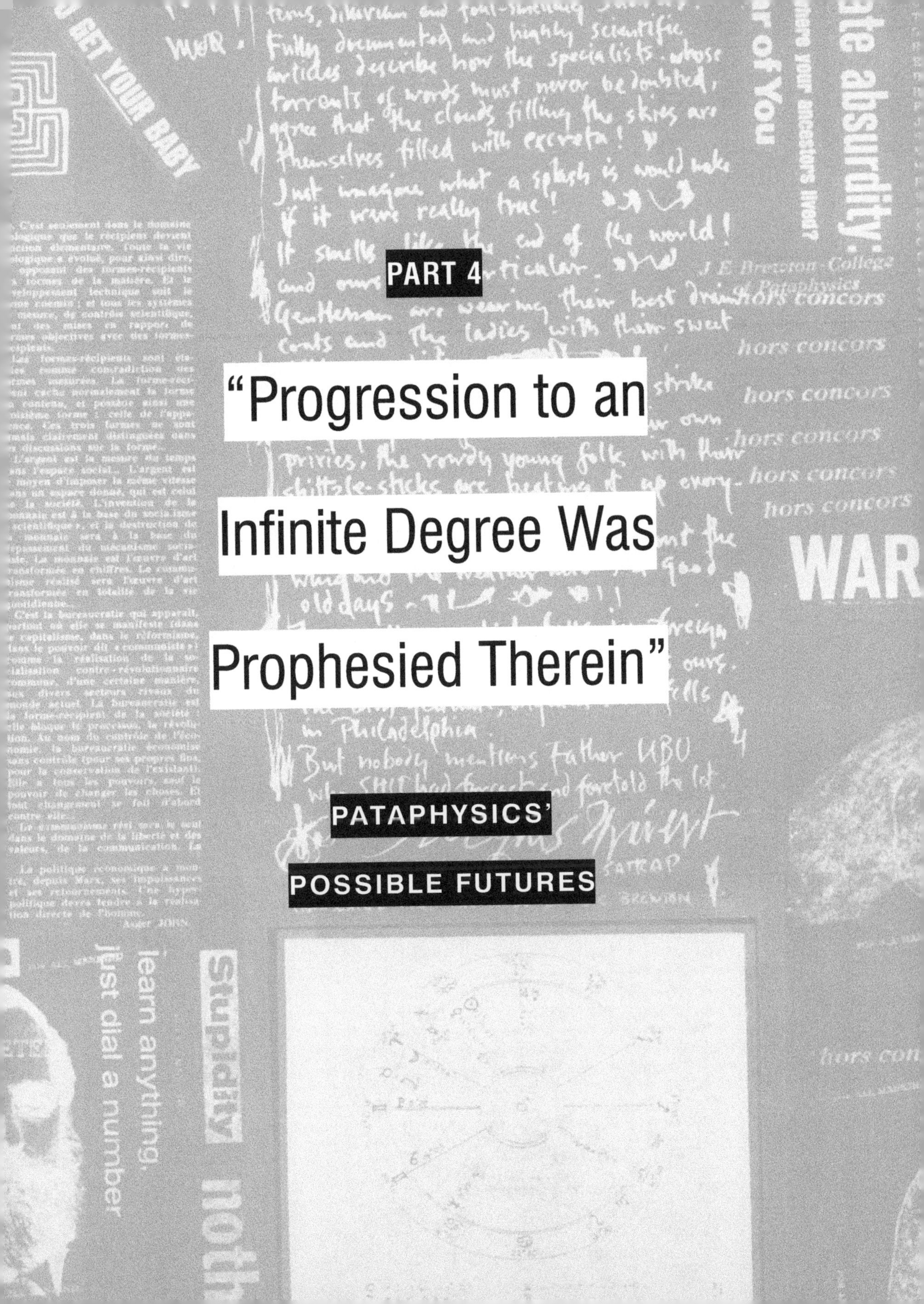

PART 4

“Progression to an Infinite Degree Was Prophesied Therein”

PATAPHYSICS’ POSSIBLE FUTURES

Chapter 14

Concerning an Unfindable Architecture

Seth McDowell

In 1969, during his appointment as Régent of the *Collège de 'Pataphysique*, Jacques Carelman published the *Catalogue d'objets introuvables*—translated into English as the *Catalogue of Unfindable Objects*.[1] This publication of fantastic inventions was a parody of the mail order catalog, presenting a series of objects that question utility and offer impossible solutions to seemingly irrelevant problems. This essay contemplates an architectural addition to Carelman's collection of pataphysical objects, and examines the relationship between radical speculations for architecture and the experimental literary movement known as pataphysics.

Architecture often finds itself chasing rapid developments in science and technology in ways that emphasize efficiency and rationality. The goal here is to deploy pataphysics in an effort to challenge the field's often overzealous reliance on scientific method in favor of a poetic appropriation of science and technology. How can the architect operate as a pataphysician? How can architecture disrupt generic assumptions with alternate futures, rooted in chimerical science and ludic theories?

A quick search reveals that there are no Google results for an unfindable architecture.[2] Perhaps this indicates that an unfindable architecture is an exception, a special occurrence, an outlier. It is an architecture on the fringe. The projects discussed here will frame architecture as a strange concoction of particular, seemingly irrelevant concerns that accidentally stumble on undiscovered territories.

Consequently, an unfindable architecture does not study the rules governing the general recurrence of a periodic incident (the expected case) so much as the games governing the special occurrence of a sporadic accident (the excepted case).[3] Translating this statement to an architectural agenda, architecture is envisioned as the exception to "the building." Architecture is imagined as the moment when "the building" becomes a manifestation of a particular person, culture, or time, and not merely the regurgitation of general, generic practices and principles. Prompting this unfindable condition is a clinamen, or unexplainable change in momentum that enables the exception.

Three examples of the exception can be examined through three design projects. They include anomalos (the principle of variance), syzygia (the principle of alliance), and clinamen (the principle of deviance). The three projects highlight design work from my architectural practice, mcdowellespinosa architects, an experimental design studio exploring the absurdity of architectural pursuits.

The anomaly—a particular occurrence that differs from every other occurrence in a system that values the norm of equivalence—"serves the will to disrupt."[4] The anomaly is a response to excess, as will be seen in a project called City of Blubber, where the excess of the contemporary city is transformed into a soft, amorphous urban terrain, situated above a relentless grid of skyscrapers. Syzygy, on the other hand, finds a way to equate things to each other in a system that values the norm of difference. This condition will be examined in a project titled Drift City—a city that is a hybrid between highway and city. The project fuses two urban enemies together, creating a transient megastructure for a migrating economy. The third mode of the exception is the clinamen, which finds a way to detour around things in a system that values the fate of contrivance. Clinamen will be investigated in a project called Water Fuel, which employs an act of material *détournement* to extract water from a defined context and reposition it within a new spatial economy.

To position architecture within this framework of the exception is a critical action allowing, if not demanding, that the field offer up more than clichés. It encourages the architect to step outside of an internalized dialogue with the tropes of architectural history, to invent or imagine new realities. It is not calling for the reinvention of the wheel; it is calling for the reimagining of the rules that govern the wheel.

It is with the exception that architecture contains some resemblance of relevance. Architecture cannot solve the urgent matters of the world—it has limitations. Architecture, by nature, creates more problems than it can solve. Thus, the value of architecture lies in its ability to offer difference within a homogeneous context. An unfindable architecture accepts this responsibility and works to celebrate the condition of the exception as a rare moment of authenticity.

The Unfindable

"Unfindable" is a strange term within the English language. Merriam-Webster defines it as "not capable of being found," suggesting a lost scenario.[5] Carelman's catalog title has been translated a few different ways: from "fantastic" to "impossible" to "unfindable." Unfindable is a provocative term in the context of Carelman's objects, whereby it suggests that a series of products is so unusual and absurd that each failed within a consumer market. Thus, the design narrative is so unconventional that it thwarts the success or appreciation of the object, rendering it "unfindable" or inaccessible to an audience.

The dilemma with pairing the terms "unfindable" and "architecture" is the suggestion that architecture could then only exist in the imagination. This is problematic to many who believe that the richness of architecture resides in the physical manifestation of form and material—an act that requires an equal distribution of art and science.

While unfindable architecture can exist in the tangible world, it is more obvious within a tradition of "paper architecture," a term used to describe the visionary architectural proposals that never make it beyond speculation. These visions are often not realized because they present drastic shifts in conventional logic. They attempt to address societal problems with a whimsical bias that flips the crisis on its head, recalibrating the logic of the problem. These paper projects are never implemented, largely because they have no audience and usually ignore traditional economic or constructability parameters. With extreme singularity they solve one problem; yet due to highly focused objectives, they instigate a whole surplus of new problems.

The unfindable condition in relation to the imaginary visions for architecture can be positioned by tracking the lineage the speculative, utopian vision. Beginning with modernism, the late nineteenth century through the 1960s presented a strategy of ideal, utopian visions. The architecture of modernity was fueled by industrialization and internationalization, and it employed emerging technologies to reach for infinite boundaries. Le Corbusier, Walter Gropius, Mies van der Rohe, and Frank Lloyd Wright, to name a few, searched for "truths" with architecture. Architecture was to embody the "essence" of the time, culture, and materials. This heroic approach led to visionary proposals like Ville radieuse (Radiant City, 1924) by Le Corbusier, where a totalitarian master plan of grand avenues, parks, and towers aimed to create a better society: "In accordance with modernist ideals of progress (which encouraged the annihilation of tradition), The Radiant City was to emerge from a *tabula rasa*: it was to be built on nothing less than the grounds of demolished vernacular European cities."[6] Design solutions fixated, with extreme isolation, on future societal conditions, creating a dramatic and freakish shift away from tradition and history. When the speculative projects of modernity did come to realization, as in Brasília (1956), they were erected as imported anomalies within the cultural landscape.

With postmodernity, paper architecture in the 1960s through the 1990s became a tool for criticism and theory. Similarly to Carelman's objects of the same time, these architectural visions were critiques of contemporary society and politics. These visions were fueled by popular culture and multinationalism, and became more theoretical, more hypothetical. The modes of representation tended to be cartoons and sketches rather than the more resolved plans and perspectives of modernity. Postmodernity approached the imaginary solution with ideology. Projects like Archigram's Walking City (1966) or Superstudio's Continuous Monument (1969) acted as critiques of the political and social ideals of modernism by offering partial, loosely delineated solutions as a counterpoint. For much of the postmodern era, the economy was not supporting architecture as a building project, and thus writing and theoretical projects became the means for developing an architectural agenda. This allowed architects to imagine new worlds—countercultural fantasies that hover over the existing cities (Yona Friedman's Ville spatiale, or Spatial City, 1959–60) or sprawl above an untouched natural landscape (Constant Nieuwenhuys's New Babylon, 1959–74).

One of these projects is No-Stop-City (1966–72) by Archizoom Associati. No-Stop-City is one of the most radical visions of the city of the future; without boundaries, artificially lit, and air-conditioned, it is simultaneously utopian and dystopian. No-Stop-City was envisioned as a "well-equipped residential parking lot" composed of "large floors, micro-climatized and artificially lit interiors."[7] Rather than serving to identify a place, No-Stop-City would be a neutral field in which the creation of identity through consumption could be unfettered." The drawings of this city depict relentless repetition of generic plots of single-family dwellings that beg for the appearance of the anomaly.

Interest in the unfindable attributes of paper architecture still exists today in a period Michael Speaks has dubbed the "supermodern."[8] With supermodernity, intelligence has replaced ideals and ideology. Knowledge is understood not as a fixed condition, but as something that is always changing. A pataphysical pursuit can be seen in projects like In-Vitro Meat Habitat (2009–12) by the design laboratory Terraform One, whereby 3D-printed extruded pig cells are used to generate a living architectural organism. The project positions design within a laboratory, and architecture is explored as a scientific experiment. This is the "supermodern" version of surrationalism. Architecture has become a poetic appropriation of science. An unfindable architecture is grown from a biological process.

Logical Absurdity

Carelman described his unfindable objects as inventions that exhibit "logical absurdity or absurd logic."[9] These two terms negate each other as do "science" and "fiction," a fundamental pataphysical motivation of opposition, as seen in Jarry's "plus-minus," first seen in *Caesar Antichrist* (1895), "where the plus-minus is embodied in the physic-stick, a revolving stick which turns across the stage creating as it does both the - and the + and describing, through its rotation, a circle."[10] This "double aspect" is aligned philosophically with the term *antinomy*. Immanuel Kant used antinomy[11] to "describe the equally rational but contradictory results of applying to the universe of pure thought the categories or criteria of reason that are proper to the universe of sensible perception or experience (phenomena)."[12]

Pataphysics is inundated with the "simultaneous opposition of seriousness and humor."[13] This is evident from its origins: Jarry, with his schoolboy friends in Rennes, coined the term as a way to describe the elaborate fables their science teacher would construct when attempting to answer scientific questions beyond his knowledge. Thus, at its origins, pataphysics was a childhood game of rigorously deploying science and fiction. This same duality of humor and seriousness is seen in Carelman's objects, where problems are solved with tongue-in-cheek solutions.

Oulipan Italo Calvino had a tremendous influence on architects who found an "extraordinary willingness to submit to the remorseless demands of an imagined and self-imposed logic, within the context of allegorical fantasy."[14] This self-imposed syntax heavily influenced postmodern design methods, culminating in the work of the Deconstructivists during the mid to late 1980s. Within this group, Peter Eisenman tends to be the most explicit about his deployment of self-imposed logics, describing his work as "cardboard architecture"—an interesting spin on "paper architecture"—because it "neglects the architectural material, scale, function, site, and all semantic associations in favour of architecture as 'syntax': conception of form as an index, a signal or a notation."[15] Working with Jacques Derrida, Eisenman attempted to establish a linguistic model for architecture, and, like Calvino and the Oulipo, used self-imposed logics to direct the architectural formation. He referred to this work as "diagrams of interiority," because it was "characterized by the desire to find internal rules and mechanisms for the discipline without any contact with the exterior world."[16] Eisenman's house series from 1967 to 1978 is a clear manifestation of this internalized spatial game.

Elements of Exception

Fundamental to pataphysics is the upheaval of empirical physics, which depends on the repeatable experiment to produce an outcome that is generalized into a law or rule. By examining the exception, pataphysics deploys experiments governed by their own singular rules, which produce unique events. Jarry states that the laws of the universe are not laws but "correlations of exceptions, albeit more frequent ones, but in any case accidental data, which reduced to the status of unexceptional exceptions, possess no longer even the virtue of originality."[17]

An exception poses a problem for those who look to categorize or rationalize. Friedrich Nietzsche argues that "the first instinct of the knower is to search for the rules, although naturally enough with confirmation of a rule nothing is as yet 'known.'"[18] Repetition has an order; it is an expected case and poses no problem, "because it implies the security of a paradigm." The instance that does not repeat has an uncertain order and is an excepted case. This surprise poses a problem because "it implies the insecurity of the paralogy."[19] The science of pataphysics is precisely focused on the logic of what logic exempts.

In *'Pataphysics: The Poetics of an Imaginary Science*, Christian Bök relates pataphysical exceptions to "deviant devices whose extravagance evoke all the ecstatic tortures of shock, noise, and speed." Shock, noise, and speed could in fact be the three key operations for producing the exception. For Bök, shock (*la scossa*) works to "short-circuit the laws that forbid perpetual motion and libidinal action."[20] Noise, on the other hand, works to continuously break down systems. A "noisiness" whose "interferent perturbance not only subverts the redundancy but also enriches the complexity of any system" can be seen in the exceptions produced by computational codes, semiotic codes of societies, or even the biologic codes of organisms.[21] The third operation for inducing an exception involves speed. Italian futurist F. T. Marinetti suggests that "to be fast results in the 'intuitive synthesis' of rectilinear forms (the prognosis of straight lines), whereas to be slow results in the 'rational analysis' of curvilinear forms (the nostalgia of undulant lines)."[22] Thus, in moments of high velocity we operate instinctively, which allows for exceptions to escape the routines of rationalization. This is a notion that is commonly emphasized in today's architectural design process, especially in relation to form-finding operations. Architects, most notably Rem Koolhaas and OMA, encourage a conceptual design process of high velocity, where interns rapidly produce an excessive amount of form studies. This high-velocity action removes contemplation from the act of making and often yields unexpected results that escape rationalized preconceptions.

Shock, noise, and speed have become design operations. The projects that follow deploy these operations in efforts to induce, respectively, the three modes of the exception: anomaly, syzygy, or clinamen. Each project builds on evolving design methods that play with these pataphysical games.

Anomaly: The Principle of Variance in City of Blubber

"Nothing, it seems, is so fascinating as the thing that does not fit." This is echoed in the popularity of "reality" television shows that present a survey of cultural freakology—social and physical misfits who offer eccentric and entertaining counterpoints to a homogenous, mainstream culture. There is also the deep fascination in popular culture of the paranormal—those strange, inexplicable occurrences that sound more like hallucinations or conspiracies than realities. The long-running radio broadcast *Coast to Coast* is a comical platform for collecting these encounters with the anomalos. Unidentified flying objects, strange animals falling from the sky, mysterious disappearances, alien abductions, levitation, and teleportation "have given rise to the modern science of 'anomalistics,' which entails the use of scientific method to evaluate anomalies, and includes areas as ufology and cryptozoology."[23]

Rigorous examination of the anomaly can largely be attributed to the work of Charles Fort (1874–1932), "who was driven by an extreme skepticism and dislike of the pomposities of scientific positivism."[24] The principle of variance is scrutinized by Fort in a pataphysical encyclopedia, whose "itinerary," according to Bök, "bombards its Victorian readers with bizarrerie, ironically documenting, as though without exception, cases of exception, be they climatological (tiny frogs, for example, falling from temperate skies) or archaeological (iron tools, for example, hailing from Neolithic times)—case after case, in which science ignores evidence in order to make aberrances fit the procrustean."[25]

"Anomaly is, after all, like a stranger, estranged."[26] The anomaly is a principle of excess, where obscurities disobey the rule that divides identity from alterity: "The anomalos is a surprise, a mutation—a 'simple apparition' without tragedy or perfidy."[27]

What does the anomaly mean for architecture? The immediate instinct is to relate the anomaly to a contextual strategy, but this just leads to tired discussions about architectural formalism and iconic aliens dropped into foreign environments by star architects. The anomaly is more interesting for architecture when it is approached by way of a methodical agenda to disobey multiple formats. This became the objective for the project called City of Blubber (fig. 14.1)—a speculative city designed by mcdowellespinosa for the 2013 Bi-City Biennale of Urbanism/Architecture in Hong Kong.

City of Blubber is an urban anomaly situated on the rational, modern city of Babylon (a fictional version of Hong Kong). It is a strange urban territory floating above Babylon's vertical extrusions of concrete and steel. Neither grid, nor zone, nor avenue organizes this space. It is a new frontier—a formless terrain, a fat, soft, amorphous, visceral monster—in contrast to the lingering effects of modernity. It is a mushy mass that engulfs its inhabitants and deforms when touched. It is a parallel world that shrinks and swells atop the waste-plagued metropolis of Babylon.

A layer of fatty tissue forms the City of Blubber, creating an urban terrain of fat folds, crevices, and sagging bulges. Just as with mammals, this layer of urban tissue is the result of metabolism, waste storage, and thermal regulation. The City of Blubber swells as a result of excess and waste. This alternate world began to emerge when Babylon, a congested metropolis of seven million people, ran out of real estate for trash disposal. The dense city had grown accustomed to generating over six million tons of garbage each year and had no sustainable plan for reducing

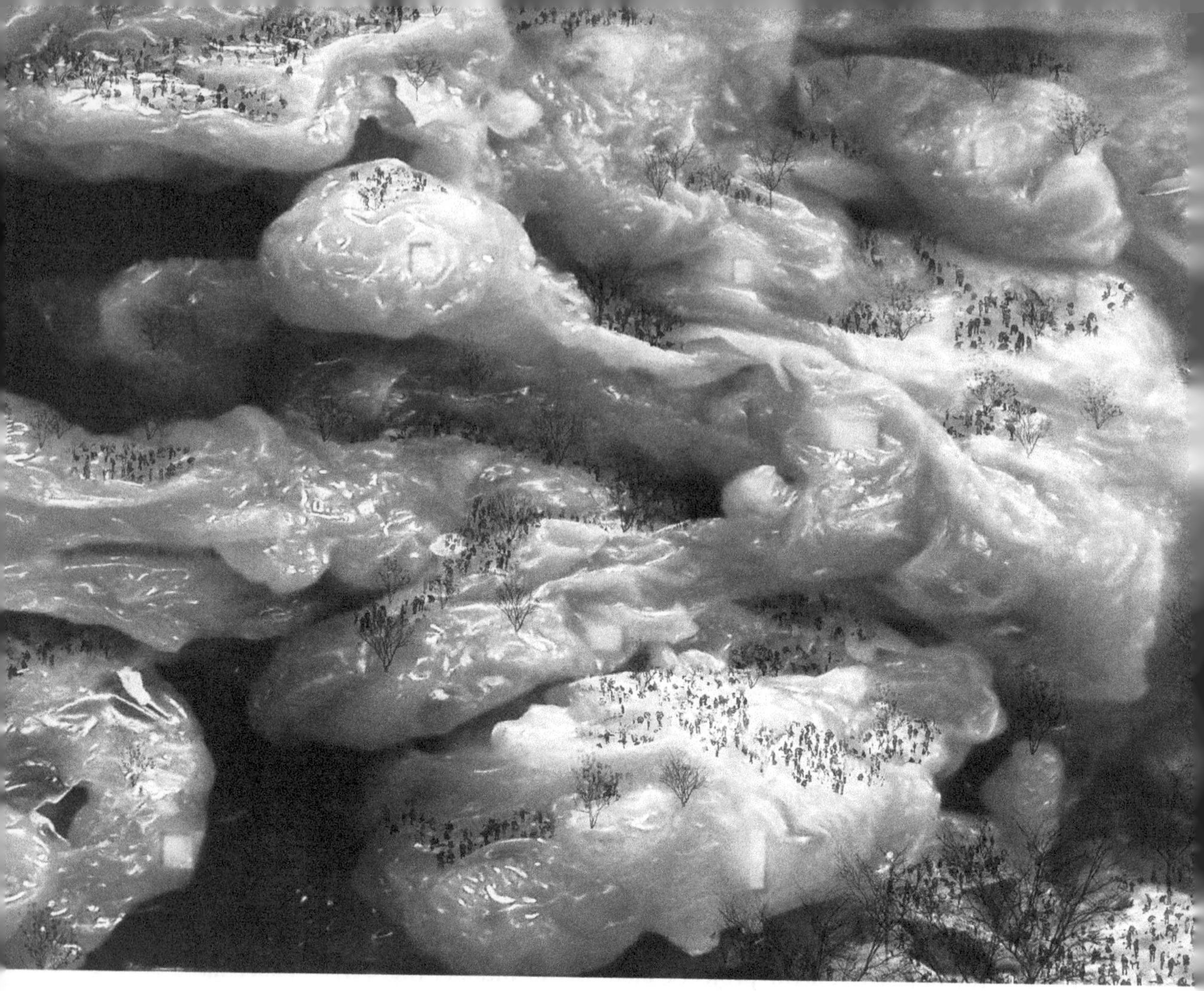

14.1. City of Blubber project. Collage showing blubber accumulation on top of the modern city. Courtesy of mcdowellespinosa architects, 2013.

or reallocating waste. So Babylon decided to address the issue with an absurd logic. Waste is perceived as a negative, unwanted material. If perception is altered, and the stigma of waste is forgotten, one could imagine waste as a raw, valuable material. With this altered vision, Babylon is a city wealthy in waste as the inhabitants generate excessive amounts of it through indulgent acts of consumption. The discarded materials littering the streets of Babylon and consuming the landfills could be exploited and transformed into a new materiality and become a resource for urban metabolism.

The City of Blubber was generated by a new infrastructural element: the biorefinery. Similar to the oil refinery's transformation of petroleum into fuels, biorefineries would come to convert corn, sugarcane, and other plant-based material into a malleable, plastic material known as blubber. In a massive plan to stabilize Babylon's waste issue, each block within the city was outfitted with a biorefinery to act as a garbage disposal for the neighborhood. These biorefineries were located in the center of each block and networked to floors of surrounding buildings. Within the biorefinery, an upstream processing step occurs, in which a mixture of fungus breaks down food waste into simple sugars, and then bacteria convert the sugars into a succinic acid. The succinic acid is then piped to the top of the city where it emerges as bioplastic blubber—a spatial and material anomaly.

The project incorporates a real, emerging science. The biorefinery concept is currently being investigated by engineers; however, the resulting urban transformation of this technology is an imaginary solution. The project was presented in the Hong Kong Biennale as a large physical model (six by six meters) and a short story. The model displayed visceral, pinkish wax formations atop the buildings of Hong Kong (the real-life Babylon).

Excess is the ingredient for urban expansion in Babylon. The transformed waste material is positioned as a new ground—a new datum supporting leisure and recreational activities for the city. The existing, gridded city acts as a foundation for this soft, urban creature. The city of modernity is the ground from which blubber accumulates. Within the accumulation, a spatial alien emerges.

City of Blubber is soft. It is resilient and resistant to destruction. Cataclysmic events only cause the terrain to ripple, vibrate, and roll. The blubber does not break. Brute force may cause the fatty mass to redistribute, but equilibrium is never disturbed. As a cushioned city, it is an ideal state of comfort. Upon touch, every surface of the city offers relief to the human body.

This project approaches design as the construction of a dystopian fictional city. The proposal is fixated on the principle of variance. It is an entire city that becomes an alter ego or pataphysical doppelgänger to the modern metropolis. It is an entanglement of two worlds, where the excess in one world generates spatial bulges in the other.

City of Blubber is a mechanism of noise. Matter (here, organic waste) is broken down with a mechanized parasitism. Marinetti argued that just as "microbes . . . are essential to the health of the intestines, so also is there a microbe essential to the vitality of art."[28] City of Blubber exemplifies Marinetti's argument, as spatial variation is generated through an atomic alchemy of excess. It is a spatial construct where nothing happens twice—instead, each event arises from its own set of exclusive accidents.

Syzygy: The Principle of Alliance in Drift City

Drift City (fig. 14.2) is essentially a design exercise that is generated by the hybridization of various fragments. In plan, a city is aligned with a highway. In section,

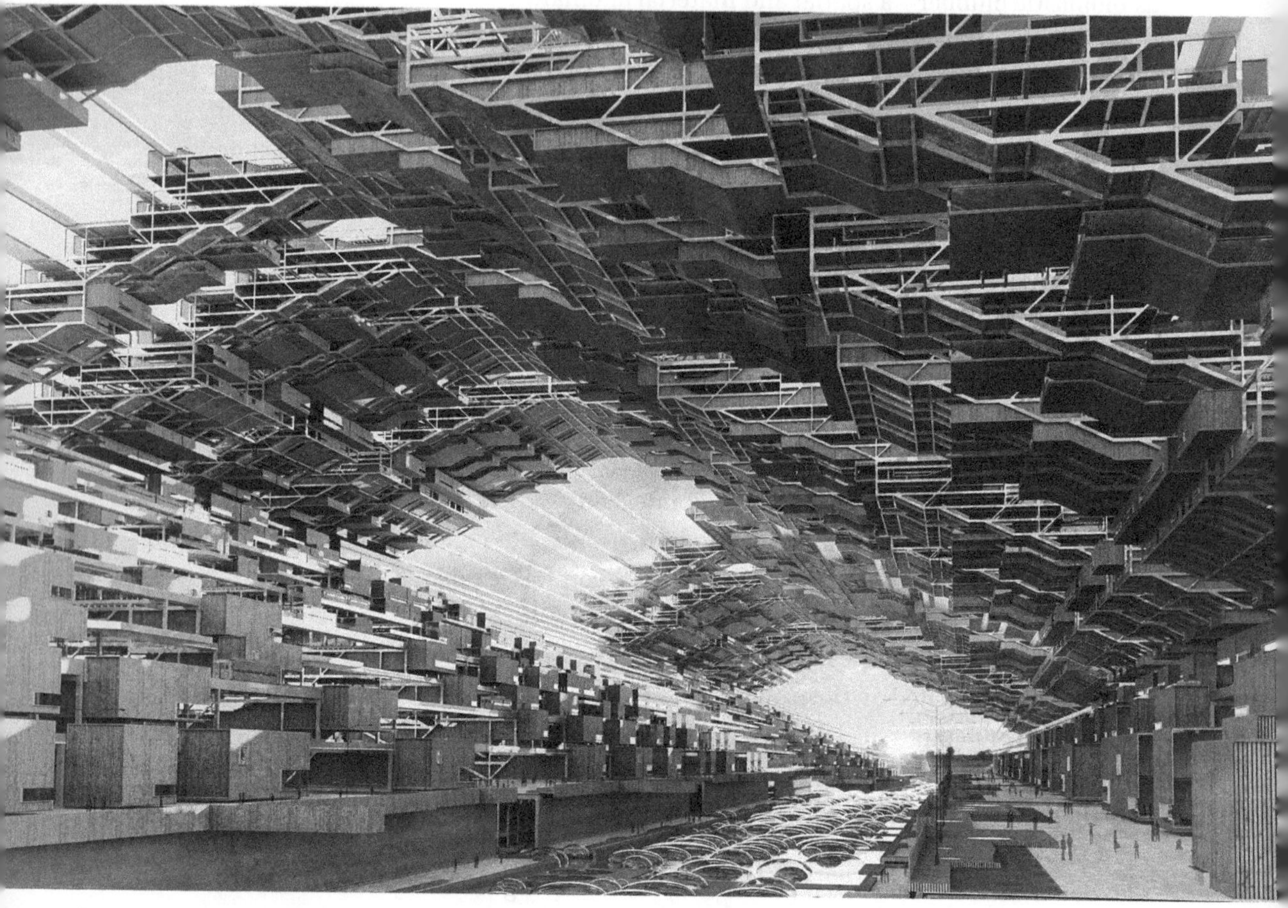

14.2. Main corridor of the Drift City project. Courtesy of mcdowellespinosa architects, 2016.

a stair is aligned with a window. In program, an industrial city is aligned with an agrarian city. All of these oppositional alignments are in response to the conceptual alignment of economic instability with public works projects.

Drift City began as a design exercise to imagine a city designed to solve an unemployment crisis. Economic instability has historically prompted two strategies for recovery. As with the Great Depression, one answer to stimulate work and money is to build large, federally funded infrastructure projects. The other is to retrain and relocate workers in hopes of decreasing unemployment. Drift City is a hybrid of the two strategies—it is an infrastructural city for a mobilized, nomadic working society. It is a syzygy of transportation and city, on a massive scale.

Home is merged with the road and the rail. The concept involves the occupation of circulation so that the street, the stair, and the landing become the framework for the home, the market, and the factory. Conceived as a linear city similar to Le Corbusier's Plan Obus for Algiers (1933), this highway city attempts to condense all aspects of a production-oriented society into one strip of infrastructure and habitation.

The title of Drift City is a riff on the surprise encounter of the syzygy, a key element of Guy Debord's and the Situationist International's theory of the *dérive* (drifting). A *dérive* involves playful-constructive behavior and awareness of psychogeographical effects, and are thus quite different from the classic notions of journey or stroll. Rather than vastly separating highway from rail, Drift City imagines them as parallel entities. This extreme redundancy allows the drifter to continuously mediate between the two modes of transportation.

There are two very different views of the Drift City. One is from a distance, where the system of highways, railways, and homes is seen as a figure in the landscape. The active city blurs together forming one striated line. Then, there is the view from within the city, where the individual drifter understands the world as a series of recognizable components that are replicated across the landscape. A complex dialogue develops between the repetition of singular components and the variation of multiple frequencies. This relates to the notion of familiarity and routine, which is often an element of the *dérive*. Here, a continuously changing environment is digested through a set of replicated, recognizable elements.

Drift City is a state of syzygy achieved by speed. Movement is relentlessly linear and induces an ecstatic velocity of stimulation. The city permits the future to outrace the past. The speed recalls Marinetti's analysis that to be fast results in the "intuitive synthesis" of rectilinear forms (the prognosis of straight lines).[29] It is a city without a beginning or end, where the primary unit of measure is velocity.

Clinamen: The Principle of Deviance in Water Fuel

Clinamen is the impetus for the "imaginary solution" for pataphysics. A project called Water Fuel investigated an approach to design that incorporated the clinamen (fig. 14.3). With an Epicurean method, we began the project with a "what if" statement. What if the world ran on water? There is no hard proof that it is possible to extract hydrogen from water, but there is also no proof that it is impossible. Hundreds of online videos depict amateur inventors burning water using improvised techniques of electrolysis. Our design project accepts water fuel as a reality and contemplates a world suddenly contending with the reconceptualization of a natural resource. The prospect of running one's car on water stimulates a plethora of questions about economy, distribution, dependence, and the commoditization of the natural resource.

Marcel Duchamp's readymades stripped objects of their functional associations—allowing the element to escape the system of control. With Water Fuel, we intended to do the opposite—to add a critical new functional association to a material, thus forcing it to also shed the inherited mechanisms of control. Water, now associated with fuel, will endure a radical swerve in materialistic desire. The project involved the design of a water fuel network that enables a profound shift in fuel distribution.

The water fuel network is a soft infrastructure that combines energy generation, fuel production, and recreation to formulate a new, floating landscape for New York City. The network is mapped at two scales across Manhattan. The first scale occurs at the edge of the island, on the water, where harvesting mats (or fueling mats) collect water and extract hydrogen by means of electrolysis. The second scale occurs within the streets of Manhattan, where current lanes for automotive traffic are converted to water scooter lanes designated by the fueling pods that hover above the street.

The key design element of this new fueling network is a modular pod (the privy pod) that functions as a public restroom and fueling station. This privy pod is conceived as an inhabitable electrolizer and extracts hydrogen from the flushed wastewater. The modules are designed in sections and the walls undulate to form storage tanks. On one side of each module water is stored, and on the other side hydrogen is stored. This extracted hydrogen feeds the fuel cells of a shared scooter network. The privy pods hover above the street and share a vertical column with other street utilities.

The entire system, from the architectural components to the transportation vehicles (scooters), is calibrated as a unitized, cellular network. This allows for the network to engage the swerve. The units allow for instantaneous shifting and incremental adjustments relative to unforeseen disturbances. Epicurus's falling particles informed the model for design, and collisions induce spatial transformations.

This clinamen results from the procedure of shock. In this project for a water fuel network, the shock is first introduced with material electrocution. Water is literally electrified in order to split hydrogen from oxygen, thus creating the fuel that

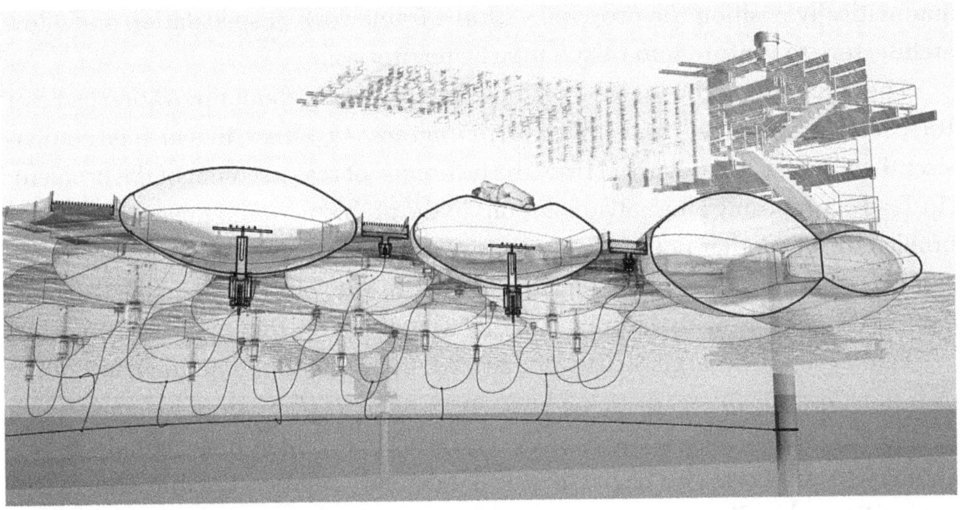

14.3. Section perspective of the Water Fuel project's bubble beach. Courtesy of mcdowellespinosa architects, 2009.

generates a new programmatic concern for the city. Then, shock is also manifested in the architectural tectonic, as the fueling infrastructure is formulated as perverse, bachelor machine–like pods that accumulate across the city. These pods are erotic devices that offer intimate space within a public street. Inside them individuals urinate, defecate, bathe, shower, or even masturbate. "Whether electric or artistic, the shock generated by such a device short-circuits the laws that forbid perpetual motion and libidinal action."[30]

What If . . . ?

Gaston Bachelard suggests that "all scientific radicalism begins with an epoch, a placing of reality between parentheses so that science might systematically explore an otherwise impossible hypothesis: it is in this area of dialectical surrationalism that the scientific mind dreams. Every question about what if leads to a science of as if."[31]

Each of the previous examples for deploying a pataphysical method for architectural speculation was initiated by a "what if" question. Each involved taking a significant event and speculating about what might happen. Marvel Comics experimented with this in its "What If" series, where each issue offers a look at familiar characters in situations they might never really face (e.g., "What if Spider-Man had joined the Fantastic Four?"). Each story takes place in a separate reality that doesn't affect the central continuity, so there are no rules and no limits. Characters can die—and often do. By opening a statement with the phrase "What if . . ." we automatically position the proposal within a framework of speculation and allow architecture to venture into risky, fantastic territories.

The "what if" approach could be linked to the writing about innovation by Peter Rice, structural engineer and author of *An Engineer Imagines*, in which he emphasizes that intelligence is derived from the technique of reassessment of the problem: "Instead of proposing alternative solutions to the problem, the engineer reassess the problem from another point of view."[32] By reassessing the problem, the engineer is able to escape objective parameters that formulate one solution. Breaking the paradigm of the "what is" with the pursuit of the "what if" allows the engineer to innovate.

Paul Feyerabend argues that, "for science to progress, the nomic truth of the *as is* must induce an escape to the ludic space of an *as if*: we need a dream-world in order to discover the features of the real world . . . which may actually be just another dream-world."[33] The pataphysical imaginary solution is a dramatic extension of Feyerabend's principle because it stresses the importance of every theory no matter how obsolete. In pataphysics, every theory has the potential to improve knowledge in some manner. This directly translates as an argument for an unfindable architecture. Architecture is not required to be physically constructed or publicly visible to build on the historical cannon of the discipline. A modest, one-off anomaly can radically propel the discourse of building.

Ultimately, unfindable architecture describes "a universe which can be—and perhaps should be—envisaged in the place of the traditional one."[34] It is an architecture that strives to construct the exception. It is an architecture that poses more questions than answers. It is an architecture of contradictions, and in these contradictions a complex, layered narrative is embedded. An unfindable architecture is an important condition for the field because it adds tension to the discourse. It encourages experimentation and seeks new solutions, however seemingly irrelevant they may be. While an unfindable architecture tends to yield an eccentric perspective, tailored to an ostentatious audience, it resonates in popular culture in the form of science fiction, a genre in debt to Jarry's pataphysics. Sci-fi novels and films have always reflected our anxieties and used fantasy to propose solutions. This is evident in today's subgenre of cli-fi, which fixates on the evolving apocalyptic vision of the effects of climate change. The importance of this work is not in its reality, but its critique of cultural fears. "Science fiction does not detail the realities of specific problems so that we might avoid them"; rather, it holds a mirror to our collective anxiety.[35] An unfindable architecture is the mirror, the recognition of how similar and fragile the world is—and how rewarding it can be to escape to a new frontier.

Notes

1. Jacques Carelman, *Objéts introuvables: A Catalogue of Unfindable Objects* (Paris: André Balland, 1969).

2. While this was once true, the search term "unfindable architecture" now offers results relating to this chapter.

3. Christian Bök, *'Pataphysics: The Poetics of an Imaginary Science* (Evanston, IL: Northwestern University Press, 2002), 9.

4. Ibid., 38.

5. *Merriam-Webster Online*, s.v. "unfindable," accessed February 1, 2021, http://www.merriam-webster.com/dictionary/unfindable.

6. Gili Merin, "AD Classics: Ville Radieuse / Le Corbusier," ArchDaily, August 11, 2013, https://www.archdaily.com/411878/ad-classics-ville-radieuse-le-corbusier.

7. Kazys Varnelis, "Programming After Program: Archizoom's No-Stop City," *Praxis: Journal of Writing and Building* 8 (2006): 89.

8. Michael Speaks first describes "supermodern" in his lecture "Future of Design," given at the University of Michigan on October 9, 2009.

9. Andrew Hugill, "The Pataphysics of the Future," lecture at De Montfort University, May 13, 2013.

10. Andrew Hugill, *'Pataphysics: A Useless Guide* (Cambridge, MA: MIT Press, 2012), 9.

11. Kant developed four antinomies; in each, a thesis is contradicted by an antithesis.

12. Michelle Grier, "The Logic of Illusion and the Antinomies," in *A Companion to Kant*, ed. Graham Bird (Oxford, UK: Blackwell, 2006), 194.

13. Hugill, *'Pataphysics*, 10.

14. Ibid., 64.

15. Iman Ansari, "Interview: Peter Eisenman," *Architectural Review*, April 26, 2013, https://www.architectural-review.com/essays/interview-peter-eisenman/8646893.article.

16. Stefano Corbo, *From Formalism to Weak Form: The Architecture and Philosophy of Peter Eisenman* (Farnham, UK: Ashgate, 2014), 18.

17. Alfred Jarry, *Exploits and Opinions of Doctor Faustroll, Pataphysician: A Neo-Scientific Novel (A Neo-Scientific Novel)* (1911), trans. Simon Watson Taylor (Boston: Exact Change, 1996), 22.

18. Friedrich Nietzsche, *Saemtliche Werke: Kritische Studienausgabe*, ed. Giorgio Colli and Mazzino Montinari (Berlin: Walter de Gruyter, 1967), 187–88.

19. Bök, *'Pataphysics*, 39.

20. Ibid., 54.

21. Jean Baudrillard, *The Transparency of Evil: Essays on Extreme Phenomena* (1990), trans. James Benedict (London: Verso, 1993), 69.

22. F. T. Marinetti, *Let's Murder the Moonshine: Selected Writings*, ed. R. W. Flint, trans. R. W. Flint and Arthur A. Coppatelli (Los Angeles: Sun and Moon, 1991), 103.

23. Hugill, *'Pataphysics*, 12.

24. Ibid.

25. Bök, *'Pataphysics*, 39.

26. Ibid., 40.

27. Jean Baudrillard, *Fatal Strategies* (1983), ed. Jim Fleming, trans. Philip Beitchman and W. G. J. Niesluchowski (New York: Semiotext(e), 1990), 26.

28. Marinetti, *Let's Murder the Moonshine*, 97.

29. Ibid., 103.

30. Bök, *'Pataphysics*, 54.

31. Gaston Bachelard, *The Philosophy of No: A Philosophy of the New Scientific Mind* (1940), trans. G. C. Waterston (New York: Orion, 1968), 28.

32. Peter Rice, *An Engineer Imagines* (London: Artemis, 1994), 80.

33. Paul Feyerabend, *Against Method: Outline of an Anarchistic Theory of Knowledge*, rev. ed. (London: Verso, 1988), 32.

34. Jarry, *Faustroll*, 22.

35. J. P. Telotte, "Science Fiction Reflects Our Anxieties," *New York Times*, July 30, 2014.

Chapter 15

Metabolic Poetics

Writing the Anthropocene

Adam Dickinson

Oil is a form of writing. I know this because I can read it in my blood, urine, and feces. As part of research for a recent book, I tested myself for a wide range of chemicals. I also had my microbiome sequenced. I found petrochemical pollution in my blood and urine in the form of pesticides, flame retardants, phthalates, and more. I discovered evidence in my gut of shifted microbial communities associated with aspects of the Western diet. I wrote about what I found in a book called *Anatomic*, which I think of as an unusual chemical/microbial autobiography in poetry that reframes the body as a kind of mobile bioregion, as a biosemiotic anatomy of interfering messages.[1] What does it mean to rethink ecological identity in the Anthropocene—that emerging era in geological history where humans have begun to significantly affect planetary biogeochemical cycles—as a function of potent intra-actions between environmental toxins and symbiotic organisms?[2] What is the ethical potential of understanding identity as a porous, membranous, trans-corporeal organization where the metabolic forces within are affected by the global metabolic forces of energy and capital without?

The Anthropocene constitutes in part, McKenzie Wark observes, "a series of metabolic rifts, where one molecule after another is extracted by labor and technique to make things for humans, but the waste products don't return so that the cycle can renew itself."[3] The social formations produced by oil and petrochemical-related industries create their own metabolic rifts by concentrating capital in massively unequal ways and accumulating forms of dependence on and desire for unsustainable products and lifestyles. Oil permeates our biological and cultural metabolism and also our literary tropes and technologies; the road trip beckons and the computer screen winks. Consequently, it requires of us new forms of literacy sensitive to metabolisms, scalar poetics, and seductive nostalgia for cheap energy. The biosemiotic effects of endocrine-disrupting petrochemicals constitute an emerging focus for ecopoetic practice and ecocritical analysis, especially through the lens of new materialisms.[4] Pataphysics, I would argue, offers a particularly helpful perspective from which to consider these deterritorialized forms of metabolic writing in the Anthropocene because of its intrinsic concerns with scale, shifted frames of inquiry and perspective, as well as détourned scientific procedures and research-creation methods—think of the psychogeographic walks of the Situationist International, imaginary encyclopedias, readymades, procedural writing, and other extraordinary and impossibly realized forms of research. I think of pataphysics as a creative/critical practice attentive to rifts, exceptions, particulars, and "diffractive methodologies," which is Karen Barad's term for the interference patterns revealed by unlikely juxtapositions resulting from intentional collisions between disciplines.[5] Diffraction, it is worth noting, might also be said to characterize the deviation or swerve of the clinamen so important to Jarry's 'pataphysics. I think of pataphysics as a mode of what Haraway calls "SF," or "science fiction, speculative feminism, science fantasy, [or] speculative fabulation," because of the ways in which it entangles contexts, reimagines stories, and exposes different patterns of worlding.[6] Pataphysics deserves attention not only as an object, but also as a potential *form* of ecopoetic inquiry conducting research at the complex and controversial nature-culture thresholds. After all, through the proliferation of toxic chemicals, the industrialized world is carrying out a kind of fantastic, reckless science project of its own on the bodies of its citizens without consent.

Pursuing a diffractive methodological approach, I will examine some recent examples of pataphysical responses to chemical pollution as manifestations of what I am calling "metabolic poetics." I define metabolic poetics as an artistic practice concerned with the potential of expanded modes of reading and writing to shift the frames and scales of conventional forms of signification in order to bring into focus the often inscrutable biological and cultural writing intrinsic to the Anthropocene, especially as this is reflected in the inextricable link between the metabolic processes of human and nonhuman bodies and the global metabolism of energy and capital. What does it mean to think about writing in a more expanded way to include the processes and effects of hormones? How might the metabolic effects of chemicals and microbes provide models for renovated poetic forms? How can writers respond to the many ways in which the global metabolism of energy and capital is inextricably linked to the metabolism of human and nonhuman bodies? In particular, I will focus in more detail on the permeable forms of identity established in relation to the "queer productivity" of toxins[7] in Jenny Sampirisi's *Croak* and Juliana Spahr's *The Transformation*. To begin, however, let me explain what I mean by biosemiotics, hyperobjects, and the pataphysics of oil.

We touch plastic and it touches us back. Synthetic chemicals have become part of the hormonal communication of what it means to be human. Just as the Anthropocene can be defined as evidence of human imprint in the fossil record—a new form of rock, Plastiglomerate, has recently been identified—so, too, can it be defined by the increasing presence of synthetic chemicals in our blood and fat, affecting hormones and potentially damaging DNA, the genetic archive of human evolutionary inheritance.[8] These chemicals "interfere with signalling and other biological processes," Bruce Lourie and Rick Smith illustrate in *Toxin Toxout*.[9] Such metabolic interventions perpetrated by these endocrine disruptors emphasize the semiotic nature of biological processes. Biosemiotics is an emerging field in theoretical biology that studies the communicative dynamics between organisms and their environment as well as the interpretive interactions within organisms at the endocrine, immunological, and reproductive system levels. As Wendy Wheeler points out, from a biosemiotic perspective "all life, not just human life and culture, is semiotic and interpretive."[10] By studying the signifying environments of organisms and the internal endosemiotic environments at the molecular level, biosemiotics emphasizes the importance of the *semiosphere*, which, as Jesper Hoffmeyer notes, "is a sphere like the atmosphere, hydrosphere, or biosphere," except that "it permeates these spheres from their innermost to outermost reaches and consists of communication: sound, scent, movement, colors, forms, electrical fields, various waves, chemical signals, touch, and so forth—in short, the signs of life."[11] The point is to demonstrate that life is a function of semiosis.

We might also say, however, that biosemiotics represents a kind of pataphysical détournement in which biology is read through linguistics. Hoffmeyer in fact concedes the unorthodox and exceptional position of biosemiotics when he decries that so many "path-breaking" biosemiotic texts have been "banished to the fringes of scientific study and acceptance" because of "their perceived radicalness."[12] One of those early path-breakers was Jakob von Uexküll, whose fantastic and surreal depictions of the signifying environments (*Umwelten*) of such dissimilar creatures as bees, crabs, houseflies, and mollusks, prompts Giorgio Agamben in *The Open* to draw comparisons to Jarry's *Ubu Roi*.[13] Indeed, biosemiotic concerns are evident in Jarry's principal treatise on pataphysics, as we learn that Dr. Faustroll "is quite literally a literary creation, his body becoming a book—a papyrus cadaver that can unscroll to divulge the secrets of a poetic vision, his eyes, like 'two capsules of ordinary writing-ink.'"[14] I would also suggest that biosemiotics focuses important attention on the ways in which interpretive frameworks generate imaginary solutions to biological circumstances such as predation (plants signal each other about insect attacks), migration (birds navigate by the stars), foraging (dung beetles read polarized moonlight), and reproduction (ring doves coo at their own ovaries to release eggs).[15] The next time you encounter a freshly mown lawn, think about how the wonderful, evocative smell is really the volatile organic compound *cis*-3-Hexenal, a distress signal emitted to stimulate antibiotic production at the wound site and to induce other plants to prime their own defense responses.

Biosemiotics has recently been taken up in ecocritical studies as part of a turn to new materialism with its emphasis on reconfigured notions of ontology and agency. Material ecocriticism, for example, as defined by Serenella Iovino and Serpil Oppermann, "is the study of the way material forms—bodies, things, elements, toxic substances, chemicals, organic and inorganic matter, landscapes, and biological entities—intra-act with each other and with the human dimension, producing configurations of meanings and discourses that we can interpret as stories."[16] The term "intra-act" mentioned here comes from Barad, who proposes a renovated conception of identity formed through what she calls "intra-action." Unlike "interaction," which is predicated on associations between discrete agents, "intra-action" presupposes that any distinctive qualities ostensibly possessed by participating agents emerge as a result of their entangled relationship. In other words, intra-action "*signifies the mutual constitution of entangled agencies*."[17] Stacy Alaimo recognizes the importance of Barad's work to new materialism as well as to environmentalism for the ways in which it challenges totalizing applications of nonhuman identity and also productively renovates critical approaches to massive extraction and emission concerns where intra-actions are occurring at numerous and diverse scales. Alaimo reorients some of these concerns through her concept of "trans-corporeality," which "reveals the interchanges and interconnections between various bodily natures." It involves critical awareness of the ways in which the body is permeated by its environment. According to Alaimo, trans-corporeal ethics encourages "us to somehow find ways of navigating through the simultaneously material, economic, and cultural systems that are so harmful to the living world and yet so difficult to contest or transform." She argues that "understanding the substance of one's self as interconnected with the wider environment marks a profound shift in subjectivity."[18] Jane Bennett's theory of vital materiality also represents an influential aspect of this developing ecocritical, new materialist approach. Her work implicitly emphasizes biosemiotic processes by considering how vibrant matter, which includes things such as electricity, chemicals from landfills, and dietary fats, has the capacity to alter human behavior and consequently political action: "How would political responses to public problems change were we to take seriously the vitality of (nonhuman) bodies?

By 'vitality' I mean the capacity of things—edibles, commodities, storms, metals—not only to impede or block the will and designs of humans but also to act as quasi agents or forces with trajectories, propensities, or tendencies of their own."[19]

Modernity, Timothy Morton proposes, "is the story of how oil got into everything."[20] He thinks of oil as a hyperobject, which, like global warming, flu pandemics, nuclear radiation, and chemical pollution, confronts us as a strange phenomenon massively out-scaling conventional human experiences of time and space. Apprehensible in many cases only with the assistance of sensitive measuring equipment, hyperobjects are omnipresent but never precisely contained in or expressed by a specific location. The nonlocality of hyperobjects is apparent, for example, in the way that endocrine disruptors, as Morton notes, penetrate the skin and "start cascading reactions . . . interfering with the production and circulation of hormones"; yet the precise consequences of this interference, such as the potential occurrence of cancer, can only be indirectly connected back to any specific chemical exposure.[21]

Questions of scale, metabolic trans-corporeality, and intra-action have been primary concerns for pataphysics since Jarry's early articulations of the science. We learn that Dr. Faustroll harnessed the power of symbiotic microbes to maintain the appearance of his distinctive facial hair.[22] In addition, the figurative laboratory of his studies, his boat, is, we might say, metabolically balanced. For example, when compelled, he expels his urine directly into the boat, which is really a sieve with a semipermeable membrane that allows the liquid to "simply pass through the mesh and rejoin the external waves," thus avoiding any metabolic rift or accumulation of pollution.[23] Faustroll's companion, however, a hydrocephalic baboon, suffers from a metabolic rift of his own that causes water to accumulate on his brain. Water is a constant concern for Jarry in contrasting ways. He famously called it a corrosive solvent, eschewing it in favor of copious and constant alcohol consumption, which he first tried at age three, becoming drunk on wine after being left alone with a friend collecting frogs.[24] In *Faustroll*, however, water is the focus of intense pataphysical study. In fact, it marks a foundational concern with signifying environments, or *Umwelten* (perceptual worlds), as well as with the scalar poetics common in pataphysical art and research. Dr. Faustroll deliberately shrinks himself down to the size of a water droplet on a cabbage leaf "in order to examine any disturbances which this change in size might involve in their mutual relationship." This shift in perspective permits him to observe how "a living eye, became presbyopic, lengthened itself along its horizontal diameter into an ovoid myopia." The scaled-down study, which metacritically and humorously reflects on both the semiotic limitations and opportunities of magnitudinally shifted perspectives, ends with the realization of formerly invisible environmental metabolisms: "Beneath everything, the chlorophyll, like a shoal of green fishes, followed its charted currents in the cabbages subterranean canals."[25]

Attentiveness to hyperobjects, metabolic processes, and semiotic materialism make pataphysics especially sensitive to the science of exceptions that defines oil production and politics. Counterintuitive practices abound in the history of oil. Intentional "sabotage" of production has frequently served to keep prices high and maintain the ruse of public imperialistic interventions that have historically masked the real private interests of oil firms.[26] In addition to creating obstacles for themselves in order make their product scarcer and more expensive, another key "method of preventing energy abundance," utilized by oil companies, "involved the rapid construction of lifestyles in the United States organized around the consumption of extraordinary quantities of energy."[27] Oil became the realization of a cultural fantasy, an imaginary solution for a future based on a hyperreality of speed and capitalist consumption. Stephanie LeMenager argues that the affective pleasures involved with driving or feeling the heat from the asphalt are evidence of the ways in which "petroleum infrastructure has become embodied memory and habitus for modern humans."[28] Love for oil and its media represent a significant obstacle to imagining alternative energy systems and social formations. The interest in preserving this fantasy has generated questionable technological practices. For example, following the 2010 BP blowout in the Gulf of Mexico, the ocean was aggressively treated with dispersants in order to make the disaster as invisible as possible to coastal communities by reducing the quantity of tar balls washing up on beaches. These remediation methods, however, turned out to be highly toxic, bioaccumulating up the food chain and inadvertently facilitating the deposit of oil on the deep ocean floor, damaging marine life at greater depths. Oil disasters necessarily affect the metabolism of biological beings who encounter them. However, in the attempt to make the spill as invisible as possible, this molecular interference was exacerbated by the dispersants, which functioned like a deliberate imaginary solution designed to sacrifice the water in the Gulf of Mexico "for the sake of the shore."[29] If this is the authoritative technological science on which safety measures and corporate-influenced government policies are based, then it is a science that represses its pataphysical roots, that "represses in itself . . . its own basis in signs, their errors and biases," which serve the preservation of corporate appearances over the metabolic health of the ocean.[30] A pataphysical approach to oil illuminates these constraints and procedures that are otherwise couched in the neoliberal language of the free market and benevolent public interest.

The Museum of Jurassic Technology, located three miles from the La Brea tar pits in Los Angeles, links important recent studies of both oil and pataphysics. A strange, updated version of a medieval cabinet of wonders, the museum presents "a specialized repository of relics and artifacts from the Lower Jurassic, with an emphasis on those that demonstrate unusual or curious technological qualities."[31] In *Living Oil*, LeMenager mentions the museum in the context of trying to understand the temporal framing of oil as technological and cultural: "The question of what endurance means for 'nature,' 'history,' and the natural history museum seems to break around what will continue to count as life-like: information or object, media or bone."[32] The Museum of Jurassic Technology is also the initial frame Christian Bök uses to introduce his book *'Pataphysics: The Poetics of an Imaginary Science*: "What Wilson [the founder of the museum] calls 'Jurassic technology' we might call Jarryite 'pataphysics'—a science of imaginary solutions, in which the critic wishes not only to study but also to evoke cases of exceptional singularity."[33] The evocation of such a singular case is embodied by LeMenager's appendix to *Living Oil*, in which she explores the metabolism of her book's production by subjecting it to a Life Cycle Assessment, conducted by a graduate of UC Santa Barbara's Bren School of Environmental Science. The results of the research are "meant to express with the baldest honesty the energy inputs required to make this book."[34] In conducting such an assessment, LeMenager employs pataphysical methods such as cataloging and shifting scales of perception. It turns out that the amount of energy needed to produce and transport one copy of her book is 6.2 kWh, which, as she notes, is more than the 3.79 kWh required to produce an American cheeseburger.[35] Her intervention raises interesting questions about what it means to consider academic and literary labor in this way, productively contextualizing an overlooked aspect of its material history. Such imaginative scholarly approaches demonstrate the value of unconventional critical responses to oil in the Anthropocene, responses I would characterize as pataphysical, given their concerns with shifting scales of perception in order to read the hyperobject of oil in a more intimate and strange manner. In effect, LeMenager reframes her own book as a form of media art, expressing its particular contribution to the metabolic rift of the carbon cycle. Jussi Parikka argues that recent modes of media art have "succeeded in deterritorializing media practices from a narrow understanding based on technologies to a wider and more innovative distribution," including chemicals, animals, geological strata, and other formations.[36] As a critic, like LeMenager, like Bök's pataphysician, who wishes not only to study but also to evoke cases of exceptional singularity, I see my own chemical/microbial autobiography, *Anatomic*, as a species of media art, as a related attempt to "reveal a whole new world of sensations, perceptions, movements, stratagems, and patterns of organization that work much beyond the confines of the human world" and also within its strange, expressive metabolic corridors, revealing flows of industrial, agricultural, and military interests.[37] In what follows, I investigate some examples of metabolic poetics that read and write oil as a form of media expressed in the particular histories and social formations of human and nonhuman bodies. Imre Szeman argues that "oil only has such significance as it does for us as a result of the cultural narratives that shape our understanding of it." In order to understand and interrogate these narratives, it is necessary to attend to trans-corporeal and intra-active bodies as forms of petromedia expressing the ways in which "oil animates and enables all manner of abstract categories," identities, and politics.[38]

Some of the most extreme acts of writing now being carried out in the capitalist Anthropocene are being performed by petrochemicals. Metabolic poetics involves attempts to respond with similarly extreme or expanded forms of writing and in so doing "make oil a more conceptually powerful part of our knowing," as Szeman suggests must happen as part of any political change.[39] If bodies and objects can be read as expressive networks and assemblages, then metabolic poetics has obvious affinities with BioArt, especially with work like Eduardo Kac's "Natural History of the Enigma," which incorporates biological material from the artist's own blood to a produce a genetically modified petunia with distinctive red veins on its petals.[40] However, in looking for more manifestly literary responses to "storied matter," as the material ecocritics would say,[41] Georges Perec might be said to have created an early example with his "Attempt at an Inventory of the Liquid and Solid Foodstuffs Ingurgitated by Me in the Course of the Year Nineteen Hundred and Seventy-Four." In this pataphysical catalog, excerpted here, Perec lists exactly what the title describes:

> One eggs with anchovy, two boiled eggs, two eggs *en meurette*, one ham and eggs, one bacon and eggs, one eggs *en cocotte* with spinach, two eggs in aspic, two scrambled eggs, four omelettes, one sort of omelette, one soya-seed omelette, one craterellus omelette, one duck skin omelette, one *confit d'oie* omelette, one herb omelette, one Parmentier omelette.[42]

Perec's list not only archives the ordinary quotidian work of a metabolizing body, but it also recalls the more contemporary exotic lists that characterize the chemical ingredients cataloged on the sides of packaged food, or the list of nutrient percentages that signify dietary caution, or even the lists of toxins obtainable via biomonitoring and toxicological studies. Moreover, the list expresses a particular culture, a form of material and social life—Who was he eating these meals with? Where did he eat them? What conditions produced them?[43]

Other examples of metabolic poetics might include the sound poetry experiments of Henri Chopin (especially his poems derived from swallowing a microphone and recording his blood circulation and digestion).[44] More recently, Evelyn Reilly's *Styrofoam* explores endocrine disruption in plastics along with a poem about Henrietta Lacks's cervical cancer cells, which, without her permission, have been used long after her death to develop drugs and profits for pharmaceutical companies.[45] Lisa Robertson's "The Seam" enacts "the urgent motions of membranes / with the mystic dialectic of toxins and hormones" as part of an investigation of gender, health, and form (aesthetic, biological, cultural).[46] Her related work with Stacy Doris, "The Perfume Recordist," is similarly metabolically focused as it seeks to "consider the meeting of perfume, hormones and degeneration."[47] Craig Dworkin's poem "Fact" is an example of conceptual poetry, not unlike Perec's dietary inventory, that lists all the chemical ingredients in the sheet of paper the poem is printed on: "Ink on a 5.5 by 9 inch substrate of 60-pound offset matte white paper. Composed of: varnish (soy bean oil [$C_{57}H_{98}O_6$], used as a plasticizer: 52%. Phenolic modified rosin resin [Tall oil rosin: 66.2%. Nonylphenol [$C_{15}H_{24}O$]: 16.6%. Formaldehyde [CH_2O]:4.8%."[48] A publication note in *Poetry* indicates that this is a work in progress, changing as the surfaces of publication change, requiring the author to adjust the content. Robert Kocik's *Overcoming Fitness* is also an example of metabolic poetics in its claims for poetry as a biosemiotic tool for talking back through germlines to challenge oil-driven politics and the limiting, systematic definitions of "fitness" they pursue.[49]

Both Jenny Sampirisi's *Croak* and Juliana Spahr's *The Transformation* employ pataphysical methods (impossible-to-stage productions, extraordinary catalogs, unconventional ethno-botanical research) to explore the metabolic processes and rifts involved in living with oil and chemical pollution. Pollution or toxicity in these texts involves an exceptional intimacy that, in addition to mutation, endocrine disruption, social disintegration, and physical displacement, produces productively queering effects such as expressions of trans-corporeal subjectivities and intra-active identities that integrate and entangle important questions about gender, sexuality, colonialism, and environment with "petrocultural" practices and relationships.[50] These books propose necessarily contingent imaginary solutions to rewriting the biosemiotic writing of petrochemicals and "prickly new cells." They express a metabolic poetics that invites an ontologically phenomenal consideration of identity alive to the permeability of bodies to energy systems, systems of production and profit, and social formations. They invite us to think of writing in broader terms; we touch the keyboard to type a poem (Who gets to write? What are the circumstances that permit this activity?), but the keyboard touches us back, the flame retardants from the plastics slip through the membranes of our skin. We have written a world out of oil, but we know so little of how it has written us. Metabolic poetics points to these serous and agential texts.

"I know I am a frog," Girl One announces in Jenny Sampirisi's self-described frog-and-girl opera *Croak*. Girl One adds, in a manner evoking both the grammar and biology of sexual reproduction, "My brothers and sisters were commas."[51] This link between language, frogs, and sexual reproduction places Sampirisi's text within the pataphysical biosemiotic lineage established by Jean-Pierre Brisset (1837–1919), who viewed the tadpole-shapes of sperm as evidence of an unusual theory of evolution featuring frogs as the progenitors of modern human bodies and languages. A pataphysician *avant la lettre*, Brisset asserts in *The Origin of Language from Our Ancestor Frogs* that "all languages preserve the memory of the period during which we lived on flies."[52] His biosemiotic approach draws a link between language and morphology whereby "human beings in effect pun physically on frogs," evidenced by the fact that "swimming humans replicate the shape of frogs splayed out," despite "[diverging] somewhat in meaning, like the approximately twinned referents in punning."[53] Brisset's fervent investigation of puns was directed toward revealing "the herpetological underpinnings of language," which is based on the parataxis of contradictory contexts, or in other words the pataphysical "syzygy of words."[54]

The relationship between linguistic and physiological puns is a significant part of the biosemiotic exploration of chemical pollution in Sampirisi's *Croak*. I would also venture that the whole book could be considered a kind of formal pun, given that it constitutes a mutated retelling of Aristophanes's *The Frogs*, complete with the croaking refrain "*Brekekekex-koax-koax*."[55] Puns recur throughout the book; however, the brief summary offered at the beginning generates a particularly significant pun on the word "limb": "Part One wherein Frogs and Girls limb along / Part Two wherein they fall in limb / Part three wherein they die" (7). "Limb," "limp," and "love" work homophonically to establish the book's primary set of intra-active concerns: toxic mutagenesis, the difficulty of resisting complacent social strictures around romantic love and political action, and queer sexuality. Of the three principal characters, which include the Narrators, the Frogs, and the Girls, it is the Narrators who function as persistent polysemous toxins, both chemically and culturally. Mediating the action as a kind of environment, they tell the story of the Frogs and Girls by metabolically altering and deforming bodies via pesticides and heavy metals, by casting them into stereotyped social constructions—the crooner Michigan J. Frog and the puppet Kermit the Frog, who repeat the tropes of conventional love and complacent sentimentalism ("If you refuse me / Honey, you'll lose me" [59])—and by adhering to a toxic logic of binaries (the repeated references to "one plus one") that does not make allowances for the very identities blurred by the effects of the chemicals these Narrators embody. They tell the story by mediating the body internally and externally, with their endocrine disruptions and their inflected forms of phatic, or bodily, communication. Early in the second act, the Narrators are presented as twinned forces of toxicity and gesture:

> ALPHA-LINDANE[319-84-6] moaned first
> ANTINOMY'S[7440-36-0] tongue slid
>
> BERYLLIUM[7440-41-7] skewed
> CADMIUM'S[7440-43-9] capitulation
> CHROMIUM[7440-47-3] ceased
> by slow degrees
>
> CYANIDE[57-12-5]
> became pliant

TETRACHLOROETHYLENE[127-18-4]
reshaped steely contours (48)

Toxins come to constitute a more complicated queering force as the book develops. They alter developmental hormone levels to blur sexual characteristics in frogs, as depicted in the largely redacted poem "frogirls" where the only legible text indicates that "males were both / completely feminized / developed into functional females that copulated" (72). Gender definitions become fluid as the frogs declare to the girls that "we will become women and you will be our prince" (57). The girls explore their own mutual attraction, turning to each other with amorous declarations: "I'm in love. With you. You're my first" (53). However, queer sexuality is itself toxically policed by the binary and systematic logic that runs through the Narrators' contributions in the book: "It's two or zero and many will choose zero that's a choice" (46). Moreover, such narratives of toxic feminization reveal another kind of social policing that associates environmental health with normalized bodies. As Giovanna di Chiro observes, "Scratch a liberal environmentalist and you might find polluted politics enforcing 'eco(hetero)normativity' lurking underneath."[56]

Is it possible to rethink the toxin by observing, as Mel Y. Chen does in *Animacies: Biopolitics, Racial Mattering, and Queer Affect*, that it beckons as well as threatens, that it "does not repel but propels queer loves"? How might we understand "the queer productivity of toxins and toxicity"?[57] In *Croak*, I would propose, the toxins create a productive queered space for the girls and frogs to understand their common "amphibious" nature, their trans-corporeal and intra-active being composed of extra limbs and useless words—"I'd like to take them. I'm in love. With you" (53)—composed of their molecularly vibrant environment, for good and ill. Sarah Bernstein argues that "*Croak* celebrates the grotesque—the leaky boundaries of skin and identity and language."[58] Acknowledging that toxins can be productively disquieting, Sampirisi points out in an interview in the *Queen's Journal* that "it really is a text that's unnerving, not just about our distorted sense of self, but also about love, lust and sex, and how in our modern world these very natural things have been mutated and transformed."[59] The final section of the book, "Catharsis," contains two short poems, including the final one, which simply states, "So it is that we failed then" (99). The failure is ambiguous, and it is this very ambiguity that productively complicates the final expressions of identity as the book comes to a conclusion. The penultimate longer poem "Lo Figrrs," an anagram of "Frogirls," which is a frequently occurring title, turns identity into a version of environmental history, recounting in very succinct terms the emergence of girls and frogs into chemical pollution ("We came into the world. . . . Metals found bodies. . . . It sunk into our breasts until we had none but those on the screen"), and social pollution, or restrictive sexist and species-ist depictions: "We came into the world and it was a café. . . . On TV, an image of a girl. On the wall, an image of a frog. . . . We understood the café as an expectation" (98). The poem closes with a short, simple expression of metabolism: "A series of happenings grow and retract, splinter and reshape the body" (98). All of this history has culminated in a human/frog body living her life having changed none of the geopolitical systems that surround her; however, she does so now with an awareness of how her identity has become co-determinate with her environment, with petrochemicals, with the cultural will to produce them: "We spoke the chemicals into the mud and into the water until they came looking for the source and climbed back into our mouths" (98). The frog/girl body at the end of the poem expresses a queer, trans-corporeal, anagrammatic identity of entangled agencies. The toxins are no longer simply toxins, they are part of her, expressed as her intra-active identity. She is a body reading her environmental history and also speaking it. The "Lo Figrrs" have become petromedia even as they feel their own frustrated incapacities.

Rethinking identity is a necessary consequence of considering the queer productivity of toxins. It is important to note, however, that in the act of such rethinking, "queer" should not simply stand in synonymously for "odd" or "strange." Rather, as Barad contends in "Nature's Queer Performativity," with reference to "queer critters" such as amoebas, stingray neurons, lightning, and atoms, "the point is not merely that identity is multiple or fluid, but rather that identity itself is at stake and at issue in what matters."[60] The queering of identity is a central concern for both Spahr and Sampirisi in the peculiar intimacy that these books create in their engagement with metabolic toxins. While both Sampirisi and Spahr challenge heteronormative depictions of sexuality and desire, the queerness operative in these texts extends beyond "human exceptionalism," as Barad suggests a broader definition of queer theory must in order to include vibrant material forces in the environment.[61]

Just as Sampirisi evokes classical literature through references to Aristophanes, Spahr echoes Ovid's *Metamorphoses* through her title *The Transformation*. This unusual autobiography, part pataphysical work of literary ethnobotany, part diagnostic study of metabolic pathogens, presents a subjectivity composed of intra-active tensions between invasive species and invasive cultures as an attempt to imagine a diffractive form of reading and writing.[62] Rachel Zolf calls Spahr's book "a laboratory to exhaustively experiment with her ideas and feelings about U.S. hegemonic practices."[63] Dianne Chisholm—writing about Spahr's books *Well Then There Now* and *This Connection of Everyone with Lungs*, but in terms very relevant to the interference patterns in *The Transformation*—argues that the formal emphasis on repetition and refrain allows Spahr "to conduct and display a systemic analysis of how politics and culture make up and complicate ecologies and nature, and vice versa."[64] The book is in part a lengthy catalog of the legacy of the passiflora (or passionflower) in colonial and environmental history, as well as in sexual, political, and artistic identity in the immediate post-9/11 American social imaginary.[65] Three American mainlanders have moved to the island for work (one of them, Spahr, got a job at the university). Their unconventional sexual and intellectual relationship, which they characterize variously as a three-legged stool and as a triangle, provokes them to think beyond binaries about margins and frames, and about the predicament of the passionflower and its effects as an invasive species. Originally named by Spanish missionaries who associated its unique physical structure with the Passion of Christ, the passionflower was received very differently by the local inhabitants of Hawai'i after its introduction in the late nineteenth century. Hawaiians instead call it "huehue haole," which refers both to a smothering vine native to the island and to people who have come from another place. Spahr declares early on that her text is "the story of how the history of the island changed them, the story of the huehue haole and the tree canopy. It cannot help but also be a story about how they were shaped by perhaps being and perhaps not being perverts, but still it is more a story about three of them who moved to an island that was not theirs."[66]

The Anthropocene is the substrate for the temporal and expressive capacities of the book.[67] "It was a time of oil," we learn in a series of epochal declarations. "It was a time of an altered environment, an environment altered by the oil economy. It was a time of invasive species. A time of climate change" (205). It was ultimately a time that proved difficult to characterize and express within the confines of conventional language: "an awkward time for them and for the word them. . . . So it was a time of troubled and pressured pronouns" (205). The "them" that responds to and results from this pressure is a subject intra-actively defined by the varied and irreducible forces that drive the three lovers involved in this relationship: "They all had their own interests and these interests intersected and overlapped with other interests and they all felt they could be shaped by each other into some new thing" (15). This intra-active identity is queer inasmuch as the question of its own formalization is continually at issue. For example, they embrace the word "pervert" (171) but resist the word "queer," despite pressure from others to define themselves in this way: "they told themselves they did this out of respect because they were not sexually involved with people of the same gender" (173). Nonetheless, the queering of identity is fundamental to *The Transformation* in terms of the strange intimacy this book explores and enacts in its metabolic entanglements with material-discursive toxins.

The queer productivity of toxins and toxicity emerges through a metabolic poetics that catalogs intellectual and physical changes in the identity of the "them" brought about by the metabolic effects of an infection first acquired in Hawai'i and then reinvigorated in New York. The narrators' difficulties in reckoning with the imperialist history of Hawai'i in terms of its cultural and biological consequences, and their subsequent decision to move to New York (from an island in the Pacific to an island in the Atlantic) only to face the disruptive and polluting specter of the terrorist attacks of September 11, 2001, all take place against the backdrop of energy politics and those "values of oil" that "defined the government that currently occupied the continent" (208). These militaristic, energy-driven politics confront them with toxins that produce damaging, poisonous effects as well as potentially productive and hopeful outcomes. The toxic dust from the collapsed towers, for example, is a constant health concern: "Words like asbestos, lead, mercury, dioxins, furans, hydrogen cyanide, benzene, xylene, chromium, polychlorinated biphenyls, aromatic hydrocarbons, and volatile organic compounds entered their daily conversation" (150). However, their complex Hawaiian experiences produce an encounter with toxins that causes unexpected metabolic effects in which political questions "bit into them and those around them with bladelike, piercing mouthparts and stabbed through the skin and then injected a saliva that teemed with digestive enzymes, viruses, and anticoagulants" (39). The bite left "some prickly new cells" in their bloodstream that affected their immune system, causing them to "now see the huge amount of historical data and position that they carried with them" (204). The result of this metabolic adjustment is altered forms of reading and writing, shifted frames of signification that spur them to reckon with the central problem and dominant activity of the book: the very construction of heuristic catalogs, maps, and charts. They are struck by the realization in the closing chapter that "they had to stop making maps that were limited by their horizontal or vertical axes. Or charts that started with two options and then spread out from there. They needed a new sort of conceptualization that allowed for more going astray than any map they had ever seen" (211). The diffractive method they devise as a result of this encounter with toxins combines diverse forms of knowing and awareness "under the sign of contradiction," exploring their own entanglements within ideological state apparatuses and colonial education systems as well as within the larger biogeochemical cycles of melting ice shelves and chemical pollution (213).

Diffracted forms of reading and writing are at the heart of what is productively achieved through these toxic encounters—especially given that the heart muscle and the vascular system provide the book with its concluding momentum: "They pumped milkweed and butterfly through their superior vena cavas. . . . And let in their pulmonary arteries the realization that they could only be colonizers who perpetuated even if they wanted to be colonizers who refused. . . . They pumped the cracking Larsen B ice shelf through their right ventricles" (211–13). Their blood, which has been altered by the toxins to make legible such diverse matters as expanded tourist industries, names of military operations, unusual island biology, expansionist language, imperial conflict, and climate change is now pumped through the body "with the hope that it would eventually reach the palm of their writing hand" (211). Their blood becomes a form of writing. It also becomes a site of trans-corporeal, intra-active identity where it is possible to read the entangled and vibrant forces producing their identity. As Barad reminds us, "*the forces at work in the materialization of bodies are not only social, and the materialized bodies are not all human.*"[68] Along with their perversions, their poetics, and their politics, the "prickly new cells," the passionflower, and the polluting dust from the fallen towers are all intra-active forces, "queer" productive toxins that mark a "shift from a metaphysics of things to phenomena," which, for Barad, "makes an enormous difference in understanding the nature of science and ontological, epistemological, and ethical issues more generally."[69] Identity is phenomenal in its material-discursive entanglements at the end of *The Transformation*, expressing, by way of its porosity and trans-corporeality, the metabolic flows of "their" biology along with those of pollution and capital.

Without oil there would be no democracy, Mitchell proposes in *Carbon Democracy*. Oil is the quintessential example of agentive, intra-active matter in the Anthropocene. The intricate connection and entanglements between modern democratic politics and carbon energy leads Mitchell to see his book not as a study of democracy and oil but as "democracy *as* oil."[70] By extension, as the work of Sampirisi and Spahr demonstrates, the energy systems of our historical moment intra-actively become part of the expression of the energy systems of biological bodies, human metabolic processes. The outside writes the inside whether we like it or not. From the results of my blood tests, I can see the multinational companies that have written their flame retardants and PCBs into my flesh—I accumulate their products. "Capitalism," Wark proposes, "is a communicable disease in the form of a disease of communication. It puts everything into communication with everything else."[71] This is the biosemiotic consequence of volatile chemicals mimicking hormones in the endocrine system. It is also the site of pataphysical responses to chemical pollution taken up by Sampirisi and Spahr in their engagements with metabolic poetics. Both books explore imaginary solutions to the extreme writing of the petrochemical Anthropocene by pursuing the productively queering effects of mutations, toxins, pressurized language, and "prickly new cells" on alternative modes of expression and on alternative perspectives when it comes to questions of gender, sexuality, colonialism, and environment. They draw attention to the importance of a diffractive, pataphysical methodology capable of broadening conceptions of literacy so that we might better attend to the reading and writing of energy systems as they are inevitably taken up in the metabolism of biological and political bodies.

Notes

1. Adam Dickinson, *Anatomic* (Toronto: Coach House Books, 2018).

2. Paul J. Crutzen and Eugene F. Stoermer, "The 'Anthropocene,'" *International Geosphere-Biosphere Programme (IGBP) Newsletter* 41 (2000): 17–18.

3. McKenzie Wark, *Molecular Red: Theory for the Anthropocene* (London: Verso, 2015), xiv.

4. For more critical analysis of connections between ecopoetics, pataphysics, and biosemiotics, see Adam Dickinson, "Better Living Through Pataphysics: The Biosemiotics of Kenneth Goldsmith," in *Time in Time: Short Poems, Long Poems, and the Rhetoric of North American Avant-Gardism, 1963–2008*, ed. J. Mark Smith (Montreal: McGill-Queens University Press, 2013), 132–51. See also Adam Dickinson, "Pataphysics and Biosemiotics in Lisa Robertson's Office for Soft Architecture," *ISLE: Interdisciplinary Studies in Literature and Environment* 18, no. 3 (2011): 615–36.

5. Karen Barad, *Meeting the Universe Halfway* (Durham, NC: Duke University Press, 2007), 25. For more on the ways in which pataphysics invites "significant conversations between disciplines," see Jerome Rothenberg, "Amy Catanzano: Excerpt from 'Quantum Poetics: Writing the Speed of Light' (Part Four)," *Poems and Poetics* (blog), January 3, 2012, http://poemsandpoetics.blogspot.com/2012/01/amy-catanzano-excerpt-from-quantum.html.

6. Donna J. Haraway, *Staying with the Trouble: Making Kin in the Chthulucene* (Durham, NC: Duke University Press, 2016), 10.

7. Mel Y. Chen, *Animacies: Biopolitics, Racial Mattering, and Queer Affect* (Durham, NC: Duke University Press, 2012).

8. See David Biello, "I Just Want to Say One Word to You: Plastiglomerate," *Scientific American*, June 8, 2014.

9. Bruce Lourie and Rick Smith, *Toxin Toxout: Getting Harmful Chemicals Out of Our Bodies and Our World* (Toronto: Alfred A. Knopf Canada, 2013), viii.

10. Wendy Wheeler, "Natural Play, Natural Metaphor, Natural Stories: Biosemiotic Realism," in *Material Ecocriticism*, ed. Serenella Iovino and Serpil Oppermann (Bloomington: Indiana University Press, 2014), 69.

11. Jesper Hoffmeyer, *Biosemiotics: An Examination into the Signs of Life and the Life of Signs*, trans. Jesper Hoffmeyer and Donald Favareau (Scranton, PA: University of Scranton Press, 2008), 5.

12. Ibid., 3.

13. Giorgio Agamben, *The Open: Man and Animal* (2002), trans. Kevin Attell (Stanford, CA: Stanford University Press, 2004), 45.

14. Christian Bök, *'Pataphysics: The Poetics of an Imaginary Science* (Evanston, IL: Northwestern University Press, 2002), 36.

15. Jesper Hoffmeyer, "Semiotics of Nature," in *The Routledge Companion to Semiotics*, ed. Paul Cobley (New York: Routledge, 2010), 39.

16. Serenella Iovino and Serpil Oppermann, eds., *Material Ecocriticism* (Bloomington: Indiana University Press, 2014), 7.

17. Barad, *Meeting the Universe Halfway*, 33 (emphasis in original).

18. Stacy Alaimo, *Bodily Natures: Science, Environment, and the Material Self* (Bloomington, IN: Indiana University Press, 2010), 2, 18, 20.

19. Jane Bennett, *Vibrant Matter: A Political Ecology of Things* (Durham, NC: Duke University Press, 2010), viii.

20. Timothy Morton, *Hyperobjects: Philosophy and Ecology After the End of the World* (Minneapolis: University of Minnesota Press, 2013), 54.

21. Ibid., 38–39.

22. Alfred Jarry, *Exploits and Opinions of Dr. Faustroll, Pataphysician (A Neo-Scientific Novel)* (1911), trans. Simon Watson Taylor (Boston: Exact Change, 1996), 7.

23. Ibid., 16.

24. Alastair Brotchie, *Alfred Jarry: A Pataphysical Life* (Cambridge, MA: MIT Press, 2011), 250.

25. Jarry, *Faustroll*, 24–26.

26. Timothy Mitchell, *Carbon Democracy: Political Power in the Age of Oil* (London: Verso, 2013), 39, 71.

27. Ibid., 41.

28. Stephanie LeMenager, *Living Oil: Petroleum Culture in the American Century* (New York: Oxford University Press, 2014), 104.

29. Ibid., 125.

30. Bök, *'Pataphysics*, 16.

31. "Introduction and Background," Museum of Jurassic Technology, modified December 16, 2011, https://www.mjt.org/main2.html.

32. LeMenager, *Living Oil*, 143.

33. Bök, *'Pataphysics*, 3.

34. LeMenager, *Living Oil*, 197.

35. Ibid., 207.

36. Jussi Parikka, *Insect Media: An Archeology of Animals and Technology* (Minneapolis: University of Minnesota Press, 2010), xviii.

37. Ibid., ix.

38. Imre Szeman, "How to Know About Oil: Energy Epistemologies and Political Futures," *Journal of Canadian Studies / Revue d'études canadiennes* 47, no. 3 (Fall 2013): 146.

39. Ibid., 147.

40. Eduardo Kac, "Natural History of the Enigma," Ekac.org, 2009, https://www.ekac.org/nat.hist.enig.html.

41. Iovino and Oppermann, *Material Ecocriticism*, 1.

42. Georges Perec, "Attempt at an Inventory of the Liquid and Solid Foodstuffs Ingurgitated by Me in the Course of the Year Nineteen Hundred and Seventy-Four" (1974), in *Species of Spaces and Other Pieces*, trans. John Sturrock (London: Penguin, 1999), 245.

43. In a poetic sense, the list expresses an inherent tension between condensing information into an ordered arrangement and implicitly acknowledging the "threat of a surfeit of information, felt most keenly when the reader wonders, politely, 'How long can this go on?'" See Bill Kennedy and Darren Wershler-Henry, *Apostrophe* (Toronto: ECW Press, 2006), 286.

44. Henri Chopin, "La Digestion" (1972), UbuWeb Sound, modified October 13, 2020, https://www.ubu.com/sound/chopin.html.

45. Evelyn Reilly, *Styrofoam* (New York: Roof Books, 2009).

46. Lisa Robertson, "The Seam," in *3 Summers* (Toronto: Coach House Books, 2016), 9–17.

47. Stacy Doris and Lisa Robertson, "From *The Perfume Recordist*," in *I'll Drown My Book: Conceptual Writing by Women*, ed. Caroline Bergvall et al. (Los Angeles: Les Figues Press, 2012), 236.

48. Craig Dworkin, "Fact," *Poetry*, July–August 2009, https://www.poetryfoundation.org/poetrymagazine/poems/52694/fact-56d23160d463d.

49. Robert Kocik, *Overcoming Fitness*, Exit 18 Pamphlet Series (Brooklyn, NY: Autonomedia, 2002).

50. Szeman, "How to Know About Oil."

51. Jenny Sampirisi, *Croak* (Toronto: Coach House Books, 2011), 56.

52. Jean-Pierre Brisset, "Jean Pierre Brisett: *The Origin of Language from Our Ancestor Frogs* (1900)," in *Imagining Language: An Anthology*, ed. Jed Rasula and Steve McCaffery (Cambridge, MA: MIT Press, 2001), 495.

53. Walter Redfern, *All Puns Intended: The Verbal Creation of Jean-Pierre Brisset* (Oxford, UK: Legenda, European Humanities Research Centre, 2001), 37.

54. Andrew Hugill, *'Pataphysics: A Useless Guide* (Cambridge, MA: MIT Press, 2012), 186.

55. Sampirisi, *Croak*, 12, 20 (hereafter cited parenthetically in the text). In his essay on the subject, Jean Baudrillard describes pataphysics' preoccupation with a poetics of impossibility, stating succinctly that "Pataphysics is impossible." Sampirisi's *Croak* is an example of a similar fascination inasmuch as "the stage directions in the book are intentionally impossible to perform for humans with the expected number of limbs. Some of the stage directions require that the performer 'grow an extra limb' or lose one, or that they use their tails. Others require that their legs split open then fuse back together or that one eye does something different than the other. They also must become like cartoons, turning teeth into xylophones and such." See Jean Baudrillard, "Pataphysics" (2002), in *The Conspiracy of Art: Manifestos, Interviews, Essays*, ed. Sylvère Lotringer, trans. Ames Hodges (New York: Semiotext(e), 2005), 215. See also J. P. King, "Jenny Sampirisi: Writer Interview," *Papirmass: Art in the Mail, Mail Made Fun*, Papirmass, February 18, 2014, accessed August 25, 2015, http://papirmasse.com/art/2014/jenny-sampirisi-writer-interview.

56. Giovanna di Chiro, "Polluted Politics? Confronting Toxic Discourse, Sex Panic, and Eco-Normativity," in *Queer Ecologies: Sex, Nature, Politics, Desire*, ed. Catriona Mortimer-Sandilands and Bruce Erickson (Bloomington: Indiana University Press, 2010), 202.

57. Chen, *Animacies*, 210–11.

58. Sarah Bernstein, "*Croak* by Jenny Sampirisi," Lemon Hound, April 17, 2013, https://

lemonhound.com/2013/04/17/croak-by-jenny-sampirisi.

59. Caitlin Choi, "The Frog Princess," interview with Jenny Sampirisi, *Queen's Journal* 17 (September 2011), https://www.queensjournal.ca/story/2011-09-27/arts/frog-princess.

60. Karen Barad, "Nature's Queer Performativity (the authorized version)," *Kvinder, Køn og forskning / Women, Gender and Research* 1, no. 2 (2012): 50.

61. Ibid., 48.

62. This book is often classified by critics as a memoir, distinct from Spahr's poetry collections. I read it as poetry in part because the press, Atelos, describes itself as "devoted to publishing, under the sign of poetry, writing that challenges conventional, limiting definitions of poetry." *The Transformation* is poetry because it is writing at the limits of writing; it is an imaginary solution to what autobiography might look like in the Anthropocene. See Juliana Spahr, *The Transformation* (Berkeley, CA: Atelos, 2007).

63. Rachel Zolf, "*The Transformation* Thinks Wit(h)ness," *Lemon Hound*, November 14, 2014, https://lemonhound.com/2014/11/14/rachel-zolf-on-juliana-spahr-the-transformation-thinks-withness.

64. Dianne Chisholm, "Juliana Spahr's Ecopoetics: Ecologies and Politics of the Refrain," *Contemporary Literature* 55, no. 1 (Spring 2014): 121.

65. The catalog functions as an entangled social and aesthetic space in Spahr's work more generally, representing, as Lynn Keller notes with specific reference to *This Connection of Everyone with Lungs*, "a twisted enlargement of the blazon" that makes room for the more overtly politicized concerns of Language writing by integrating details about violence and pollution. See Lynn Keller, "'Post-Language Lyric': The Example of Juliana Spahr," *Chicago Review* 55, no. 3 (Autumn 2010): 78.

66. Spahr, *Transformation*, 21 (hereafter cited parenthetically in the text).

67. Spahr and Joshua Clover cowrote *#Misanthropocene: 24 Theses*, which coarsely inveighs against the destructive and self-serving forms of life generated by Western petroculture, particularly the violence operative on scales of greatly varying magnitude. The #Misanthropocene "makes oil-drum pyramids it makes ships of a size called Malaccamax. It makes endless small plastic representations of the African jungle or plains animals and fish ingest them and vomit them up or don't and there they sit in their stomachs and then they die." See Joshua Clover and Juliana Spahr, *#Misathropocene: 24 Theses* (Oakland, CA: Commune Editions, 2014), 4.

68. Barad, *Meeting the Universe Halfway*, 235 (emphasis in original).

69. Ibid., 33.

70. Mitchell, *Carbon Democracy*, 5.

71. McKenzie Wark, "Furious Media: A Queer History of Heresy," in *Excommunication: Three Inquiries in Media and Mediation*, ed. Alexander R. Galloway, Eugene Thacker, and McKenzie Wark (Chicago: University of Chicago Press, 2014), 202.

Chapter 16

Pataphysics and Computing

Andrew Hugill and James Hendler

This chapter argues that the explosive encounter between the subjective ambiguities of pataphysics and the objective precisions of computer systems has been, and continues to be, liberating for both. For example, to program a quantum computer, a circuit is inscribed on an infinitely progressing "staff" that resembles musical notation. The behavior of the qubits (a qubit is the fundamental unit of quantum information) is manipulated through a series of operations. Their entanglements and superpositions evoke three pataphysical conditions: *antinomy* (the simultaneous coexistence of mutually exclusive opposites); *clinamen* (a small swerve or deviation within a predictable field); and *syzygy* (the surprising encounter of apparently unrelated entities). The qubits form a set of "prophecies" that collapse when the result is read, like a piece of music being performed, which locks down the infinite variations that different artists could make in interpreting the written score.

This staggering aspect of quantum computation extends a pataphysical presence that has a history almost as long as computing itself, passing from Jarry's mathematics and its progeny in the *Collège de 'Pataphysique*, through the literary applications of the Oulipo and Speculative Computing, through the evolution of artificial intelligence, through the pataphysics of Silicon Valley in the 1960s and 1970s, into more recent experiments with the semantic web, new programming languages and, most recently, quantum computing. There is a pattern to all these developments: an initial period of playful inventiveness during which pataphysics has been most active, followed by a gradual withdrawal of the pataphysical spirit as commercial or other forces take over.

Pataphysical logic subjects existing forms of knowledge to critical judgment. Its serious humor introduces apparent absurdity into a rational context, both establishing and exceeding the limits of coherence. This divergent process challenges the overwhelming dominance of convergent thinking in computing. Convergent thinking takes available data and facts to arrive at a "correct" solution. Divergent thinking uses an initial stimulus to generate an array of spontaneous, nonlinear, and free-flowing outcomes, that is, imaginary solutions. Pataphysics is a wellspring of such creativity and often characterizes the initial phase of developments in computing. Quantum computing is currently in that initial stage. It is to be hoped that the realization of its full potential will not lead to the usual convergent degradation.

Pataphysics is a science of the particular. It reverses the ways in which normativity and exceptionalism are typically considered. For pataphysicians, every phenomenon is an anomaly. Things are characterized by the way they do not fit rather than by their common features. There is no general state from which they depart. This is a condition that at first glance resembles art more than science. As Jarry's friend (and dedicatee of *Ubu Roi*) Marcel Schwob, wrote, "Art stands in opposition to general ideas, describes only the individual, desires only the unique. It does not classify; it declassifies."[1] But Jarry's innovation was to declassify the classified while simultaneously classifying the declassified. He combined artistic and scientific thinking in a way that anticipated present-day blurrings of disciplinary boundaries and the surprising new combinations of knowledge made possible by digital technologies. Part of his genius lay in his awareness that pataphysics was beyond him. Whereas Franz Liszt professed to the Princess Carolyne von Sayn-Wittgenstein that he had "hurled his lance into the future,"[2] in Jarry's case it would be more accurate to say that he fired his pistol into the future, not caring whether the bullet hit its target or swerved into the neighbor's children.

The chapter divides into four sections: "Computing *for* Pataphysics," which surveys pataphysical engagement with computing from Jarry's mathematics to the Oulipo; "Computing *with* Pataphysics," which investigates the relationship between pataphysics and artificial intelligence (AI) and the patacritical methods of speculative computing; "Computing *by* Pataphysics," which describes two working examples of how pataphysics has been embedded in computation; and "Computing *as* Pataphysics," which examines the pata-mechanics of quantum computing.

Computing for Pataphysics

Jarry the writer could not have anticipated modern computers and still less the notion of a *science* of computing. Yet, as Linda Klieger Stillman points out, "his textual machinations employ algorithms and calculations that prefigure binomial coding."[3] Jarry was fascinated by physics and mathematics. He "read the work of James Clerk Maxwell and other British scientists, and became intrigued by a universe that was a model of field theory, descriptions of interconnected energies, and electromagnetism."[4] Jarry's engagement with the sciences of his time was far from merely parodistic. Indeed, the abstractions of algebra and geometry to him represented a kind of scientific perfection.[5] In his brief text "Jarry inconnu," "Baron" Jean Mollet set out to debunk the myth that Jarry was nothing more than an eccentric poet:

> His predilection was chiefly for mathematics, in which he was excessively gifted. Indeed, he kept up a long correspondence with foremost mathematicians. I remember one day when I was to fetch him for lunch, I found him barefoot, in his underpants, shirtless, his eternal bowler hat upon his head, tracing numbers with a piece of chalk on the wall of his apartment. As I was hurrying him along, for we were late, he said, "What! I'm ready and I was waiting for you; look, I have my hat on."[6]

Jarry's use of mathematical symbology goes back as far as *César-Antichrist* (1895), in which the plus-minus becomes the physick-stick, the uprooted phallus of Comte de Lautréamont that "leaps about so." The minus sign spins across the imagined stage, its rotations turning it into a plus sign, prompting this speech of the Fess:

> The Pataphysician, axiom and principle of the identity of opposites, clamped on to your ears, and you, flying-fish, to your retractable wings, is the dwarf atop the giant, beyond metaphysics; he is, through you, the Antichrist and God as well, horse of the Spirit, Minus-in-Plus, Less-which-is-More, kinematics of the zero left in our eyes, polyhedral infinity.[7]

For the symbolist Jarry, mathematical signs offered the most fertile possibilities, since they represent not just abstractions but "truths," whose limits and fixity may be challenged and tested. Like the constraints governing his physical existence, they were also fodder for his anarchic imagination. They became atomic units of potential meaning that may be turned and deflected by a clinamen or a syzygy. Just as the "r" in "merdre" deviates the meaning of the word, so the infinity sign in *Faustroll* alters the formulation of equations. It is not so much that the mathematical symbols acquire a life of their own (as in Edwin Abbott's fantasy *Flatland*) but rather that the logic of the mathematics itself is subject to pataphysical operations. This is characterized by an ironically extreme precision couched in a didactic manner. Dr Faustroll is described, as if from a physics textbook:

> [. . .] le docteur Faustroll était un homme de taille moyenne, soit, pour être exactement véridique, de $(8 \times 10^{10} + 10^9 + 4 \times 10^8 + 5 \times 10^6)$ diamètres d'atomes;[8]

> [. . .] Doctor Faustroll was a man of medium height, or, to be absolutely accurate, of $(8 \times 10^{10} + 10^9 + 4 \times 10^8 + 5 \times 10^6)$ atomic diameters;[9]

Jarry's treatment of algebra quite literally reaches its apotheosis in the celebrated definition of the surface of God. Faustroll plays a game with algebraic symbols in order to furnish a pataphysical proof. Once again, it is delivered in a didactic mode that exaggerates the precisions of its formulae. The definition is superficial, focused on surface rather than substance, but it nevertheless sees the resulting surface as evidence of the substance beneath. God occupies a three-dimensional space of indeterminate dimensions emanating from a single point: a metaphysical triangular projection. It is at this point that that the pataphysical precision begins:

> Let x be the median extension of one of the Persons a, $2y$ the side of the triangle to which it is perpendicular, N and P the extensions of the straight line $(a + x)$ in both directions *ad infinitum*.
> Thus we have:
>
> $x = \infty - N - a - P.$
> But
> $N = \infty - 0$
> and
> $P = 0.$
> Therefore
> $x = \infty - (\infty - 0) - a - 0 = \infty - \infty + 0 - a - 0x = - a.$[10]

Is this an example of Jarry's prescience? In his conception of space and time, extension could apply to both duration and distance. Polynomial algorithms are in a class called "P" and run in time proportional to a polynomial factor of their input size (for example, n^2 for n inputs). Other algorithms grow exponentially in time (for example, $2n$ for n inputs) and are known as non-polynomial, or NP, algorithms. The pataphysician must then surely ponder if it is purely a coincidence that the most important conjecture in computing, still unsolved after more than seventy years, is whether these two classes are the same or, as a computer scientist might set out to prove, whether "P = NP"?

Geometry is just as important as algebra in Jarry's writings. The pedantic specifications of Achras's polyhedra confront the misshapen blob that is Ubu, the very embodiment of the "hairy ball" theorem of mathematician Henri Poincaré that states, in its modern version, "You can't comb a hairy ball without creating a cowlick" (a cowlick is the spiral of hair that arises when you try). The pataphysical version of this algebraic topology might say: You can't decorate Ubu's belly without creating a *cornegidouille.*

In the post–World War II years, the *Collège de 'Pataphysique* continued to develop Jarry's mathematical speculations, most notably through the work of Boris Vian, whose *Calcul numérique de dieu . . .*[11] included such rich formulations as:

Dieu = deux + i – x = 2 + i – x
Dieu + Dieu = Dieux = 2 + i
(2 + i – x) + (2 + i – x) = 2 + i
4 + 2i – 2x – 2-i = 0
2 + i – 2x = 0
x = (2 + i) / 2 = 1 + (i / 2)
Dieu = 2 + i – 1 – i / 2 = 1 + i / 2
[. . .]
Deux + Deux = 4
(Dieux – i) + (Dieux – i) = 4
Dieux + Dieux – 2i = 4
(mais Dieux et Dieux, ça fait toujours Dieux!)
Dieux – 2i = 4
Dieux = Deux + i = 2 + i
2 + i – 2i = 4
2 – i – 4 = 0
i = –2
Dieu = 1 – 1 = 0.

Vian's interest in numerical precision extended beyond the purposes of the immediate text to more general speculations about mathematics. For example, he commented on the function of the equals sign:

> Entire volumes could be written about the equals sign, which has a self-negating quality since it always connects two members which, were they truly equal, would not need to be indicated as such; it would be self-evident, or rather not so self-evident since there would only be one of them; from which, incidentally, follows an entirely new algebra in which this sign has been removed, so that whenever one writes 1, that stands for 1 = 1; one day we will develop such a thing.[12]

Given its original predilection for mathematics, it is not surprising that pataphysics became intertwined with computing fairly early in the latter's evolution, most notably through the work of the Oulipo in the 1960s.[13] Academic criticism has generally recognized the Oulipo for its literary achievements; indeed, it is usually viewed as a literary movement whose best-known exponents are Raymond Queneau, Georges Perec, and Italo Calvino. In fact, the Oulipo's primary purpose is to make *potential* rather than actual literature, which it does by the creation of rules whose logic frequently resembles, or exploits, computational processes and which occasionally go under the name of "algorithms." It makes a distinction between the "basic research" involved in constraint construction and the "applied research" of writing. François Le Lionnais emphasized that "method is sufficient in and of itself."[14] The literary outputs of the group are therefore, if not exactly a by-product, at least the "icing on the cake" of this core activity.

In the early days, there were links between the Oulipo and "Nicolas Bourbaki," the collective pseudonym of the group of mathematicians who advanced set theory as a basis for mathematics. Queneau attended a Bourbaki conference in 1962, and other Oulipians, such as Claude Berge and Jacques Roubaud, also had connections with the group. Bourbaki influenced structuralism, and it is not hard to see the way in which Oulipian constraints, with their anonymizing effects, anticipated the general evolution of critical theory toward the transition point marked by Roland Barthes's essay "The Death of the Author" in 1968.[15] The mathematical basis of Oulipian thinking was perhaps most explicitly stated in Queneau's *Les fondements de la littérature: D'après David Hilbert* (1976),[16] in which he translated Hilbert's *Foundations of Geometry*, replacing the words "points," "lines" and "planes" with "words," "sentences" and "paragraphs."

Computers were an important part of the Oulipo's early efforts. Their use for both reading and writing is described in the *Atlas de littérature potentiel*,[17] mainly focusing on the efforts of Paul Braffort and others to realize the combinatorial possibilities of Queneau's *Cent mille milliards de poèmes* (1961) and the multicursal structure of *Un conte a votre façon* (1967). Jeremy Douglass comments on the display of early computer game techniques in this simple tale, which include "recursion, branch convergence, paratextual branches, retracing, false branches, and more."[18] Such characteristics seem, on the face of it, to lend themselves very well to computational methods.

As Mark Wolff recounts in his detailed discussion of the Oulipo's use of computers, this work had been preceded by collaborations with Dmitri Starynkevitch, who was the developer in 1957–59 of the programming language "Programmation automatique des formules" (PAF).[19] This resembled Fortran and ran on a relatively small computer called the CAB500, which had been designed by the Société d'électronique et d'automatisme (SEA). Starynkevitch had used random number generation to produce an imaginary telephone directory, something that fascinated the Oulipo. The directory was made by selecting names of people and streets from a given list comprising surnames created arbitrarily from alternations of open and closed syllables.[20]

In 1975, the Atelier de Recherches et Techniques Avancées (ARTA) created a program that produced poems from the *Cent mille milliards*... in response to the user's name and the length of time taken for its input. However, the computer's preference for random selection presented a significant problem, since the Oulipo explicitly wished to avoid aleatoricism (using chance to generate artworks).[21] Queneau himself became quite skeptical of the Oulipian potential of computers for this reason.

An offshoot of the Oulipo named ALAMO (Atelier de littérature assistée par la mathématique et les ordinateurs) was founded in 1980 by Paul Braffort and Henri Roubaud, and included other Oulipians such as Marcel Bénabou and Paul Fournel. This group continued the Oulipo's previous combinatorial and algorithmic work, but also added an "application" level, which allowed word substitutions from a vocabulary such that grammatical sense was maintained; and an "implication" level that aimed to deploy recursion in text-generating programs, such that "the very logic of the text is controlled by the program: a global syntagma comes into play and becomes manifest as a supervisor of local syntagmas."[22] This implication level proved very difficult to achieve, however, and is still not fully realized. The ALAMO eventually produced "litware" programs, which essentially progressed by defining rules, then allowing the author to filter the results using the structures of preexisting works.

Similar groups have developed this approach still further. TEAnO (Telematica, Elettronica, Analisi nell'Opificio), for example, which was formally founded in Florence in 1991 after eight years of work, developed computer systems to produce "manufactured aesthetic goods" or, in other words, algorithmic tools for automated artistic creation.[23]

The difficulty that the Oulipo encountered at the heart of the question of how to use computers in creating potential literature was one of automatism. The closer to artificial intelligence the work of ALAMO or TEAnO became, the more problematic was the Oulipo's involvement. This was because, as Wolff points out, "the Oulipo does not seek to replace the human writer who is at the center of the Oulipian universe."[24] Wolff describes how they turned instead to the pataphysical clinamen to realize two algorithms for reading texts: the Mathews' Algorithm and variations on Queneau's matrix analyses of language. The latter offered the possibility of quantitatively analyzing an author's style, although Queneau was more interested in their mathematical properties. Wolff concludes:

> [Harry] Mathews and Queneau offer two algorithms for creating meaning with language that demonstrate the Oulipo's efforts to imagine potentialities for literature, "if need be through recourse to machines that process information."[25] We can operationalize these algorithms with computers for literary analysis "if need be," but the interest of the algorithms lies not in what they help us see in a given text but in the way they invite us to play rigorously for play's sake.[26]

Literary analysis, however, has also turned out to be fertile territory for pataphysics and computing. The evolution of the digital humanities as a discipline has produced an interest in pataphysics as a critical framework. Johanna Drucker, Jerome McGann, Bethany Nowviskie, and colleagues at the University of Virginia developed a theory and practice of speculative computing. SpecLab wove both 'pataphysics and probability theory into "a probabilistic rather than a mechanistic conception of text."[27] It elaborated a "'patacritical method" that challenges the self-identity of an object by adopting a punning approach that encourages "sleights, swerves and deviations."[28] Exceptions are treated as rules, and "bugs and glitches are privileged over functionality." Speculative computing therefore "struggles for a critical approach that does not presume its object in advance."[29] Instead, the aim is to "allow subjectivity to be mapped," for example by using meteorological metaphors in collective acts of critical activity that include drawing.[30]

The latter activity was part of an early project to create an Ivanhoe Game[31] that critically examines the celebrated novel by Walter Scott by deploying a 'Patacritical Demon as "a way to express the way we can understand a 'text' or other artifact as an indeterminate field of potential within which a reader intervenes."[32] The interventions in this case included new texts, animations, drawings, and so on. The 'Patacritical Demon was an elusive and incomplete project that nevertheless still "stands as the energy and sign" of the SpecLab. It gave rise to some novel computational techniques, such as temporal modeling of subjectively interpreted temporal relations, and subjective meteorology, a system of mapping personal weather. The resulting software is a gamelike environment that takes graphical and textual input from the user who stands in a "double parallax" relationship to the discourse field.

SpecLab's attempt to harness the pataphysical spirit in a critical context has ultimately produced a collection of digital humanities tools. These included Collex (an online collections development environment) and Juxta (a textual collection tool), both of which were eventually subsumed into the NINES (Networked Infrastructure for Nineteenth-Century Electronic Scholarship) project. This seeks to create a "federated" (rather than top-down and centralized) network for digital humanities scholarship, built on a semantic web infrastructure.[33] The pataphysical impulse that provided the initial energy for the SpecLab was clearly important to the development of NINES, whose philosophy continues to privilege subjective interpretation over supposedly objective data-gathering, and so challenges received wisdom about the neutrality of technology.

Computing with Pataphysics

At the same time that pataphysicians were beginning to play with computers, the early pioneers of the personal computer were being strongly influenced by the radical ideas conveyed to them through the celebrated issue 13 of the *Evergreen Review* titled "What is Pataphysics?," published in 1960. This critical period of evolution in digital technology has been well documented in Fabrice Florin's documentary *Hackers: Wizards of the Electronic Age* (1985) and John Markoff's *What the Dormouse Said* (2005). Apple's celebrated exhortation to "think different" in the 1990s may partly have emerged from what was learned from pataphysics.

Among the pioneers were Ted Nelson, the visionary who coined words such as "virtuality" and whose Project Xanadu anticipated hypertext and the World Wide Web; and Howard Rheingold, whose work in the 1980s with virtual communities such as the *Whole Earth Catalog* and The WELL prefigured the rise of social media. Both these individuals acknowledge openly the importance of pataphysics. The Pataphysical Studios in San Francisco remain highly active today, including about a dozen core members and a wider connected community. They are influential in the "maker culture" of technology-based DIY, and have run education workshops based on their Pataphysical Slot Machine. They are currently building a "Time Machine," inspired by Jarry's text *Commentaires pour servir à la construction pratique de la machine à voyager dans le temps* (1899)—loosely translated as *How to Construct a Time Machine*—comprising an interactive multimedia installation that invites you to meet characters from the past, present, and future.

Pataphysics has also played a part in the evolution of AI, thanks to the challenges of its need to accommodate illogicality, inconsistency, and paradox. AI has a long history that goes back to classical speculations on the possibility of thinking machines; long before the rise of the electronic computer, philosophers were asking the question "Could a machine think?" As modern computation came into existence, the polymath Alan Turing set out a challenge as to how this might be resolved.[34] He proposed a test called the "imitation game," although it is probably better known by its informal name: the Turing Test. Turing suggested that when a person had a conversation with another unseen entity, if they could not tell the difference between whether they were talking to a person pretending to be another person (Turing suggested a man pretending to be a woman) or a computer pretending to be a person, then the computer could be said to have passed the test—that is, the computer could be considered intelligent. While many have questioned the adequacy of the Turing Test, and others have claimed to pass it, Turing himself took the position that possibly the hardest part would be dealing with illogic, inconsistency, and paradox. In his own words, "It is not possible to produce a set of rules purporting to describe what a man should do in every conceivable set of circumstances."[35]

As the question of potential machine intelligence became more immediate with the exponentially increasing power of computers, the field of artificial intelligence was born, and rapidly developed into two camps. One group, the "neats," believed that AI could be achieved by the application of logic and rigor. The other group, the "scruffies," thought that a logical approach was not going to lead to what was needed. For example, take the following apparently self-contradictory syllogism:

> All birds fly
> The penguin is a bird
> The penguin doesn't fly

To deal with handling unusual birds like penguins and kiwis the "neats" were forced to invent complex logical means, or to come up with probabilistic ways to deal with reasoning that "most birds fly"; while the "scruffies" were content to live in a world in which rules were routinely violated. Like Turing they argued, "If a machine is expected to be infallible, it cannot also be intelligent."[36]

In the past few years, a new contender as the way to achieve artificial intelligence has emerged. Models of computation based on a rough approximation of the neurons in the human brain have been a part of AI since the beginning, but the 2010s saw a rapid development of the power of these models. Dubbed "deep learning," complex neural models have led to huge increases in the capabilities of the computer to process speech, images, and language, often at seemingly superhuman levels of competence.[37] Despite their incredible power, these deep learning systems also come with a new variant of the neat/scruffy problem. The systems turn out to be very susceptible to the pataphysical clinamen, which is "the smallest possible aberration that can make the greatest possible difference."[38] In this case, the aberrations are so small as to be undetectable by humans. Consider the two images of a pig in color plate 19, which are apparently identical. When the background noise shown in the middle image is added to the first image, resulting in the second image, deep learning categorizes the pig as an airliner. This clinamen has been viewed as a technical problem by computer scientists, but the pataphysical scruffy may well see it differently.

AI has become pataphysical in the sense that it is both generating and analyzing imaginary solutions. Those "human" attributes of error, stupidity, and failure are the ones that make it more creative. The need is no longer to win the imitation game, it is to redefine the rules of the game itself. Since 'pataphysics is the science of the laws governing exceptions and contradictions, then the extent to which deep learning systems strive to disallow them is a new way to limit the extent of pataphysics in AI, as the "neats" have done in the "good old-fashioned AI" paradigm of logic above everything. This extent may ultimately be free of human input, but it will always present a challenge to human rationalism.

Computing by Pataphysics

A different kind of challenge has been to undermine the rationalism of computers themselves. Classical computer logic finds physical expression in binary states within the integrated circuits of microchips. Their logic gates are programmed at the machine level to enact on-off conditions as a positive or negative charge. These states are programmed using binary numbers, which open and close the logic gates in sequence at extremely fast speeds. The results are the logical operations that define classical computing: 1/0, TRUE/FALSE, OR/NOR, XOR/XNOR, AND/NAND. These contradictory motions find a parallel in the pataphysical plus-minus, or antinomy. As Jarry wrote, "Thus—because already—we know that *opposites are identical*."[39]

To have computers reason illogically is a theoretical impossibility, because the need for structured reasoning drives the algorithmic process itself. However, there are existing systems of many-valued logics, which describe an indeterminate value that is sometimes called the *included middle*. Jan Lukasiewicz's classic paper of 1930 introducing his three-valued logic system describes an intermediate truth-value I:

> I can assume without contradiction that my presence in Warsaw at a certain moment of time next year, e.g., at noon on 21st December, is not settled at the present moment either positively or negatively. It is therefore possible but not necessary that I shall be present in Warsaw at the stated time. On this presupposition the statement "I shall be present in Warsaw at noon on 21st December next year" is neither true nor false at the present moment.[40]

D. A. Bochvar's ontological system, developed in 1939, similarly treats I as "undecided,"[41] whereas S. C. Kleene's later epistemological system refers to I as "unknown."[42] We may perhaps discern here an unintentional echo of Arthur Rimbaud's "Je est un autre." More recently, Jan Aldert Bergstra and Alban Ponse have proposed that the value D should be substituted for I to express divergence.[43] This takes us somewhat closer to pataphysical ideas, but a detailed perusal of their system shows that D and I are interchangeable and remain indeterminate. The m-valued systems of Emil Post dispense with the true/false distinction altogether, but only to effect "a cyclic shift in the truth-values."[44] Fuzzy logic introduces a degree of controlled variability into the reasoning process, but still accords with the fundamental principles of binary architecture.[45]

All these solutions are incomplete in terms of pataphysical science. Since the ideal state of scientific logic is incarnated in the computer above all other products, it seems the best we may achieve is to subvert its logical processes in order to deliver pataphysical results. One example of an attempt to do just that is the programming language PRASCAL.[46] This makes interventions within the traditional PASCAL language. The name PRASCAL is itself an example of that, because the addition of an "R" puts a rascal into PASCAL.

PRASCAL precedes the standard mathematical operators +, –, *, and / with an apostrophe to denote the pataphysical element. We may express the implied crossing of levels of abstraction thus:

<Physics> '+ <Physics> ::= Metaphysics
<Metaphysics> '+ <Metaphysics> ::= Pataphysics
<Pataphysics> '– <Metaphysics> ::= Metaphysics
<Metaphysics> '– <Physics> ::= Physics
<Physics> '* <Metaphysics> ::= Pataphysics
<Pataphysics> '/ <Metaphysics> ::= Physics

To illustrate this, consider a frog as an instance of physics and Heqet (the ancient Egyptian frog goddess) as an instance of metaphysics. A hoquet (hiccup, or antiphonal musical technique) may then be, by a clinamen, an instance of pataphysics. This gives us the following example:

frog '+ frog = heqet
heqet '+ heqet = hoquet
hoquet '– heqet = heqet
heqet '– frog = frog
frog '* heqet = hoquet
hoquet '/ heqet = frog

PRASCAL replaces Boolean logic with a new form: Uboolean. In Boolean there are two possible states: True (T) and False (F). Uboolean logic allows a third state, the FalsTrue (FT), in which something is simultaneously false *and* true. The following truth tables present the consequences of Uboolean logic. Consider the outcome when this is applied to the basic conjunction (AND). Here, z = x (AND ∧) y:

When x is False and y is False, z is False
When x is False and y is True, z is False
When x is False and y is Falstrue, z is False
When x is True and y is False, z is False
When x is True and y is True, z is True
When x is True and y is Falstrue, z is Falstrue
When x is Falstrue and y is False, z is False
When x is Falstrue and y is True, z is Falstrue
When x is Falstrue and y is Falstrue, z is Falstrue

Similar tables may be derived from disjunction (OR) and negation (NOT) and the exclusive disjunction (XOR). The FalsTrue is not some indeterminate, undecided, divided, or even paradoxical instance of an included middle. Rather, it is an explosive combination of irreconcilable states of affairs whose only possible outcome is an imaginary solution. This cannot be instantiated, because there is no generalizable example of an imaginary solution arising from a FalsTrue condition. Any such example is by definition exceptional. Herein lies the crucial distinction: Uboolean logic is inherently subjective and particular.

To exemplify the consequences of Uboolean logic, consider the case of wave-particle duality. Given that Albert Einstein, writing in 1905, concluded that light is both a wave and a particle (thereby simultaneously contradicting both the Newtonian particle theory and the Maxwellian electromagnetic wave theory), we may test his conclusion as follows:

> Is light: having nothing to do with particle (NotP), particle plus something else (PPlus), or only particle (OnlyP)?
> Is light: having nothing to do with wave (NotW), wave plus something else (WPlus), or only wave (OnlyW)?

This results in the following:

X (Light with particle) is)	*Y (light with wave)*	*Z = X ∧ Y (light*
F (NotP)	F (NotW)	F
F (NotP)	T (WPlus)	F
F (NotP)	FT (OnlyW)	F
T (PPlus)	F (NotW)	F
T (PPlus)	T (WPlus)	T
T (PPLus)	FT (OnlyW)	FT
FT (OnlyP)	F (NotW)	F
FT (OnlyP)	T (WPlus)	FT
FT (OnlyP)	FT (OnlyW)	FT

In PRASCAL, this would be expressed as follows:

```
writeln('Is light: having nothing to do with particle (NotP), particle plus
    something else (PPlus), or only particle (OnlyP)?');
Readln(answerP);
writeln('Is light: having nothing to do with wave (NotW), wave plus some-
    thing else (WPlus), or only wave (OnlyW)?');
Readln(AnswerW);
If (AnswerP = 'NotP') then LightP := F
If (AnswerP = 'PPlus') then LightP := T
If (AnswerP = 'OnlyP') then LightP := FT
If (AnswerW = 'NotW') then LightW := F
If (AnswerW = 'WPlus') then LightW := T
If (AnswerP = 'OnlyW') then LightW := FT
```

```
Light := LightP and LightW
If (Light = T) then writeln('Pschitt');
If (Light = F) then writeln('Fruck');
If (Light = FT) then writeln('Ha ha');
```

Another attempt to introduce pataphysical logic into a classically constrained scenario is the Syzygy Surfer, a new kind of search engine that operates on the World Wide Web. It is worth recalling that the web itself to a large degree emerged from the field of physics rather than computer science. The inaugural paper proposing a networked hypertext system for managing information that became the World Wide Web was written by Tim Berners-Lee in 1989 at CERN, the celebrated particle physics laboratory in Geneva.[47] In 2001, Berners-Lee, Hendler, and Ora Lassila published "The Semantic Web," which proposed an extension to the web "in which information is given well-defined meaning, better enabling computers and people to work in cooperation."[48] Many millions of web domains conform to semantic web standards, and its principles underpin much of the recent evolution of the web. One consequence is that the technology is becoming increasingly convergent in both its design and results. The process of disambiguation that is necessary for it to work effectively means that it has largely fallen into the hands of the "neats," leaving less room for the contradictions and exceptions of pataphysics.

The semantic web seeks to understand the meaningful relationships between online things that are implied in links. It does this partly by exploiting the metadata that sits one layer above the data. The languages of the semantic web provide some relatively simple metadata relationships, such as defining one class of objects to be a subclass of another, or to encode some facts about a relationship between two objects (a collection of such statements being an "ontology").

The ontologist, that is, the person making the categorizations, must decide in advance how things will be grouped. Thus, for example, if one wanted to create a description of a number of recipes and to define which ones were vegetarian, the ontologist must decide where to put milk, eggs, fish, and other controversial items. Whereas a vegan would want a recipe with cheese to be excluded from this category, some other user might not. On the other hand, to the pescatarian, the salmon with goat cheese should be grouped with the vegetarian foods. The ontologist can get around this problem by creating multiple categories—ovo-lacto, fish-included, et cetera—but there still must be a decision made as to what to call all these categories and whether or not to include a hierarchical distinction.

But it is possible to take a very different view of this web of knowledge. A pataphysical ontology is one in which the laws governing exceptions and contradictions are expressed through a syllogistic platform for transcendent eccentricity provided by Resource Description Framework (RDF) triples. In RDF, each entry to the data store has the following attributes: <object..> <relation..> <value..>. For example, a blue balloon would be <balloon..> <hasColor..> <blue..>. The <relation> part of the RDF triple provides us with opportunities to insert pataphysical terms. We give this layer of pataphysical intelligence the name *patadata*.[49]

Patadata can draw on the "flaws" described by Cory Doctorow in his "metacrap" thesis: "people lie, people are lazy, people are stupid, schemas aren't neutral, metrics influence results, there's more than one way to describe something."[50] Patadata designers make use of the Panalogy Principle proposed by Marvin Minsky and Push Singh to represent entities from multiple viewpoints. This states, "If you 'understand' something in only one way then you scarcely understand it at all . . . but if you represent something in several ways, then when one of them fails you can switch to another."[51]

Patadata has so far found its most telling application in the Syzygy Surfer. This search engine does not take you where you want to go, but somewhere you did not expect to go and are glad you went there when you arrive. The user experience differs from random search engines such as The Useless Web or Randominio. Rather, it echoes the kind of surprising yet charming encounter that is captured in Jorge Luis Borges's celebrated description of the entry for "animals" in the *Celestial Emporium of Benevolent Knowledge*, the Chinese encyclopedia described in "The Analytical Language of John Wilkins."[52] We expand Borges's text by looking at some examples of the evocative relations that the categories depend on, as follows:

> those that belong to the Emperor (Borges)
> culturally specific, royal, possessive (Hendler/Hugill)
> embalmed ones (Borges)
> past, preserved (Hendler/Hugill)
> those that are trained (Borges)
> made uniform, commonalities (Hendler/Hugill)
> and so on.[53]

The first step for the ontologist/pataphysician is to decide how things will be grouped. This is not constrained to simple categories and relations; in fact one could use, for example, the fourteen classes from Borges as categories and define a sorting of objects into these. More challenging, however, would be defining the sorts of relations that would cause us to decide which objects might go into these classes. Stating that these relationships exist is nonproblematic, but defining their features unambiguously would be arbitrarily hard.

The objective of the Syzygy Surfer project is to find precise, unambiguous algorithms that the computer can apply to the growing metadata-based knowledge on the web but that when realized can enable a human to envision the existence of relationships that the machine would be unable to represent or use. This behavior, properly done, should enable the machine to produce a nonrandom encounter that the human may see as either logical or surprising or both but that will let the human conceptualize the inherent ambiguity that the machine is incapable of directly creating. The "neat" aspect of the algorithm couples with the "scruffy" ambiguity of human thought.

If we take, therefore, a user input of the word "table," a syzygy could end up looking for a document that includes chair, periodic, and dissecting. These are fed to a traditional text search, and it produces documents such as the Tom Lehrer song about the periodic table of elements, a blog entry in which author James Howard Kunstler "dissects" modern life in suburbia, and the web page for the US national clearinghouse for management of squamous cell cancers. A clinamen for "table," on the other hand, could take a definition such as "an abstract, a table of contents, a graphical representation"[54] and end up with the phrase "hierarchical anthophyllite visually, ebony water," which, when fed to a search engine, produces results ranging from a small company in New Jersey to the search history from a Shanghai-based search engine. Anomalous search results are made from the negation of the topic. We model this by searching for documents that do not include related terms. Through the Panalogy Principle, we can see that "table" is commonly related to furniture, to science, to philosophy, to legs, et cetera, so we search for the occurrences of table that are *missing* these common referents. This leads to topics such as the HTML table construct, the ASCII table, a book called *The Table*, and a video on table tennis.

Now let us consider some rather more creatively inspiring examples. Figures 16.1, 16.2 and 16.3 contain some of the results we get using these operations, when we take terms from Borges's "Chinese encyclopedia" and show what is produced by applying specific patadata principles (syzygy, clinamen, and anomaly, respectively) to specific search terms (fabulous, mermaid, and trained, respectively).

The Syzygy Surfer has been most pataphysically implemented by Fania Raczinski, who applies a set of "patalgorithms" to *Faustroll* (color plate 20).[55] These operate on text in three ways: by substituting hyponyms, hypernyms, and holonyms for synonyms of words from *Faustroll* (clinamen); by substituting antonyms for the synonyms (syzygy); and by finding words that have a Damerau-Levenshtein distance of one or two (meaning, there are one or two spelling errors) from words

16.1. Screenshot of results of a syzygy search on "fabulous" using the Syzygy Surfer, 2011.

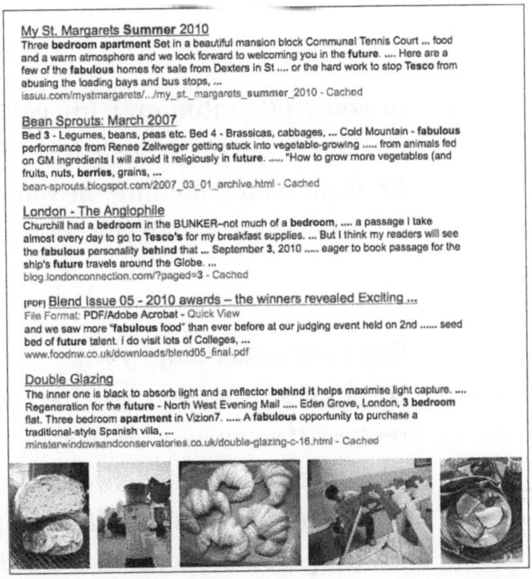

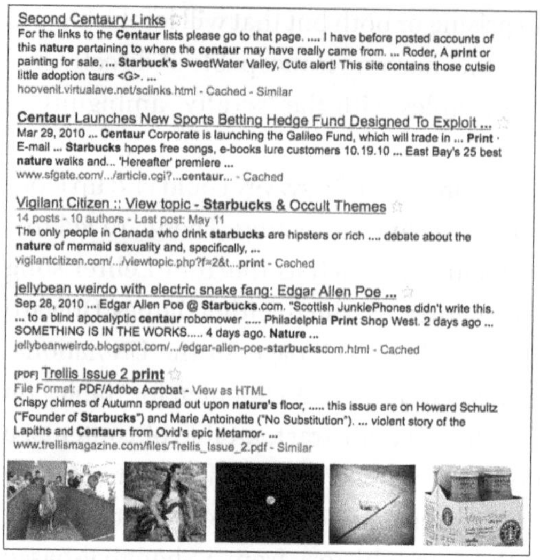

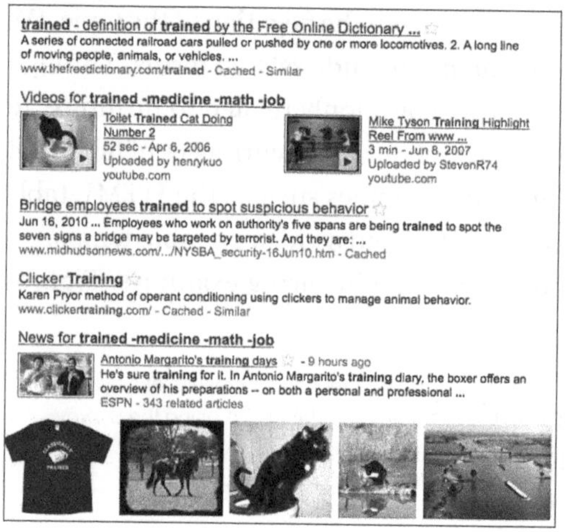

16.2. Screenshot of results of a clinamen search on "mermaid" using the Syzygy Surfer, 2011.

16.3. Screenshot of an anomaly search on "trained" using the Syzygy Surfer, 2011.

in *Faustroll* (antinomy). Image and video algorithms work by translating a Flickr or Bing string from English to French, then French to Japanese, then Japanese to English, then matching the output to Flickr metadata. The results are displayed on-screen as a golden spiral.

Computing as Pataphysics

"If physics proposes: 'you have a brother and he likes cheese,' then metaphysics replies: 'If you have a brother, he likes cheese.' But 'Pataphysics says: 'You don't have a brother and he likes cheese.'"[56] Georges Perec's celebrated syllogism is presented as an example of Jarry's three-step sequence: physics → metaphysics → pataphysics. In quantum mechanics the third step is the starting point. "You don't have a brother and he likes cheese" stands as a perfect statement of quantum entanglement, in which each particle cannot be described independently of the other, even when the particles are separated by a large distance. The quantum wave form instantaneously unrolls physics, metaphysics, and pataphysics in an infinite progression. Thus, we claim, quantum mechanics is pata-mechanics.

Quantum entanglement is the phenomenon at the heart of quantum computing. In accordance with quantum mechanics, qubits may be in a superposition of a 1 or 0 quantum state; in other words, they may be added together (superposed) to produce another quantum state. Quantum mechanics thereby "symbolically attributes the properties of objects, described by their virtuality, to their lineaments."[57] To put it another way: Erwin Schrödinger's physics places a cat and some radium in a box. When the box is open, a metaphysical dice roll (rather than God) will tell us whether the cat is alive or dead. But in pataphysical quantum mechanics, the cat is both alive *and* dead. As a consequence of this, metaphysics has largely been rendered redundant. In 1944, Einstein famously wrote to Max Born:

> You believe in the God who plays dice, and I in complete law and order in a world that objectively exists, and which I, in a wildly speculative way, am trying to capture. . . . Even the great initial success of the quantum theory does not make me believe in the fundamental dice-game.[58]

The very existence of quantum computing is a demonstration that Einstein was wrong and that physics, like pataphysics, now accepts that something chance-driven and arbitrary is indeed fundamental to reality. Metaphysics is an irrelevance in this narrative, whichever viewpoint is taken. Instead, we now have a computing machine that can only be programmed by physicists or pataphysicists. We have consequently only just begun to become aware of its possibilities. The pataphysical era is truly upon us.

In quantum computers, the Josephson effect requires that the central chip is immersed in liquid helium at very low temperatures (within a few millikelvin, which is very near absolute zero), making it one of the coldest places on Earth. There is an echo here of Jarry's contrast between the frozen state of Life and the dynamic condition of Being.[59] In "How to Construct a Time Machine," Jarry opposes the motion of Bergsonian time to the rigidity of space. The structure of the machine must isolate time travelers from "the action of Duration" by making them "transparent to these physical phenomena, [allowing] them to pass through us without modifying or displacing us."[60] In the case of quantum computers, *each individual machine* affects the outcome of the quantum calculations performed on it due to the complexities of the physics that dominate individual qubits in different devices. In other words, each quantum computer is exceptional in its subjectivity, whose dynamic nature vanishes from the moment it is perceived (frozen). To draw a musical analogy, the same quantum calculation could end up in different states depending on: the exact machine it is run on, like playing a piece on a different piano; the way the program is interpreted, like two performers reading the same piece of music; and the unique way in which the instrument itself is constructed, like a piano that reproduces exactly what its maker hears rather than what the composer has in mind.[61]

At the heart of the quantum computer is the entanglement of qubits. In traditional computer memory, adding energy to a 0 turns it into a 1. In quantum computing, adding energy changes it from 0 to 1 and back to 0 and on and on ad infinitum. The intermediate phases (neither zero nor one) more closely resemble the antinomial states of the FalsTrue in PRASCAL than any included middle. The qubits are linked to one another, but can only stay entangled for very short periods of time. The period of this "coherence" determines the outcome of a computation, and is unique to that particular occasion on that particular machine. It follows that what works in a simulator is not likely to work in a real machine, because the computation becomes incoherent. When the qubits are no longer coherent, the computation becomes meaningless. Pataphysics both establishes and exceeds the limits of coherence.

The computation itself is modeled using imaginary numbers—that is to say, the square roots of negative numbers—which cannot exist in the real world. This derives from the nature of quantum mechanics itself. Metaphorically, the real is what became true when we opened the box containing Schrödinger's cat and can be represented by real numbers. The imaginary is what did *not* become true and may be represented by imaginary numbers. As physicist Matthew Francis observes:

> I used to give a talk in graduate school called "Imaginary Numbers are Not Real" . . . I still agree with most of what I said back then, but I've changed my rhetoric a bit: I now say imaginary numbers are real, in the sense that they provide meaning to the results of real physics experiments. If the quantities they characterize exist in nature, I say complex numbers are as real as any other mathematical entity—not as a Platonic ideal, but as a true description of the Universe in which we live.[62]

The "real physics experiments" he mentions include the celebrated double-slit experiment, which demonstrates that photons (i.e., light) are both a wave and a particle. The Schrödinger equation, which describes this quantum condition, uses imaginary numbers because that is how mathematicians represent such antinomies in the complex plane.

It is therefore still splendidly unclear how we will eventually get a useful answer out of a large-scale quantum computer. Perhaps the piano piece turns into a tuba solo, or a horse, or a smile. Currently, quantum computing is a gigantic imaginary solution, enacted on individual machines whose processes are arbitrary and whose outputs can be useless. Which begs the question: what is this technology *for*? At present, the conceptual limitations of human engineering mean that all the effort is being expended on getting it to produce "correct" answers. But in fact it could be producing creative, interesting answers! Now is the time to realize the pataphysical potential of quantum computing, which has a serendipitous quality somewhat like the early days of the web, in the sense that it is unknown and unpredictable. We have fired our metaphorical pistol, but we do not know how the bullet will travel: "Meanwhile, Faustroll, finding his soul to be abstract and naked, donned the realm of the unknown dimension."[63]

Conclusion

Most computers today are still driven by classical logic. Each of the topics above tries to find a way to exploit or contradict this in order to capture the particularities of pataphysics. In each case the result is an explosion of creative energy. But ranged against this are the deadening effects of the forces that usually prevail in the design and construction of computer systems. More often than not, these are driven by financial imperatives. The early days of the internet saw a flourishing of creative freedom expressed in the concept of "surfing" that contrasts sharply with the Google-, Facebook- and Amazon-dominated state of the web today. The philosophical urges that gave rise to artificial intelligence have largely been driven underground as the potential uses of this technology have been fought over and concretized as products, and deep learning companies strive to be the next mega-technology giant.

The abiding hope is quantum computing, which most essentially embodies pataphysics. Richard Feynman famously declared, "I think I can safely say that nobody understands quantum mechanics."[64] This is also true of pataphysics, as expressed in *'Pataphysics: A Useless Guide*: "To understand pataphysics is to fail to understand pataphysics."[65] Their similarities, however, go deeper than just mutually incomprehensible phenomena. It is through them that we are most likely to realize Jarry's predictions of supplementary, alternative universes. As he observes, "God—or myself—created all possible worlds, they coexist, but men can hardly glimpse one of them."[66] Quantum computers, such as they are, are only just starting to compute *anything* reliably. This makes them some of the most pataphysical entities on the planet today, a situation that cannot last forever. Nevertheless, we can and should do something to seize this opportunity. As Steve McCaffery has remarked, "It falls to we pataphysicians to continue Jarry's project without knowing what it was."[67]

Notes

1. Marcel Schwob, "Vies imaginaires" (1896), in *Alfred Jarry: The Carnival of Being*, ed. Sheelagh Bevan (New York: Morgan Library and Museum, 2020), 4.

2. Ronald Taylor, *Franz Liszt: The Man and His Music* (Oxford, UK: Oxford University Press, 1987), 262.

3. Linda Klieger Stillman, "Ubu, the Pataphysician and Tyrant: Jarry, Miró, Kentridge," in Bevan, *Alfred Jarry*, 75.

4. Ibid., 74.

5. Keith Beaumont, *Alfred Jarry: A Critical and Biographical Study* (Leicester, UK: Leicester University Press, 1984), 306.

6. Jean Mollet, *Jarry inconnu* (The unknown Jarry), in *A True History of the College of 'Pataphysics*, ed. Alastair Brotchie, trans. Paul Edwards (London: The Printed Head III (10/11), 1995), 92.

7. Alfred Jarry, *Caesar-Antichrist*, in *Adventures in 'Pataphysics: Collected Works I*, ed. Alastair Brotchie and Paul Edwards, trans. Paul Edwards and Antony Melville (London: Atlas Press, 2001), 142.

8. Alfred Jarry, *Gestes et opinions du Docteur Faustroll, pataphysicien* (1911) (Paris: Éditions de la différence, 2010), 43.

9. Alfred Jarry, *Exploits and Opinions of Doctor Faustroll, Pataphysician (A Neo-Scientific Novel)* (1911), in *Selected Works of Alfred Jarry*, ed. Roger Shattuck and Simon Watson Taylor, trans. Simon Watson Taylor (London: Eyre Methuen, 1996), 182.

10. Ibid., 254–55.

11. Boris Vian, *Calcul numérique de dieu par des méthodes simples et fausses* (Paris: Cymbalum Pataphysicum, 1977).

12. Ibid., 9.

13. The Oulipo began as a Subcommission of the *Collège de 'Pataphysique.*

14. Jacques Bens, *Oulipo, 1960–1963* (Paris: C. Bourgois, 1980), 88.

15. Roland Barthes, *Image, Music, Text* (1977), trans. Stephen Heath (London: Fontana, 1993), 142–49.

16. Raymond Queneau, *Les fondements de la littérature: D'après David Hilbert* (Paris: Bibliothèque oulipienne, no. 3).

17. Oulipo, *Atlas de littérature potentielle* (Paris: Gallimard, 1981), 295–331.

18. Jeremy Douglass, "Command Lines: Aesthetics and Technique in Interactive Fiction and New Media" (PhD diss., University of California, Santa Barbara, 2007), 142.

19. Mark Wolff, "Reading Potential: The Oulipo and the Meaning of Algorithms," *Digital Humanities Quarterly* 1, no. 1 (2007): 8.

20. Bens, *Oulipo*, 162–63.

21. Ibid., 157–58.

22. Paul Braffort, "La littérature assistée par ordinateur," *Action poétique* 95 (1984): 18. Cited in Wolff, "Reading Potential," 8.

23. Paolo Ferrara et al., "TEAnO, or the Computer-Assisted Generation of Manufactured Aesthetic Goods Seen as a Constrained Stream of Technological Unconsciousness," paper presented at the International Conference on Generative Art, Milan, 2000.

24. Wolff, "Reading Potential," 9.

25. Warren F. Motte "Clinamen Redux," *Comparative Literature Studies* 23, no. 4 (1986): 263.

26. Wolff, "Reading Potential," 18.

27. Johanna Drucker, *SpecLab: Digital Aesthetics and Projects in Speculative Computing* (Chicago: University of Chicago Press, 2009), 20.

28. Ibid., 26.

29. Ibid., 29.

30. For more on the relationship between pataphysics and digital humanities projects that emerged from the University of Virginia, see Johanna Drucker, Jerome McGann, and Brandon Walsh's chapters in this volume.

31. Johanna Drucker and Geoffrey Rockwell., "Reflections on the Ivanhoe Game," *TEXT Technology*, no. 2 (2003): vii–xvii.

32. Drucker, *SpecLab*, 29.

33. Jerome McGann and Bethany Nowviskie, "NINES: A Federated Model for Integrating Digital Scholarship" (white paper, NINES September 2005), accessed February 9, 2021, https://nines.org/about/wp-content/uploads/2011/12/9swhitepaper.pdf.

34. Alan M. Turing, "Computing Machinery and Intelligence," *Mind* 59, no. 236 (1950): 433–60.

35. Ibid., 452.

36. Alan Turing, "Lecture to the London Mathematical Society," February 20, 1947: 124.

37. Yann LeCun, Yoshua Bengio, and Geoffrey Hinton, "Deep Learning," *Nature* 521 (2015): 436–44.

38. Christian Bök, *'Pataphysics: The Poetics of an Imaginary Science* (Evanston, IL: Northwestern University Press, 2002), 45.

39. Alfred Jarry, "To Be and to Live," (1894) trans. Paul Edwards, in *Adventures in 'Pataphysics*, 200. Author's italics.

40. William Kneale and Martha Kneale, *The Development of Logic* (Oxford, UK: Clarendon Press, 1962), 570.

41. Nicholas Rescher, "Many-Valued Logic," *Topics in Philosophical Logic* 17 (2007): 66.

42. Stephen Cole Kleene, *Introduction to Metamathematics* (New York: Van Nostrand, 1952): 332.

43. Jan Aldert Bergstra and Alban Ponse, "Kleene's Three-Valued Logic and Process Algebra," *Information Processing Letters* 67, no. 2 (1998): 95.

44. Rescher, "Many-Valued Logic," 76.

45. Dan E. Tamir, Naphtali D. Rishe, and Abraham Kandel, eds., *Fifty Years of Fuzzy Logic and Its Applications* (London: Springer, 2015).

46. Andrew Hugill and Hongji Yang, "PRASCAL: A Pataphysical Programming Language," *International Journal of Creative Computing* 1, nos. 2–4 (2016): 133–53.

47. Tim Berners-Lee, "Information Management: A Proposal" (1989), https://www.w3.org/History/1989/proposal.html.

48. Tim Berners-Lee, James Hendler, and Ora Lassila, "The Semantic Web," *Scientific American* 284, no. 5 (2001): 34.

49. James Hendler and Andrew Hugill, "The Syzygy Surfer: (Ab)using the Semantic Web to Inspire Creativity," *International Journal of Creative Computing* 1, no. 1 (2013): 20–34.

50. Cory Doctorow, "Metacrap: Putting the Torch to Seven Straw Men of the Meta-Utopia," version 1.3, August 26, 2001, http://www.well.com/~doctorow/metacrap.htm.

51. Marvin Minsky, *The Emotion Machine: Commonsense Thinking, Artificial Intelligence, and the Future of the Human Mind* (New York: Simon & Schuster, 2006), 6.

52. Jorge-Luis Borges, "The Analytical Language of John Wilkins" (1952), in *Other Inquisitions, 1937–1952*, trans. Ruth C. Simms (Austin: University of Texas Press, 1993), 101–5.

53. For the complete list, see Hendler and Hugill, "Syzygy Surfer."

54. See http://dublincore.org/2010/10/11/dcterms.rdf.

55. Fania Raczinski, "Algorithmic Meta-Creativity" (PhD diss., De Montfort University, 2016), https://dr.physics.wtf.

56. Georges Perec, "Qu'est-ce que la pataphysique?," Radio-Sarrebrück interview, quoted in *Subsidia Pataphysica du Collège de 'Pataphysique* 7 (1968 vulg.): 52.

57. Jarry, *Faustroll*, 22.

58. David A. Shiang, *God Does Not Play Dice: The Fulfillment of Einstein's Quest for Law and Order in Nature* (Lexington, MA: Open Sesame, 2008), 1.

59. Jarry, "To Be and to Live," 200.

60. Alfred Jarry, "Commentaire pour servir à la construction pratique de la machine à explorer le temps," *Mercure de France*, no. 110 (February 1899): 387–96. Translated into English in 2013 as "How to Construct a Time Machine" by Roger Shattuck; see https://www.patakosmos.com/database-open-access/Machine-time-jarry-en.pdf.

61. Andrew Hugill, "Thirty Minutes for Diplacusis Piano," 2018, http://www.andrewhugill.com/music/thirtyminutes/.

62. Matthew Francis, "Imaginary Numbers Are Real," *Galileo's Pendulum* (blog), June 9, 2012, https://galileospendulum.org/2012/06/09/imaginary-numbers-are-real/.

63. Jarry, *Faustroll*, 99.

64. Richard Feynman, *The Character of Physical Law* (Cambridge, MA: MIT Press, 1965), 129.

65. Hugill, *'Pataphysics*, 2012.

66. Jarry, *Caesar-Antichrist*, 190.

67. Steve McCaffery, email to Andrew Hugill, March 15, 2015.

Chapter 17

Pataphysics and the Academy

Orchid Tierney

In 1948, the *Collège de 'Pataphysique* in Paris was established for the promotion of "learned and inutilious research."[1] The *Collège*'s head—its Inamovable Curator—was none other than Dr. Faustroll himself, the title character from Alfred Jarry's pataphysical novel *Exploits and Opinions of Dr. Faustroll, Pataphysician* (1911). Over the years, a number of prominent scholars, writers, and artists joined the *Collège*'s ranks, including Raymond Queneau, Luc Étienne, Jean Baudrillard, Umberto Eco, Joan Miró, Man Ray, and Max Ernst. Members, like Jean Baudrillard, also wrote extensively on pataphysics, making the *Collège* a type of virtual academic center for hyperrational inquiry. The *Collège* continues to publish its "research" through various official organs, beginning with the *Cahiers du Collège de 'Pataphysique* in 1950 and, since 2014, the *Publicateur du Collège de 'Pataphysique*. The *Collège* is, in one sense, a speculative endeavor that revels in the satirical idea of the academy and its bureaucratic hierarchies, institutional branches, and publication channels through which the language of academic excellence and innovation are sharply brought into focus under the paradoxical umbrella of "learned and inutilious research."

Yet, is it all a joke? Is the *Collège de 'Pataphysique* nothing more than a localized art experiment, a single anomaly in the otherwise serious endeavor of academic inquiry? Or does the *Collège* represent a broader epistemological enterprise where the satirical registers of pataphysics—and its conflation of fabrication and truth—are deliberately imposed on the academy's notions of useful and productive knowledge? The *Collège de 'Pataphysique* is, in fact, one of several fake or imaginary academies, established in a number of countries, including Spain, Chile, Argentina, Canada, Japan, and Australia. Many of these fake institutions are inspired by, or gesture toward, the pataphysical or speculative sciences. Some of these universities—or "ubuniversities," to borrow a term from Andrew Hugill—maintain a muted online presence as small Facebook groups, online communities, or blogs that restrict their activity to advertising local pataphysical exhibitions, offer portals to image galleries and discussion groups, or provide information about the science of imaginary solutions.[2] Some of these fake institutions may not exist at all. Social network groups such as the Institut Pataphysique Arménien simply repost pictures of textual curios, manuscript pages, or audio files without necessarily framing either their documents or digital archives in the context of pataphysics.[3] Other groups—like the Vilnius's Pataphysics Institute, located in the bat-riddled Paneriai tunnels of Lithuania, and the Melbourne Institute of Pataphysical Studies—are either permanent or temporary extensions of established multimedia or performance collectives and art museums that are interested in interrogating the relations of activist or scholarly methods of inquiry to the pataphysical sciences.[4] As Andrew Hugill has noted, pataphysics in these digitally expanded contexts often takes on a rather amorphous form that varies "between the precisely knowledgeable and the vaguely evocative."[5] Pataphysics, in other words, loosens its already imprecise definition as it spirals with a life of its own when released into cyberspace.

Still, dismissing such social network groups and fake academies as merely jocular or playful experiments that fluidly skirt the pataphysical edges would be missing the point. Indeed, why should the idea of the academy *not* become subject to—and an object of—pataphysical inquiry? Some groups, like the London Institute of 'Pataphysics or the Académie Québécoise de 'Pataphysique in Canada, not only publish their pataphysical "research," but also organize performances, meetings, exhibitions, and even conferences. In this light, they publicly enact the science of imaginary solutions within a larger community outside of a much smaller pataphysical society.[6] These institutions draw on the cultural currency of the academy as a legitimate system of organizing knowledge and publishing innovative research. In the process, they also stress the useless functions of pataphysics—and its delight in obfuscating the real and invoking the imaginary through wordplay and abstruse texts—thereby defamiliarizing the serious role of the university as a producer of useful knowledge. The convergence of pataphysics with the idea of the academy raises the question why a speculative science, which emphasizes ambiguity, should readily map onto the institutional frames of higher education. Is there something inherently pataphysical about the idea of the academy that insists on the inclusion of speculative sciences in serious spaces committed to lucid research and learning? Does "pataphysics pervade . . . the Academy," as Andrew Hugill claims, or does the science of imaginary solutions contest the normative regimes of research and learning that marginalize or exclude alternative modes of education and pedagogy?[7] Is the academy already a pataphysical entity?

This essay brings to the fore a literary tradition of the parodic institution. Rather than documenting the history of the *Collège de 'Pataphysique* or its variegated offshoots (already thoroughly accomplished by Andrew Hugill's and Christian Bök's respective research),[8] I consider more broadly the kinds of critiques that the science of imaginary solutions makes toward the humanities and, by extension, the field of pedagogy and scholarship.

I will examine a literary example of what I call the "patacademy." The Colleges of Unreason, as illustrated in Samuel Butler's satirical novel *Erewhon; or, Over the Range* (1872), interrogate the idea of the academy and its organizational frames taken to the utmost extreme. Does the science of imaginary solutions—and specifically a poetics of potentiality—provide an apparatus for cultural critique of a neoliberal higher education made particularly volatile both by market forces and sophistry of the emergent managerial state of the contemporary university? At stake in this argument is the extent to which the patacademy can be seen as a response to the novel pressures facing the reconceptualization of the traditional university and learning in the late nineteenth and twentieth centuries. If the patacademy opens up a discursive space to examine the present state of the university and its surrounding discourses of excellence in research and education, two examples of parodic institutions—one in the nineteenth century and one in the twenty-first—bring to the fore whether a pataphysical approach to education and pedagogy might in fact offer a useful uselessness—or a useless usefulness—to education.

The second half of this essay will turn to the possible utility of an absurd pedagogy or "patagogy." The online UnderAcademy College, created in 2011 by digital writer and artist Talan Memmott, offers a twenty-first-century example of a patacademy that seriously experiments with a humorous mode of learning and instruction. The UnderAcademy College performs a way of thinking through the bureaucratic neoliberal condition of contemporary higher education by decentralizing and *détourning* pedagogical spaces. Novel patagogies do not propose a radical replacement of normative teaching strategies. Rather, they are supplemental—or, to adapt the words of Alfred Jarry, they become universal practices "supplementary" to those normative ones currently practiced in contemporary academic settings.[9] Pataphysical pedagogies provide another way to reimagine how institutional practices of instruction can be refocused from the logic of management to a logic of enactive knowledge.

The Unreasonable College

If the *Collège de 'Pataphysique* recalls a broader literary tradition of parodic institutions, one that engages with absurd practices of speculative learning, then such institutions might imply a desire to satirize the perceived dysfunctions of a knowledge economy gone awry. The Grand Academy of Projectors in Jonathan Swift's *Gulliver's Travels*, for example, indulges in the promotion of counterproductive knowledge through the development of "new Rules and Methods of Agriculture and Building, and new Instruments and Tools for all Trades and Manufactures" to increase production of an endless stream of commodities.[10] Such experiments, however, are entirely arbitrary and useless. "None of these Projects," says the narrator, "are yet brought to Perfection," and, as a result, the fictional kingdom of Laputa has become grossly impoverished.[11] The Grand Academy of Projectors reflects a literary anxiety toward an emergent technoscience of the period that produces nonsensical knowledge with little concern for its practical application. Indeed, the Grand Academy's Knowledge Engine, for example, is a proto-computer that generates new combinations of words without any concern for their syntactical meaning. These irrational projects contest rigorously academic standards that not only stress lucidity in writing and research but also the elitist academic spaces that manage the creation of, and restrict access to, so-called legitimate knowledge. In this regard, the Grand Academy of Projectors is a partially open space of unproductive knowledge whereby everyone—provided they have financial means rather than the ability—can become a bona fide cultural worker with the aid of a proto-computer. As one professor in speculative learning tells the narrator, "Every one knew how laborious the usual Method is of attaining to Arts and Sciences; whereas, by his Contrivance, the most ignorant Person, at a reasonable charge, and with a little bodily Labour, might write Books in Philosophy, Poetry, Politicks, Laws, Mathematics, and Theology, without the least Assistance from Genius or Study."[12] The Grand Academy of Projectors underscores an epistemological disconnect between pragmatism and a nascent technoscience that undertakes needless abstraction with little regard for the outcome.

Of course, this disconnect could also be seen as less a social anxiety of techno-progress than, as David Alff claims, an evisceration of the eighteenth-century language of projects that "attempts to place a risky venture beyond the realm of argument by making argumentative claims for its causal determinacy."[13] If the Grand Academy of Projects is a rejection less of knowledge institutions than of the language of projects, Samuel Butler's Colleges of Unreason offer a different critique of fields of learning. In Butler's 1872 satire *Erewhon*, the intrepid hero Mr. Higgs discovers the dystopian kingdom of Erewhon. Erewhon's location is never explicitly revealed in the novel, although the first three chapters are likely based on Butler's experiences of living near the Upper Rangitata River in Canterbury, New Zealand, where he managed the Mesopotamia Sheep Station in the early 1860s.[14] Erewhonian youths, notes Higgs, attend Colleges of Unreason where they receive formal instruction in the subjects of inconstancy, evasion, and hypothetics. Hypothetics—taught in the obsolete hypothetical language—stresses "a preparation for the extraordinary" while the "study of Unreason rests upon developing those faculties which are required for the daily conduct of affairs."[15] Higgs's descriptions of the irrational liberal arts education, in effect, underscore the value of confusion and ambiguity in the pursuit of rational inquiry. "To teach a boy," states Higgs,

> to open his eyes to these possibilities, and so to prepare him for all sorts of emergencies, is the object of this system of hypothetics. To imagine a set of *utterly strange and impossible contingencies*, and require the youths to give intelligent answers to the questions that arise therefrom, is reckoned the fittest conceivable way of preparing them for the actual conduct of their affairs in after life. (130–31; my emphasis)

If irrationality leads to rationality, what of the reverse? At what point does hyperrationality become simply illogical? By training Erewhonian students in the studies of the exception—that is to say, the "impossible contingencies"—the Colleges of Unreason set up an imaginative curriculum that focuses on a poetics of potentiality and the unrealized states of possible realities. Such practices see unreason as a complement—rather than the opposite—of reason with an outcome that checks the ossification of rational thinking created by "hard and fast lines" of obstinate ideas (132). Unreason, in other words, permits speculative inquiries into possible solutions by tempering extreme rationality, which, if left unchecked, prevents skeptical study into commonly held beliefs. "There are no follies and no unreasonablenesses so great," according to Higgs, "as those which can apparently be irrefragably defended by reason itself, and there is hardly an error into which men may not easily be led if they base their conduct upon reason only" (132). The ideological stance of these colleges then speculates that reason itself contains its own complement. "Without unreason," suggests Higgs, "reason itself" would be "non-existent" (132). It follows, according to the unreasonable ideology of the colleges, that "the more unreason there is, the more reason there must be also" (132). Rationality and irrationality are, in fact, the obverse of the proverbial coin, and the combination of both is necessary to guide appropriate scholarly inquiry into the systems of beliefs that govern the world at large.

This complementary relationship between reason and unreason betrays Butler's fraught relationships with scientific thought and Christian orthodoxy as conditional forms of knowledge and tradition, which, if left separately to their own devices, stilt useful creative and critical inquiry. Yet the Colleges of Unreason also serve as biting allegories for a system of Victorian education that rewarded sophistry through aggressive coercion. As a Professor of Wordly Wisdom makes clear to Mr. Higgs, the purpose of Erewhonian education was not to "help students think for themselves" but to ensure that they think and say exactly as society does (132). In this sense, the Colleges of Unreason seem to reject a radical yearning for a new utopian pedagogical practice in Butler's Victorian society. Instead, they point to the failure of standardized education that favor rhetoric over a creative participatory and pragmatic culture. As Butler writes in his *Note-Books*, "The more I see of academicism the more I distrust it":

> Don't learn to do, but *learn in doing*. Let your falls not be on a prepared ground, but let them be bona fide falls in the rough and tumble of the world; only, of course, let them be on a small scale in the first instance till you feel your feet safe under you. Act more and rehearse less.[16]

For Butler, play involving trial and error is an essential learning strategy and it is an idea embraced by some parodic institutions, such as the UnderAcademy, which I will discuss below. Suffice to say, the Colleges of Unreason echo Butler's own bitter experiences with Victorian education. Butler was homeschooled in his early years by his father, the Reverend Thomas Butler, who subjected his son to particularly severe beatings. As his biographer Clara Stillman suggests, his violent treatment was perhaps typical for nineteenth-century protestant Puritan family.[17] Nel Noddings argues that Butler may have "wanted to think freely and 'possess' his own thoughts" and, thus, "he advocated that all students should be encouraged (not forced) to think creatively and critically."[18] In this regard, the Colleges of Unreason reflect a contradictory program. On the one hand, they appear to codify the problems facing Victorian instruction that, to Butler, must have seemed particularly totalitarian as they stressed the passive absorption of knowledge rather than encouraging the active participation of students during their educational development. The Colleges of Unreason pronounce the failure of a humanist education in which reason and unreason are both subsumed into mindless repetition of unexamined knowledge, staged in unoriginal rhetoric. On the other, the Colleges of Unreason express a delight in linguistic play that is almost pataphysical. Indeed, the study of hypothetics is a refusal to preclude the possibilities of imagination and stresses a world of potentialities in which active thought overtakes rehearsed habits.

The Colleges of Unreason predate Jarry's notions of pataphysics, but his fake science hardly existed in a historical vacuum where the discourses of hyperrationality and irrationality were not already in play. Butler's stress on forms of conditional knowledge, on developing disciplined, rigorously scientific approaches to contingencies and ambiguities in the literary imagination, underlie a rhetoric of exception even if the Colleges of Unreason might be better viewed as a moral commentary on the failings of a Victorian society anchored in the circulation of unoriginal rhetoric. Yet if the Colleges of Unreason propose a useful uselessness of knowledge, must education—as a means of facilitating knowledge regardless of philosophical or political framework—necessarily imply its utility? As the Vice-Curator-Founder Irénée

Louis Sandomir suggested in the inaugural harangue of the *Collège*, does "the word College . . . not imply Education?"[19] Indeed, as he writes, "Education, does that not imply usefulness, or the pretense of utility? Utility, is that not seriousness? And the word serious, is that not anti-pataphysical? These terms are all equivalent."[20] And so I return to the question: Is there utility in a useless pedagogy?

Pedagogies of the Absurd

The Melbourne Institute of Pataphysical Studies, the *Académie Québécoise de 'Pataphysique*, the London Institute of 'Pataphysics, and the now-defunct SpecLab at the University of Virginia emphasize the role of performance and play through workshops, creative performance, multicultural activism, and ludic critical activity in their cultural mission in a manner that enunciates the partiality of knowledge over notions of objective truths.[21] If performance or subjective interpretation of knowledge and information is an integral method for student learning, as Samuel Butler suggests in his *Note-Books*, parodic institutes and research groups staged in speculative inquiry may also beg the question: How can pataphysical play be seriously incorporated into the regimes of pedagogy? The UnderAcademy College illustrates an absurdist approach to expand the possibilities in both curriculum and instruction. Established in 2011 by its "Provisional Provost," the digital writer and artist Talan Memmott, the UnderAcademy College is "an unaccredited undergraduate, graduate, and post-graduate institution" that emphasizes its anti-degree status.[22] The college is not, however, anti-academic. According to its mission statement, the UnderAcademy "situates itself as a shadow-academic environment offering alternative courses and anti-degree programs in a variety of subjects."[23] Past courses have included fanciful subjects such as "Advanced Macaronics: Neology, Subjectivity and the Problem of Persuasion," "Meme on Meme Action," "Underwater Procrastination and Advanced Desublimation Techniques," "Grammar Porn," "WTF 1001," "You Can Say That Again: Mass Culture Tautologies Today & Tomorrow-Today &c.," and "Meme Cultures, Alienation Play, and Gestic Play."[24] For prospective students, the college offers three anti-degrees: Calidus Parvulus (crafty little one), Paratus Adversario (prepared adversary), and Caput Magnum (big head), with each anti-degree successively building on the expertise of the previous. This hierarchy reflects a degree structure similar to a bachelor, master, and doctorate in a more condensed framework. The Calidus Parvulus, for example, can be completed with four courses, while the Paratus Adversario requires students to undertake an additional class and complete a thesis project. Upon "graduation," students receive an "official" UnderAcademy College certificate, rendered as a PDF. As of 2021, this patacademy still maintains an infrequent Facebook presence with Mark Marino taking over as the Probationary Provost in 2019.

The fakulty [*sic*], called Digressors (as opposed to professors), have included a number of scholars, artists, and writers who have a background in digital scholarship and new media art, such as Mez Breeze, cris cheek, Maria Damon, Christopher Funkhouser, and Rob Wittig. As Talan Memmott states, the Digressors themselves are artists and writers, who are often "interested not only in the subject of the course, but in exploring methods of dissemination and instruction, while also learning something about the subject through interaction with the participants."[25] Classes are conducted entirely online and invite a form of "critical play and production."[26] Seminars and assignments have taken a variety of forms. In Rob Wittig's "WTF 1001" class, for example, students created fake whiteboard lectures and notes in both academic and pseudo-academic spaces before reverse-engineering the course's own syllabus.[27]

Since 2011, nearly six hundred students have participated in various UnderAcademy College classes. The digital context of the courses permits a flexibility in instruction, whereby the lines between instructor and student are often not clearly marked. Not only do the roles of instructor and student often merge, but the zones between the parodic and real academy become contested. Memmott's course "Banality-Based Banality," for example, was a repetition of a module in a digital cultures course that Memmott taught at the Blekinge Institute of Technology in Sweden.[28] Despite the humor with which UnderAcademy College courses engage, the college demonstrates a serious endeavor to encourage the acquisition of digital skills and new media theory by applying such skills to the investigation of popular culture. In the process, the UnderAcademy College attends carefully to knowledge production rather than production of qualification. As the late literary critic Simon Leys suggested, "An ideal university . . . would deliver no degrees, nor give access to any specific occupation, nor award any professional qualifications. The students would be motivated by one thing only: a strong personal desire for knowledge—the acquisition of knowledge would be their only reward."[29] By the same token, the UnderAcademy College redirects a student focus from qualification to the acquisition of enactive knowledge.

By conducting the classes informally online through Google Docs and tumblr posts, and by allowing students to opt in rather than opt out, the UnderAcademy short-circuits the bureaucratic apparatuses of traditional universities as well as the discourses of excellence by encouraging free play, ambiguity, and blurring the roles of the instructor and student. The courses themselves involve culture-jamming, whether by using memes in place of the traditional essay or reverse engineering the syllabus at a course's conclusion. In this sense, the UnderAcademy College fosters creative and critical experimentation that underscores conditional knowledges predicated on the possible rather than objective knowledge. Like the Colleges of Unreason or the pataphysical institutes of the twentieth century, the UnderAcademy

College refuses to foreground goal-orientated outcomes in the classroom, leaving the potential of both curriculum and lesson to the needs of the student. In other words, performative learning is what generates critical experiential knowledge.

Yet what is really at stake in such an experiment as the UnderAcademy College? Can it offer a solution to the breakdown of the traditional academy? In short, it doesn't. The UnderAcademy College is not a replacement for traditional methods of learning and instruction. It proposes that supplemental spaces of pedagogy and knowledge economies can also exist within and without traditional practices of education and scholarship. Reimagining a dynamic website as a knowledge producer brings to the fore the kinds of digital practices of pedagogy that traditional universities are themselves undertaking through massive open online courses (or MOOCs). At the same time, it is worth attending to how the patacademy might help us understand the rise of the neoliberal university. In 1998, Bill Reading argued that universities faced increasing pressures from the neoliberal market and have responded by reinventing themselves as corporate entities. These changes have been motivated, he suggests, by the decline of the nation-state: "The University is no longer primarily an ideological arm of the nation-state but an autonomous bureaucratic corporation."[30] Such changes can be seen in the so-called dialogues of excellence that replace the traditional cultural mission of the academy, liking it to a bureaucratic organization.[31] Over two decades later, David Sessions echoes a similar idea: universities are "major economic actors, not only in market-oriented competition for students but in the commodification of ever greater swaths of their activities, including faculty research."[32] Austerity measures, administration bloat, and the decline in tenure-track jobs have destabilized the traditional university. Governor Mike Dunleavy's decision to cut 41 percent of state funding for the University of Alaska is one example that the academy is viewed as a corporate entity, at least in the United States. In the shift from the traditional university to a knowledge-producing corporate organization, everyone can be "excellent," but only because everyone is streamlined by the same managerial infrastructure and budgetary constraints. This shift is perhaps none too different from the effect of the proto-computers for the uneducated, who could buy their way into the Grand Academy of Protectors.

In such a state of affairs, it is worth considering if satirical colleges like the *Collège de 'Pataphysique* and the UnderAcademy College embody what Alan Liu has termed the "ethos of the unknown," in which those who participate "inside the system of contemporary knowledge can paradoxically, and with more than the normal (normalizing) irony of cool, seem to stand outside it."[33] If, as Liu suggests, "the academy can no longer claim supreme jurisdiction over knowledge," different kinds of learning and knowledge economies foreground the idea that the academy is hardly a stable historical subject. The sacred halls of the university are not lost—if they existed in actuality at all—but instead have dispersed into other spaces where partial and situated knowledge is set above objective interpretation and the passive absorption of facts.[34] "Learned and inutilious research" in this instance is really better understood as a pragmatic "speculative learning" that complements the preexistent forms of scholarship and instruction found in the traditional university and resists the commodification of the neoliberal university. Ludic, performative, imaginative, and irrational activities are supplemental to critical forms of pedagogy and scholarship. Indeed, as our intrepid adventurer Mr. Higgs reminds us, "reason would be non-existent were there no such thing as unreason."[35]

Notes

1. Alastair Brotchie, ed., *A True History of the College of 'Pataphysics*, trans. Paul Edwards (London: Atlas Press, 1995), 77.
2. Andrew Hugill, *'Pataphysics: A Useless Guide* (Cambridge, MA: MIT Press, 2012), 33.
3. See Institut Pataphysique Arménien, http://vk.com/club72872718.
4. See Rupert, "Vilnius' Pataphysics Institute," accessed October 16, 2016, http://www.rupert.lt/en/past/the-opening-of-vilnius-institute-of-pataphysics/#; and Hernan Palacio, "The Melbourne Institute of Pataphysical Studies," http://www.patafisica.net. Patakosmos, a self-declared "Pataphysical Terrestrial and Extraterrestrial Institute Tourist Map," offers a world "PATAmap" that documents various pataphysical institutes, presses, websites, theater groups, and videos across the globe. See Patakosmos, "Pataphysical Terrestrial and Extraterrestrial Institute Tourist Map," http://www.patakosmos.com/institutes-map.
5. Hugill, *'Pataphysics*, 25.
6. See London Institute of 'Pataphysics, "Institutum Pataphysicum Londiniense," accessed March 2, 2016, http://www.atlaspress.co.uk/theLIP; and l'Académie Québécoise de 'Pataphysique, http://www.pataquebec.org.
7. Hugill, *'Pataphysics*, 33.
8. See ibid.; and Christian Bök, *'Pataphysics: The Poetics of an Imaginary Science* (Evanston, IL: Northwestern University Press, 2002).
9. Alfred Jarry, *Exploits and Opinions of Dr. Faustroll, Pataphysician (A Neo-Scientific Novel)* (1911), trans. Simon Watson Taylor (Boston: Exact Change, 1996), 21: "Pataphysics will examine the laws governing exceptions, and will explain the universe supplementary to this one; or, less ambitiously, will describe a universe which can be—and perhaps should be—envisaged in the place of the traditional one."
10. Jonathan Swift, *Gulliver's Travels* (1726), ed. Claude Rawson and Ian Higgins (Oxford, UK: University of Oxford Press, 2005), 165.
11. Ibid.
12. Ibid., 171.
13. David Alff, "Swift's Solar Gourds and the Rhetoric of Projection," *Eighteenth-Century Studies* 47, no. 3 (2014): 251.
14. Roger Robinson, "Butler, Samuel," *Dictionary of New Zealand Biography*, 1990, http://www.TeAra.govt.nz/en/biographies/1b55/butler-samuel.
15. Samuel Butler, *Erewhon and Erewhon Revisited* (1932), introd. Desmond MacCarthy (London: Dent, 1959), 131–32 (hereafter cited parenthetically in the text).
16. Samuel Butler, *The Note-Books of Samuel Butler* (1912), ed. Henry Festing Jones (London: Dutton, 1917), 104 (my emphasis).
17. Clara Stillman, *Samuel Butler: A Mid-Victorian Modern* (New York: Viking Press, 1932), 21.
18. Nel Noddings, "Samuel Butler," in *Fifty Major Thinkers on Education*, ed. Joy A. Palmer (London: Routledge, 2001), 154.
19. Quoted in Brotchie, *True History*, 34.
20. Ibid.
21. Johanna Drucker, *SpecLab: Digital Aesthetics and Projects in Speculative Computing* (Chicago: University of Chicago Press,

2006), 5: "Speculative computing is not just a game played to create projects with uncertain outcomes, but a set of principles through which to push back on the cultural authority by which computational methods instrumentalize their effects across many disciplines. . . . We defined speculative computing to push subjective and probabilistic concepts of knowledge as experience (partial, situated, and subjective) against objective and mechanistic claims for knowledge as information (total, managed, and externalized."

22. Talan Memmott, "The UnderAcademy College," https://underacademycollege.wordpress.com.

23. Ibid.

24. Ibid.

25. Talan Memmott, email to the author, March 20, 2015.

26. Ibid.

27. Rob Wittig, "Fake Whiteboard Lecture Notes: WTF 1001," December 1, 2012, http://robwit.net/?p=385.

28. Talan Memmott, email to author, March 20, 2015.

29. Simon Leys, *The Hall of Uselessness: Collected Essays* (New York: New York Review of Books, 2011), 463.

30. Bill Reading, *The University in Ruins* (Cambridge, MA: Harvard University Press, 1998), 40.

31. Ibid.

32. David Sessions, "How College Became a Commodity," *Chronicle Review*, January 14, 2020, https://www.chronicle.com/interactives/how-college-became-a-commodity.

33. Alan Liu, *The Laws of Cool: Knowledge Work and the Culture of Information* (Chicago: University of Chicago Press, 2004), 9.

34. Ibid., 21.

35. Butler, *Note-Books*, 132.

Contributors

Charles Bernstein is Donald T. Regan Professor, Emeritus, of English and Comparative Literature at the University of Pennsylvania. His most recent books are *Topsy-Turvy*, *Near/Miss*, and *Pitch of Poetry*, from which the essay in this book is excerpted. His current research is interested in pataquerics.

Marc Décimo is Professor of Contemporary Art History at the University of Paris-Nanterre. His most recent book is *Sciences et 'Pataphysique*. He has published over twenty books on *art brut*, Marcel Duchamp, and the history of linguistics.

Adam Dickinson is a professor of Creative Writing and Poetics in the Department of English Language and Literature at Brock University. His most recent book is *Anatomic*. His scholarly and creative work focus on intersections between science, poetry, and the environment.

Johanna Drucker is the Breslauer Professor of Information Studies and Distinguished Professor at UCLA. Her book *Visualization and Interpretation* is forthcoming. She has published widely on topics related to visual epistemology, history of writing, experimental poetry, graphic design, and digital humanities.

Craig Dworkin has published four scholarly monographs, including, most recently, *Radium of the Word: A Poetics of Materiality*; he is currently completing a pataphysical investigation into Robert Smithson's *Spiral Jetty*. He teaches literary history at the University of Utah.

Catherine Hansen is Specially Appointed Assistant Professor at the University of Tokyo, where she teaches literature and writing. Her work on the Bucharest-based "Infra Noir" group and mid-century surrealism can be found in the *International Encyclopedia of Surrealism* and in *Cabinet* magazine among other places. She is co-editor/author of *In Search of the Third Bird: Exemplary Essays from the Proceedings of ESTAR(SER), 2001–2020*.

James Hendler is the Tetherless World Professor of Computer, Web, and Cognitive Sciences and Director of the Institute for Data Exploration and Applications at Rensselaer Polytechnic Institute. He has authored over four hundred books, technical papers, and articles in the areas of semantic web, artificial intelligence, agent-based computing, and high-performance processing. His most recent book is titled *Social Machines: The Coming Collision of Artificial Intelligence, Social Networking, and Humanity*.

John Heon, a founding co-director of the Philadelphia Avant-Garde Studies Consortium, is an independent scholar specializing in the psychology, politics, and aesthetics of humor in modern/postmodern literature and visual art. His book in progress, *Articulate Art: Language, Literature, and Humor in the Works of Bruce Nauman*, examines Nauman's oeuvre in the context of avant-garde black humor and the comic theories of Nietzsche, Freud, Bergson, and Wittgenstein.

Ted Hiebert is Professor of Interdisciplinary Art and Director of the MFA in Creative Writing & Poetics at the University of Washington Bothell. He is the author of *In Praise of Nonsense: Aesthetics, Uncertainty, and Postmodern Identity*, and *Ludic Dreaming: How to*

Listen Away from Contemporary Technoculture (with David Cecchetto, Marc Couroux, and Eldritch Priest), and translator (with Alastair Brotchie) of *101 Words of Pataphysics*, a key-words compilation by the *Collège de 'Pataphysique*.

Andrew Hugill is Professor of Creative Computing at the University of Leicester. He is the author of *'Pataphysics: A Useless Guide*. Other publications include *The Digital Musician* (now in its third edition), *Thirty Minutes for Diplacusis Piano* (part of the Aural Diversity project, led by Hugill), and "The Business School in the Anthropocene: Parasite Logic and Pataphysical Reasoning for a Working Earth" (in the journal *Academy of Management Learning and Education*).

Steve McCaffery teaches at the University at Buffalo, where he is the David Gray Endowed Chair Professor of Poetry and Letters and a rotating Director of the Poetics Program. Author of over forty-five volumes of fiction, poetry, and criticism, he was a founding member of the Canadian College of "Pataphysics, the Toronto Research Group, and the Four Horsemen. As well as publishing articles on pataphysics, McCaffery has also published on Milton, the Picturesque, contemporary poetry, and architecture. His "Pataphysics of Auschwitz" can be found in his latest book of criticism, *The Darkness of the Present: Poetics, Anachronism, and the Anomaly*.

Seth McDowell is an architect and Associate Professor at the University of Virginia. He is the author of *Water Index: Design Strategies for Drought, Flooding and Contamination*. His work, which focuses on materials and construction as the catalyst for architecture, has been recognized nationally and internationally by such organizations as the Architectural League of New York, the Museum of Modern Art in New York City, and the Hong Kong Institute of Architects.

Jerome McGann is University Professor Emeritus and John Stewart Bryan Professor Emeritus at the University of Virginia and Visiting Research Professor at the University of California, Berkeley. He recently published a book of illustrated poems, *Children's Ours / Of a Certain Age*. He is currently involved in building an interpretive online research platform for studying Jaime de Angulo's twenty-five-hour-long oral prose poem *Old Time Stories*.

Anne M. Mulhall is a Government of Ireland Postdoctoral Fellow in Comparative Literature at Trinity College Dublin (2020–22). She broadly researches the intersections of the contemporary literature and philosophy of work with radical thought across Europe, the United States, and Russia. Her manuscript on the French philosophical collective Tiqqun is currently being revised for publication. She is also preparing a manuscript on the temporalities of the workplace between the financial crisis of 2008 and the pandemic.

Marcus O'Dair is Associate Dean of Knowledge Exchange and Enterprise at the University of the Arts London. He is the author of *Distributed Creative*. He is a musician, writer, and academic who has published in such venues as the *Guardian*, the *Independent*, and *Pitchfork*.

Katie L. Price is Associate Director (Lang Center for Civic and Social Responsibility) and Visiting Assistant Professor (English) at Swarthmore College. Her fields of inquiry include contemporary poetry and art, socially engaged art, and public humanities. She publishes poetry as well as criticism and is currently completing a creative manuscript that explores what she calls pataclinical poetics.

Jean-Michel Rabaté is Professor of English and Comparative Literature at the University of Pennsylvania, co-editor of the *Journal of Modern Literature*, co-founder and senior curator of Slought Foundation, Philadelphia, fellow of the American Academy of Arts and Sciences, and author and editor of more than forty books and collections of essays on modernism, psychoanalysis, and continental philosophy, most recently the monograph *Beckett and Sade.*

Michael R. Taylor is Chief Curator and Deputy Director for Art and Education at the Virginia Museum of Fine Arts and the author of *Man Ray: The Paris Years.* He is also a curator of modern art and scholar of Dada and Surrealism, with a particular focus on the work and ideas of Marcel Duchamp.

Orchid Tierney is Assistant Professor of English at Kenyon College. She is the author of the poetry collection *a year of misreading the wildcats.* Her scholarship explores atmospheres, waste, and waste management in contemporary Anglophone poetry.

Brandon Walsh is the Head of Student Programs at the Scholars' Lab at the University of Virginia Library. He recently published "Frustration Is a Feature: Ugly Feelings and the Digital Humanities" in *Pedagogy: Critical Approaches to Teaching Literature, Language, Composition, and Culture.* He has published a range of articles and open educational resources on digital humanities, digital pedagogy, and text analysis.

Index

REFIGURING MODERNISM

ARTS

LITERATURES

SCIENCES

(A Series Edited By)

Jonathan Eburne

Refiguring Modernism features cutting-edge interdisciplinary approaches to the study of art, literature, science, and cultural history. With an eye to the different modernisms emerging throughout the world during the twentieth century and beyond, we seek to publish scholarship that engages creatively with canonical and eccentric works alike, bringing fresh concepts and original research to bear on modernist cultural production, whether aesthetic, social, or epistemological. What does it mean to study modernism in a global context characterized at once by decolonization and nation-building; international cooperation and conflict; changing ideas about subjectivity and identity; new understandings of language, religion, poetics, and myth; and new paradigms for science, politics, and religion? What did modernism offer artists, writers, and intellectuals? How do we theorize and historicize modernism? How do we rethink its forms, its past, and its futures?

(Other Books in the Series)

David Peters Corbett *The World in Paint: Modern Art and Visuality in England, 1848–1914*

Jordana Mendelson *Documenting Spain: Artists, Exhibition Culture, and the Modern Nation, 1929–1939*

Barbara Larson *The Dark Side of Nature: Science, Society, and the Fantastic in the Work of Odilon Redon*

Alejandro Anreus, Diana L. Linden, and Jonathan Weinberg, eds. *The Social and the Real: Political Art of the 1930s in the Western Hemisphere*

Margaret Iversen *Beyond Pleasure: Freud, Lacan, Barthes*

Stephen Bann, ed. *The Coral Mind: Adrian Stokes's Engagement with Architecture, Art History, Criticism, and Psychoanalysis*

Charles Palermo *Fixed Ecstasy: Joan Miró in the 1920s*

Marius Roux *The Substance and the Shadow*

Aruna D'Souza *Cézanne's Bathers: Biography and the Erotics of Paint*

Abigail Gillman *Viennese Jewish Modernism: Freud, Hofmannsthal, Beer-Hofmann, and Schnitzler*

Stephen Petersen *Space-Age Aesthetics: Lucio Fontana, Yves Klein, and the Postwar European Avant-Garde*

Stefanie Harris *Mediating Modernity: Literature and the "New" Media, 1895–1930*

Michele Greet *Beyond National Identity: Pictorial Indigenism as a Modernist Strategy for Andean Art, 1920–1960*

Paul Smith, ed. *Seurat Re-viewed*

David Prochaska and Jordana Mendelson, eds. *Postcards: Ephemeral Histories of Modernity*

David Getsy *From Diversion to Subversion: Games, Play, and Twentieth-Century Art*

Jessica Burstein *Cold Modernism: Literature, Fashion, Art*

Adam Jolles *The Curatorial Avant-Garde: Surrealism and Exhibition Practice in France, 1925–1941*

Juli Highfill *Modernism and Its Merchandise: The Spanish Avant-Garde and Material Culture, 1920–1930*

Damien Keane *Ireland and the Problem of Information: Irish Writing, Radio, Late Modernist Communication*

Allison Morehead *Nature's Experiments and the Search for Symbolist Form*

Laura Kalba *Color in the Age of Impressionism: Commerce, Technology, and Art*

Catherine Walworth *Soviet Salvage: Imperial Debris, Revolutionary Reuse, and Russian Constructivism*

Jo Applin, Catherine Spencer, and Amy Tobin, eds. *London Art Worlds: Mobile, Contingent, and Ephemeral Networks, 1960–1980*

Erik M. Bachman *Literary Obscenities: U.S. Case Law and Naturalism after Modernism*

Lori Cole *Surveying the Avant-Garde: Questions on Modernism, Art, and the Americas in Transatlantic Magazines*

Elizabeth Pender and Cathryn Setz, eds. *Shattered Objects: Djuna Barnes's Modernism*

Sam Rose *Art and Form: From Roger Fry to Global Modernism*

Diederik Oostdijk *Bells for America: The Cold War, Modernism, and the Netherlands Carillon in Arlington.*

Jessica Gerschultz *Decorative Arts of the Tunisian École: Fabrications of Modernism, Gender, and Power*

Anna Lovatt *Drawing Degree Zero: The Line from Minimal to Conceptual Art*

Molly Warnock *Simon Hantaï and the Reserves of Painting*

Octavio González *Misfit Modernism: Queer Forms of Double Exile in the Twentieth-Century Novel*

Mark Antliff *Sculptors Against the State: Anarchism and the Cosmopolitan Avant-Garde (London-Milan-Paris)*